Mother Love

Mother Love

The Mystical and Psychic Bond that Shapes our Lives

Cassandra Eason

ROBINSON
London

Robinson Publishing Ltd
7 Kensington Church Court
London W8 4SP

First published in the UK by Robinson Publishing Ltd 1998

A copy of the British Library Cataloguing in Publication data is
available from the British Library

ISBN 1-85487-954-5

Printed and bound in the EC

Contents

CONTENTS

CONTENTS

Introduction

Her Mother Love rose in a great tidal wave and swamped me.

Joyce Webb from Dorset
on seeing the ghost of her mother

*M*other love and maternal instinct have been central to humankind from the time when Mother Earth was first worshipped. Today mothering is still regarded as the fundamental psychological and perhaps psychic human relationship. Its cornerstone is love of the deepest, most enduring and altruistic kind. This book draws from myth, history, literature, sociology, psychology, biology, religion, news stories from around the world, and my own extensive ongoing research into maternal intuition, telepathy and premonition.

Maternal intuition is one of the least researched aspects of psychic experience and yet one to which almost all of us can relate. Mothers can also draw upon superhuman strengths to save their children in life-threatening situations. But motherhood is not just composed of magic and spiritual links. A mother may show patience and care that last a lifetime for a sick or disabled child, and sacrifice her own happiness or even her life for that of her offspring. Yet when mother love turns sour it can lead to appalling tragedy. The book also studies darker aspects of motherhood—neglect and even murder—and asks how the purest love can turn to most violent hatred. It looks also at mothers falsely accused of abuse—women who have found themselves unable to protect their children and may never recover from the injustice.

From my own research I have discovered that the severing of the maternal bond by death is often the single most traumatic event in a person's life, whether the relationship was close or parent and child were estranged by events. The majority of letters I receive concerning mothers are about death, which leaves a profound sense of grief and loneliness even where the child has children of his or her own. And the loss of a child has no parallel within the human condition.

> As a mother a woman is another person than the woman without child. She carries the fruit of the night for nine months in her body. Something grows into her life that never again departs from it. She is a mother and remains a mother even though her child dies. For at one time she carried the child under her heart and it does not go out of her heart ever again.
>
> *An Abyssinian noblewoman quoted by*
> *Leo Frobenius in* Der Kopf als Schicksal

I have been surprised and moved by the number of letters I have received from women who gave away their babies at birth and still recall, thirty or more years later, the first moments of love with their child and the agony of parting. In some cases they were happily reconciled with their lost children years later. In other instances time proved too great a barrier.

Each section of the book examines a different aspect of motherhood, the influences that mould it and the powers and emotions it triggers, using the words of men and women from the UK, US, Australia, New Zealand, South Africa, Europe, Japan and India. Although the book considers the influence of mothers on the lives of heroes, royalty and dictators, it concentrates primarily on the experiences of ordinary men and women and those who mothered them, whose stories are no less remarkable.

Whatever our circumstances, we all have a mother who for good or ill has influenced our lives in profound ways. Even if she is no longer with us, she lives on in our hearts, and in our unconscious as well as conscious actions. A wise friend of mine once said that if you have children, you die a mother. If not, you die a mother's child.

Motherhood is surrounded by more ideals, expectations and trials than any other role. Mothers in every age have shared their children's pains and sorrows. Spartan mothers from the sixth century BC, whose goal was to produce strong healthy boys for the war machine, sent young sons into battle with the words, "Return from battle with your shields or on them." They would sooner their children were among the honoured dead carried back by their comrades on their shields than among the cowards who threw down their weapons so they could flee. Yet those same mothers were depicted on vases of the period, weeping bitterly as the battalions departed.

Many single mothers in the harsh world of the seventeenth century were forced to leave their children in foundling hospitals, some with pathetic notes attached to them such as, "I am unable to subsist any longer." They were the lucky ones. Unwed women whose infants died at birth were often executed for infanticide. For example, in Prussia at this time unmarried mothers of dead babies would be buried alive, while in Sweden they were burned at the stake.[1]

In the UK during the earlier decades of the twentieth century, unmarried mothers as well as those with post-natal depression were routinely assigned to mental hospitals and in some cases disappeared for the rest of their lives, with devastating effects upon the abandoned children as cases in this book will tell.

Even today, motherhood can be a source of profound sorrow. Dana Raphael, Director of the Human Lactation Center in Westport, Connecticut, who has spent more than thirty-five years observing thousands of mothers and babies, speaks of the dilemma of "mothers in the less developed countries who often must choose which child is to get the little bit of extra food and live and which they must break their hearts over and bury".

Set against this is the modern whiter-than-white Mum of the advertisements who combines career, designer baby, caring sharing partner, glowing good looks and model girl figure with the ability to whip up home-made apple pie: a secular combination of the sensual warrior goddesses of the Classics and the Madonna. The reality is very different from the media image. Mothers are warmer, more self-sacrificing, and prone to laughter and tears in equal quantities.

I have tried to reflect the emotions of people who have written to me or telephoned in response to the extensive appeals I have made, as well as those who write to me after reading other books I have written. Where possible I have reproduced their words. I am aware of areas I have not covered, but this book is not enough even to scratch the surface. The mother-child link stretches backwards through history and forwards to unborn generations, an elusive but unbreakable silver cord from Palaeolithic cave to twenty-second-century space station and beyond, where mothers will still pace the midnight hours with wakeful infants. It outlasts civilizations, and will endure until the end of the world.

PART ONE

The Magical Bond of Motherhood

The Lifesaving Link

Telepathy uses the language of the soul. With mother
and child there is tremendous soul-flow, as there is
between all people who are in love.

Joe Cooper, author and paranormal researcher

The Mother/Infant Connection

Annette was enjoying a rare evening at the cinema with her husband
when an inexplicable sense of danger made her rush home to save her
baby's life. At the time she and her husband were employed as cook
and waiter in a hotel in Surrey, and lived with their six-month-old
daughter in a little cottage nearby. "We could only rarely go out
together as we each had different days off," she said. "But on this
occasion we both got an evening off together to see a film in the
nearest town, which was about six miles away. One of the hotel staff
had volunteered to babysit and we set off to catch a bus.

*"We had not been in the cinema for more than a few minutes when a
terrible uneasiness came over me. I could distinctly smell burning. I
fidgeted a lot and my husband asked what was wrong. I told him I
could smell burning. He said I'd probably dropped a bit of my
cigarette. I stooped and had a look on the carpet but there was no
sign of any glow. The smell persisted and eventually I told my husband
I was leaving. He followed me reluctantly, muttering something
derogatory about women.*

*"As we boarded the bus for home I prayed for it to go faster. At each
stop I almost died. At last we were sprinting down the lane leading to the*

3

cottage. The smell of burning was now very definite to me though my husband still could not smell anything. We reached the door which I literally burst in. As I did, dense smoke poured out and a chair by the fire burst into flames. I rushed through to the bedroom and got the baby out while my husband dragged out the unconscious babysitter. She had fallen asleep and dropped her lighted cigarette into the chair which had been smouldering."

The incident happened in 1936, and the baby is now grown up and the mother of six children and living in America. But it is as inexplicable now as it was then and has remained for me the most remarkable example of the mother/child bond transcending time and space. Annette's own explanation, recorded in the archives of the Alister Hardy Research Centre for Religious and Spiritual Experience in Oxford, England, is: "I believe God sent me home to save my baby."

Many women do see a religious significance in such dramatic examples of maternal intuition. Annette responded to a smell of burning that prompted her on an unconscious level to recognize a danger to her infant. Maternal intuition at its most dramatic is inexplicable in scientific terms. This "power" seems to operate as an automatic radar from a mother to her infant that enables her to detect unvoiced distress or unseen danger to her child whether they are together or miles apart.

Eleanor, who lives in Christchurch in New Zealand, wrote to tell me how a voice in her head warned her of danger and stopped her inadvertently killing her son:

"When my three sons were young, I never went out in the car without ensuring they were clear of the driveway. One day when my youngest son was about two years old, I checked that the boys were inside and went to the garage, then backed out slowly. A loud and urgent voice yelled 'Stop!' in my head and I jammed on the brakes. As I got out I found my son lying on the driveway with his head inches away from one of the back wheels. How he had got out I do not know, but he had obviously fallen.

4

After that incident I always trusted my intuition concerning the children."

The maternal automatic radar is strongest before an infant has a sense of his or her own danger and the ability to take effective action. Maternal telepathy is the most common and easily understood of all psychic phenomena. Many people have experienced a paranormal cry of distress to a greater or lesser degree with their own offspring or can recall an incident in their own upbringing or family history when Mother or Grandma "knew". The instances of fathers experiencing this sense of danger on a psychic level are comparatively few, so why should women have these promptings?

A survey on the medical differences between males and females carried out by the British magazine *She* in March 1997 may offer a clue to women's heightened sensitivity. Rita Carter, the journalist who investigated the findings, reported on brain scans, which indicated that when women were asked to think sad thoughts the areas of their brains that registered emotion showed up to eight times more activity than those of men. This suggests that they might actually feel more sorrow, making women much better than men at empathizing with others. The image of women as intuitive, caring souls could be a real reflection of their biology. Women seem to be exquisitely attuned to their babies' crying, while men are better at picking up faint animal noises—a hangover perhaps from the time when they had to keep their ears pricked for prey while hunting.

Taken a step further this fine tuning in women may extend to a psychic level, so that not only does the mother wake before the baby cries (see p. 39), but she can actually tune into the infant's psyche and take over its own warning system by using a telepathic link. Is this possible?

The psychologist Carl Jung was foremost in recognizing what he called synchronicity or meaningful coincidences and saw the mother/child relationship as one in which telepathic bonds are at their strongest. Jung's own mother Emilie had evolved psychic abilities and kept a diary in which she noted down all the strange occurrences in her life. Jung's maternal grandmother also had second sight. So Jung was part of a psychic chain. Such maternal influences suggested to Jung the possibility that the human mind and spirit did have many channels of communication that could not be explained in biological terms and that these "abilities" were inherent in the mother/child bond. He himself dreamed of his mother's death at the time she died (see p. 147).

Jung's private secretary, Aniela Jaffe, became an analytical psychologist in her own right. She explains that to Jung synchronicity was the fourth principle which "must be added to the recognized triad of space, time and causality".[1] Jung believed: "The mother/child relationship represents an archetypal situation *par excellence*. For a long time after the birth the two form a psychophysical and later a psychic unity. Normally a strong psychic bond persists throughout childhood. It has its roots as much in the unconscious as in consciousness. Hence a much smaller impetus is needed for synchronistic phenomena than with people with whom the unconscious bond is weaker and who are not contained in the one and the same archetypal situation."

There are experiences that cannot and should not be judged by materialistic criteria of frequency and statistical significance. Just as scientists cannot take a lover or a grieving widow or widower into a laboratory and quantify their love or grief, so there are no tools for measuring maternal links beyond rudimentary tests on lactation. The effect of breastfeeding on maternal intuition is discussed in a later chapter but my own research suggests that bottlefed babies are no less connected by this intangible power in times of crisis.

The cases in this chapter illustrate the sixth-sense communication of danger from the protective psyche in which the mother envelops her young child. A mother in a completely different room from her baby may detect the child's silent distress even when others in the same room as the infant notice nothing. This destroys the argument that it is a change in the baby's sounds or even breathing pattern that alerts the mother.

Carolyn, a mother of five children who lives in Salt Lake City, Utah, trusted her instincts and so saved her child:

"Our first child, born twenty-five years ago, was bottlefed and given her own room with all of the modern paraphernalia that society deems necessary. The last four were breastfed and spent the first four or five years of their life in our room, either in our bed or on a mattress on the floor. I recall many nights when I woke moments before my child needed me.

"I felt an especially close bond with my second daughter Sarah and was told by family that we were too close. I remember one evening when she was about eight months old. I was in the kitchen and she and her sister were in the living room with my husband. I rushed to the living room where my husband was reading and my older daughter was playing. The baby was lying in the corner on her stomach apparently quite happy. I flipped her over and saw that Sarah was silently choking on a balloon. My husband and daughter were not aware of the emergency."

This is a particularly interesting example because the mother-link was working through walls even though the people right in the room with the baby were totally oblivious to the infant's danger. Furthermore it was a second child, not the first where maternal anxiety would be expected. The link persisted, because a similar incident occurred when Sarah was about four, and again Carolyn was the only person alerted to the danger.

"We were in the kitchen preparing dinner. Sarah was standing beside me and was eating some carrot sticks. In the midst of a normal noisy dinner hour I realized that Sarah was completely quiet, her head was down and she was stamping her foot. It seemed to her older sister Monica, who was twelve at the time, that she was playing. I can't explain what made me feel something was wrong but I knew. I stopped what I was doing and turned her around. Her face was purple and she was unable to speak or breathe.

"Monica says she will never forget that look on Sarah's face and neither shall I. After a moment of sheer panic and total confusion about what to do things suddenly slowed down and I was able to think clearly. I remembered an article I read just one week before in the Sunday newspaper demonstrating a technique to save the lives of choking victims. It is called the Heimlich Manoeuvre, named after the man that invented it. If a person is choking, you stand behind them, wrap your arms around their body and clasp your hands together, then quickly and firmly thrust back up and the foreign object or food pops out. It worked. The carrot sticks just popped right out and her normal colour returned almost immediately. Sarah did start to cry though because she felt I had been rough with her and she didn't understand why.

"We all had a big hug and it was only afterwards I really panicked, thinking of what might have been. Monica is now a mother herself and while she was staying here with her children I spoke to her of the experience as I wanted to test my memory. It was over twelve years ago, but Monica remembered it exactly as I did."

One writer on the pyschic link between parent and child comments: "We call ESP paranormal because no sensory channel has yet been discovered which mediates the information. However, ESP may be a natural and normal part of the parent/child relationship. Perhaps all parents and offspring share a lifelong ESP connection, a link that knows no geographical barrier, and if so perhaps the paranormal is not so paranormal after all."[2]

Another interpretation of the life-saving call cites the intervention of a deceased relative. In cases of maternal involvement, I have found that such an interpretation usually involves warnings from the deceased mother or grandmother of the mother herself. Maria, from the Isle of Wight, felt on looking back on a life-threatening experience that her dead grandmother had issued the warning. Maria, now a radio presenter in Dorset, responded to a sudden urge that allowed no time for conscious deliberation and saved her baby from serious injury.

"When my youngest daughter, Veronica, was about nine months old we were following the usual evening ritual most mums know of sharing a bath filled with ducks and toys. We would splash about together then I would get out, dry myself and get dressed in the bathroom while she played with the ducks. But on this particular evening I was drying myself with my back to the baby when suddenly I turned round, snatched her out of the bath and clutched her close to me.

"Veronica screamed with the shock of my grabbing her. Seconds later a heavy terracotta plant pot that was screwed into the ceiling came crashing down. The pot smashed into the water, denting the bath where Veronica had been sitting. I held Veronica until she stopped screaming. I can remember saying, 'Thank God, thank God, thank you whoever you are who saved my baby.'

"Afterwards I felt it was my dead grandma who had warned me. There are no two ways about it. The baby would have been dead had I not snatched her away so suddenly."

The word telepathy, from the Greek *tele* (distant) and *pathe* (occurrence or feeling) was coined by Frederic W.H. Myers, a founder of the Society for Psychical Research in 1884. Myers was an eminent Victorian psychical researcher, poet, psychologist and Inspector of Schools. To Myers telepathy was more than mind-to-mind communication without normal sensory mediation.

He believed that telepathy was "the inward spiritual aspect of the outward gravitational law". Just as gravity bound the constituents of the cosmos together, slowing down their headlong rush to decay and disintegration, so telepathy, the gravity of the mind, held together the warring factions of the personality, which were always threatening to fly apart.

This profound concept of telepathy saw it as an intangible binding force, ineluctably drawing together mindstuff from many quarters both within and beyond the psyche of the individual. Myers did not exclude the fragmented intelligences of the dead or otherwise discarnate beings. The implication of Maria's grandmother in her experience would therefore have posed no problems for Myers.

Peg, an Oxfordshire woman, woke up suddenly to find her mother shaking her and telling her, "Wake up quickly, it's the baby. He needs help urgently."

Not stopping to wonder why her mother hadn't gone to the baby herself, Peg jumped out of bed and rushed to the baby's room. The infant's face was turning blue; another minute and he would have choked. No medical reason could be found for the attack.

Much later Peg sank back exhausted into bed, glad that her little one was safe. Only then did the strangeness of the experience strike her: her mother had been dead for three years and had never even seen the child. Peg believed her mother had been sent back by God to look after her baby and was thereafter sure her mother was helping her to care for her son.

For the majority of women, the psychic bond is rooted not in the world of spirit but in the mortal love between mother and baby. It may even be that reliance on expertise can blunt the instinct. I myself was trained in teaching and psychology and when I had my first child I wanted to be the perfect mother. I read babycare books by the score, knew all the theories and yet had absolutely no intuitive links with my first two children. I can remember agonizing about how I was going to adjust my eldest son Tom's infant feeding schedule to incorporate British Summer Time, and howling my head off in hospital because I thought Tom had a fatal intestinal blockage since his feeding bottle remained full although he had been sucking at it for five minutes. An experienced nurse passing through the ward pointed out that the teat had no hole.

Common sense, let alone sixth sense, departed as dependence on expertise dominated my early mothering. Neither as a teacher of young children nor with my own oldest two did I have what seemed to be a natural bond, precisely because I believed that psychology had all the answers.

Of course, medical advice should never be ignored. However, doctors are increasingly recognizing that many mothers "know" when a child is ill, even in the absence of major symptoms. The mother of Ingrid, a UK journalist on a national magazine, was a nurse, but her training proved less effective than Ingrid's sixth sense in a crisis.

"I was at my mother's house in Scotland," said Ingrid. "Rory was four months old and was just sitting up and teething. He was grabbing at everything and chewing on it. He was propped up by a chair, playing with a brightly coloured box, chewing the corner of it, and I was putting my make-up on. I turned round and noticed his ears were red. Immediately, I felt really panicky. I'd never panicked like that before with him, though naturally I worried like most first-time mums. 'Phone the doctor,' I said to my mother.

"*Mum was a nurse and always erred on the side of caution. But she thought I was over-reacting. It was nearly Christmas and the central heating was full on. 'It's just because the house is so warm and Rory's overheated,' she said.*

" *'Get the doctor,' I insisted. I was really scared.*

"*My mother told me: 'He won't come out so near to Christmas. Don't worry, Rory's all right. Just take off his jersey and he'll cool down.'*

" *'No, phone an ambulance, now,' I persisted.*

" *'Well, if you're that worried,' my mum said, 'Dad will drive you to the doctor.'*

"*The baby was playing quite happily all this time and didn't seem ill. My mum thought I was being a fussy first-time mother but I knew something was really wrong. 'We've got to phone the ambulance,' I remember saying. 'We must get him to hospital at once.'*

"*By the time we'd called Dad and were still debating, Rory's ears had swollen to twice their normal size, but he still seemed fine. Mum still thought it wasn't anything serious, but I picked up the baby. 'Take me straight to casualty,' I told my dad.*

"*It was very frosty and about four o'clock in the afternoon, and as we went out to the car Rory's face was starting to swell. By the time we got to the hospital, his body had swollen to about twice the normal size and his head was like a football.*

"*I rushed into casualty shouting: 'Help me, please! My baby's very ill,' and I realized they were taking me seriously and treating it as an*

11

emergency. The doctor injected Rory with an antihistamine drug, but the swelling didn't go down. Rory was kept in hospital overnight and the doctor said it was the worst allergic reaction he had ever seen. It could have been disastrous because with the swelling his trachea was closing up, so if I hadn't got him to the hospital so quickly, I dread to think what might have happened. I sat by him all night, frightened I'd lose him because he looked so ill. But by the morning the swelling had gone down and then I couldn't wait to get out of the place with my baby.

"It upsets me even now to think of it though Rory is eight. The doctors didn't know what caused the reaction, but they said it might have been that I had taken some antibiotics the week before and was breastfeeding Rory. I wonder whether he was allergic to the brightly coloured dye on the box he was chewing. But whatever, there was no reason when his ears went red for me to suspect there was anything wrong other than what my mum said, that Rory was too hot."

Often mothers who describe psychic links are ones who trust their own innate warning system and seem to relax into motherhood. The experiences tend to occur with one particular child in the family, not necessarily the one who is most alike. Ingrid explained that her second son Leo, is "my soul mate. He is so like me, physically and every other way. I dote on him and have tremendous tolerance of him. I relate to him. But in spite of this it is with my first son, Rory, that I have this incredible intuitive bond. I have always felt that he needed me to look after him. He has always been sensitive and highly strung. I always woke before Rory woke, but I didn't with Leo. I knew Leo was all right. It was more than exhaustion that let me sleep till Leo yelled."

Maria, who lives in Victoria, Australia, told me about the closeness of her bond with her second child, Alexander. "Alex and I have a special rapport," she said. "One incident has left me with no doubt of the special ties a mother and child have. I was in the kitchen washing dishes and Alex, aged around eleven months (he had started walking by nine and a half months), was running around in our lounge. It's very much a child-proof room so I was confident he could come to no harm. But while I was working I kept getting a fidgety, odd feeling that wouldn't go away. This uneasiness rapidly became a very strong feeling of 'Do something'. I kept trying to ignore it. But then it was like a light that filled a black room. 'Alex!' I dropped everything and ran into the other room. There he was about to put a fistful of sewing needles into his mouth. How my sewing box got into the lounge I'll never know, as it is always up high in another room. But it was just lucky I got the message that Alex was in danger."

Where does the psychic power originate? Dr Jan Ehrenwald, at one time consultant psychiatrist at the Roosevelt Hospital in New York City, believed that the oneness in the womb continues after the child's birth and that mother and child are still joined on a deep unconscious level. This channel remains open for future psychic communication. The psychic bond between mother and infant is even stronger than that between mother and adult offspring. Some mothers can recall psychic experiences from their own childhood. It may be we were all psychic as children, but in some of us the awareness was obliterated by the disapproval of adults. Motherhood is the time that dormant intuitive potential is reactivated, perhaps especially in those who can still recall inexplicable experiences from their own childhood. Maria says that her psychic path started in childhood.

"I was ten years old and remember looking at my tea and then having a vision of someone telling Mum that her dad had died. The image became so strong that I had to speak the words, 'Mum, Grandpa's dead.' Within minutes my aunt was knocking on the door with the bad news.

"I now have two children of my own and feel that this childhood sense has carried into my adult motherhood. My first born, Veronica, as a baby would sleep quite soundly but then I'd wake in the night, or even just be sitting watching television, and I'd get a stirring. I'd say to myself, 'No, Veronica, don't wake up.' But within maybe thirty seconds of saying that, she'd wake. I was always annoyed that I could sense she would

wake up. It was almost as if I was waking her by just thinking about her, rather than the baby sending me a message."

Maternal Psychic Power and Infants

Once children become mobile the hazards change, although the child still may have no perception of danger. Many mothers become adept at sensing a crisis, and the more relaxed the mother and the lower her conscious anxiety levels, the more easily the instinctive "radar" can operate. Barbara, who lives in Hull, England, described how a sudden urge to rush to her eldest son Mark saved his life:

"When Mark was about three years old, he was upstairs playing in the spare bedroom. I was downstairs in the living room with my younger son Paul when I had a strong urgent feeling that Mark was in great danger, although I could hear him playing happily. I took the stairs two at a time and reached the room just as he was about to insert a hair grip into the line socket on the skirting board. I have no doubt Mark would have been killed. How I knew he was in danger I will never know but I am glad I did not question my intuition.

"The feeling that was like no other I had experienced returned some years later. I was in the back room of our present house when I felt urgently I must rush to my youngest and fourth child Jane whom I could hear coming downstairs. Again had I not acted promptly the consequences would have been horrific. Jane, who was only three years old, had fastened a leather belt over the balustrade at the bottom of the stairs and placed her neck inside it like a noose. She jumped from several stairs up with the belt round her neck and I caught her in mid-air, seconds before disaster struck.

"I do believe that children and their mothers have a close psychic link which protects children in times of danger. I still always know if my grown-up children are in trouble or danger."

Coincidence? Why then did Barbara and other mothers in this

chapter describe the feeling as different from the normal free-floating anxiety? Why was Barbara not constantly dashing to check the children? One common feature of these experiences is that the mother acts in an unusual and seemingly irrational way that only later is understood. Such experiences might happen once or twice in a mother's lifetime and stand out years later as being of great significance. It is not that the mothers have forgotten the countless occasions when their anxieties were not justified, but that these moments stand out as having an entirely different quality and intensity. Generally a mother who wonders, "Should I check?" is not experiencing the urgent "go now" or total panic of the true crisis connection.

Elaine lives in Salt Lake City in Utah. Some years ago, she and her husband were living in the Los Angeles area with their son Matt who was almost five.

"I was in Palm Springs setting up a conference for the Nature Conservancy. I had taken my neighbour along for the ten days away from home. Matt would spend the mornings at his pre-school and the afternoons with a friend from school. Then his dad would pick him up on the way home from campus. As my neighbour and I were getting ready to drive back to LA from Palm Springs we decided to get a quick bite to eat so that we would miss the rush-hour traffic. As we were waiting for our order in the restaurant I had the most horrible feeling come over me. I told my neighbour I must call home to check on Matt. She kept telling me not to worry but I knew things were not right. I put in a call to home and when no one answered and the answering machine didn't come on I was even more sure things were not well. So I proceeded to call my neighbour's husband. He told me he didn't know anything. Later he told me this was not true. He hadn't wanted to upset me before I spent two and a half hours on the road.

"We ate our dinner in silence and left soon after. The drive home was the worst in my life as I was still convinced something terribly wrong had happened. My neighbour's husband came out to meet us as we drove up.

He told me that Matt had fallen through a glass door and was going into surgery shortly. He had severed several tendons in his right hand. I was able to arrive at the hospital in time to be with Matt for a couple of minutes before his surgery. All turned out well and now at twelve he has full use of his hand. When Matt was very little and still nursing I would wake up in the night and the morning before he would, knowing that he would wake up in a matter of seconds."

Elaine's neighbour lied to save her distress, but this did not satisfy her unconscious knowledge.

The telepathic link does not only warn of danger. In a time of apparent crisis, it can also work to reassure the mother that things are not as bad as they look. Louise, mother of Craig, two, and Alex, four, who lives in the south of England, told me: "You should listen to yourself, trust your instincts and develop them. Last summer Alex got lost on the housing estate where I live. I was starting to cry and get upset when I thought: 'Wait a minute, this is all superficial. I know Alex is all right because I can feel he's still there. He hasn't gone from me.' Instantly I relaxed and within a few minutes Alex turned up at a friend's house."

Louise described the link "as if the cord between mothers and children was cut physically but not psychologically".

Once a child can talk, the bond becomes a two-way process and moves closer to the conventional definition of telepathy. But because it is a telepathy that exists in actual situations, it is not as clear-cut as the card-guessing experiments in laboratories.

It can happen that the child uses this link to reassure the mother. Donata lives in Mainville, Ohio. Her daughter Hope, now six, was born when Donata was thirty-eight. She believes that "the intense birthing and bonding Hope and I experienced contributed to her abilities to communicate with myself and her father on deep, unconventional levels.

"As early as a year, Hope could point to an object, particularly the bathtub drain handle. Within minutes it would break. Today she can

often tell who is calling before I answer the phone or whether her father is home long before we pull into the driveway.

"When she was almost two, I went out for the afternoon leaving her at home with her sister. While on the interstate I was forced off the road by a truck. Although I was not injured the incident was upsetting because the trucker did not stop.

"When I arrived home Hope and I went out into the backyard to play in the sandbox. I sat in a lawn chair vividly recalling the truck incident in my mind, as I wrote a letter of complaint to the company whose truck had caused the near-accident. After a few minutes, my little girl, who could barely talk, said, 'No big truck come in this yard, Momma.' I had not mentioned a word to her or her sister about the event but Hope was able to pick up the information simply by being close to me. For days she assured me our house and yard were safe from big trucks."

We do not know at what point the child begins to home into his or her mother's distress, but it is only when the child can put thoughts into words that we gain evidence of this. Mary, now a mother herself, living in County Cork in Ireland, can still recall this link between herself and her mother.

"When I was young, my mother had taken my brother to our summer place to do some work on the house. About five o'clock in the afternoon, I knew something dreadful had happened to my mother. The feeling was so strong, I knelt down and started to pray. My mother sometimes had a tendency to choke so my immediate thought was it was that. But later I heard that she and my brother had gone for a walk to the beach and at about five o'clock she had fallen down the concrete steps leading on to the beach and hurt herself badly, though not dreadfully.

"I never had the feeling again till when my own son was about three. We had moved house and although we always meant to fit locks to the upstairs windows we never got round to it. My mother and sister had come over and we were sitting having afternoon tea when I stopped mid-sentence. 'I've got to go to the little one,' I said and rushed upstairs to my husband's office where my son was at the open window. He had climbed

on to my husband's desk, somehow opened the window and was within two inches from falling out from the upper floor."

What then are the implications of the mother/child intuitive link? Not that mothers should be perfect, ever-smiling Madonnas, nor scorn the expertise of health professionals, but that they should trust their own wisdom and listen to their inner promptings. Whatever our age, it is never too late to start listening to what our children and mothers are saying on a spiritual rather than earthly level. As author and paranormal researcher Joe Cooper says, we can open ourselves to the "soul-flow" and let the earthly mistakes and barriers dissolve into acceptance and love or, if the relationship is fatally flawed, into understanding and perhaps forgiveness.

The Continuing Connection

O vain boy, do not think so highly of yourself. Your strength is nothing, your shrewdness is nothing. It was not these that saved you from the eagle, but the strength of your mother's thoughts.

Native American legend

The Maternal Bond and Adolescents

As a child gets older, the maternal radar becomes less evident, but still operates in times of crisis. What is more surprising is that where the mother is no longer sufficiently close physically to rush to her child's aid, the power can, it seems, be transmitted as a psychic force that gives the child actual physical strength or protection at the time of danger.

Daphne, who lives in Scotland, described this strange phenomenon:

"My teenage son Alistair was out driving in March 1982 when an unexpected blizzard hit. I was standing by the dining room window watching enormous snowflakes fall when I suddenly heard his voice call 'Mum, help me.' I said to my husband, John, 'There's something wrong with Ali.' John said it was just the snow making me nervous.

"About an hour later Ali appeared in a terrible state covered in snow. 'I've rolled the car but I've got it home,' he said. The car had crashed through a hedge and down a bank into a field. But Alistair had managed to right the heavy car, get it back on to the road and drive it home.

"When we saw where he had gone through the hedge and where he had landed we could hardly believe he could have managed it. Had I sent him the extra strength he needed? I asked him later what he was thinking. He replied: 'I think I said "Mum, help" or something like that.'"

Judi, who lives in Indiana, believes that she was able to transmit instant protection to her eighteen-year-old son Corey, although she did not understand on a conscious level how he could be in danger since he was apparently safe at high school.

"It was in May 1989, about two weeks before the dismissal of school for the summer. The seniors were going to celebrate Senior Skip Day about which I knew nothing. Corey, along with many of his classmates, had planned to skip school that day to have a party at the country home of a friend who had graduated the previous year. Neither did I know that Corey had borrowed a motorbike from his older brother.

"Around noon as I was standing in my kitchen looking out of the window, I was suddenly filled with intense fear and immediately thought of Corey. I told myself this was ridiculous because I knew Corey was in school and was just fine. But the feeling grew stronger and I began shaking and crying uncontrollably. Then my mind was filled with the words: 'Pray for Corey.' I did not hear the words with my physical ear but the feelings were so intense I could not ignore them and I stood there shaking and praying to God that He would surround Corey with His love and protection. When I was able to calm myself I went into the living room and sat on the sofa, still shaking, trying to understand what had happened to me.

"Ten minutes later the telephone rang. It was Corey's best friend telling me Corey had just been involved in a motorcycle accident and the Emergency Services had been called to transport him to hospital although he had not been badly hurt. I ran next door and got my father to come to the hospital with me because I was so afraid of what I would find.

"While Corey was in X-ray, the deputy sheriff who had investigated the accident arrived in the Emergency Room. He told me Corey

definitely had his guardian angel with him in the crash. As Corey rounded a curve in the highway, the back tyre of his motorcycle hit loose gravel which caused him to lose control of the vehicle, throwing the motorcycle across the highway and Corey into a small ditch running along the side of the road. Corey skidded along the ditch on his stomach, passing directly between a cement culvert and a pile of rocks. If Corey had veered even a couple of inches in either direction he surely would have been killed. After passing between the culvert and the rocks, Corey then rolled on to the highway into the path of a truck. Because the truck driver was alert and had seen what was happening he had slowed the truck or he would have hit Corey.

"There was nothing left of the motorcycle but the gas tank. Corey sustained minor injuries for what he had just gone through: a cracked clavicle and abrasions to his hands and his face from which he has no scars. As near as I can figure I was having my experience just as Corey was involved in the accident."

The experiences of Daphne and Judi involve more than simply crisis telepathy, since both mothers were not only aware of an offspring's danger but, they believe, influenced a positive outcome.

Lucille was living in England while her daughter Donitza was in America. One night Lucille had a terrifying dream. "It concerned my daughter who unfortunately had fallen for a man who swaggered around like Errol Flynn. He nearly killed my young and beautiful daughter in her Manhattan apartment. She cried out to me the moment he attacked her with a knife. I woke up thunderstruck and perspiring and sent out my love and protection to her. Miraculously she survived, I believe because I was with her then in her hour of danger as I had been with her throughout her childhood when she called out for me."

Could it be that spontaneous protective telepathic power is an extension of what Freud called original archaic communication, whereby women in hunter-gatherer societies protected husbands, brothers and sons who were hunting? If so, it may be that special rituals were carried out to ensure a safe return: perhaps the origins of protective sympathetic magic. For example, among Oceanic tribes mothers and sisters would leave food in the pot after a meal so that menfolk hunting far away would not be hungry. They would not sleep before two in the morning so that enemies would not sneak up unawares upon the absent menfolk. When a man married, his wife would take over the protective ceremonies.[1]

A Canadian Indian legend relates how a mother sent strength to her son via her thoughts:

A widowed squaw and her son lived by the sea. One day the boy went to hunt beavers but was seized by the Great Eagle who carried him to his nest on a high cliff overlooking the sea to feed his young.

His mother wept for him but an old woman who had learned the secrets of the fairies said: "Little good the men of your tribe can do you. You must aid him with your thoughts."

That night when the boy slept his mother came to him in his dreams and said: "Tomorrow when the Great Eagle swoops down to kill you, brace your knife point upwards against the rock and he will be pierced to death. You are not strong enough to cut through his feathers but he is powerful enough to destroy himself."

The boy did as he was told and the Eagle was impaled. Then he killed the young eagles but could see no way to escape from the nest.

That night his mother again came to him in a dream and said: "Foolish boy, why do you not use the thoughts I send you? Skin the eagle then crawl inside his skin. If the wide wings can hold him in the air they can likewise hold you. Drop from the cliff and you will land safely on the beach."

Thus the boy escaped and back at his village he boasted of his strength and cunning. But the wise old woman said: "O vain boy, do not think so highly of yourself. Your strength is nothing, your shrewdness is nothing. It was not these that saved you but the strength of your mother's thoughts."

It may be that even in societies where logic has overlaid instinct, these channels are accessible in times of crisis in situations where the maternal psychic bond is well evolved.

How then could this power operate? Could it be a form of psychokinesis, literally movement by the mind, a power most popularly associated with the UK psychic Uri Geller and with poltergeist activity that is often hypothesized as being fuelled by the mindpower of an adolescent. It may be that all mothers have the ability to use psychokinetic power to some extent.

There are no scientific experiments to test this maternal link. However, experiments have shown that people are aware of being stared at, even though the subject cannot see the person who is looking at him or her, which would suggest that we can affect other people's behaviour and maybe a situation by mindpower. The effect can occur when the viewer and the subject are in separate rooms or even buildings. In one experiment at the University of Adelaide in 1983, subjects were intermittently viewed by closed-circuit television in different rooms 60 feet apart and scored significantly above chance in awareness of when they were being watched. In a later experiment at the Mind Science Foundation at San Antonio, physiological recordings registered differences in basal skin resistance in subjects while they were being watched unawares on CCTV.[2] Such powers might be especially strong between a mother and child, although this has not been researched as yet.

In less urgent situations, telepathy alerts a mother to unvoiced distress of an adolescent so that she is able to contact the child through earthly channels to offer reassurance and help, as when I felt compelled to leave my work one morning and go to the leisure complex where my eighteen-year-old son worked, about two miles from my home. Tom no longer lived at home and, as with many adolescent boys, contact was extremely cordial but intermittent, usually when he had a minor crisis. When I arrived another employee was in Tom's place and told me my son had just been taken to hospital, having been involved in an accident a few minutes earlier. At the hospital I discovered Tom was not badly hurt, although his arm had been damaged and he was cut and bruised.

Belinda, who lives in the south of England, left her seventeen-year-old daughter Judy at home while she went off for a few days' holiday with her husband, brother and sister-in-law in the West Country. Judy had a full freezer, enough money and instructions to go to her grandmother round the corner if there were any problems. Since Judy had happily stayed at home alone on earlier occasions, enjoying the freedom, Belinda had no unusual worries about her daughter until, four days later, "I had a sudden feeling that something dreadful was wrong with my daughter, not the normal teenage escapades, and that I must go home at once. I went to my husband and said, 'I'm sorry but we've got to go home right away. Something's terribly wrong with Judy.'"

"My husband insisted I was being stupid, especially as I couldn't tell him anything definite, only that she needed me. I tried to explain to my sister-in-law because I knew I was spoiling everyone's holiday. But I was determined that if my husband wouldn't take me, I'd go back on the train. All the way home, my husband said I was being an absolute fool, and an over-anxious mother.

"When we got home, Judy was in a terrible state. She hadn't told me before we went away but she was pregnant and in those four days suffered a miscarriage. She had phoned her gran but she was very narrow-minded and had refused to help. My daughter didn't know who to turn to. She'd even been too frightened to call a doctor.

"Though Judy and I had had our arguments and still do and hadn't even been especially close in a conventional way, she was so relieved to see me. We were able to sort things out. It turned out she had been pregnant with twins and had lost one of them. We talked it through and I promised to help her to look after the second child when it was born. In a funny way we started to look forward to it. But she miscarried the other twin too. Had I not gone back, who knows what would have happened? I was there when she needed me."

Had Belinda detected some signals in her daughter before she left of a serious crisis looming? What is remarkable in all such cases is that the moment when the mother feels the panic and the actual crisis are so finely attuned.

Jane, who lives in Lancashire, was naturally slightly worried about her twenty-year-old son Jake who was in India with friends. However, the timing and intensity of her fears became suddenly concentrated as she picked up the distress signals of her son on the other side of the world. She woke in the middle of the night, feeling very ill and frightened and sure that something was wrong with Jake. Jane begged her husband to help her raise the fare to India and was actually planning her journey two or three days later when her son wired home for his return fare. Jane later discovered that his friends had travelled on to Kathmandu, leaving Jake camping alone, when he suddenly became ill. He had been delirious for three days with what eventually turned out to be hepatitis.

"Crisis" Bonds with Adult Children

Once a child has his or her own home and perhaps a partner, the link with the mother tends to be weakened as bonds form within the new family. However, mothers and daughters seem to remain especially close, and in a crisis a mother may pick up her daughter's pain or distress when the daughter may not have contacted her mother to avoid worrying her. About 80 per cent of adult maternal links are between mother and daughter. Marjorie, who lives in Chester, England, was especially psychically close to her youngest daughter Brenda.

"It happened the day before Christmas. I found myself prowling round my flat. I could not understand what was going on. I then knew something was wrong and I asked the question out loud, 'What's wrong?'

"I heard the name Brenda. The voice came from the middle of my ribs and though I could not describe the tone, I knew something was seriously wrong with Brenda, who lived thirty miles away. My grandson answered the phone and I asked where his mother was. He said she was out and then handed the phone to his stepfather. I again asked where Brenda was and Brenda's husband told me at first that she was out, then

when I pressed him for details admitted, 'There's been a bit of a an accident.'

"Brenda had slipped down the stairs and caught her leg in the banister. She had broken her leg in three places and had just gone to hospital in the ambulance. Her husband and son were about to follow her in the car when I phoned. Brenda was in really bad pain.

"I have always been aware of a different level of communication, but I used to think I was alone and different from other people. I would wake in the night when the children were small and know something was wrong. It was usually something minor, for example they had fallen half out of bed, the bedclothes had slipped off or one was developing a temperature. I only ever woke if something was wrong, and could not go back to sleep unless I had checked.

"When my eldest daughter Linda was a young toddler, I woke in the middle of the night with a start and knew that she was going to fall off a chair on to the fire at my mother's house. I could see her dress burning and hear her screams.

"Next time we visited my mother, I took our spark guard with us on the bus, which must have looked odd. When we got to the house, I insisted on putting the guard round the fire and sure enough that day Linda fell off her chair against the guard which prevented her slipping on to the fire. It had never happened before or since."

Marjorie's unconscious had obviously been warning her that an unguarded fire was dangerous, so the context of her anxiety is quite explicable. However, as with many of these experiences, the warning came immediately before the moment of danger. It is this timing in incident after incident that makes the experiences so uncanny.

"Crisis" Bonds with Mothers

As Marjorie has grown older, there has been a subtle change in emphasis so that the power is two-way in times of crisis and Brenda can detect her mother's unhappiness. "Brenda will know at once if there is anything wrong with me. One day I was really upset and was sitting crying on my own. Brenda rang up. 'Now stop it,' were her first words. 'Stop what?' I asked. 'You know. You're upsetting everything here with your crying.'"

Even a young independent woman can link into her mother's need, even across oceans. Barbara, who is a mother herself and lives in Leeds, England, recalled how she was halfway across the world when she detected her mother's distress:

"I am the youngest of three children and was not particularly close to my mother. In 1985 when I was twenty-three and my mother was fifty, I was travelling through Israel and Egypt with my boyfriend who is now my husband. I had phoned home from Israel ten days earlier and everything was absolutely fine. But in the middle of the night I woke with a start. I desperately needed to phone home as I was suddenly aware that there was something wrong with my mother.

"I was in Aswan so I knew I would have to wait until eight o'clock in the morning, then queue up at the telegraph office. I was in a dreadful state for the rest of the night. When I finally got through, my father answered the phone and told me that my mother was in intensive care. Some treatment she had been having had gone wrong, the chemicals had poisoned her body.

"We could not get a flight back from Cairo so had to trek back to Tel Aviv before we could get home. My mother did recover. I have never before or since experienced such an overwhelming feeling, though I am now a mother myself. I am very sceptical of all psychic matters and would not have believed it possible."

Julia from Manchester, England, had a similar experience over an even greater distance, although her first concern for her mother came as a forewarning.

"When I was twenty-two I travelled from the UK around New Zealand for a year. On my second day in New Zealand I had a vivid dream I was back with my mother and saw that she was covered in lumps. I was so

27

disturbed I rang home the next day but my mother assured me she was fine.

"Eight months later in mid-August I had an unexpected sudden urge to contact my mother, although her letters had been quite regular and as usual full of everyday news. I went to the call box and dialled home. My mother was a teacher and it was mid-afternoon in the UK so, being the school holidays, I felt she might be at home. When she did not answer I became even more alarmed, although I knew logically that there was no basis for my panic, since she could have been shopping or visiting friends, I had never felt so concerned before and so I rang my father at work, which again I had never done before, and asked if Mum was all right.

"Dad gasped, 'But you're not supposed to know anything's wrong.'

"My mother was having emergency surgery that afternoon to remove a huge lump in her womb that was blocking her bowel. It is of immense comfort to me to know that my mother and I have such clear communication, a connection that I understand now that I have children of my own."

The psychic link passes down the generations, as this account from Vera in Christchurch, New Zealand, illustrates. Vera, who is now seventy-five, wrote:

"I know there to be great depth [of communication] between a mother and child. My mother was my sister, my friend, the person who listened to my happy stories and my tales of woes. She shared my secrets and I listened to her advice which was always right.

"My eldest daughter Lynette contracted tubercular meningitis. She was unconscious for a long time and the drug that saved her life destroyed her hearing. One morning I received a message from the hospital that she was coming home and I should pick her up as soon as possible.

"I was very upset as my youngest daughter, only a baby, was also very ill in hospital. In addition I had young twin daughters to care for. I had no transport and no money and did not know how I would manage to get a sick child home as well as visit my little one in hospital. Although my mother lived a considerable distance from my home, suddenly, as if by

magic, there she was on her bike, two bags on the handlebars full of food and treats for the children.

"I cried with relief. Her words were, 'I knew I was needed.'

"Mum gave me money to pay for a taxi to go to the hospital and collect Lynette, visit my baby and come home in comfort, while she cared for the twins. She had cycled more than nine kilometres laden with bags."

Later Vera's psychic link allowed her to repay her mother's kindness.

"One evening after dinner my husband and I were doing the dishes. Suddenly I threw the tea towel down and almost screamed at my husband, 'Quick, take me to Mum's house.'

"He did not ask why I and we soon reached my parents' home. My father came to the door. 'You must have been sent,' he told me. I rushed to the bedroom and found my seventy-five-year-old mother on the floor in a dreadful state and close to death. My father had not known what to do and had not even sent for help. Mother was taken to hospital and operated on for a fractured femur, and spent three months in hospital. I was an only child and my mother and I were very close. I am positive she sent me a cry for help, or was it God in His wisdom guiding me to her in her moment of dire need?

"One day when my mother had been in hospital for some time, I had a strong urge to go to her and packed her a set of day clothes and a warm rug, although I had not been told she was being discharged. I was determined to bring Mum home with me regardless of what the hospital staff said. When I arrived I noticed tears in her eyes and the nurse said she had been going to ring me to tell me to fetch my mother, but I had just turned up. Mum told me as I dressed her, 'I prayed for you to come. I was going to come out even in the nude.'

"I am especially in tune with my own youngest daughter. It can be quite uncanny how her thoughts and mine are the same. I worry sometimes when she goes away but she says, 'I shall know if you need me,' as I did with my mother all those years ago."

Understanding the Link

As with Marjorie and Brenda, the telepathic bond seems to be stronger with certain children than with others. It seems not to depend on similarity of personality or even intensity of love, but on the vulnerability of a particular child.

Sarah, who lives in Maryville, Washington, still knows when something is wrong with either of her adult sons and experiences physical symptoms of their distress, although actual contact between them is intermittent. Her daughter is equally close but the psychic link is not perhaps needed:

"I have ESP with my boys who are forty-three and forty-two but I don't have it with my daughter who is forty and I am not sure why. Whenever something is wrong with one of my boys, especially my second son Richard, my hair will feel that it is standing on end and I get a headache that will not go away until the problem corrects itself.

"When Richard was fifteen and going out for a Saturday evening, I told him I wanted him home by 11 p.m. at the latest. All evening I was worried as I knew something was going to happen. I had not said anything to him, except be extra careful, and he said, 'Oh, Mom.' By 9 p.m. I knew something was seriously wrong but I did not know what. At 11 p.m. Richard walked in with sticking plaster on his arms and head. I discovered that at exactly 9 p.m. he was riding on the back of a motorcycle behind his friend and they had run into a brick wall. They had been taken to the Emergency Room at the local hospital and his friend's father brought them home at 11 p.m. I only ever had that feeling when there was a disaster. It was very different from the usual anxiety that is inbuilt if you have teenagers.

"Years later, when Richard was in his thirties, I had an intensely painful headache that lasted for ages. I told my husband something was wrong with one of the boys. Sure enough about two weeks later, my second son called me and I asked him if he had been in hospital recently. Richard was shocked. 'How did you know, Mom?' he asked. He had

been admitted to hospital with pneumonia but had not wanted to worry me.

"Two years ago Richard had a job washing trains at a turnabout and fell off an engine. At the moment he fell, the hair stood up on my arms and I knew something bad had happened.

"Richard is now forty-two and working with a carnival erecting and dismantling the children's rides. Last month I had such a bad headache I told my husband that Richard had hurt himself again. Sure enough, Richard had fallen off the top of a ride that he was working on and had bruised his ribs.

"Sometimes when I am really worried I silently ask Richard to call and pretty soon the phone rings. It is Richard to ask me what is going on. There is invariably a crisis in his life that he had not wanted to worry me about."

Perhaps the secret of maternal bonds, intuitive or just loving on the earthly plane, lies in the ability to let children go, because rarely does a possessive mother have links of any kind with her children. The cords of love are not tight and constricting. Where there is animosity, the psychic link disappears or may not even develop. As children grow older the connection in a non-stifling relationship becomes a two-way protective net of concern. I am convinced that love is the key to the magical bond of motherhood.

The Link of Love

I can see pictures in your mind.
Five-year-old Dom to his mother Cathy

Everyday Maternal Telepathy and the Young Child

Children are highly skilled at "mind-hopping", reading the thoughts of others. In the mid-1970s Dr Ernesto Spinelli carried out tests in Britain with children as young as three years old and demonstrated that small children had considerable telepathic powers. He found that three-year-olds did best of all, but the apparent ability declined from then on until at the age of eight the results, like those of adults, were the same as chance guessing.[1]

I corresponded with Dr Spinelli who told me that in his view telepathic powers come from the same source as ordinary thought, but that in the young child this ability has not been suppressed by learning. Telepathic powers, he believes, are a form of externalized thinking that disappears once the child learns to do his thinking inside his head.

My own research suggests that in the majority of telepathic experiences involving young children they are reading the mother's mind. What is more, although many incidents occur, not surprisingly, in the pre-school phase, the mother/child everyday psychic link is one that survives well into adulthood, long after in experimental terms normal telepathic powers have declined. Wendy from Hampshire relates: "I was washing my hair and thinking I hadn't seen my bridesmaid Julie for some time. Within seconds four-year-old Jo piped up, 'When are we going to see Aunty Julie again,

Mummy?' The friend had not been mentioned in conversation for some months and there was no reason why Jo should ask the question unless she was picking something up from me telepathically."

Naturally, since the child often spends more time with the mother than anyone else in the early years, it could be argued that he or she is likely to pick up on the mother's concerns. But such experiences also occur with working mothers which would suggest that it is the nature of the mother/child bond rather than unbroken proximity that is a key factor.

In Ontario, Rebecca tries to make quiet moments during her working day in which she sends mental messages to her son in his crèche. She told me: "Since my son Alex was born, we've had an amazing connection. He sleeps with my husband and myself, but invariably since his birth I've always awakened just before he does. Now I'm back to work, Alex is in day care at my work site. Whenever I have a moment I like to stop in my day and send him a mental 'I love you' message. The staff have commented that almost any time I call down by phone, Alex points and moves towards it when it's me and only when it's me. When they buzz to let me in through the security door Alex walks over to the gate as if he knows it's me. It doesn't matter what time of day I visit, he seems to know intuitively. I had often thought I'd work at my psychic connection with my children but I am so busy that I never seem to find the time. So I'm pleasantly surprised that our telepathic connection has developed effortlessly."

Nor, as is sometimes argued, does the mother necessarily speak aloud without realizing it. Often the child will pick up a thought from another room and come running. Ann, of Leicester, England, recalls: "Years ago my eldest child, aged four, was playing in our lounge, cutting pictures out of an old catalogue. I went into the kitchen to cook, and was thinking how much I would like a ring with stones set all round the band. A few minutes later my daughter came into the room and said she had a present for me. Out of all the things she could have cut out of the catalogue she had brought me a

33

ring almost identical to the one I had been mentally designing."

Debra, who lives in Cornwall, recalled several telepathic incidents with her daughter:

"Charlotte began reading my mind when she was three years old. When my own mother was very ill a couple of months ago, I heard the news during the evening while Charlotte was sleeping (Charlotte has slept twelve hours a night since the age of ten weeks).

"I got very upset inside. Charlotte woke crying, saying she was hurting. She was very distressed and had to sleep in my bed hugging me all night. When we moved apart, she woke. There had been nothing wrong with her prior to this and she was fine the next day.

"The mind-reading first began when I watched a television programme about a scan on a pregnant woman. It reminded me of the scan I had with Charlotte's brother, Toby, who is now fourteen and a half months old. There is a gap of two years and two months between the children. I had the scan at twenty weeks. Charlotte and my husband came. Charlotte got upset when the radiographer and her assistant started touching my belly and tried to get on the bed to pull me off. My husband had to take her out of the room.

"The morning after the programme as we drove in the car we passed a local school which is reminiscent of the hospital building. We have never been back to the hospital since the scan. Charlotte said to me out of the blue, 'Is that the hospital where the baby was on the television and I got upset with the ladies and tried to get you off the bed?' I had not mentioned the scan or programme at all, but still had it in my mind.

"The next mind-reading happened when I was writing something on the calendar and noticed the date was 19 May. This was an old flame's birthday and I thought to myself, 'I wonder what David will be doing for his birthday?'

"Charlotte was out in the garden on her bike and started singing 'Happy Birthday'. Then she came in and asked me whose birthday it was.

"On another occasion we went for a walk to the beach I lived opposite as a child. I told Charlotte that I had two dogs and we used to open the

THE LINK OF LOVE

front door and run down the cliffs and on to the beach. I was thinking to myself about the occasion when my grandfather had put leads on the dogs. Because they were so accustomed to scrambling over the edge themselves, the dogs pulled my grandfather over with them. He was not injured, just badly shocked and bedraggled, and it made me smile to myself. Charlotte looked at me and asked, 'Who did the dogs pull over the cliff, Mummy?' Again she had spoken my thoughts."

For Julia of Berkshire it is not a case of one or two particular incidents standing out, but a process which has grown since conception and occurs constantly. Lawrence is her second child.

"I knew the moment I had conceived him. I wrote to tell my friend I was pregnant the next morning. It was strange because I had two years of fertility treatment before I conceived my first child Laura and I was booked to go and see the doctor for more treatment as I wanted a second child. I said to the doctor on the first visit, 'I think you should be careful examining me in case.' To his surprise I was pregnant. Throughout the pregnancy Lawrence was my son. I never thought for one moment he was a girl. Laura was much wanted but Lawrence was a part of me. I knew exactly what he would be like and I always saw him at about three years old. When Lawrence was three, he was the child I had imagined.

"Once Lawrence was born, I woke before he did and was totally in tune with his needs and emotions. I know a second child is easier anyway but this was almost magical. As he grew, Lawrence read my every thought. I would think, 'I wonder where I put my sewing box?' and he would arrive from another room with it in his little hands. Or I would notice a mark on the furniture and think I must polish that and instantly there was Lawrence from another part of the house with my polish. No words were necessary, nor even visual contact."

It is noticeable that the parents most prone to experience "routine" telepathy, as opposed to "crisis" telepathy are those who do not dash about frantically stimulating their offspring with lots of toys and activities, but are content to let the children get on with childhood in their own way. This offers children space for intuitive channels to flourish.

James E. Peron, director of the Childbirth Education Foundation in Richboro, Pennsylvania, says: "There exists a very special psychic bond between a mother and her child. There are those who dismiss any such link. There are even those who argue that it is not necessary for infants to bond with their parents at birth. Yet if we look at the relationship of mother and offspring in the animal world, we see this bond and innate communication link highly developed. Are we to believe that it does not exist in the highest form of mammalian life?"

Dr Spinelli did not test the telepathic bond between mother and children. However, Dr Elaine Shrager at New York University carried out trials in which a mother communicated different colours to her child in another room. Children scored higher when their own mother rather than someone else's communicated the information.

Yet the mother/child sixth-sense connection is not a purely genetic one, a fact which may be disappointing for those who anticipate that one day we shall be able to explain the link in terms of DNA strands. Close intuitive bonds are often found between children and their foster and adoptive parents. Rita Laws of Oklahoma, a researcher into the maternal psychic bond who has six adopted children as well as three birth children, found that the psychic links between herself and her birth son Joaquin and her adopted son Jesse were not only equally effective but also painful. When Joaquin and Jesse were four and three and a half years old Rita developed a toothache in the left lower middle molar.

"The tooth looked fine but it hurt a lot. After about a week of this it stopped. Then the same tooth directly across on the other side began hurting too. After that stopped, both molars began to hurt very badly at the same time. The dentist could find nothing wrong and sent me to a specialist. The specialist did X-rays and an examination but also found absolutely nothing wrong. I went home discouraged and confused.

"The next morning the toothaches were gone and I was thrilled. But

after breakfast Joaquin complained of a toothache. When I looked in his mouth I was horrified to see the lower molar on the left side was half eaten away with decay. The tooth was all but lost. And then Jesse mentioned that his tooth had been hurting too. I looked in his mouth and saw a lower molar on the right side in the same horrid condition! Both boys had to have crowns put on those bad teeth but after that was done I never experienced the phantom toothache again. And I now supervise tooth-brushing more carefully."

What is the purpose of the link in everyday life? Rita sees it as vital to the well-being of the child: "I believe that this phenomenon has several purposes, not the least of which is to afford the helpless baby or younger child extra protection from harm. This might explain why the frequency of events declines as the child gets older. For example the mother who wakes for no reason, only to find the baby has kicked off his blanket, is afforded the opportunity to re-cover the infant and provide protection from a chill. This has happened to me innumerable times."

She also advises mothers to note such experiences so that they can show their children the importance of the bond. "I would advise mothers to record psychic events to give a child later, lest they are forgotten. I dearly wish my mother had recorded some for me."

"Routine" Telepathic Links Between Mothers and Adult Children

Enid from Berkshire is in her fifties. Her son David, a sailor, is in his thirties. Enid always knows when David is going to telephone although during his long periods at sea he often cannot get a shore line from one week to the next. She will suddenly say to her husband: "We can't go out. David is going to ring." Five minutes later David phones from the Falklands or Fiji. This does not surprise Enid. "Why shouldn't I know? David and I have always been close from when he was a baby."

37

Many people can identify with the phenomenon of telephoning their mother on impulse to find that her number is engaged because she is phoning them at precisely that moment, although it is not a regular time or day to call. These everyday links are so common as to pass largely unremarked, but on examination are quite startling.

Sylvia was in her thirties and living on the Isle of Wight. Her mother Thelma, who was living in Hong Kong at the time, related this example: "One day I dialled the code for England and began to dial the Isle of Wight code. But before I could do so I heard Sylvia's voice asking, 'Mum, is that you?' She had started to dial my number and we connected. We didn't have a regular day or time to phone but we'd been thinking about each other quite strongly prior to the call."

It is very hard to dismiss maternal "magic" as mere coincidence. Helen, who lives in Southampton, has found that technology has weakened her son's intuitive powers: "Until recently when I wanted to contact my son who lives in Bournemouth, about thirty miles from my home, I used to concentrate on him and whisper 'Call Mum' over and over again. He always called very shortly afterwards to ask what I wanted. Recently he bought a message pager and it is no longer such fun. Because I can contact him, he doesn't trust his intuition any more."

Doreen lives in Wiltshire. Her son Eric used their telepathic connection to wake Doreen after a night out: "When he was in his late teens Eric had a habit of forgetting his key and would quietly wait outside using telepathy to wake me. Sometimes it would be well after midnight when I woke up and realized he was there. He was a bit embarrassed to tell me how he woke me. He says he thought to me, calling me in his mind, and after a while I woke, realizing he needed me to open the front door. It never failed."

Julia, who lives in Essex, has discovered that the link she and her sister had with their mother has extended to her own relationship with her children:

"I am the mother of two lovely little boys, aged twenty-eight months and

eight months, and my husband often comments on the way that I 'hear' them waking or calling out shortly before they make any sound. Isn't this the case with all mothers? My mother and I live a hundred miles apart but often jam the telephone simultaneously, although we have no regular time to call each other. As the phone rings, I usually say, 'Oh, that will be Mum.' I am invariably correct. The only time I have ever dialled and found my mother's phone to be engaged is when she is phoning my sister.

"When my sister was expecting her first child, my mother had terrible dreams one night. She awoke wet with sweat and suddenly experiencing a great sense of relief. Mum noticed the time was 1 a.m. The following morning my brother-in-law rang at breakfast time to announce that baby Ella had been born at exactly 2 a.m. They live in France with a one-hour time difference from us.

"I used to find all this fairly incomprehensible, but now I understand there will always be a psychic link with the flesh of my flesh, bone of my bone. Surely this must have a genetic basis, with the survival of the species having relied on the mother being attuned to any distress or alarm affecting her child. My husband agrees that sensing our baby waking before he can cry is a wonderful thing, thanks the stars it does not apply to dads, rolls over and has a good night's sleep."

Lin, who also lives in Essex, told me of the link between herself and her mother:

"Our psychic link is a great source of interest to the rest of the family, and though I am quite sceptical I have to admit that some of the incidents are very amusing.

"We can go round a large supermarket separately with separate trollies and find we have identical shopping at the checkout, although we do not live together or have the same family needs.

"When I had a birthday this summer she joked that I had not read her mind this time as I usually did, regarding my present. I had not even thought of it because I had decided that for once it would be nice not to know. In the evening I was watching television with my husband when suddenly I had a vision flash in front of my eyes of a wooden garden seat.

I phoned my mother immediately and told her, 'I know.'

"My mother was disgusted with me for spoiling her surprise. She had to admit that was what she had bought me, although it was not something I had expressed any interest in previously. As usual it was the perfect present.

"I think of my mother and she phones me within seconds. We send the same cards to the same people when we have bought selection boxes without the other's knowledge and written them separately. When my parents have an argument I feel a sense of gloom but not depression. It is a strange feeling. I know the atmosphere is not right even though I live about ten minutes' walk from them. When my mother phones to say she has had a tiff with my dad, I know already. Mum and I never argue. We always laugh and agree and sometimes I feel as if we are one, like twins. We speak long sentences at the same time. I hear myself speak and see her mouth moving with the same words.

"I was given a brand-new baby blanket when my daughter was born. One windy day, I had taken Lucy and Steven to deliver Steven at school and by the time I got there I realized that I had lost my treasured blanket. I felt sick. How could I have been so careless? It had been folded up in the tray underneath the pram. I retraced my footsteps several times but there was no sign of the blanket. I gave up hope, and next day went to the shop where it had been bought and purchased a new one.

"Three weeks passed and we had been to south Devon for two of those weeks. After we came home, I received a phone call from Dad: 'We were on the bus going home and Mum saw your blanket draped over somebody's wall. She went back to get it for you.'

"It turned out that on the windy day I had lost the blanket, it had blown over a garden gate and was hidden in a lot of bushes. The owner of the house had come home from a three-week holiday in Spain, found the blanket in her bushes and put it on her wall. Mum instinctively knew the flash of white out of the corner of her eye, as the bus sped by, was my blanket. Mum and Dad have often found things I have lost out in the street without even knowing that I had lost them."

Such instances are frequently dismissed as mother and daughter having similar tastes or being familiar with the other's preferences. That is part of the story. However, the sheer volume of incidents, and the ability to sense when a mother or daughter is distressed miles away, suggest that the bond is not merely chance. The result is a wonderful sense of being linked to another person, loved and cherished even when apart. As I have said, these bonds are not born out of possessiveness and the mother and daughter usually lead happy, separate lives. Such psychic hugs are the ingredients that allow people to function without the need to check every five minutes that they are valued. Psychic bonds comprise links of gossamer lit by sunlight, and are never chains of steel.

Mother and Daughter Labour Pains

A strange phenomenon is the sharing of labour pains between mother and daughter. A remarkable example comes from Carmel who lives on the Isle of Wight.

"I shared all three of my daughter Sue's pregnancies. The first time I had a lot of symptoms, such as morning sickness, cravings, pains and swelling, and indeed had a very small gynaecological operation to ease the problems. I did not associate them with Sue's pregnancy, but once she had the baby I was fine.

"When Sue became pregnant for the second time, I had problems right from the start. As well as the cravings, twinges and sickness, my stomach started to swell and my menstruation became very light. I was seen by a gynaecologist, but not my usual one, as my stomach was continuing to grow. He said that there was a large growth in my womb and that I would need a hysterectomy. I was so distressed that he offered me a scan so that I could see the growth for myself.

"To everyone's astonishment the scan showed there was nothing there. I talked to my own gynaecologist some weeks later, as I was still swelling, and he asked me if I had undergone any unusual life changes recently. I told him reluctantly that I had had problems the last time my daughter

had been pregnant. He did not laugh but explained that he himself had shared his wife's pregnancy and advised me just to wait.

"Once my daughter gave birth, my stomach went back to its normal size. It was very awkward in the village where I live, as I did not have a boyfriend. However, before long everyone was joking about my sympathetic pregnancy.

"My daughter got pregnant for a third time much earlier than she had expected. Her husband would not let her tell me as he said if I did not know about the pregnancy I would not get the symptoms. However, I started to experienced sickness, cravings and pain. I was worried I might have cancer. One morning I woke up desperate for bacon and eggs which I do not normally like. I went to the village shop to get some, and on the way back called in to see my daughter and son-in-law. I told them I did not know what was wrong with me and explained about the eggs and bacon. My son-in-law went white. My daughter had also been craving bacon and eggs that morning and she told me about the new pregnancy.

"I had been with my daughter for her first two labours and it was agony for me as well. The second time I woke in the morning with terrible backache. Sue had experienced a few pains but did not think she was in labour. I insisted she contacted the midwife and our pains began to alternate. As she had a contraction, I missed out.

"When her due date was near the third time, I woke in pain one morning and went to my daughter's house. Sue had a few twinges but again I insisted that the midwife was called. The midwife examined her and said she had to go to hospital at once or the baby would be born in the ambulance. I could not go as I had to look after the other children.

"I went to the first shop in the village and had to rest on the counter as I had the most horrendous contraction. When I reached the second shop I had another terrible pain followed by relief and I told the shopkeeper the baby had been born. When I got home my daughter telephoned me on her mobile phone to say exactly that. We checked the time and it was the moment I had the pain in the second village shop."

Maternal telepathy defies distance. Even though Ann and her mother were thousands of miles apart, her mother knew when Ann was in labour with her second child. At the time Ann, who now lives in Kailua, Hawaii, was living in California while her mother was out to dinner in Ohio, the other side of America.

"At the dinner table, Mom laid down her fork and knew, she just knew, when I was pushing that baby out. She felt my presence so strongly, two thousand miles away. I called her shortly after the birth to tell her the good news and she wasn't the least bit surprised since she already knew the baby was born.

"My mom and I are very close as friends, not just as mother and daughter. We often pick up the phone to call each other at the same time and write letters to each other on the same day."

There are countless examples of mothers and adult children, especially daughters, maintaining the bond, even to a third generation. Many are so commonplace as to pass unnoticed; all are evidence that love need be no more than a phone call away.

PART TWO

In the Beginning

The Mother Goddess
in History and Myth

(℘)

Greeting to you, Sun of the Seasons,
As you travel the skies so high,
With your strong step on the wing of the heights,
You are the happy mother of the star.

From the Sun Woman of Ireland,
a traditional Gaelic prayer

*A*lmost from the moment that primitive peoples were able to appreciate the miracle of motherhood, the Mother Goddess has been worshipped. Her image has been found among all cultures and at all times as an archetype of motherhood, containing the elements of creation and destruction, birth and death, fertility and barrenness. She has been seen as Mother Earth, Mother of the Moon and sometimes the Sun, the controller of the tides and seasons of the year, the regulator of the human life cycle, death and rebirth.

As the hunter-gatherers evolved towards agricultural life, the Mother Goddess also changed from the mother/lover of the god of the Hunt to represent the goddess of the Corn. In time she became the consort of the Sky Father, but always kept her control over fertility and the earth. She fulfilled a basic need for a personalized figure who was not as remote as the Father God, and would mediate between him and mere mortals. Although she might be destructive as well as creative, she offered the comfort and security of an idealized human mother to worshippers.

The earliest statues of the Mother Goddess date from 20,000–18,000 BC; for example one found at Lespugue in France's Haute

Garonne is carved from the ivory of a mammoth. There are no hands and feet and her legs are tapered to a point, possibly to stand in the earth. Her curved body suggests she is about to give birth. The pregnant, featureless Mother Goddess was an icon of fecundity of earth and mankind for thousands of years and similar figures have been found worldwide. With their prominent breasts and hips, in later periods these statues were dressed in girdles and necklaces and wore headdresses. Surviving examples are frequently stained by smoke, suggesting that they were placed by the hearth as household gods. All are powerful in their simplicity.

Earth and fertility goddesses, stemming directly from the Mother Goddess, retain their potency even today in remote Indian villages, where the temples of the great gods are regarded as less important in everyday life and worship than the little shrines of the local goddesses. These maternal deities have many names and are responsible for the fertility of the fields surrounding their village. However, they are also a source of comfort, especially for women who wish to become pregnant, mothers and children. People relate to these humbler goddesses as they could not to the remoter consorts of the great gods: Parvati, the creative wife of Shiva, Kali his destroyer wife, or Lakshmi, Vishnu's wife. What is most remarkable is that these village goddesses have not changed in essence for more than 5000 years.

The Mother in the Moon

When was the moon first associated with the Great Mother? Surely, the answer must be from the moment mankind first looked upwards and recognized, in her changing cycles, connections with the female reproductive cycle. Ever since, the moon has been linked to motherhood through countless ages and cultures.

The first trinity of huge carved stone goddesses, representing the three main cycles of the moon and dating from 13,000–11,000 BC, was found in a cave at the Abri du Roc aux Sorciers at Angles-surl'Anglin. The Triple Goddess of the Celts reflects the lunar cycles of maiden, mother and crone, an image repeated throughout the classical world. Vestiges of moon worship can be seen in the myths of less technologically developed cultures today, where there is frequently a belief in the Woman rather than the Man in the Moon. Such moon women are usually mothers.

The Creek Indian Moon Mother   The Creek Indians of south-eastern America tell how a young girl woke and was thirsty. Her own mother was tired and refused to bring her daughter some water. The child began to cry. The Moon Mother took pity on the child and sent down dew to drink. The child agreed to return to the sky with the Moon Mother and can be seen on the face of the moon with the little basket she took with her.

The Samoan Moon Mother   Sina, a Samoan mother, went out with her sleeping child at twilight to make cloth. As the moon rose it looked like a breadfruit and, since she was hungry and wanted to feed her child, Sina implored the moon to come down so that they might eat some of the delicious fruit. The moon became angry at this impertinence and snatched up Sina and her child. They can still be seen at certain lunar phases, the mother weaving her cloth, her daughter at her side.

Sun Mothers

In other cultures the sun is seen as the Great Mother. In Lapland, for example, Baiwe, the Great Mother of the Sun, blesses the land with plants and gives reindeer as well as human mothers fertility. Baiwe is depicted not in human form but as a geometric design, for example as a lozenge with rays emanating in all directions in the centre of a sacred shaman drum. Mother of all animals, she is offered only female animals in sacrifice. A Lapp hunter who is lost will erect a sun ring on a pole to contain the sun, so that she will not set before he has found his way home.

Wotjobaluk Sun Mother The Aborigine Wotjobaluk tribe of Victoria, Australia, tell of a time before there was light when people used bark torches to find their way in the darkness. A mother left her young son to look for yams. She became lost, wandered over the edge of the world and came up on the other side, becoming distressed when she could not find her child. Taking her bark torch, she climbed into the sky so that she might see where her infant was, and at last found him patiently waiting. Each morning the Sun Mother repeats her journey, and each evening she goes down to the west where she feeds her waiting child.

The Mother Goddess and her Consort

During the Bronze Age, from about 3500 BC to 1250 BC, the Moon and Earth Goddesses were given names and their cycles taken to reflect the birth, maturity, death and rebirth of first the Great Mother's daughter and later her son. The latter image persisted throughout the Greek and Roman empires, eventually culminating in the union of Sky Father and Earth Mother, Zeus and Hera, Jupiter and Juno.

The son of the personified Mother Goddess became her consort and eventually her superior, although the Mother remained vital for the continuation of both agriculture and the life of the god himself. The traditions of Sumeria and ancient Egypt whereby the Father God was sacrificed and restored by the Mother Goddess persisted into the Greek and Roman worlds: the cycles of Innana and Tammuz in Sumeria and Isis and Osiris in Egypt, where the rebirth was linked with the annual flooding of the Nile.

The Anatolian Cybele was worshipped in the Roman Empire as the Great Mother of the Gods and a temple erected to her honour on the Palatine Hill in 204 BC. Cybele in turn became associated with the classical Corn Goddess Demeter/Ceres whose daughter Persephone was doomed to the underworld for part of the year, accounting for the dearth of crops in the winter as Demeter searched for her daughter in a variation on the annual death/rebirth cycle. Though the supreme goddess Hera was definitely subordinate to Zeus on Mount Olympus, she used her guile to influence events and protect those under her auspices, not least women and the states of marriage and childbirth.

Ancient Egyptian Mother Deities

Isis   Ancient Egypt has a greater profusion of goddesses associated with fertility and motherhood than any culture apart from the Hindu. Indeed, a main focus of Mother Goddess worship in the Roman Empire was the Egyptian goddess Isis. Originally the sister/ wife of Osiris, Isis was the mother of Horus who became the principal Egyptian solar deity. Isis is perhaps best remembered in her icon as a mother suckling the infant Horus, an image thought by some to have been the prototype of later Christian images of Madonna and Child. Certainly her influence is pervasive in the dark-skinned Black Madonnas of Europe, for Isis was traditionally portrayed as a black figurine. Her Latin epithet was Stella Maris, or "star of the sea", a name later given to the Virgin Mary.

It was Isis who in accordance with the death/rebirth tradition retrieved and reassembled the body of Osiris after his murder and dismemberment by his brother Seth. In this connection she took on the role of a goddess of the dead and of funeral rites. Isis magically impregnated herself by the corpse and subsequently gave birth to Horus, so continuing the cycle of life.

Hathor   An Egyptian cow goddess who was also the daughter of Nut and Re, Hathor was regarded in early Egyptian mythology as the mother of the sky god Horus, but was later replaced in this capacity by Isis. Hathor then became a protectress of Horus. She was

51

depicted either as a cow or in human form wearing a crown consisting of a sun disc held between the horns of a cow. Her name appears to mean "house of Horus", referring to her role as a sky goddess, the "house" denoting the heavens, depicted as a great cow.

Her principal sanctuary was at Dandarah, where her cult had its early focus, and where it may have begun. At Dandarah, she was particularly worshipped in her role as a goddess of fertility, of women, and of childbirth. At Thebes she was regarded as a goddess of the dead under the title "Lady of the West", associated with the sun god Re on his descent below the western horizon. The Greeks identified Hathor with Aphrodite.

Taueret   The Great One, Taueret, the Egyptian hippopotamus goddess known to the Greeks as Theoris, was the protective deity of childbirth. She was depicted with the head of a hippopotamus, the limbs of a lion, the tail of a crocodile, human breasts, and a swollen belly. This appearance was meant to frighten off any spirits that might be harmful to the child.

Taueret was often depicted in the company of the dwarf god Bes, who had a similar function. Taueret was popular among ordinary Egyptians as a protectress. Pregnant women commonly wore amulets bearing the goddess's image and her role was carried into Greece.

The Mother Goddesses of the Northern Tradition

The Celtic Goddesses   Danu was the Earth Goddess and Great Mother of the Gods. She was not their actual mother, but as the early creator ritually mated with the Father God Dagda, symbolized by the chief of the Celtic tribes, to ensure fertility of the land as well as the continuation of human and animal life.

Although Brigid or Bride, the Triple Goddess, is often depicted on fertility images, for example that found in the Well of the Triple

Goddess at Minster in Kent (see next chapter), the Celtic goddess that most closely parallels the Mediterranean corn goddesses Demeter and Ceres is Cerridwen. As Goddess of the Grain, she is most famed for her role in the legendary poet and bard Taliesin's childhood. The consort of Tegid Foel, Cerridwen had a daughter, Creirwy, and a son, Afagddu. According to the legend of Taliesin, Cerridwen prepared a brew in a great cauldron which was to give her son Afagddu the gifts of inspiration and knowledge to compensate for his ugly appearance, and set her foster child Gwion to stir it. However, Gwion tasted the brew and so obtained its benefits. Cerridwen, realizing what had happened, pursued the boy. During the chase she and Gwion transformed themselves into a variety of creatures, and at last Cerridwen in the form of a hen swallowed Gwion in the shape of a grain of corn. However, this only impregnated Cerridwen, and she later gave birth to the rejuvenated Gwion. She wrapped the infant up in a leather bag and threw him into the river. The child was rescued by a fisherman who, struck by the child's beauty, named him Taliesin ("radiant brow"). This is yet another version of the transformation by death and rebirth ritual that symbolizes the Great Mother throughout many cultures.

Teutonic Mother Goddesses

Like the All Father Odin, Frigg his consort appears under many names and guises, Ostara, Freya, Hulda, Mother Holle, Bertha, all of which are different aspects of the Mother Goddess. As Frigg or Frigga, she is goddess of women, marriage and motherhood. Her jewelled spinning wheel formed Orion's belt and she was patroness of northern housewives, often being depicted with a distaff. Though she had knowledge of the future she would never reveal it. She was the mother of Baldur, the god of light, Hermod the messenger and Tyr the Spirit Warrior.

As Ostara, Goddess of Spring, or Oestre in her more youthful aspect, she is remembered at the festival of Easter, her sacred animal the hare transformed into the Easter rabbit. In Germany the first eggs of spring were offered to her, gaily painted.

In her role as Valfreya, the Lady of the Battlefield, Frigg recalls the Northern tradition of mother warrior goddesses, beings of magical power who ride the sky, mail-clad, and lead the spirits of the slain to a spiritual resting-place. She is said to be the guardian of a fountain called Quickborn, the waters of rebirth. She invited devoted husbands and wives to her hall after death that they might never be parted again. However, in accordance with the downgrading of mother goddesses, Frigg had no temple of her own and was worshipped alongside Odin.

As Hulde or Mother Holle, the Mother Goddess presided over the weather. When it snowed people said that she was shaking her feather bed; when it rained she was washing her clothes. White clouds were her newly bleached linen hung out to dry. She gave flax to mankind and taught women how to spin.

Finally as the White Lady or Bertha in Germany she cared for the souls of unborn children, who helped the Goddess of Agriculture to water the plants.

The Native North American Mother Goddess

Goddesses in the conventional sense are not normally associated with the Native North American Indian tradition. However, Canadian and American Indians see the earth as female and believe that she gives birth to all people, animals and plants, all of whom are living creatures of equal standing.

In traditional folklore, the earth is sometimes called Mother Turtle, upon whose back the weight of the world is carried. A Wichita creation myth describes how the "first woman lay on her back naked in the sun and slowly sank into the earth as her nipples turned dark as if suckling a child until her entire body was absorbed, after which the earth became fruitful".

Among the Hurons, the female creation myth is one of suffering as well as joy and tells how new life comes out of death. The lunar deity, Aataentsic, was the first mother and was carried to earth on the backs of swans when she fell from the Upper World. On the original island of earth, she gave birth to a female child. This infant grew up and died giving birth to twin boys, Iouskeha and Tawiscaron, who brought conflict and destruction into the world.

It was left to Grandmother, Aataentsic, to mediate between the brothers and encourage Iouskeha, who created everything useful for human beings. However, when Iouskeha eventually killed Tawiscaron, Aataentsic was so distressed that she also left the world, making her home in the four great Huron villages of the dead in the west so that she might care for her dead grandson.

The Cherokee creation myths concern a primal couple, Selu and Kanati, who are ruled by Mother Sun. Selu is the Corn Mother from whose body come corn and beans. Among many Native North American agricultural peoples corn is female, a primal source of life endowed with both intelligence and remarkable powers. The Corn Mother's symbol is the perfect ear of corn without a single missing or misshapen kernel, often placed as part of a healing medicine bundle.

The Return of the Mother Goddess

We approach the known through the unknown.
Archaeology, history, prehistory, tradition, legend,
folklore, mythology, paganism and Christianity and
human emotions are all entwined. No one knows the
answers and perhaps never will. All we can do when we
touch the Triple Goddess image is to marvel that her
power has been reawakened to restore fertility to a
spiritually arid world.

> Brian Slade, custodian of the
> sacred Triple Goddess Image at Minster

*W*e have seen how the Mother Goddess was worshipped in times past. But what relevance does she have today? Can we dismiss the superstition of our far-off ancestors and relegate their artefacts to the dustier corners of our museums? Evidence that the power of the Mother Goddess may still exist today has come from a small corner of England where wells once sacred to the Mother Goddess have been excavated.

Sacred wells date back to the beginning of recorded time, for water has always represented life and health and the well formed the centre of any community. In pre-Christian times wells were regarded as entrances to the womb of the Earth Mother, so many became associated with fertility and were visited by women who wanted to have children, but had difficulty conceiving. Just as the Catholic Church has its Walsingham and Lourdes where women pray to the Virgin Mary for a child, so the Mother Goddess had her ancient fertility wells and standing stones that retained their primal powers.

Celtic historian Dr Anne Ross wrote: "I have listened to many tales in Gaelic of wells having powers of fertility. One well in the Isle of Skye, called Tobar an Torraidh, was, as its name suggests, believed to create pregnancy when the water was poured over silver and drunk. This was in latter days used to make barren cows pregnant, but one very old man told me that in previous times the women themselves used it and believed unquestioningly in its powers. We have lost so much of our contact with forces that do, I believe, exist in all kinds of things. There is a very great deal that science is unable to explain but is well attested."

However, it would seem that such powers are not totally consigned to history. Brian Slade, historian, archaeologist and author, is convinced that the power of the Mother Goddess has been re-awakened in Britain with the discovery of the Triple Goddess fertility image in one of the three sacred wells that Brian's archaeological team has successfully excavated at Minster on the Isle of Sheppey.

Already five "miracle" babies have been born as a result, it is believed, of the Goddess's renewed power at Minster, and hundreds of childless couples visit Brian's home from all over the world to touch the image.

The Triple Goddess Well was originally inside Minster Abbey, founded in AD 670 by the widowed Queen of Kent, later St Sexburga. The saint, herself a mother and grandmother, used this and the other wells in the immediate vicinity for healing. Like many Christian wells in Britain and Ireland, the Minster Abbey well was originally dedicated to Brigid, the Triple Goddess. Brigid was said to have been the midwife and later foster mother of Christ and anointed his head with three drops of water from her sacred well, so uniting the old religion with the new. The sixth-century St Brigit of Kildare in Ireland took over this quasi-maternal role and became patron saint of childbirth with her feast day on 1 February, the old festival of Brigantia.

Teresa Kewley, an American author and expert on natural mothering practices, recalls the traditional Hebridean prayer of a woman in labour:

> Come to my help,
> Mary fair and Bride,
> As Anna bore Mary,
> As Mary bore Christ,
> As Eile bore John the Baptist
> Without flaw in him.
> Aid thou in my unbearing,
> Aid me, O Bride.

The Triple Goddess Well was excavated in 1990–1. Ian, one of the archaeologists, was up to his waist in well water when he picked up the twisted and unrecognizable piece of rusting metal that was to change his life. Experts confirmed the metal image was of a three-headed pregnant woman, with no legs, squatting as though about to give birth, possibly dating from pre-Celtic times.

It is speculated that the metal image either was thrown in the well by a rich childless woman or was the original mould for wax fertility images. The latter theory is strengthened by the discovery of fragments of beeswax in the well that, pieced together, made up the Triple Goddess image. From Celtic times and perhaps even earlier, votive images depicting the part of the body that needed healing would be cast into sacred wells. The images of swollen bellies were powerful pleas for a child from the mother of all life.

Ian thought little of his discovery and placed it with other artefacts, eager to get home to his wife Sharon, distressed after a series of late miscarriages indicated that her chances of carrying a baby to full term were remote. Doctors told her that they could not find the cause. Nine months later, almost to the day that Ian retrieved the image, Sharon gave birth to a healthy baby girl and went on to have a second child.

A "miracle" baby was also born to Maggie, the wife of another Ian, a medical research scientist. Maggie also despaired of carrying a baby to full term. Ian commented: "I really believe that the Mother Goddess played her part. Don't ask me for the mechanisms of how it happened. I just believe now that the world can work in a different way from the one we scientists think."

Maggie knew nothing of the votive offering Ian had made, so it was not a question of suggestibility. Indeed, as Brian Slade commented on the birth of Sharon and Ian's infant: "If the couple had known with their rational minds the significance of the image, then the birth of their children could have been explained away as mind over matter. I think that the explanation for such images lies in the powers they unconsciously reawaken in us. If you go back far enough over the centuries to the number of pregnant women and those wanting children who visited the shrine, then a sympathetic energy source is created. When an empathic person comes to Minster or is connected to the Goddess image by a votive offering, he or she may be influenced by those energies in a physical way."

Krystyna, who lives in Kent, is still struggling to have a child. Her story is told in the following chapter. She wrote to Brian Slade after her visit to Minster. "When I touched the Goddess at your home, I felt a tremendous energy coming out of her and into my fingers, just the same as touching powerful ley lines. There is definitely something very special about her."

Since the image has been found, the presence of the Goddess herself has been witnessed by many at or close to the Well of the Triple Goddess. Pilgrims have reported seeing a lady dressed all in white who disappears when approached. "Like a bride on her wedding day" is how she was described by one observer. Christians interpret the presence as a vision of the Virgin Mary, while others call her simply the White Lady, an old Celtic term for the goddess Brigid and the reason brides are still dressed in white in many parts of the world where the Celtic influence has prevailed.

Wonderful music and distant chanting in a strange tongue have been heard. A strong scent of flowers is also noticed by pilgrims as they push coins as votive offerings between the paving cracks. Above all is a sense of overwhelming love and peace.

Brian has seen a manifestation of the Goddess in his home close to the site. "Sitting upright in bed, in the very early hours of the morning on the first day of spring in 1996, I suddenly saw, glowing brighter than any light at the foot of my bed, a beautiful woman dressed in loose flowing white robes who then disappeared. I have seen the White Lady several times before out of the edge of my eye and field of vision, indistinctly pass my bedroom door."

One couple's pilgrimage had a happy ending. Shelley and Julian from Sussex turned up at Brian's home, and he allowed them to touch the figure and the ancient baby's birth bracelet, a fertility image uncovered from the third well to be excavated. In a letter to Brian Slade they wrote: "We visited the Well in March when we were just starting our third attempt at IVF treatment. We had been trying for a baby for eight years. You were so kind and spent time with us explaining your work and allowing us to touch the Goddess. We have never contemplated believing in anything like that before but we were desperate and somehow it gave us our hope back. We visited the second healing Well also and I drank the water once the embryos were implanted. We also touched the baby's birth bracelet from the third well. You opened your door to us without an appointment and welcomed us and now we want to let you know we believe that you and the Goddess and the other kind people we met helped us to achieve our dream. Our baby is due on New Year's Eve."

Diane, who touched the Triple Goddess image, had powerful dreams for two days after she returned home.

"I saw the Isle of Sheppey, perhaps 2000 years ago, much larger, green, surmounted by Minster Hill. The whole hill bubbled with tiny springs among the groves. The surrounding countryside was a mass of creeks and inlets with floating coracles and huts on stilts rising above the marshy land. There was a priestess of immense wisdom and stature, one of a royal clan, trained in the arts of Druidic wisdom and wearing robes of dove grey. She had heard of the well on top of the sacred hill and come on a pilgrimage.

"It was this priestess who had the original metal Triple-Headed Goddess image made for herself and the wax seals for her entourage. The

image was worked and empowered by a craftsman priest, so that it would have special qualities instilled and reflected into the water. The image was offered to the Goddess in a special ceremony. I feel the priestess may have returned to help rediscover the properties of the wells. I sensed her presence as I walked around the sacred sites and when she appeared in the dream she told me, 'You have only to touch my talisman to feel the power of creation.'"

Brian suggests possible reasons for the unleashing of the Goddess's ancient powers.

"I believe that there was something very special about my archaeological teams, a unique coming together of circumstance and forces that activated some dormant repository of wisdom and power. Ian, the archaeologist who due to youth, strength and enthusiasm spent more time than anyone else working at the bottom of the Well of the Triple Goddess, was extremely worried about his wife's health and her seeming inability to carry a baby to full term. Hence for those many hours, days, weeks that Ian worked digging out the Well, gradually getting nearer and nearer to the fertility goddess image at his feet in the well-bottom, he was constantly praying consciously and unconsciously for his wife and for the baby they longed to have. In effect Ian was carrying out the same ritual that thousands of husbands and wives had performed at the Well over thousands of years. In addition he worked for hours on end immersed up to his waist in the sacred fertility well water, as pilgrims would have done centuries before as part of their rites. Finally he completed the ancient ritual by touching the image.

"By fulfilling all the ancient ritualistic requirements to have a baby, I believe he acted as the catalyst by which the ancient powers were restored to the Well of the Triple Goddess and thereafter the other two wells in the immediate vicinity.

"I believe also because the team were not paid, but acted out of love for archaeology and the site, which as locals they treasured, they came to the Well in the spirit in which positive powers could be harnessed. Coincidentally the youngest member of the team was born on the

Feast of the Goddess at Imbolc, the beginning of February.

"My belief is strengthened by the fact that another archaeologist working on the Well seems to have been blessed by the Goddess. Ray, an older archaeologist, also worked in the holy waters and touched the Triple Goddess image when it was found. His son and daughter-in-law, desperate for a baby, and unable to conceive, journeyed to my home to touch the fertility goddess image and nine months later their daughter was born."

We do not understand the complex relationship between the spirit and the body, but for pilgrims who come from around the world to touch the image and drink the waters, the Goddess promises at least a focus for hope and positive energies.

The Goddess and Modern Motherhood

.I suddenly looked up to see the most beautiful sight I'd ever seen: the blackness melted away and there in a radiant and brilliant shining light stood the Great Mother. She was smiling in that benign, all-accepting smile that a mother gives her child, and she reached out to reassure me. She let me know that all was well, and the baby was well and on its way, and for me not to give up.

Lisa's experience while giving birth to her daughter

*M*any pagan women today still look to the Mother Goddess for inspiration and protection as they become mothers themselves. Lisa, a Wiccan practitioner who lives in Berkshire, explained:

"I realized that I was pregnant whilst in a magic circle with Jim, my husband. Immediately after an act of magic that I normally perform without incident, I suddenly collapsed in a heap and was far too dizzy to continue. We had been trying to conceive for several weeks, but it was too early for me to take a pregnancy test. Once I fell over, I realized that we had been successful in our attempts, and a pregnancy test a few weeks later confirmed it!

"At that point I decided to quit ritual magic for the duration of the pregnancy. I felt that the formation of our baby Skye was where all of my energy and focus should be directed, and so I settled down to savour what I hoped would be and proved to be an extremely magical and fulfilling pregnancy.

"When I was seven weeks pregnant with Skye, I started to bleed. This frightened me incredibly because I had miscarried at nine weeks only five months before. Until this point, I had been feeling fine and still felt pregnant, but I was scared none the less. I took a week off work, and Jim and I left London to go to spend a week in Wiltshire with our friends. Once I put my feet up, the bleeding seemed to be stopping. We had some lunch, enjoyed the stones at Avebury, and decided that a visit to Bath probably wouldn't be too much for me.

"However, once we arrived at the Bath museum, I suddenly passed more blood. I was really terrified now. I sat alone on a stone bench and there made my desperate plea to the Goddess to let me have my baby. The Goddess and I have had many a conversation, but my need was never greater than at that moment. I then made my way to the actual Baths and, when I thought no one was looking, stepped between two columns at the water's edge and scooped up three great handfuls of the healing Bath waters and anointed my belly, all the while visualizing myself heavily pregnant and full of energy and good health. I thanked the Great Mother and the magical waters and sat on a bench until my companions had finished the museum visit, and then headed back to Wiltshire. The bleeding did stop then, and occurred only once or twice more during the rest of the pregnancy.

"I had the usual strange pregnancy dreams that I think most women get and in hindsight I now believe on a few of those occasions Skye presented herself to me in her true form. I wondered at first if the tiny body forming within mine held the spirit of the baby that I had miscarried and I did have a dream where I was assured that the baby within me was a totally separate entity, and the first little soul that had left me had a different agenda now. Strangely, this gave me a real sense of completion with the earlier miscarriage. I wanted a daughter so desperately that I think I convinced myself that I was carrying a boy. I convinced absolutely everyone else too, except my best girlfriend who still gloats over the fact that she was right! In actual fact, I call my daughter 'the son I never had' because she is turning out to be a terrific tomboy.

"I went into labour at 11 p.m., at the beginning of May 1995, on Beltane, the start of the Celtic summer. We had had a quiet day. It was our third wedding anniversary and it was also three days past my due date. I had been bothered by a backache for most of the weekend, so when the first unmistakable contraction came—just as we were going to bed—I wasn't too surprised. We stayed up for a couple of hours, but decided that we should try and sleep. Jim helped me put on the tens machine [an electrical pain control device], and we went off to bed. I soon found that as soon as I would drop off to sleep, another contraction would wake me up, so I spent most of the night pacing the upstairs hall and climbing in and out of the bathtub, trying to remove and replace the tens machine on my own!

"I was planning a water birth, so I used my time in the bathtub to go deep within myself. I found that by applying the same visualizing techniques that I use in healing work, I was able to psychically check on the baby during the labour. I felt a tremendous sense of excitement in spite of contractions that were increasingly causing me to chew on a towel to keep from screaming.

"We went into hospital the following morning at 9 a.m. I wrote pagan on my birth plan and hospital chart. The midwives and consultant were very interested, and asked a lot of questions. The consultant was particularly impressed by the Sheelagh-na-gig statue [a Mother Goddess figurine from Ireland] that we brought as a focus point for me. We brought music and incense and candles to the hospital with us, but as the labour was advanced, we only got as far as setting up the tape player before it was time for me to get into the birthing pool.

"In the pool is where things started to get incredibly intense. I knew that this would probably be the only time I would give birth (as we already had Jim's older girls in our family) and so I was determined to get through it as naturally as possible. I wanted to experience every sensation because I had read so many accounts of women who had had epidurals and then felt cheated because they couldn't feel their baby coming out. I used an exercise taught to me in my Craft training to get myself to an alpha level, but I think the experience of labour puts you between the worlds anyway.

"All of the pain was in my lower back, so with each contraction I either got on my hands and knees in the water or hung over the edge of *the pool while Jim dug into my lower back with one of those wooden ball massagers from the Body Shop. I can't really call it a massage because I was commanding him to do it harder and harder. After the birth I had a terrific bruise and he had terribly sore arms! During this, I would try to zero in on the Sheelagh-na-gig and mentally invoke the Goddess to assist me in opening up and to keep the baby safe during the birth.*

"This went on for a couple of hours, but then the pain was so bad that I felt I couldn't manage without at least gas-and-air. The first canister was wheeled in and the midwife showed me how to use it. I am not a drinker or drug user, so the impact that came from the gas-and-air really sent me to the Other Side. Jim was the only thing that I could see from the mundane world; everything else was a sort of misty dark outer/inner space. The water was the perfect temperature and depth to allow me to lose the understanding of where my body ended and the infinite began.

"Even though the pain was still there and obvious, my consciousness seemed to expand far beyond the confines of my body. Even Jim faded from view during the contractions, and after who-knows-how-long this was going on, I suddenly looked up to see the most beautiful sight I'd ever seen: the blackness melted away and there in a radiant and brilliant shining light stood the Great Mother. She looked like All Women to me, and not at all like I might have guessed. She was huge, much bigger than the room, but somehow I could see all of her. She was smiling in that benign, all-accepting smile that a mother gives her child, and she reached out to reassure me. She let me know that all was well, and the baby was well and on its way, and for me not to give up. I was amazed by the sight of her and I couldn't take my eyes off her. I can only describe the Goddess as a huge, shimmering, all-encompassing Love, and her confidence in me was both humbling and empowering. I don't know how long she was there, and I cannot remember her going away, but she must have changed her appearance or disappeared entirely because I could have never broken my gaze.

"After that, the midwife told me that I was acting as if it might be time to start pushing, and I had to get myself out of the pool for an internal examination. Jim and the midwife got me, plus the gas-and-air canister that I was still clutching, over to the bed. I was told I could start

pushing when I liked and they offered to help me back into the pool. Once I had solid ground under me, though, I decided to stay out of the water. In the end this turned out to be a good decision as the labour slowed to the point where I ended up on a drip and, after two hours of pushing, finally agreed to a forceps delivery. Still, I hadn't taken any drugs beyond the gas, and once they got her head out, I was able to give that final push to send my baby into the world.

"As a mother, you know that words cannot describe the feeling of your child being born. In spite of being half out of my mind with pain and exhaustion, I was aware as it happened that this was the greatest moment of my life. Everyone in the room (at this point I had a doctor, two midwives and the head of midwifery as well as Jim) was cheering, and I could tell from her angry, lusty hollering that the baby was all right. They laid her on her back across my belly immediately, and her arms were raised and quivering with shock and/or anger and I could hardly believe I was holding my own child.

"Jim was beyond being able to speak. Even now I am filling with tears as I recall the moment I realized that I had my little girl at last. I said her name 'Skye', and she soon went quiet and started looking around. The midwife took her and cleaned her up and then we were left to spend our first two hours as a family. When I put Skye to my breast, I was again moved beyond words at how the Goddess manifests in woman as Mother. I may never give birth again, but even through this one experience I feel that I could never know a moment more Divine."

Lisa told me about bringing up her daughter in the pagan faith:

"I am a woman, a mother, and a Witch. These three aspects of my life make up most of my identity. They are inextricably linked and for me, I could not have felt complete in any one aspect without the other two. In my twenties I embraced a pagan philosophy that had really begun to form (or was remembered) in my childhood. I felt a kinship with nature and the magical realms that I was lucky enough to carry with me into adulthood. I dreamed of my own family through many years of searching for fulfilment, and made many mistakes along the way. When at last I

found my spiritual home in Wicca, everything else fell into place. I found myself through the self-examination and disciplines of my Craft teachings, and a few years later found my husband Jim, also a Witch. Together we have created a home and live very happily with our beautiful daughter.

"Becoming a mother has touched me more deeply than I ever could have imagined. I am sure that every mother, pagan or otherwise, has felt and appreciated the magical connection between mother and child: eyes and hearts locked together during a breastfeed; waking to silence in the middle of the night, only to hear the baby wake and cry out moments later; being able to recognize one's own child's cry in a room full of noisy babies. Being a pagan has brought all of these experiences into a spiritual focus that has brought me closer to the Goddess in a way that I don't think could have happened if I hadn't chosen to become a parent. It has allowed me to experience the Mother Aspect firsthand; it gave new meaning to the moon cycles of a woman, it allowed me to become the microcosm of the great Earth Mother as I watched my own body grow and give birth to a new life. It gave me the protective instinct of Sekhmet [the lion-headed Egyptian goddess of fertility], when I realized that I would fight to the death to protect my child. It showed me the true and profound power of the female body; to create and sustain life within the body, to bring forth that life and nurture it with a perfect food made by the body.

"All of these are precious gifts to me as they are all a reflection of my deepest spiritual belief and faith. When my daughter is older, I will share with her what I have learned. For now, we just walk in the forest or along the river and Jim and I give her the opportunity to explore her environment. Through books and Disney videos she already has an image of fairies, elves and other magical beings. We try to encourage her to see the spirit in the tree or in the running water. We collect stones and leaves just to look at and admire their colour or shape. Some we take home, but most we leave where we find them. Skye loves these adventures and I am so happy to be part of her experience.

"On the Sabbats, the main Wiccan festivals, we and our friends celebrate with seasonal games, activities, myths and feasts, and the

children in our lives are always eager and excited to join in. Skye is still a bit young for much of it, but even a two-year-old can dance around a maypole, pick berries, plant seeds and help bake bread or biscuits. It's exciting to think that the Wheel of the Year will have deep significance to her; that Samhain [the end of October] and Beltane [the beginning of May] will hold the same magic and excitement that Christmas held for me as a child.

"I don't know if Skye will ultimately choose Wicca as her spiritual path, but I feel that growing up in a pagan home will give her the best tools for making choices in her life. She will learn to be aware of her environment and will feel a part of it; not above or outside it. Hopefully this will inspire her to care for it and for others around her, and to encourage others to do the same. Wicca is self-governing, and I hope that Skye will have integrity and confidence in herself.

"Having a Goddess as well as a God in her life will certainly give her a better spiritual balance than either Jim or I had as children. I wish for her to be strong and sure of her Self, and not be afraid to challenge or be challenged. Paganism certainly provides a framework for this, and regardless of the spiritual path she chooses, if any, I believe that growing up with these values will help her immeasurably in her life.

"Recently, I had an experience in walking home from work along the Thames. I was making my way along a towpath between the river and a pasture where about a hundred or so cows were grazing. One cow decided to follow me whilst mooing her head off and incited the rest of the herd to do the same. I found it pretty unsettling, and the next morning I was not looking forward to passing the same herd again on my way to work. I was thinking about it while I was changing Skye's nappy, and she suddenly looked up at me and said brightly, 'Mama, lots and lots of cows!'

"This is the sort of connection that I imagine will happen with greater frequency as Skye grows older and more articulate. She reads my mind effortlessly, she sees and converses with any number of astral beings, and she can transport herself to any dimension she chooses through her incredible imagination. I think she has as much, if not more, to teach me than I have to teach her. She is a perfect child of the gods; unspoiled and

*innocent of the limitations humankind have created for themselves. I
believe that my greatest gift to her would be to teach her to stand with
one foot in each world: the magical and the mundane, so that she will
live her life fully and in true happiness, and perhaps inspire others
towards the same."*

Because the image of the great Mother of Fertility is so powerful it
is easy to forget the sorrow of women who cannot have children,
whose mother love is left unfulfilled, an aching wound for the
potential children who may never be conceived or if conceived are
lost within hours and days. Where the woman concerned looks to
the pagan Earth Mother for help, where none is forthcoming it can
seem a betrayal of the fundamental beliefs of the faith, the greatest
trial of all.

Krystyna, who lives in Rochester, England, wrote in April 1997:

*"I have not yet reached motherhood and do not know if I ever will. I am
a writer and produce and edit my own magazine* Homeground, *a Kate
Bush fan magazine which reaches its fifteenth birthday on 18 May. I am
not ashamed of our infertility. I am also currently undergoing my fourth
attempt at IVF.*

*"Infertility has to be handled with sensitivity. Many people will not
even tell their friends and family that they are having trouble conceiving,
let alone that they are having treatment. It is at this time that we need
our friends and families the most. The infertility path is a very lonely,
frightening and isolating one and we need all the support we can get.
Infertility is such a vast and emotive issue and only those who have
struggled to conceive, or who still haven't achieved that first much-
wanted child, will ever really understand.*

*"Those who have children often can't understand, usually because
they haven't had to try very long or the child has been conceived by
accident. Some who do have children don't value them as the precious
little beings they are, probably because they achieved them so easily.
There is nothing romantic about infertility. It is a hard fact for some of
us and for some it may never be resolved.*

"*Sometimes it can feel as if the whole Mother Goddess thing becomes distant, intangible, that we are not part of the cycle of creation and procreation. Indeed infertility goes against the grain of what the whole Mother Goddess belief is about so that somehow we are mocked by what we believe in—a belief in the mother aspect of God, the creative, powerful, sexual Feminine and the ultimate in creation, the procreation of a child. This is a true testing of faith.*

"*Infertility, the inability to create a child when it seems that almost every other living thing can, affects the way you feel about yourself as a woman, as a sexual woman, as a creative woman. Instead the womb becomes tomb and we become the goddess of Death, Hag before our time, destroying ourselves in our frustration and anger at our inability to create our child. Where is the Rite of Passage for the infertile woman? We do not pass from Maiden to Mother but from Maiden to Crone, leaving a vast aching emptiness made more hollow and resounding by the eventual onset of the menopause, the final blow, a time in my life I know I will dread if I have never been able to have children.*

"*Feelings run similarly so for a man, the sower of seeds that can become new life. When his seed will not grow, he feels less of a man. No part of you is left untouched by infertility, woman or man. As a couple it can bring you closer, but if you are unlucky it can tear you apart. I have been one of the lucky ones, though it leaves us bruised and battered, physically for me and emotionally for both of us. It invades your sex life. The making of babies and making love become two separate things and that can be quite a healing realization. Woman bear the scars in the most intimate places. We are bruised and stretched and pierced by various surgical instruments, used in attempts at procreation.*

"*Subfertility or infertility is one of the major life crises, comparable in my experience only with death. Some of your friends don't know how to deal with it, avoid talking about it, ignore you even, the same way as people deal with the bereaved.*

"*There was and is folklore attached to fertility but what spells are there when your infertility is virtually incurable and your only hope is through technology? A positive frame of mind is good magic enough and rituals can help emotionally and spiritually, if not physically, but what* can you do if your body is not cooperating with your mind, heart and intention? Can miracles happen? I hope they can.

"I for one have tried everything. I have been to standing stones, sat on the Avebury Mother Stone, have touched the Minster Triple Goddess image. I have touched the Cerne Abbas Giant. I have prayed. I have dreamed and hoped and despaired. I have been kissed and blackened by so many Morris Men I have lost count. They have put their hats on my head. You are supposed to become pregnant within the year. I have opened myself up to any possible beneficial influences in the hope that my poor infertile body will by some miracle release the eggs that would become our beautiful children.

"I have not exactly lost faith in these things, it is more that I do not expect to find any solutions. I still kissed Jack in the Green through his green leaves at the Sunrise ceremony at Bluebell Hill near Maidstone, Kent on 1 May. Our dear friend Max was inside the Jack again this year and he gave us Black Jack sweets as little fertility offerings from him and Jack to us to wish us good luck. But I do not hang on to any of these things now working for us. I just share in their good vibes and don't dare get carried away on it. The truth is that my body does not work properly and the real truth of this I found out from my professor at a leading London hospital recently. I have a condition called polycystic ovaries, and together with my husband's low sperm count our only chance of becoming pregnant is through a technique called ICSI [Intra Cytoplasmic Sperm Injection] where a single sperm is injected into an egg.

"We have been trying for a baby for ten and a half years. We were told in 1990 there was no hope after years of investigations and tests on my husband Peter and myself. In 1992 we changed our GP and she said that ICSI had been recently developed and suggested we tried again. After three more years of waiting I had my first ICSI attempt which began in August 1995. This was the great unknown. The procedure involves many drugs and a nasal spray which shuts the body down into a false menopause so that the doctors can control your body with further drugs in the form of daily injections for about two weeks. These start the follicles in the ovaries growing the little fluid-filled sacs where hopefully eggs are also growing. Progress is monitored throughout with blood tests

72

and vaginal scans. Sometimes my treatment has had to be cancelled because I have over-responded to the drugs.

"The eggs are retrieved under sedation, easier and less risky than a general anaesthetic, but a very painful experience as a probe with an ultrasound-guided needle is plunged through the muscles of the vaginal walls on right and left sides and pierces the ovaries several times. The follicles are drained of their fluid and if we are lucky there is an egg in the fluid. The pain is like something I have never experienced. But we do anything to have the chance of a child. The third time I had this operation was in November 1996. I had over-responded to the drugs and it was decided I should go for egg collection, but have any resulting embryos frozen for transfer into my womb when I am out of danger of hyperstimulation, where the body and lungs can fill with fluid post egg retrieval. At worst this can lead to a stroke and one woman in the UK has died from hyperstimulation. Twenty-two eggs were collected. Of these ten could be used and we had six embryos frozen so I could recover for three months and then have a maximum of three transferred.

"The day after any egg retrieval is crucial. That is when you are told if any embryos have resulted after incubation for twenty-four hours. The wait for the phone call from the hospital is nerve-racking.

"The most spiritual part of ICSI and IVF is when those precious little embryos are transferred into the womb. For me it is not without physical pain, though with gentle and understanding consultants and nursing staff my experience of this has now been eased. The last transfer I had was in February 1997, using three of my tiny frozen embryos. It was a very Tribal experience and one I will always treasure.

"Because of the pain I had previously, I requested sedation to make the experience easier for me and less traumatic for our potential children. Our embryologist asked if I could go ahead with the procedure without sedation and I agreed providing she was very gentle with me and took her time. Our embryologist sent for a midwife and she took me through relaxation, holding my hand and stroking my hair and talked of oceans and white beaches. Peter held my other hand. The two female embryologists gently eased the catheter into the body and passed our three precious embryos into my womb, a very moving, very conscious

experience. Quite suddenly there is life at its very beginning inside me, very conscious conception and, as many agree, the best part of IVF. We are usually shown the embryos on a television screen prior to transfer, images that remain with me.

"For a few days I dare to hope, for a few days I am pregnant. I watch my body for every sign that I may be properly pregnant this time. I pray so hard, ask my Mother Goddess for protection, ask her to look after our little ones, ask her to keep us all safe. I pray our little ones will stay.

"There is a two-week wait of something approaching hell. Almost everyone going through IVF would say the same. The total and utter feelings of despair, shock and a depth of misery rarely felt when the pregnancy test showed negative yet again. A few days later, the bleeding begins and then all hope of being pregnant bleeds away. Our dreams and hopes of being pregnant, being parents, all gone. I dream of rushing into our bedroom with my magic wand showing a positive test result and leap on Peter and tell him he will be a daddy. How I have longed to see the look of joy in his beautiful, dark dragon eyes. The utter hopelessness of never feeling our child or children growing inside me, never to feel my breasts and tummy swell or be throwing up at the smell of coffee, having an aching back or fearing the unknown as the birth approaches. There is so much blood and pain in my emptying belly, so many tears, so many questions as to why it didn't work again. The body breaks, the heart breaks. I truly feel that I will break.

"At the bottom of my garden is the most beautiful blossom tree and under its gaze we have buried the blood which has held our tiny children, those tiny embryos, little clusters of cells which held so much hope for us. A sunflower stone marks the place where we buried our seven tiny embryos from three failed ICSI attempts. It is vital to us to have a ritual to mark that our potential children were there for a short time and we mark their loss, our loss of those children and ourselves as parents. We have to grieve and when the time is right and we have healed as best we can we let them go. I wonder if their little spirits play in our garden around that beautiful tree. I wonder too if they will return to us next time or the time after and try to come through the gateway we create through flesh and technology.

"There are many private rituals Peter and I have done together to welcome these little souls because there is spirit going on here too, not merely biology, and nothing has been wasted, not energy or intention. Nothing is ever wasted. And so I have entered, with some trepidation, the fourth ICSI attempt. My body pumped full of drugs, injections begin in two weeks' time and we go down that path again. I am so scared of yet another negative pregnancy test and all the grief that follows. I don't want to have to be on my knees sobbing my guts out into that tiny grave under our blossom tree. I don't want to have to say goodbye yet again to our hopes and dreams of those little children. I don't want to have to write yet another little goodbye card to our tiny children to go into their grave, signed Mummy and Daddy. I want my children here. I want to hear them laughing and playing in the garden like the children next door have been doing this afternoon as I have been writing this.

"There are those who judge techniques such as IVF and condemn the professors and consultants who work in such fields, accusing them of playing God. I would say to any of them, let them walk a few miles in our shoes. I totally believe in what we are doing, and know if the treatment was to be successful we would do our best to give our children a happy life. They would be loved and how dearly I wish to share with them all the places special to us. The truth is that they may never be, that is the reality we have to face.

"Meanwhile we watch as our dearest friends experience their first pregnancy, a little boy called Jake, due to be born in September. I was the first person to be told the news. I was happy for them but it brought my own infertility smack up close to my face and for a few days I went through hell, experiencing close and raw all the feelings of that infertility and all the lost children. Everything came rushing in madly at me, something I did not expect. Thankfully the little child has brought my friend, his mother, and me closer. Seeing babies and pregnant women brings the pain close yet it is the thing I desire more than anything in my life, the heaven and hell, this strange kind of limbo. My friend's tummy grows bigger and rounder and she looks so beautiful. When she isn't looking I take a few glances of her lovely tummy. At times I want to ask her if I can see her tummy, bare and round, protecting little Jake, but I

am scared of intruding on this private time. I may never see another pregnant tummy.

"Between now and Jake's birth my fourth ICSI attempt will be over and done with. It would be wonderful if I became pregnant too. But I know the reality will probably be different. At best we may have more little embryos to add to our remaining two frozen ones so we can have a few more transfers. I know I will continue on this path until I have exhausted every possibility and until someone tells me I have to stop.

"Knowledge is power and I do not believe in being a victim of treatment, more that we and the medical profession are working as a team to try to have our children. Laughter is as vital as the ability to cry and let the many sometimes completely overwhelming emotions move through you, rather than bottling them up. It's not doom and gloom all the time, but it is always there in my mind.

"Not a minute goes by without thinking about having a child, thinking about my treatment, or going into some daydream about our future children and the things we would do together. Despite everything I dare to hope, because without hope and trying to be positive there is no point in even attempting this ICSI treatment. This is a form of magic in itself. But every waking and sleeping moment the hopes, fears and dreams are there. There are babies in my dreams, babies that turn into dolls on waking, leaving me haunted and feeling my sense of loss, dreams of giving birth in every possible position, dreams of girl babies, boy babies. I wake up and my belly is empty as before and sometimes tears fall.

"Jake's birth will be another important time, not only for our friends but for us. I long to hold Jake, yet I know the agony I will feel as I take his delicate little body in my arms for the first time and look into his eyes and touch his tiny fingers and toes and I know I may never experience holding my own child for the first time, looking into his or her little face and touching those tiny fingers and toes. I know I may cry long and hard and hate my own inefficient ovaries again. But laying my own pain to one side, I want to hold little Jake and love him and, if I can, be there as a friend as he grows and play with his bears and toys with him, play silly games and see the world a little through his eyes. I want to see him laugh

and be happy and I wish all the good things in life for him and maybe he'll have children of his own continuing the cycle. And maybe I'll hold his children on my knees in my old age, if I have no grandchildren of my own. We infertiles not only lose our children but our grandchildren. I am thirty-two now and will give myself another eight years if I am able (sanity, finances, body permitting) to continue along the ICSI path for that long. There will be new developments in those years to come and maybe we will eventually have our much-wanted child. It will take more than a miracle, though I hear miracles do happen."

Krystyna's fourth attempt at ICSI failed and she is taking a six-month break to allow her body to recover for a while.

PART THREE

Ideals of Motherhood

The Virgin Mary, Perfection of Motherhood

> But Mary kept all these things, and pondered them in
> her heart.
>
> *Luke 2:19*

*T*his chapter is not a definitive guide to the incredibly complex
doctrine concerning the Virgin Mary, but an examination of her
role as daughter and mother in an attempt to see how the idealized view
has influenced maternal aspirations of modern women.

The History of the Virgin Mary

There are remarkably few references to Mary, mother of Jesus, in
the Bible. Knowledge of her birth and childhood comes from early
Christian writings, especially the *Nativity of Mary*, sometimes
called the *Protoevangelium of James*. It is these texts that reveal the
names of Mary's parents, Anna and Joachim. They also tell that as
a child Mary was dedicated as a virgin of the Temple in gratitude
for her birth. Intriguingly, the origins of "The Cherry Tree Carol"
can be found here too. The haunting lines reveal the unbridled
anger of Joseph, masked in the gospels, that Mary was with child
(see p. 167).

Because the *Protoevangelium* was written less than sixty years after
Mary's death, it is claimed to be accurate because memories of her
life were still vivid. But even here, the images capture only the

landmarks in her life and the backcloth remains intriguing. We can only guess at the world within.

It is difficult over a distance of 2000 years to see beyond the Madonna to the ordinary mother, the Mary behind the ideal, lovely whether in sorrow, joy, humility or splendour. It is hard to imagine her fears, her joys, her private thoughts, her bewilderment, the moments of boredom, her humorous interchanges at the well with other women. Did she ever wish even momentarily in the dark of the night that her son was just an ordinary boy?

Yet it is precisely because Mary was an earthly mother, not a remote goddess living on a high mountain or born on celestial plains, that people worldwide, not only Catholics, do call on her for help and consolation and tell her their private worries and fears, confident that she will understand. Even when the cult of Mary as Queen of Heaven, which began in the fifth century, was at its height, her call has always been from the heart, one that instinctively goes back to the root human need to be mothered, understood and forgiven. Mary is the personalized face of divinity, the touchstone for many mothers as well as their children throughout the ages. Unlike the Mother Goddess and pagan deities, she reveals no cruel or warlike tendencies, but endures. Because she lost her son, yet sought no revenge, she is the Mater Dolorosa, the grieving mother, who shares the sorrows of all who have lost a loved one.

Mary the Daughter

According to tradition, Anna and Joachim were a childless couple of a Jewish priestly family. Anna asked God for a child and Joachim went into the desert to make an offering to God. Here he received a vision that his wife would bear a child. At the moment of Joachim's vision, an angel announced the same news to Anna. The joyous couple met at the Golden Gate of Jerusalem and this moment is taken to represent the conception of Mary.

Anna promised: "As the Lord my God lives, if I bear a child, whether male or female, I will bring it as a gift to the Lord my God, and it shall serve Him all of its days" (*Nativity of Mary* 4:1).

The major events in Mary's life recorded in the apocryphal sources and legends of her life begin with Mary's conception and end with the Coronation of the Virgin Mary in heaven after her death.

"In her ninth month Anna gave birth to a daughter, as the angel had said And she nursed the child and called her Mary" (*Nativity of Mary* 5:2). "Day by day Mary grew strong; when she was six months old, her mother settled her on the ground to see if she could stand. And Mary walked seven steps and returned to her mother" (*Nativity of Mary* 6:1).

Jacobus Voragine gives us precious snippets of her daily life, for example being taught by her mother to sew, embroider and read.[1] Scenes of Mary and her mother are depicted on the St Anne Altarpiece created by Gerard Davis about 1500–20 and now in the National Gallery of Arts in Washington.

When Mary was three, Anna kept her promise and brought Mary to the Temple to be dedicated. "And the priests took her and placed her on the third step of the altar, and the Lord God put grace upon her and she danced for joy with her feet, and the whole house of Israel loved her" (*Nativity of Mary* 7:3). "And her parents went home marvelling and praising God, because Mary did not turn back after them (*Nativity of Mary* 8:1).

How could Anna bear to leave her little daughter? Because she believed that Mary was the child of God and had made a promise. Did she weep for the loss of her child? Did the young Mary cry for her mother? Those brought up in a secular tradition find such concepts hard, especially where we are used to public displays of emotions and analysis of every nuance of feeling.

"And Mary lived in the temple nurtured like a dove, and received food from the hand of an angel" (*Nativity of Mary* 8:1).

Mary remained at the Temple for ten years. She took a vow of life-long chastity while in Temple service. At the age of thirteen, she was sent home by the Temple priests to be betrothed to Joseph, a

Nazarean carpenter, for her protection. Mary after the birth of Jesus probably lived the humble life of a Jewish wife and peasant in Roman-occupied Palestine.

Mary the Mother

Mary has been represented in Christian art as the ideal mother: Raphael's *Alba Madonna* (1511; National Gallery of Arts, Washington) depicts her maternal love for her infant; Michelangelo's *Pieta* (1499; St Peter's Basilica, Rome) is an exquisite marble statue of Mary cradling her dead son.

According to the New Testament, Mary was a virgin, probably in her early teens, when she conceived Jesus through the intercession of the Holy Spirit. Mary was greeted by the angel Gabriel as "highly favoured, the Lord is with you" (Luke 1:28), a unique biblical phrase indicating, it is said, the pre-existing holiness given to her by the grace of God.

Gabriel told Mary of her son: "He shall be great, and shall be called the Son of the Highest: and the Lord God shall give unto him the throne of his father David: and he shall reign over the house of Jacob for ever; and of his kingdom there shall be no end" (Luke 1:32–3).

We know both from the Bible and from the *Protoevangelium* that Joseph was visited by an angel who assured him that Mary's son was indeed the child of God and that he could marry her with honour. Mary's *Magnificat* offers the only soliloquy attributed to her in the Bible. In this beautiful hymn of praise she says: "For behold from henceforth all generations shall call me blessed, for he that is mighty hath done to me great things and Holy is his name" (Luke 1:48). In the biblical representation nothing is revealed of Mary's emotions during the pregnancy, the birth or the visits from shepherds and Wise Men with precious gifts, apart from the enigmatic words "But Mary kept all these things, and pondered them in her heart" (Luke 2:19). This phrase is echoed through her life. Mary was in the background throughout Christ's earthly ministry. One of the most significant interchanges between mother and son was when Jesus was twelve years old. He was missing, and Mary and Joseph had to turn back on their long journey from Jerusalem home to Nazareth. After three days they found Jesus in the Temple questioning and listening to the Doctors. Mary said, "Son, why hast thou dealt with us thus? Behold, thy father and I have sought thee, sorrowing." And he said to them: "Wist ye not I must be about my Father's business?" (Luke 2:48–9). Again Mary did not understand but "kept all these sayings in her heart".

Mary's final act of love to her son recorded in the Bible is her vigil with him in his death agony. When Jesus saw his mother and the disciple John whom he loved, he said to his mother, "Woman, behold your son." Then he said to John, "Behold, your mother." (John 19:26–7). Because Jesus gave his mother to the disciple at the Cross, it was said that she became symbolically mother of all who followed Christ. Mary's words on this final occasion are not recorded. Indeed the last words we have were spoken at the wedding at Cana, where she told Jesus there was no wine and he performed the miracle with the water. His mother said to the servants, "Whatever he sayeth unto you, do it" (John 2:5).

Mary is seen among the disciples at Pentecost, but it is not known how she spent her last days, or even for certain where she died. Jersusalem and Ephesus both claim to be the place of her death; Jerusalem is considered to be the more likely.

The belief in her Assumption into heaven, declared dogma by Pope Pius XII in 1950, dates from the sixth century. From then on her role as intercessor for mankind was increasingly accepted. Born without original sin thanks to her own Immaculate Conception (declared dogma by Pope Pius IX in 1854), Mary is traditionally believed to have remained a virgin after Jesus's birth. The purity and obedience to God of this second Eve enabled Christ as a second Adam to sacrifice himself to redeem the sins of mankind.

In a secular age it can seem hard to imagine a little girl who danced for joy in the Temple, who sewed next to her mother, became a

Temple handmaid and followed the path ordained for her. Mary did not understand the son who could leave his family to engage in learned discussion with the greatest Jewish teachers, but nevertheless she accepted and later followed him, never deserting him even in the last hours. It is above all the quiet acceptance of her destiny that makes the Madonna not an impossible act to follow but, like many mothers, a woman who did her best.

The Black Madonna and the Marian Folklore Tradition

It came about on a bright summer's day
Small rain from the sky did fall
And our saviour asked his mother dear
If he might play at the ball.

"O yes," his mother Mary said,
"O yes my little young son.
But don't let me hear any mischief of you
In the time that you are gone."

So it's up the hill and down the hill
Our sweet saviour ran,
Until he spied three rich young lords
A-playing in the sun

"Good morning, good morning,
Good morning all," said he,
"And which of you three rich young lords,
Will play at ball with me?"

"Oh we're all lords and ladies' sons.
Born in the highest hall,
You're a poor carpenter's son.
And we won't play at ball."

So he built him a bridge of the beams of the sun
And over the river ran he,
Those three young lords followed after him,
And drowned were all three.

So Mary mild brought home her child,
And laid him across her knee.
And with a bundle of withy twigs,
She gave him lashes three.

The Bitter Withy (folk song)

"*T*he Bitter Withy" would have been sung or heard by English peasant women who visualized the Virgin Mary as a mother like themselves with their hopes, fears, troubles—and unruly children. The willow or withy tree was sacred to the ancient Goddess of Death. In a similar humanizing vein is the following story from the Brothers Grimm's collection of German folk tales. It tells of a poor woodcutter with a daughter for whom he could not care.

While the woodcutter was chopping wood there suddenly stood before him a tall and beautiful woman with a crown of shining stars on her head. She said to him: "I am the Virgin Mary, mother of the child Jesus. Thou art poor and needy. Bring thy child to me and I will take her with me and be her mother, and care for her."

The child was fed on sugar-cakes and milk, wore golden clothes and had angels for her companions. However, when she was fourteen she disobeyed the Virgin Mary by opening a forbidden door, and was cast from heaven into a prison of thick thorns for refusing to confess her sin.

A handsome king rescued her from the thorns and married her, but she was struck dumb by her refusal to admit her sin. When her first two sons were born, the Virgin Mary appeared to her and said, "If thou wilt tell the truth and confess that thou didst unlock the forbidden door, I will open thy mouth and give thee back thy speech, but if thou perseverest in thy sin, and deniest obstinately, I will take thy new-born child away with me."

On each occasion the Queen refused, and the Virgin took the child out of her arms and went away to heaven.

The following year the Queen gave birth to a beautiful little daughter, and for the third time the Virgin Mary appeared to her in the night and said, "Follow me." She took the Queen by the hand and led her to heaven, and showed her there her two elder children, who were playing with the ball of the world. When the Queen rejoiced thereat, the Virgin Mary said, "Is thy heart not yet softened?"

But for the third time the Queen answered, "No, I did not open the forbidden door." Then the Virgin let her sink down to earth once more, and took from her likewise her third child.

The Queen was accused of devouring her children and condemned to be burned at the stake. As the fire began to burn round about her, the hard ice of pride melted, her heart was moved by repentance, and she thought, "If I could but confess before my death that I opened the door."

Rain fell from the sky and extinguished the fire. The Virgin Mary descended and told the Queen, "He who repents his sin and acknowledges it, is forgiven."

Then she gave her the three children, untied her tongue, and granted her happiness throughout her life.

This tale takes quite a harsh view of the Madonna mother, showing what might in modern terminology be called "tough love", as expressed in "The Bitter Withy". This more assertive, unforgiving aspect is also reflected in folk tradition and in the mysteries of the Black Madonna statues, symbols, like the Hindu goddess Black Kali, of the mother of death as well as life.

The Black Madonna

The Black Madonna is an image of the Virgin Mary and her child that either turned black from some natural cause, such as candle smoke, tarnish or a chemical imbalance of the paints, or were naturally black when they were carved. Such images were found all over medieval Europe, and their origins and purpose are shrouded in uncertainty.

Many of their sites were previously dedicated to fertility goddesses; other are associated with the Holy Grail, the Gnostic sects of the eleventh and twelfth centuries, and the Crusaders. The most famous Black Madonnas are at Chartres in France, Czestochowa in Poland and Montserrat in Spain. A group of post-Renaissance Black Madonnas whose coloration is more directly related to the racial and ethnic types appropriate to their geographic location also exists, the most famous being Our Lady of Guadalupe in Mexico.

Some Black Madonnas are said to be Christianized versions of the Egyptian Isis and the infant Horus, and thus rooted in the pre-Christian concept of saviour gods who died and were reborn in annual cycles, descending ultimately from the Mother Goddess of Palaeolithic and Neolithic times. In this tradition, the dark skin represents the Mother Goddess's underworld or fallow winter aspect, Goddess of Death and rebirth as well as birth; the fact that Black Madonna shrines are frequently found near caves, wells or mountains reinforces the connection with the Mother Goddess. The Black Madonna of Monserrat was found by shepherds in a cave, while the original Black Madonna of Chartres (said to be of Druidic origin) stood in a grotto underneath the medieval cathedral with its own healing well, dating back to time immemorial. The statue was burned in the town square during the French Revolution. The statue of the Black Madonna of Czestochowa, the Lady of the Sorrows, has been carried many times into battle, and her cheek is scarred by two sabre slashes.

According to the legend of the Virgin of Guadalupe, an Indian named Juan Diego had a vision of the Virgin Mary while he was gathering herbs on a hill near Mexico City in 1531, ten years after the Spanish conquest and the introduction of the Catholic faith, which Juan had adopted.

The Virgin appeared on a hilltop and told Juan to go to the bishop and instruct him to build a shrine to her at the place where Juan had the vision. But the bishop would not listen to Juan, telling him he was insane and demanding proof.

Three days later the Virgin again appeared to Juan. This time she told him to go to a barren hillside and pick the roses he would find there. Juan knew that only cacti ever grew on that stony slope, but he obeyed. He was amazed to find the roses, and took them to the Virgin. She wrapped them in his cloak, whereupon they disappeared and an image of the Virgin appeared on the cloth. The bishop declared that it was a miracle and built the church to honour her. She then became the patron saint of Mexico.

On 12 December, the day of the Virgin of Guadalupe, Mexicans commemorate this miracle. Little boys dress up as "Dieguitos" in memory of Juan Diego, wearing serapes, sandals, and painted moustaches. There are Guadalupe churches in many towns in Mexico, but many people try to visit the original site outside Mexico City. There, at the Basilica of Our Lady of Guadalupe, they view the miraculous cloak, which is enshrined in its own altar. They also take part in her festival on her fiesta day. The *concheros* perform a ritual circle dance of both men and women, dressed in Aztec clothing. Some travel on foot or on donkeys for days, and some arrive in limousines. Young and old, rich and poor bring gifts for the Virgin.

The Virgin of Guadalupe is so adored by Mexicans that a reproduction of the image she is said to have left on Juan Diego's cloak 465 years ago appears in nearly every home and workplace, including the windshields of city buses and the bumpers of long-haul trucks.

Mary Magdalene, the Gypsies' Madonna

Many of the Black Madonnas are found in the crypts of churches and cathedrals, struggling to reconcile the purity of Mary with the hidden powers of the Mother. A widely held theory associates Black Madonnas with Mary Magdalene who some legends say married

Christ at the wedding at Cana where he turned water into wine, and sees the infant in her arms as the son of Jesus.

According to the folklore and mythology of Provence, Mary Magdalene migrated from the Middle East to Ste-Marie-de-la-Mer, a small village on the French Mediterranean. The myth speaks of her coming by boat with a small entourage thirteen years after the Crucifixion. She reportedly spent the last thirty years of her life in seclusion at the cave of St-Baume in the French Alps. Although the literature in the monastery that is currently at St-Baume contains this story, it has never entered the mainstream of Christian history.

In the Auvergne and Provence, where there is the highest concentration of Black Madonnas in the world, many local fêtes are held in her honour. On 24 May the Gypsy Festival of the Black Madonna is held at Ste-Marie-de-la-Mer. Gypsies from all over the world gather to venerate Sarah, Queen of a French Gypsy tribe, who is the patron saint of the Gypsies and is reputed to have been a member of the group that travelled with Mary Magdalene across the Mediterranean to France. In another legend Sarah rescued Mary Magdalene from the sea by casting her mantle on the waves after the boat began to sink.

The Fruit and Flowers of the Virgin Mary

In parts of Europe, the strawberry is the fruit of the Virgin Mary. On St John's or Midsummer Day, Mary accompanies children when they go strawberry-picking. On that day no mother who has lost a child will eat a strawberry for fear that there will be none left for her infant in heaven.

Various flowers are associated with Marian festivals because of the time they bloom.

Snowdrop   Often in full bloom at Candlemas (2 February), this is the first spring flower dedicated to the Virgin Mary. On the day following the Feast of the Purification of the Blessed Virgin, held on Candlemas, her images are still in many churches removed from altars and replaced by scattered snowdrops.

Cuckoopint   Known as "Our Lady's flower", its silver-white blossoms appear at Lady-tide (25 March) which is also close to the feast of Ostara (see p. 53).

Lily   At the Feast of the Visitation (2 July) instituted by Pope Urban VI to commemorate the visit of Mary to her cousin Elizabeth, the Madonna lily is used as a symbol of Mary's purity and innocence. In depicting the Annunciation, artists of the later period of Italian art, on the edict of the Pope, showed Gabriel carrying a spray of Madonna lilies in his hand.

Rose   Mary is often called the Rose of Heaven. According to a legend, St Thomas, not believing the reports about the resurrection of the Virgin after her death, had her tomb opened. Inside, instead of her body, he found the tomb filled with lilies and roses.

The rose is used in Italy all through the month of May, Madonna's month. Both red and white roses have been dedicated to the Virgin Mary from the days of the early Church. The rose was said to have first appeared in Bethlehem when a young Christian girl was condemned to be burned at the stake. She prayed for help and angels came and turned the flames into red and yellow flowers. As a result many pagans were converted.

Visions of the Virgin Mary

☙

She looked at me immediately, smiled at me and signed
me to advance, as if She had been my Mother.
Bernadette of Lourdes

*D*uring the past 150 years, visions of the Virgin Mary have
appeared mainly to children, often simple peasant children
who then express complex ideas far beyond the range of their normal
vocabulary. The visions may last weeks, months or years, as in the case
of Medjugorje.

Lourdes

The most famous visions of Mary were seen at Lourdes in the French
Pyrenees by Marie Bernadette Soubrious. Born on 7 January 1844,
she was the eldest child of François, an impoverished miller.
Bernadette was frequently ill with asthma and caught cholera which
further weakened her health. On 11 February 1858 Bernadette, then
fourteen, experienced a vision of the Virgin Mary while collecting
firewood on the banks of the River Gave near Lourdes. This was the
first of eighteen visions over a period of six months.

Bernadette said she saw "a golden-coloured cloud, and soon after
a Lady, young and beautiful, exceedingly beautiful . . . placed herself
at the entrance of the opening, above the rose bush. She looked at
me immediately, smiled at me and signed to me to advance, as if She
had been my Mother. She was dressed in a white robe, girdled at the
waist with a blue ribbon which flows down all along Her robe. She

holds on Her right arm a Rosary of white beads with a chain of gold shining like the two roses on Her feet."

Bernadette's accounts were subject to enormous scepticism. She was questioned exhaustively by Church and State authorities but despite her youth and intellectual limitations she remained serene and never deviated in even the most minor details from her original accounts. One of the most significant apparitions was the ninth, on 25 February 1858. Bernadette, by this time accompanied by a crowd of about 400 people, began to dig with her hands. Muddy water surfaced, which she scooped up and three times threw away. At last Bernadette drank the water. The witnesses laughed because her face was covered with mud, but by late in the afternoon, on the spot where Bernadette had knelt digging, the trickle had become flowing water which hollowed its own channel in the topsoil. No chemically recognizable therapeutic properties have been found in the water, despite exhaustive testing, but nevertheless countless people have claimed that they have been cured of ills, some life-threatening, at the grotto.

The tenth apparition occurred on 27 February 1858. In the morning Bernadette was once again at the grotto, undaunted by the non-appearance of the Lady the previous day. The Lady appeared and told Bernadette to instruct the priests to have a chapel built in that place.

On Wednesday 7 April, 1858, the seventeenth apparition provided evidence for those watching that miraculous events were indeed occurring. The number of people travelling to the grotto was steadily increasing, especially after the mysterious Lady had finally identified Herself as the Immaculate Conception, an amazing theological concept for a simple shepherdess to express.

At six in the morning, Bernadette was once more kneeling in prayer in front of her beloved grotto, enraptured. The Lady was standing in the niche. This vision lasted for almost forty-five minutes and, as usual, Bernadette was praying throughout. Several witnesses described how Bernadette's rosary was in her left hand and a large lighted candle in her right. As her right hand joined her left, the flame of the big candle passed between the fingers. Although fanned by a fairly strong breeze, the flame produced no effect upon the skin which it was touching.

This continued for fifteen minutes until Bernadette, still in her ecstasy, advanced to the upper part of the grotto, separating her hands. Bernadette finished her prayer and the splendour of the transfiguration left her face.

This was not the first time the phenomenon had occurred at the grotto. Finally the visions were acknowledged by the Church and work began to create the huge pilgrimage site that is probably the most visited in the Christian world. The muddy trickle of water discovered by Bernadette now produces 27,000 gallons of water each week.

Like almost all child visionaries, Bernadette did not find riches in worldly terms as a result of her vision. She and her family continued to live in poverty. She entered the convent of the Sisters of Charity in Nevers in 1866 and did not even attend the consecration of the basilica at Lourdes in 1876. She suffered increasingly poor health until she died at the age of thirty-five.

On 8 December 1933, the feast of the Immaculate Conception, Bernadette was declared a saint by Pope Pius XI. The body of St Bernadette remains in the main chapel of the convent of St Gildard in the city of Nevers, France, and to this day is incorrupt. Around her shrine are inscribed the words spoken to her by the Virgin Mary: 'I do not promise that you will be happy in this world, only in the next."

Fatima

Fatima is a village in the centre of Portugal about seventy miles north of Lisbon. During the First World War three peasant children, eight-year-old Lucia Santos and her two cousins, Francisco and Jacinta Marto, saw an angel on three separate occasions and, later, the Virgin Mary herself. Portugal's republican government, which had driven out the monarchy in 1910, was hostile towards religion and the children were treated very cruelly. They were placed in prison and threatened with torture unless they admitted they had lied. However, the children still insisted they had seen the Virgin.

They said she had appeared to them on Sunday 13 May, 1917. As usual, Lucia and her two cousins went to a cave to eat their lunch at noon, after tending the sheep. Suddenly a bright shaft of light pierced the air. As the children descended the hill, there was another flash of lightning and standing over the foliage of a small holm oak was a beautiful lady, surrounded by rays of brilliant light, dressed all in white.

She told the children that she had come from heaven and that she wanted them to return at the same hour on the thirteenth day for six consecutive months. She promised that she would appear to them each time, finally giving unmistakable signs of her presence. At each successive apparition, news of Fatima spread. It was predicted that the October visitation would offer incontrovertible evidence that it was the Virgin Mary herself. On 13 October, there was a crowd of more than 70,000. At about ten o'clock in the morning it began to rain heavily. Midday, the expected time of the apparition, passed. As people began to leave, Lucia saw the flash of light that always preceded the vision.

The rain stopped and the sun began to come out. As usual, the apparition of Mary settled over the tree which had been dressed with ribbons and flowers. Mary told Lucia in the vision that a chapel must be built on the site, that the war which was decimating Europe would end and soldiers would return to their homes before too long.

Mary opened her hands, which let forth a flood of light. As she rose into the sky, she pointed towards the sun and the light gleaming from her hands brightened the sun itself. Suddenly a cry came from the crowd. The sun became pale as the moon. To the left of the sun, the children saw St Joseph holding in his left arm the child Jesus. St Joseph raised his right hand and together with the Holy Child made the sign of the Cross three times over the crowd. Although only the children saw this vision, the crowd were transfixed by the pulsating sun.

The Portuguese newspaper *O Dia* reported on 14 October 1917: "As if at a bolt from the blue, the clouds were wrenched apart, and the sun at its zenith appeared in all its splendour. It began to revolve like the most magnificent firewheel that could be imagined, taking on all the colours of the rainbow and sending forth multicoloured flashes of light, producing the most astounding effect. This sublime and incomparable spectacle, which was repeated three distinct times, lasted for about ten minutes. The immense multitude, overcome by the evidence of such a tremendous prodigy, threw themselves on their knees."

Later, people found that their clothing, which had been soaked in the downpour, was quite dry.

As at Lourdes, the young visionaries did not find earthly happiness. Francisco and Jacinta were victims of the flu pandemic of 1918 and died in 1919 and 1920 respectively. Lucia is the sole surviving visionary, and at eighty-eight years of age she remains a cloistered nun at a Carmelite convent in Portugal.

Pope John Paul II is firmly convinced that the Madonna saved his life when he was seriously wounded by a would-be assassin's bullet in St Peter's Square on 13 May 1981, the anniversary of the first Fatima apparition. As the Pope turned to look at a young girl in the crowd wearing a picture of the Virgin of Fatima, a shot aimed at his head missed. The Pope spoke with Lucia from his hospital room. While he was recuperating from his wounds he read everything he could about Fatima, and he has since visited Fatima twice.

Medjugorje

Since 24 June 1981, in a small village in former Yugoslavia named Medjugorje, the Virgin Mary has been appearing to six young people from the village: Ivan, Jakov, Marija, Mirjana, Vicka and Ivanka. It is said that the Virgin will give each of the six visionaries a total of ten "secrets" of events which will occur in the near future. Some of the secrets pertain to the whole world while others concern the visionaries themselves. Only one of the secrets has been revealed so far by the visionaries. Mary has promised to leave a visible sign on the mountain where she first appeared.

When each of the six visionaries has received all ten "secrets", the Virgin will stop appearing to them. Two have received all ten secrets, and the other four have received nine. Three warnings will then be given to the world and they will be witnessed by Mirjana. After the three warnings, the permanent visible sign will be left on the mountain where Mary first appeared in Medjugorje. The permanent sign, it is said, will lead to many healings and conversions before the messages become reality.

Vicka Ivankovic, one of the original child visionaries who has seen the Virgin Mary every day for fifteen years, often talks to people around the world as well as to pilgrims at Medjugorje about her experiences. According to her, "Our Lady says: 'As a flower cannot live without water, so we cannot live without God's grace. For the prayer of the heart can never be learned; the prayer of the heart can only be lived, by making one step forward day after day.'"

Marija says; "Each time the meeting with Our Lady makes me marvel as much as if it were the first time. I never ask for anything special. But speaking about the details, I can say that it is magnificent to see Our Lady for Christmas when she appears with baby Jesus in her arms. Two years ago she came with the 'big' Jesus on Good Friday. He was in wounds all over, in torn clothes and with a crown of thorns on the head. Our Lady says, 'I have come for you to see how much Jesus suffered for you,' and so we saw Him both when he was a baby and at the moment of his passion, of his death. Well, I point this out because it refers to Jesus, but as for Our Lady, I couldn't single out anything, for all her appearance is simply magnificent."

Vicka describes the daily visions: "Each time before Our Lady comes, we see a light three times, which is a sign that she is coming.

When she appears, she has a white veil, a crown of stars on her head, her eyes are blue, the hair black, the cheeks rosy; she is hovering in the air on a great cloud, so she does not touch the ground. For some greater festivities, for example Christmas and Easter, or for her birthday, she wears a robe of gold."

Of the original visionaries, Vicka, Ivan, Marija and Jakov have visions on a daily basis, Mirjana on her birthday and Ivanka once a year on the anniversary of the first apparition. The apparition takes place always at the same time: at twenty to six in the wintertime, or at twenty to seven in the summertime. Pilgrims may see signs of blessing such as the spinning sun or their rosaries changing colour. It is said that such signs mean it is time for the chosen person to make a change in his or her life.

In the first months of the apparitions in Medjugorje, supernatural events were particularly numerous. These signs were witnessed by many people, especially those of the hamlet of Bijakovici, in which all the visionaries were born.

Manifestations of light that assume many forms are some of the most frequent signs witnessed at Medjugorje. The first of these was seen on 27 June 1981. On that day, the Virgin Mary's coming was preceded by a brilliant light that illumined not only the village but the entire area, and was seen by everyone. The next day the people gathered on Mount Podbrdo saw the light which immediately preceded the Virgin Mary's visitation to the five visionaries who were present.

The sign observed on 2 August 1981 was like the dancing of the sun in Fatima on 13 October 1917, which was the miracle Mary had promised the three little shepherd children, so that people would believe. At the end of the event, a white cloud came down over the mountainside. It moved towards the sun, which continued to spin briefly and then returned to its normal state. The entire phenomenon lasted about fifteen minutes.

One of the most important signs that has been observed is the word *MIR* ("peace" in Croatian) which was written one evening in large bright burning letters in the sky above the cross on Mount

Krizevac. This particular sign has been observed numerous times and was seen by the pastor and the people from the village. The village has escaped damage from the war in Croatia although all the surrounding area has been affected.

Michael W. Petrides, director of the Psychiatric Outpatient Clinic's mental health services for Catholic charities in the diocese of Norwich, Connecticut, commented on 10 September 1993:

"Five alleged visionaries tested were found to simultaneously look at precisely the same spot (even though no reference point was visible) within one-fifth of a second of each other when the Blessed Virgin Mary allegedly appears. Such synchronization can only be explained by some external 'object' holding their gaze—but one which those around them could not see.

"During the same one-fifth of a second, there are simultaneous kneeling and the cessation of eye movements. There is no eye movement during the entire apparition which can last from three to forty-five minutes. There is also the simultaneous raising of their heads and gazing upwards while remaining fixated on a spot moving upwards when the apparition is finishing.

"Two of the alleged visionaries do not blink at all during the apparition. The eyeball normally dries when there is no regular blinking, fifteen to twenty times a minute, to moisten the cornea, but lacrima secretion does not seem necessary during the apparition. The other alleged visionaries blink about half the normal rate.

"There is no reaction to pain during the apparition. When touched with an algometer, which causes a cutaneous lesion or skin burn, there was complete absence of sensitivity. The alleged visionaries react normally to pain at other times.

"Electroencephalographic (EEG) tests confirm that the alleged vision-aries' brain functioning is normal and healthy. EEG tests rule out the possibility of epilepsy or psychotic hallucinations. The alleged visionaries are not asleep or dreaming either. Hysterical neurotic reaction or pathological ecstasy is also ruled out by the EEG testing.

"To test visual stimulation further, a 1000 watt light bulb was placed

in front of the eyes of the alleged visionaries during the apparition. Not only is a 1000 watt light bulb usually painful to the eye but also it would normally cause increased blinking and influence alpha rhythm.

"There was no blinking movement of the eyelids to the 1000 watt stimulus. There was an interesting pupillary response. The pupil contracted as one would expect in bright light but there was no change in alpha rhythm to the 1000 watt light. This is scientifically inexplicable and never seen before."

The current attitude of the Church after fourteen years of scrutiny is a kind of provisional approval. Both the Pope and the former bishops are treating and nurturing Medjugorje as a legitimate place of pilgrimage.

Why should Mary appear to children rather than learned academics or the great of the Churches? Perhaps they are all too busy with their noses in books to look at the sky? Perhaps they would question, argue points of doctrine, and we need the eyes of children to see the Mother Mary? Perhaps as a mother she is drawn to children. The life of young visionaries is strange. Among the tourist stalls and media hype they alone do not profit, nor do they seek to do so. They are not promised happiness in this life, but as some of them have suffered illness and premature death there are many questions for non-believers: why, for instance, should so many of them suffer, having seen the Mother who is the inspiration for all others? They have seen others healed and asked nothing for themselves.

Countless private visions of Mary go unrecorded, unauthenticated, and lack the spinning suns or rosaries of gold. Vicka commented that she saw the Virgin Mary as a woman of our times and not some remote figure from the past. Mary has come a long way from the little girl who danced with joy in the Temple. It is an onerous burden to be Mother of the world.

Mothers in the Church

Just as a person's experience of fathering affects his or her expectations and perceptions of a male priest, so the experience of being mothered affects expectations and perceptions of a female priest.

The Reverend Jean Wadsworth

Mother of the Flock

Liberal and mainline Christian denominations, for example the Presbyterian Church in the USA, the United Church of Canada and the Methodist Church, have been ordaining women for decades. Liberal Jewish groups, including Reform Judaism, have also accepted female rabbis. However, the Roman Catholic Church and the Orthodox Churches continue to refuse to ordain women. Indeed, Bishop Angelo Scola, head of the Lateran University at the Vatican, stated as recently as January 1997: "The Church does not have the power to modify the practice, uninterrupted for 2000 years, of calling only men to the ministering priesthood, in that this was wanted directly by Jesus."

In 1995 the Church of England, despite fierce opposition from women as well as men, overcame the last obstacles to the full ordination of women priests and opened the floodgates in a previously paternalistic calling. Other Anglican Churches such as the one in Australia were still holding out against female ordination as late as December 1996. What are the effects of having a Mother rather than a Father of the Flock?

I asked the Reverend Jean Wadsworth, vicar of the parish of the

Holy Trinity in Rotherhithe, London, about being Mother to her parishioners. She proved a humorous, compassionate woman and answered my questions, spoken and unvoiced, about her maternal role, which she said provoked a great deal of thought.

"Concerning your questions about my being Mother of the Flock, theologically and in theory the female priest has the same role as the male priest. In practice, there are different expectations and different emphases. There are undoubtedly some people who play the same games with their female vicar as they did with their mother. I have had to tease a number of very competent men and women who will try and trip me into being a 'kind mummy' when they do things wrong or forget to perform some task for the church. I have had to remind them that they are grown men and women who take responsibility for themselves. Some people, thankfully only a few, react badly when 'Mummy' is not automatically kind, indulgent and forgiving in circumstances where they would respect a man (Daddy) for ticking them off or for being firm.

"You ask if I feel maternal towards my parishioners. I care for them and care about their welfare and their spiritual growth. I love them I suppose. I certainly don't feel indulgent towards them, but if I think about it I suppose I am maternal in the type of motherly role I experienced from my mother and two grandmothers. That is the love of a firm Northern type of mother who wanted the best for her offspring and wouldn't let them get away with less than the best. I think the fashionable phrase is tough love.

"I have been privileged to work with some very caring male priests who are very maternal, very involved with their parishioners' cares, griefs and joys, so I do not see the male and female roles as different in terms of nurturing. I do know some female priests who are just as cool and detached as any of the more remote male priests I have met. There are always fantastic expectations about priests. We are always expected to be better than others, whether we are male or female, hence the tabloids' glee at 'Vicar Sex Shock Horror'. Even parishioners make my heart sink when they make remarks such as 'Your faith must help you through, it's

so strong' or 'Of course I don't suppose you'll understand the sexual temptation I've had, you being a priest.'

"At least one middle-aged lady was honest when she told me, 'I don't like hearing priests saying that they are frightened or worried. I want you to be strong for your flock.'

"However, some parishes, particularly where clergy celibacy is favoured, can be very possessive about 'their Father/Mother' and very annoyed if he or she is seen to be particularly friendly with someone of the opposite sex. I have known some churchgoers be really angry at seeing priests kissing friends, even though done openly in church.

"However, my own church is very liberal and relaxed, like a number of parishes. With increasing self-knowledge through psychology and an increasing air of tolerance in society, I think that people try to face their fantasies of Earth Mother/Virgin Mary. But people on the fringe, that is those who come for baptisms, weddings, funerals, who don't go to church but are C of E, are the ones who seem to me to be in the grip of the greatest fantasies and expectations. So many of these expectations are negative: so many come in fear and trembling as if they are up before the Great Headmaster/mistress or the Great Judge. They obviously brace themselves to be lectured, questioned, rejected, and are surprised, even sometimes disappointed, when they are not.

"On the other hand a small minority will brazen it out, coming in with lots of demands and reminding me of the kids I taught at school who were frightened but were no way going to show it.

"Perhaps, on reflection, there is something of the fear of the Mother Goddess in some of the above. Many years ago, long before there were women priests, I noticed that some people, particularly men, were very afraid of women and women's power. Some are very uneasy if women sit quietly at meetings and say nothing. I remember about twenty years ago driving back from a meeting with three male colleagues and being interested in the different interpretations we put on the behaviour of a very high-powered lady at the meeting. Two of us appreciated her quietness, her listening ability. The other two were very angry with her, interpreting her silence as anger, as withdrawal of affection, Mummy again. One even described her as sitting simmering, and the description *he gave of her was of a volcano about to erupt. As he was a person who needed to dominate and control any group he entered, I felt that he could not understand that others might wish to listen and to cooperate. Many times I have noticed that certain men, not all by any means, find women's cooperative approach and their networking very threatening."*

The Churching of Women

The purification of women after the birth is a custom that is dying out except among traditional faiths where the old ritual is evolving into a celebration of family life. The Churching of Women had its roots in early pagan beliefs that the woman in birth was open to all kinds of influence, malevolent as well as benign, as well as the concept of original sin. However, even in its earlier forms there was always the sense of thanksgiving for safe delivery, at times when childbirth was still very hazardous.

Rituals whereby a new mother is isolated for a period after the birth and then re-introduced, sometimes by special ceremony, can be found in many cultures and ages. One of the main reasons for the mother and infant being isolated, often in a specially constructed building, immediately after birth was to keep them safe from infection, and it also gave the mother a rest period before she had to return to the fields or in later times the factory. However, as with many religious taboos, there is a fear that the mother has come in contact with powerful other-worldly forces during the act of giving birth. Death has its own taboos and rituals.

The first biblical reference to the purification of women that has shaped both Jewish and Christian ritual is found in Leviticus 12, where a woman who gives birth to a son is counted as ritually unclean for forty days and for twice as long after the birth of a female child. After that period of purification, the mother is to go to the Temple and bring the required offerings to the priest who makes atonement for her.

Luke 2 relates how the Virgin Mary brought Jesus into the

Temple and was purified on the fortieth day after the birth. In accord with Jewish practice, five shekels were offered to God to buy back the first-born son.

The purification of a mother after childbirth did not officially find its way into the rites of the Western Church until about the eleventh century. In the 1552 prayer book the concept of cleansing the mother was removed and the ritual given its modern name of "The Thanksgiving of Women after Child-birth, commonly called the Churchynge of Women".

The Puritans abandoned the ritual during the Interregnum, much to the indignation of mothers who wanted a special ceremony to mark their safe delivery from childbirth, and many arranged secret ceremonies.

The rite was reinstated after the Restoration of Charles II in 1660 but was never as popular as before. Only women in wedlock might be churched. Unmarried mothers had to repent of their sins openly in church on a Sunday before they were allowed to participate in the ceremony.

In Eastern Orthodox churches the emphasis has always been on mother with child rather than mother alone. There are prayers on three different occasions: a blessing on the day of the birth of the child, the naming of the child on the eighth day after birth, and prayers for mother and child in the church forty days after the birth. On the fortieth day mother and child go to church together for the first time. The child is carried through the church building where special prayers are said in each part. In the case of a male child the baby is also carried into the sanctuary where the priest says the *Nunc Dimittis*, alluding to the presentation of Jesus at the Temple.

Saints of Motherhood and Childbirth

St Anne In medieval times throughout Europe, the story of the Virgin Mary's mother Anna assumed great importance in Christian art and religion. Her cult was in evidence as early as the sixth century when the Emperor Justinian dedicated a church to her in Constantinople. Her feast spread across Europe to England and Ireland. There was a feast in honour of the conception of St Anne in tenth-century Naples and it was observed in England at Canterbury from the eleventh century. By 1584 the universal Church celebrated her life as a model of ideal Christian marriage.

Anna is frequently depicted holding her daughter or grandson, the Christ Child, in her lap. Her feast day is on 26 July.

St Margaret of Antioch   A third-century saint, Margaret is said to have overcome a dragon in prison during her persecution by the emperor Diocletian. One version of her life story says she was a princess, driven from her home because of her Christian beliefs, raised as a shepherdess by peasants. Beautiful and innocent, she resisted the amorous prefect of Antioch, who had her imprisoned. She was swallowed by Satan in the form of a dragon, but he was forced to release her when she made the sign of the Cross within him. Tortured by fire and water, she performed miracle after miracle before being beheaded.

Her return unharmed from the dragon's belly made her a natural patron of safe childbirth She is said to have promised pregnant women protection if they called upon her. Many churches, especially in Norfolk, are dedicated to her and her voice was heard by St Joan. Her cult was suppressed in 1969. Her feast day is 20 July.

108

Mother's Day: Celebration or Sentiment for Sale?

I urge that on that day all persons wear a white flower in acknowledgement and honour of the one who went down into the shadow of death for us.

Governor Marion E. Hay, Washington state

The Origins

The earliest Mothering celebrations can be traced back to the spring celebrations of ancient Greece in honour of Rhea, the Mother of the Gods, daughter of Uranus and Gaia, the original sky and earth deities. Another source is the spring festival known as Hilaria dedicated to Cybele, the Phrygian mother goddess who controlled fertility. Her cult was introduced into Rome about 250 BC and rites were performed for three days from the Ides (15th) of March.

The origin of Mothering Sunday is obscure. It may be that the ceremonies in honour of Cybele came to England with the Roman invasion and mingled with the rites of Celtic mother goddess worship. These were adapted by the early Church for veneration of the Virgin Mary as Mother of Christ, especially around the date of the Annunciation. In the Catholic tradition, the Golden Rose is blessed by the Pope on the fourth Sunday in Lent and traditionally given to the royal lady whose pious deeds or intentions have been most in evidence. If no one merits it, the rose is kept in the Vatican.

An alternative suggestion is that the concept of Mother Church was substituted for Mother Goddess by early Christian missionaries and the custom grew of visiting the church of one's baptism on the former pagan spring festival. St Paul referred to the Church as "Jerusalem above who is our mother".

From medieval times, servants and apprentices in England celebrated Mothering Sunday on the fourth Sunday in Lent. On that day they would go back to their mother church, the church in which they had been baptized. They would also take the opportunity to visit their homes, bearing small gifts or mothering cakes for their mothers, and slowly the significance of the ceremony shifted from the church to the mother.

A source for these customs is Robert Chambers' *Book of Days*, written in the 1860s. He recorded countless customs developed over the preceding centuries and talks of "the harshness and general painfulness of life in old times that must have been greatly relieved by certain simple and affectionate customs which modern people have learned to dispense with. Among these was a practice of going to see parents, and especially the female one, on the mid-Sunday of Lent, taking for them some little present, such as a cake or a trinket. A youth engaged in this amiable act was said to go 'a-mothering'. And thence the day itself came to be called Mothering Sunday. There was also a cheering and peculiar festivity appropriate to that day, the prominent dish being furmety, which we have to interpret as wheat grains boiled in sweet milk, sugared and spiced. In the northern part of England and Scotland there seems to have been a greater leaning towards steeped pease fried in butter with pepper and salt. Pancakes so composed passed by the name of carlings. So conspicuous was this item that the day became known as Carling Sunday in these regions."

The mothering cake, or simnel cake, was a very rich fruit cake that Lenten rules dictated was saved for Easter. First boiled in water and then baked, it sometimes had an almond icing. At other times the crust was flour and water, coloured with saffron. The word simnel comes from the Latin *simila*, a high-grade wheat flour. The cake is mentioned in a poem by Robert Herrick, the seventeenth-century

Metaphysical English poet, entitled "To Dianyme, A Cermonie in Glocester".

> I'll to thee a Simnell bring
> Gainst thou go'st a-mothering.
> So that when she blesseth thee,
> Half that blessing thou'lt give me.

The custom of Mothering Sunday persisted as an important occasion until the nineteenth century. The historian John Brandt writes: "It was customary in the eighteenth and early nineteenth centuries for servants and others working away from home to be given a holiday so that they might visit their mothers and present them with a cake of their own or their mistress's making. And little nosegays of violets and other country flowers gathered from the hedgerows as they walked home along the country lanes. Whole families attended church together and there was a dinner of roast lamb or veal at which mother was treated as queen of the feast she prepared herself and everything was done to make her happy."

No doubt the changes in working and living habits brought about by the Industrial Revolution had much to do with the decline of Mothering Sunday in Britain. As one old lady growing up at the turn of the century in industrial Wales told me, "I heard nothing about Mother's Day as a child. We had no money for presents and such shows of sentiment would have been frowned on."

However, interest in the festival has revived, perhaps because of the great popularity of Mother's Day in the United States, which has triggered a new lease of life for Mothering Sunday. In the United Kingdom millions of Mother's Day cards are sold and gifts range from half-price offers for ten pin bowling, a free box of chocolates at the supermarket on the purchase of a bunch of flowers, to a free car wash and wax for mothers with wheels. With secularization, the media has taken over from the Church, with poetry competitions and chat shows on estranged mothers. It is tempting to blame the secularization and indeed standardization of Mother's Day throughout the world on the American influences. That is unfair since the American festival itself had religious as well as patriotic roots.

Mother's Day in the US

Mother's Day is observed in the US on the second Sunday in May. It was first suggested in 1872 by Julia Ward Howe (who wrote the words to the "Battle Hymn of the Republic") as a day dedicated to peace. Ms Howe held organized Mother's Day meetings in Boston, Massachusetts every year.

However, the founder of the modern Mother's Day is usually considered to be Anna M. Jarvis, who was born on 1 May 1864. Ironically Anna was never a mother herself but remained a spinster throughout her life. She dedicated the festival to her own mother, Mrs Anna Reese Jarvis, a minister's daughter who for twenty years conducted Sunday school classes in the Andrews Methodist Church in Grafton, West Virginia.

Anna Jarvis worked as a teacher in Grafton before moving with the rest of her family to Philadelphia. Anna's mother died in Philadelphia on 9 May 1905, and Anna was determined that her life should be honoured. Anna felt strongly that adult children neglected their mothers and so began a letter-writing campaign in the years after her mother's death, contacting ministers, businessmen and congressmen in the hope of gaining support for an official recognition of mothers on a special day by religious services.

The first Mother's Day observance was in fact a church service held in Grafton at Anna Jarvis's request on May 10 1908. Another was held in Philadelphia on the same date. These occasions were tributes to Anna's own mother, rather than mothers in general, but were the catalyst for a wider recognition of mothers on this day.

The carnations, which have now become an integral feature of Mother's Day in many lands, were used by Anna because they were her own mother's favourite flowers. The flowers, however, rapidly came to symbolize mothers everywhere.

Jane Stewart, an American lecturer and editor, wrote soon after the first Mother's Day: "Large jars of white carnations, the floral emblem of mother love because of its sweetness, its purity and endurance, are set about the platform. These fragrant flowers may be the gift of those who have lost their mothers or those who wish to show respect and honour to a mother at a distance. At the close of the service, one of these white carnations is given to each person present as an appropriate souvenir of Mother's Day."

In time, red carnations became the symbol of a living mother and white ones were worn as a sign the mother had died.

Official recognition soon followed. In 1910 the first Mother's Day proclamation was issued by the governor of West Virginia. Oklahoma celebrated it the same year and in the state of Washington, Governor Marion F. Hay proclaimed: "I urge that on that day all persons wear a white flower in acknowledgement and honour of the one who went down into the shadow of death for us."

By 1911 every state in the union celebrated Mother's Day. It was also being celebrated in Mexico, Canada and South America. The Mother's Day International Association was incorporated on 12 December 1912, with the purpose of promoting and encouraging meaningful observances of the event.

In 1913 the House of Representatives unanimously adopted a resolution requesting the President, his Cabinet, the members of both houses and all officials of the federal government to wear a white carnation on Mother's Day. On 9 May 1914 President Woodrow Wilson issued his Mother's Day proclamation: "I do hereby direct the government officials to display the United States flag on all government buildings and the people of the United States to display the flag at their homes or other suitable places on the second Sunday in May, as a public expression of our love and reverence for the mothers of our country."

What of Anna Jarvis? Having tended her mother until her death, Anna then assumed care of her blind sister, Elsinore. Although the festival she had instigated was gaining international acclaim, she became distressed at the commercial nature of what she saw as a purely religious celebration. The cards, flowers and other gifts, she felt, destroyed the whole point of the festival which was to elevate, not sentimentalize, maternal love and sacrifice.

Her own life began to disintegrate. She lost her property, her sister died and her own sight began to fade. By November 1944 she was ill and without money. Friends paid her expenses at a sanatorium in West Chester, Pennsylvania and she died there on 24 November 1948. The creator of the festival of mother love died without anyone to call her own.

Perhaps, however, she would have been pleased that in the US and Canada the week from the first Sunday in May to Mother's Day itself has been designated Christian Family Week.

Mother's Day in France

Napoleon himself had called on France to honour mothers. He wanted to celebrate "a great festival for mothers, children and the family every spring when nature is reborn, because it is to my mother that I owe everything".

However, there was no special ceremony until American troops came to France during the First World War and were seen wearing their Mother's Day carnations. France had suffered hideous loss of life in the war and there was a feeling in government circles that mothers should be encouraged to have large families. Mother's Day became a focus for promoting motherhood.

On 16 June 1918 the first French Mother's Day was organized at Lyon under the influence of a colonel of the Croix-Laval. Prizes to mothers of big families were given, one by the President of the Republic. Seven thousand people gathered at the Trocadéro in Paris for a ceremony during which the gold medal for the supreme French family was presented to Mme Marcelle Comblet-Sue, mother of thirteen children.

From 1926, Mother's Day became an annual event. In 1935 the daily paper Le Matin proposed raising a monument to mothers and this was inaugurated by President Lebrun in 1938. Some associations wanted the "sublime mothers" to be awarded the Order of the Nation.

In the post-war years, dutiful women, the mothers of large families, became the object of the country's gratitude. Marshal Pétain, faithful to his motto "Work, family, fatherland", tried to promote the family as the basic unit of France, the indispensable building block of civilization. He was convinced that the nation could be rebuilt only through the development of strong family units, which depended on the return of women to the home. "The heart of the family, the light in the home is the mother," said the newspaper *Le Foyer* (*The Home*). Some argue that this policy was, as in other post-war nations, a cynical ploy to provide employment for the returning soldiers by getting the working women back into the kitchen.

In 1941, the festival of mothers of large families became the National Mother's Day and all mothers were celebrated, not just those of large families. On 24 May 1950 Mother's Day was enshrined in law and fixed on the last Sunday in May, marking the end of the week of mother and child.

Mother's Day Around the World

Mother's Day in Australia is on the second Sunday in May. Pat, a grandmother from Brisbane, described how she tries to avoid the inevitable commercialization of the festival: "I always ask my grandchildren to give me a plant of white chrysanthemums and when it is finished I plant it in the garden. I have quite a selection of cuttings now. This year, my daughter gave me a photograph of their reaffirmation ceremony and a blue flowered nightie.

"I believe that it is up to the individual family to keep the day simple and avoid commercialization. I am convinced so long as we are all together that is what matters."

Amelia, a great-grandmother living in Christchurch, New Zealand, told me: "Sad to say, our country has adopted the American way, that is the second Sunday in May, sad because the occasion has become so commercialized and secularized. However, some churches do recognize the English Mothering Sunday on the fourth Sunday in the season of Lent. So many of the old ways are being lost and this is a pity."

A South African mother recalls the decline in the significance of Mother's Day in her country: "When I was a child in the fifties, Mothering Sunday was celebrated in all the local churches. I remember in the Anglican Church all the children being given little posies of flowers for our mothers. Nowadays that is largely forgotten and modern children celebrate Mothering Sunday on the second Sunday in May with little treats such as breakfast in bed and gifts of chocolates and toiletries. Within the black communities mothers are very specially revered because they hold their families together, and poorer children who cannot afford to buy their mothers a present would draw a picture or make her something at school."

Mothering Sunday was introduced into Japan after the Second World War and is usually celebrated on the second Sunday in May. Children with a living mother traditionally wear a red carnation. Those whose mothers have died wear a white one. A retired Japanese businessman living near Tokyo commented: "I have noticed that few people wear carnations nowadays. Instead they present their mothers with gifts and red carnations. Sadly these days the high esteem of motherhood no longer exists and you read horrible cases in the paper of maternal neglect, for example a mother who left her small child locked in a car for hours while she went gambling."

In Thailand Mother's Day, which has been celebrated only in recent years, is associated with the reverence for the Queen and so has retained some spiritual significance. A spokesman for the Royal Thai Embassy said: "Even under the constitutional monarchy, the King is respected as the paternal head of the nation while the Queen is loved and cherished by all Thais as the embodiment of the ideal mother. The King's birthday, 5 December, is celebrated throughout the country as Father's Day while 12 August, the Queen's birthday, is celebrated as Mother's Day.

"During the traditional New Year period (2–14 April) people return to their families to pay respect to the elders and visit their relatives. So important is this occasion that in Thailand 14 April has been officially designated Family Day.

"But Mother's Day is only part of a wider, lifelong concern for mothers in Thailand. Even though many young people have to work in the cities, one of the prime responsibilities placed upon children is care of their parents in old age. As yet this is still not regarded as a burden, as has happened in many parts of the West. Rather grandparents still have an honoured place in the family and their advice is actively sought in rearing grandchildren and great-grand-children."

In Germany Mother's Day, 12 August, became a national holiday in 1935. Norah who lives in Berkshire is German. She told me: "I came to England in 1989 to study and never went back. In Germany Mother's Day was first celebrated between 1922 and 1923. Now Mother's Day in Germany is more or less as it is in the UK except celebrated later in the year.

"In my family we never really celebrated it. My parents disliked the idea because they felt it was abused by the Nazis who celebrated mothers as machines to produce children. My own mother thinks that everybody should be special every day of the year. Even so I usually send her some token or gift to show that I am thinking of her."

Mother's Day in Iceland was first celebrated nationally in 1934 on the fourth Sunday in May. It was changed to the second Sunday in May in 1980. According to Erla Hulda Halldorsdottir, head of Iceland's Library of Women's History, the festival was first suggested in 1932 by a priest in Akureyri and in 1934 a women's organization called Maeorastyrksnefnd, the Mother Assistance Committee, cele-brated Mother's Day on 27 May. Erla says: "Some people have celebrated Mother's Day as a family occasion and sometimes flowers have been sold to collect money for poor mothers. The last few years shopkeepers and florists have advertised during the days before Mother's Day, but I cannot remember ever having given my mother flowers or presents on this day."

In Argentina, Mother's Day is celebrated on the third Sunday in October and as it is a special occasion the whole family gathers together.

In Austria, Mother's Day is celebrated on the second Sunday in May. It was initiated by Marianne Hinisch (1839–1936), the founder and head of the Austrian Women's Movement, in 1934, following the American custom.

Mother's Day was introduced into Norway in 1918 from America, but is celebrated on the second Sunday in February.

However, the majority of countries that recognize the festival, including Belgium, Denmark, Finland, Italy, the Netherlands and Turkey, celebrate Mother's Day on the second Sunday of May after the American tradition.

Sam comes from Israel, although his family roots were in Toledo in Spain. His family were driven out of Spain by the Inquisition, settled in Morocco and eventually moved to Israel. He now runs a sandwich bar near the British Museum in London. Sam said that for him the mother did not need a special day to be remembered. "Every day is Mother's day. My mother is my friend and when she grows old I will take care of her so that my children will in turn take care of their mother. When a mother is old, my people do not put her in hospital or hospices. We treat her with the loving care she gave us. When I go and see my mother I always take her flowers and a present. We come from many countries and settle in Israel, but many of us believe in the ancient ways, that the mother is the centre of the family, and so we would not insult her by having a special Mother's day. She is always our mother, every day."

As the world becomes increasingly secular and the demands of industrialized and modern technological society eat into traditional values in the East as well as the West, it is all too easy to lose any meaning of Mother's Day in an orgy of consumerism. The interests of commerce can and do engulf any festival, but consumerism is ultimately controlled by public demand. We do not have to buy our mothers elaborate cards or expensive bouquets. It is possible for any family to resist these pressures and to have a meaningful celebration.

However, there is a real danger that if mothers are revered on a single day, then during the rest of the year the hero-mother struggles on unappreciated. In the words of John Brandt, "Mother was treated as queen of the feast *she prepared herself*."

Life doesn't change.

PART FOUR

The Hand That Rocks the Cradle

Royal Mothers

A royal doctor congratulated Victoria immediately after
the birth of the Prince of Wales, saying, "You have a fine
boy, Ma'am." She replied: "Prince, you mean."

*F*ame and motherhood are uneasy bedfellows. The French film
star Brigitte Bardot is said to have called her unborn son a
tumour which fed on her and commented: "I'd rather have given birth
to a little dog than a child. They're faithful, obedient and never answer
back."

Joan Crawford's adopted daughter wrote *Mommie Dearest* about
the horrors of life with the American film star who posed lovingly in
front of the cameras but harnessed her children in their beds at night,
beat them and made them scrub floors.

Enid Blyton, the children's writer, declared in old age, "My books
are my children." The public face of the author who gathered her
young fans around her for story-reading sessions contrasted sharply
with the private woman who is said to have been indifferent,
resentful and even, as has been implied by her younger daughter
Imogen, unkind to her own children.

This chapter centres on the most difficult task of all, being Queen
of England and a mother, two roles that would almost seem
impossible to reconcile. Duty to the nation inevitably comes before
the concerns of family life, and however much a queen may love her
children, her position as head of Church and State and Mother of
the Nation predominates. Royal families are perhaps at their best in
official photographs, whether, as in Victorian and Edwardian times,
ramrod straight with the boys in sailor suits and the girls in frilly
dresses or the action shots of modern young royals.

"The House of Hanover, like ducks, produces bad parents," the Royal Librarian, Sir Owen Moreshead, once commented. "They trample on their young." It might be fairer to say that it is the institution of monarchy rather than parental failings that makes intimacy in the archetypal family of the nation an exception rather than rule.

In 1897, Britain was swept with a wave of patriotic fervour as the country prepared to celebrate the Diamond Jubilee of Queen Victoria. Portraits showed her with her nine children and numerous grandchildren gathered about her. She was known as the Grandmother of Europe because her children had married into royal houses throughout the Continent. Victoria was exceptionally fond of her grandchildren and insisted that one of them should always be with her. To satisfy her whim a little prince or princess might be suddenly shipped halfway across Europe to join the widowed Queen at Windsor or Balmoral or her holiday home Osborne House on the Isle of Wight.

How good a mother was Queen Victoria? She hated pregnancy and was contemptuous of women who bred like "rabbits and guinea pigs". In her journal she referred to her first pregnancy as "being caught" and was unreasonably furious whenever she found herself pregnant again. Her last two labours were eased by the new wonder drug of the time, chloroform. To her, babies were unpleasant "frog-like" beings.

She did not approve of breastfeeding but employed wet nurses. Victoria was not amused to learn that not only had her daughters Vicky and Alice fed their own babies, but also that Vicky suckled one of Alice's during an illness.

Small children were, in her view, best when they were clean, clothed and quiet and could be handed back to a nurse when they had outstayed their welcome. Victoria's journal describes a "nightmare journey" by train from London to Windsor when the elder children were still toddlers. Somehow their nurses had been separated from the royal party and Victoria and her ladies had to cope on their own. Her journal recounts that the children "were taken with tearing spirits and a rage for climbing, crawling, poking into corners and upsetting everything, and after a little time being tired, cross and squally for hours".

During the children's early years their father, Prince Albert, spent more time with them than Victoria did. Indeed, he was the one who imported the beautiful Swiss Cottage to Osborne House for the children to play in. The cottage still stands in the grounds, along with the small fort Albert ordered to be made for the children.

Osborne House is sumptuous with its statues, pictures and grand staircases. But the children's quarters, approached by a narrow stair, are far more spartan, although this was typical of an age in which upper-class children were believed to be prepared for life by the absence of luxuries in their nurseries. Children who worked in factories had an even harder life. Victoria opposed the Ten Hour Bill which would have limited their working hours because she was afraid it would alienate the factory owners in her government.

The Queen is said to have thought that beating schoolchildren was degrading, but it is related that when her mother, the Duchess of Kent, said it was upsetting to hear a whipped child cry, she replied: "Not when you have eight children, Mama."

Victoria's own childhood made it hard for her to develop any insight into normal family life. Her father died when she was a baby and she was torn between a possessive manipulative mother and an equally scheming governess who used every opportunity to usurp the mother's role.

Her father, Edward, Duke of Kent, was the fourth son of George III. He entered the army where he was a brave soldier in war but a martinet in peacetime. Her mother, Victoire, had married a man of forty, Emlich Charles, Prince of Leiningen, when she was only seventeen. The marriage was made for the economic convenience of her impoverished father, the Duke of Saxe-Coburg-Saalfeld. The marriage might not have been a great success but they did have two children, Charles, born in 1804, and Feodora, born in 1809. In 1814 the Prince died, leaving her in the tiny palace at Amorbach, in

Germany. Two years later the Duke of Kent came looking for a wife, proposed and was accepted by Victoire.

They settled in Amorbach where Victoria was conceived. But when the birth was imminent they hastened back to England. The Duke was a superstitious man and a Gypsy in Malta had told him that he could become the father of a great queen. At the time it had seemed an unlikely prophecy, but should it come true then only Kensington Palace would be the suitable birthplace for a future Queen of England. He and his wife undertook a seven-day journey through appalling weather to arrive home on 24 April 1819. Queen Victoria was born on 24 May. The following year her father died of a chill.

Victoria's half-brother Charles remained in Germany, but the Duchess of Kent decided to stay in England with Victoria and Feodora. Outwardly, the Duchess may have resembled a plump and amiable German housewife, but inwardly she was burning with ambition. The Prince Regent's daughter, Charlotte, had died in 1817, and it appeared increasingly possible that Victoria might become Queen. If she did, then the Duchess realized that she herself would wield immense power, especially if Victoria inherited the throne before she came of age. She was determined that Victoria should be prepared to become ruler although she concealed from her daughter the possibility that the crown was within her reach until she was eleven years old. When told of the possibility, Victoria is said to have burst into tears and declared: "I must be good. I will be good."

Nothing was to be left to chance. At night the young Victoria had to sleep in Mama's bedroom. During the day she was not left alone for one minute. Somebody had to supervise her education and Louise Lehzen, a clergyman's daughter from Hanover, was engaged. With the assistance of lesser governesses, she won the trust of the young princess, teaching her history and even helping her to dress a collection of 132 wooden dolls. She encouraged Victoria to keep a diary, something which became a life-long habit.

Victoria had the company of her half-sister Feodora, who was fifteen when Victoria was born, and their friendship lasted until

Feodora's death in 1872, but beyond the palace walls she saw little of normal family life to contrast with her own claustrophobic isolation. Among her few playmates were the daughters of her mother's Comptroller, Sir John Conroy. But Victoria never allowed herself to forget her position: as she once said, "You must not touch those, they are mine. I may call you Jane but you must not call me Victoria."

Conroy was to play a large part in Victoria's early life. An ambitious man himself, he urged the Duchess on and sought to establish a secure place for himself under Victoria should she become Queen. He became close to the Duchess and gradually the household split into two camps: on the one side the Duchess and Conroy, on the other Victoria and Fräulein Lehzen, who was becoming mother in all but name to the girl.

The Duchess was disliked by her royal brothers-in-law and George IV ignored her and her children for years. But in the 1820s visits were exchanged and the King was charmed by Victoria. However, the Duchess became anxious that the old man's interests were turning towards Feodora, forty years his junior and now a beautiful young woman. She began to worry that her well-laid plans could be upset if George asked for Feodora's hand. Despite the huge age gap between the two, most ambitious mothers would have been delighted at the prospect of marrying a daughter to a king; especially if the daughter might bear him a child who would inherit the throne. But the Duchess looked beyond this. She wanted to be not just the mother-in-law of the King but the mother who held the reins while waiting for the Queen to come of age. The answer was a quick marriage, and in February 1828, to Victoria's distress, Feodora left England to marry Prince Ernest of Hohenlohe-Langenburg.

Victoria felt more isolated than ever and in 1829 matters came to a head when she found her mother and Conroy in what she considered a compromising situation. There is no possibility that the pair were lovers—had there been a hint of such a scandal the children would have been swiftly removed from the care of the

Duchess. To Victoria even a passing kiss would have been out-rageous, and her hostility to the pair increased when she saw her mother as little more than a pawn of Conroy. Lehzen knew what had happened and used the situation to widen the breach in the household.

In 1830 King George IV died and was succeeded by his brother, who became William IV. The new King made no secret of his contempt for his sister-in-law's ambition and at his birthday in August 1836 he prayed at dinner in front of a hundred people that his life might be spared until his niece was old enough to reign unaided by her mother's regency. His wish was granted, for Victoria turned eighteen on 24 May 1837.

On 20 June 1837 William IV died and Victoria became Queen. Now the tables were turned and the child who had been kept in her place was the first lady of the land. Within a month of being proclaimed Queen, Victoria had moved into Buckingham Palace. A great shock was in store for her mother. No longer would the child sleep in the Duchess's bedroom. She insisted on settling her mother at the far end of the building while Louise Lehzen was put into quarters next door with a connecting doorway. In case of night-mares, which were frequent, the Queen would turn to the governess.

The Duchess took her revenge on Victoria's nineteenth birthday. She gave her a copy of *King Lear*, Shakespeare's bitter depiction of the ingratitude of daughters.

Relations deteriorated to such a pitch that when Victoria sent her mother a note meant to make up the quarrel the Duchess refused to believe she had written it. There seemed little chance of reconcilia-tion between them until Victoria married Prince Albert in 1840. The German Prince worked hard to draw the Duchess back into the family circle. The main obstacle was Lehzen who wanted to remain everything to the Queen, her substitute daughter, and was anxious to keep mother and child estranged.

Lehzen was also resented by Prince Albert for her undue influence over the Queen. His opportunity to remove her came when Victoria's first child, Vicky, was fourteen months old and the

Prince of Wales two months. Vicky was not gaining weight and Albert feared that Lehzen, who was in control of the royal nursery, was over-doctoring the child. Victoria defended her confidante but Albert threatened to leave the court unless Lehzen went. So, bearing a title and a pension, Lehzen returned to Germany. Victoria never saw her again. It was a sad end for the "surrogate" mother who never had children of her own, but probably the only way Victoria could move into womanhood.

There was now a remarkable improvement in her relationship with her own mother, who gradually became a source of advice and comfort to Victoria herself and became close to her grandchildren, especially Alice who shared her love of music. When her mother died, Victoria was heartbroken, weeping over the baby books and mementos that her mother had collected over many years. In her way the Duchess had always done what she believed to be her best for Victoria, and if she craved power herself, so have many others who have pushed their offspring along a pre-ordained path.

Nevertheless, it was Albert who welded Victoria's own children into a family unit. After his death, Victoria found it hard to relate to her children, apart from her daughter Alice and the young Princess Beatrice. Albert Edward, Prince of Wales, later Edward VII, wavered between times when he could do no right for Queen Victoria and others when he was indulged. At such moments Victoria refused to acknowledge her eldest son's philanderings and became angry with any who tried to inform her.

Queen Victoria set the template for royal family life. For decades after her death, the members of the royal family tried to step into those moulds. Individual members, treated as gods by fawning courtiers and expected to act as saints by a public eager for living fairy tales, have either succeeded in eradicating any human weakness, good as well as bad, or been condemned for failing to uphold the tradition.

Edward VII's second son George became heir to the throne when his elder brother Albert Victor (Eddy) died in 1892, and married his brother's intended bride, Princess May of Teck, the following year.

George, rather than his reprobate older brother, was the favourite of his beautiful mother, Alexandra. It is easy to condemn Alexandra for her possessiveness, but her husband's infidelities may have thrown her back, like many scorned women, to seek the missing love from her children. She declared that she and her second son shared the bond of "Mother and Child—which nothing can ever diminish or render less binding. Nothing and nobody will ever come between me and my darling Georgie boy."

Such sentiments hardly offered a firm foundation for a demonstrative relationship between George and his wife, notwithstanding the natural reserve inbred into majesty. Certainly George found it difficult to show physical or verbal affection to his wife and children, although there is no doubt the couple were devoted and loved their children. Indeed, many affectionate letters were sent between husband and wife and from the royal parents to the children. But theirs was a world in which the family moved in ways pre-ordained by the Victorian court. The royal family lived their most intimate moments in public from morning till night, and had to act out the regal parts expected of them.

King George frequently commented: "I was frightened of my father and I'm damned sure that my children are frightened of me." Queen Mary was too nervous of her husband to prevent his bullying them. To her, George was King and must be obeyed unquestioningly. A more overtly affectionate side of Queen Mary was occasionally revealed towards the young princes and their sister when her husband was not present. But for most of the time the children only saw their parents for an hour a day, and the sadistic nurse would make sure that David, later Edward VIII, was seen in a bad light by pinching his arm and making him cry.

Queen Mary, like Queen Victoria, disapproved of her eldest son's behaviour, but would often turn a blind eye to it. She could not forgive the Abdication, unable to condone his weakness in putting love before the throne, even if she could understand.

The happy royal family par excellence was created by Queen Elizabeth, now the Queen Mother, who like Queen Mary was more regal than those born to the job. On her marriage to the Duke of York, and after the birth of the "little princesses", as they were popularly known even when teenagers, she stage-managed the family image of "us four". There were pictures—not just the dull sepia photographs, but moving images for Pathe and the other newsreel companies—of the princesses and their mother, often dressed in powder blue or pastel shades, singing at the piano, playing board games around the fire, stroking the dogs, patting the horses.

The family became the inspiration for every hearth and home in the UK and indeed further afield. This positive image was especially important in maintaining national unity during the war years and was based on genuine affection. But it provided few opportunities for the airing of any emotions of the less positive kind. The King might swear while pruning his bushes, but the Queen never stopped smiling and waving and fun was perhaps centred on charades and pantomimes rather than spontaneous joy.

Crawfie, Marian Crawford, the royal governess who gave up her own child-bearing years to remain with the "little princesses" into adulthood, perpetuated the saccharine image in her world-selling book, *The Little Princesses*, written after she left royal service. Crawfie was cut off by the royal family for betraying few more intimate details than that the young Princess Elizabeth methodically arranged her sugar crystals while the more impulsive Margaret Rose gulped hers down, or that the future heiress to the throne folded her clothes neatly on her bedroom chair and placed her shoes at precise right angles to the chair.

"Doing a Crawfie" became a family expression for letting out intimate secrets.

Like other royal children, the little princesses knew more of the world of the nursery than that of their parents. In January 1927, when Princess Elizabeth was nine months old, her parents were sent on an official tour of Australia and New Zealand for six months. There is little doubt of the present Queen Mother's genuine unhappiness at leaving her baby for the first time: "I felt very much leaving on Thursday. The baby was so sweet, playing with Bertie's buttons, it quite broke me up."

The carriage drove round until the Duchess had regained her composure and could leave with a smile and wave for the adoring public. Princess Elizabeth was left in the care of her grandparents and George V proved to be more overtly affectionate with her than he had been with his own children.

Queen Elizabeth the Queen Mother was far more empathic and at ease with people than her mother-in-law or elder daughter, who even as Queen would fall silent as her socially skilled mother took centre stage. When George VI died, Elizabeth was even more anxious not to upstage her mother.

Few can deny the Queen Mother's human touch, which revealed itself during her wartime walks through the bombed East End of London and in her support of her husband in his gruelling duties, crippled as he was by shyness and a stammer when kingship was thrust upon him. So her strengths should not be underestimated. She assumed the role of favourite mother and later grandmother of the nation more readily than Queen Mary had done. In family life there was love and laughter, but she closed her eyes to anything controversial or unpleasant and, it is claimed by critics, simply blanked out any who offended her.

Margaret was billed as "the lively child, the rebel", as befitted the younger daughter, whereas the future Queen was the "serious conformist". At what point image merged into reality or which came first is not recorded in the numerous royal biographies. What is certain is that the present Queen has inherited or acquired her mother's gift for ignoring what is not pleasing in her family life, symptomatic of the hereditary royal tendency to rise above baser emotions.

After Prince Charles was born on 14 November 1948, he was brought up for the first few months of his life in the rented family home, Windlesham Moor in the Surrey countryside, seeing his parents at weekends, until the family took up official residence at Clarence House in London in June 1949. This separation is a sign not of maternal indifference, but that Princess Elizabeth was no more or less maternal than the majority of aristocratic mothers, among whom such practices were normal.

In November 1949 Princess Elizabeth flew out to Malta to join Prince Philip where he was stationed with the Navy. Charles remained with his nannies and under the care of his grandparents. He spent Christmas at Sandringham without his parents.

Princess Elizabeth came home on 28 December but departed to join her husband in March, returning to Britain in May to await the birth of Princess Anne. She faced the choice of being with her husband or her child and chose her husband. A similar decision was taken for a short period years later by the Duchess of York when she chose to be with Prince Andrew, not long after the birth of Beatrice, when Andrew was about to go away to sea for a considerable period.

In September Prince Philip left again for Malta and Princess Elizabeth followed in December. Charles spent another Christmas with his grandparents, this time with his young sister.

On 24 November 1953 the new Queen Elizabeth and Prince Philip began a six-month tour of the Commonwealth. After five months the children were brought to Tobruk where five-year-old Charles formally shook hands with his mother in greeting, after she had welcomed the VIPs. This has been frequently contrasted with pictures of the late Princess of Wales embracing Prince Harry warmly when they were reunited on the royal yacht *Britannia* in Toronto in 1991, after a much shorter parting. The difference is forty years and a different emotional climate.

Like Queen Victoria, Elizabeth left the running of the family to her husband. Much is made of the fact that she saw the older children for an hour in the morning and evening, but otherwise left their care to the nannies, a continuation of her own upbringing. Yet it is reported that she cried when, before a tour, her young son promised to care for his sister. Of course Prince Charles must have minded not being cuddled and played with and being the centre of his mother's universe. Countless wealthy children sent away to boarding school at a young age cry into their pillows and would exchange their privileged lives for a mother to tuck them up and pack their lunch boxes every day.

The younger children were given more of Queen Elizabeth's time, but still were primarily brought up by paid carers. It was not a sign of bad mothering, but a way of life.

Queen Elizabeth knew Charles was unhappy at school, especially the spartan Gordonstoun where he was badly bullied. But she did not intervene, and neither did his grandmother. Queen Elizabeth, like Queen Mary before her, did not stop her husband bullying her son, believing that Prince Philip should have the final say with the children, and that the future King must be physically and emotionally strong.

Three of her children have experienced failed marriages. The late Princess of Wales and the Duchess of York entered a world where duty was all, where princes traditionally could commit adultery or neglect their wives and a blind eye would be turned. Modern women like Diana Spencer and Sarah Ferguson expected more.

It is comforting that Prince Charles has shown affection to his sons in public during the period of intense sorrow after their mother's death. That Diana was a good mother is not in question. "They mean everything to me," she frequently said. "I always feed my children love and affection." The quiet dignity of the young princes at the funeral was a fitting tribute to the love and loyalty their mother inspired.

Mothers of the Famous

The hand that rocks the cradle
Is the hand that rules the world.

William Ross Wallace

A man who has been the indisputable favourite of his
mother keeps for life the feeling of a conqueror, that
confidence of success that often induces real success.

Sigmund Freud

*E*very mother thinks her offspring is a second Picasso, Shakespeare
or Margot Fonteyn. Whether that child gets a job in a bank or film
studio, drops out to backpack round the world or settles down with 2.4
children and a mortgage, there is always a lingering sense of "if only"
mingled with maternal pride, joy and anxiety, whether the child is
sixteen or sixty.

I have looked at examples of famous men and women from
history and the modern world in some detail to see if there are
certain characteristics that mark out a mother who will push her
child to fame and fortune. Whether this brings happiness for child or
mother is another matter. For the child who becomes the property of
the world may have little time for his own family, although he or she
may provide generously in material terms.

What is clear is that the mothers of successful people tend to be
strong, determined women, perhaps widowed or with a weaker
partner in the intellectual rather than physical sense, the matriarchs
of the family. They also, as Freud says, have a total belief that a
particular child—usually the eldest or only child—is special. The
child is nurtured in the belief along with the maternal milk. For

example, Duke Ellington, held by many to be the most influential jazz composer and band leader ever, was inspired by his mother. By the standards of American Negroes in the early years of this century his parents were well off. But it was not an easy world for a black man to grow up in, let alone flourish; he would become famous playing at the Cotton Club where blacks were allowed to work and entertain but not to enter as customers. However, he had that magic confidence instilled by his mother who told him from an early age that he was blessed. In return, Ellington was devoted to her and never stopped showering her with gifts and compliments. When she died in 1935 the strain brought him close to a nervous breakdown. He wore a gold cross in his mother's memory for the rest of his life.

There are exceptions, weak mothers who reared world-changers. Florence Nightingale's mother, for example, sought a conventional path for her in marriage and could not understand her daughter's crusading. What is certain is that the mother, whether as an inspiration or catalyst for change, influences the path of the great and infamous for good or ill.

The Heroes

Napoleon Buonaparte   The prime characteristics necessary to mother a powerful person—strength and a total belief in the ability of the child to succeed—were possessed in abundance by Letizia Buonaparte, mother of Napoleon, the self-made Emperor of France who nearly brought all of Europe under his control.

Napoleon is unlikely to have inherited his iron will from his father Carlo. Although a leader of the Corsican resistance, Carlo submitted to the French in return for recognition as a member of the French nobility. He was a spendthrift and once frittered his entire annual income on a single party. In sharp contrast, Letizia, who had married Carlo when she was fourteen, was a tough woman who ruled her family with a rod of iron.

Napoleon was to say of his own determination: "I had the instinct that my willpower was stronger than other people's. I had to get what I wanted." Like other famous men, he found himself responsible for his family at an early age. He joined the French army at the age of sixteen and was commissioned as an officer in the artillery. So badly was he paid he had to cut down on food to send money to his mother, who by now was a widow bringing up his brothers and sister on her own. Napoleon had a very Mediterranean attitude to women: "We Westerners have spoiled everything by treating women too well. We are quite wrong to make them almost our equals. The Eastern peoples have been much more sensible," he once said. But this chauvinistic attitude did not impress his mother. When Napoleon was Emperor and tried to make her kiss his hand in homage, her fan came down smartly on his knuckles. Even at the height of his power she refused to spend a penny more than necessary, saying that she might one day have to "find bread for all these Kings I have borne".

His attitude towards his own mother did not conflict with his belief in mothers as breeding machines, whose three main roles were in the bed, the home and the church. Indeed, he declared that the greatest woman, living or dead, was she who had the most children. Letizia was a prime candidate, having given birth to eleven children, eight of whom survived. She died in her mid-eighties, having outlived her famous son.

Abraham Lincoln   The 16th President of the United States is considered by many historians to have been the greatest man to have held that office. He guided his country through the Civil War, the most divisive and threatening experience.

His father Thomas Lincoln was physically strong and brave, and must have inspired Abraham with courage and the ability to withstand hardship. Yet had it not been for the determination of his stepmother, Abraham might have remained an illiterate farmer like Thomas. Shortly after his mother's death in October 1818, his father married his childhood sweetheart, a widow with three children. When she arrived, Sarah Bush Johnston brought clothes for her stepchildren and set the chaotic place in order. Ten-year-old

Abraham was her favourite, as she recognized even then the qualities that made him different from other rough country boys. To her, his sensitivity and awareness of moral dilemmas were not signs of weakness, but qualities that reflected her own wider perspective of the world. Indeed, Abraham became closer to his stepmother than to his own flesh and blood, especially his father who found it hard to understand his tall, gentle son. Sarah would try to keep the peace between them. In her old age she said: "Abraham was always a good boy, the best I ever saw. His mind and mine, what little I had, seemed to run as one and move in the same channel."

From the first she encouraged Abraham's zeal for learning. There was a tiny schoolhouse four miles away and Sarah saw to it that Abraham attended at every opportunity, although he was often needed on the farm and lessons had to be paid for in produce that could be ill-spared from feeding the family. Nevertheless Sarah made sacrifices, determined that Abraham should fulfil his potential.

As Abraham moved from success to success, he never forgot his stepmother. Before taking office as President on 4 March 1861, he rode by freight train to Illinois and travelled eight miles on rough tracks to the cabin where Sarah Bush Lincoln lived. The old woman wept as Abraham took her in his arms. But they were tears of joy, though she knew she would probably never see her Abe again. He had fulfilled her faith in him and that was the only reward she wanted.

Mother Teresa When Mother Teresa won the Nobel Peace prize in December 1979 she asked for the banquet to be cancelled and the money to be put to charitable use. She declared: "I accept the prize gratefully in the name of the poor to be used to feed the starving and build homes for the lost and lonely, for lepers and outcasts."

It is often said that Mother Teresa's children were the sick and starving people of Calcutta. She was known to the poor as Mother. It was the influence of her own mother Dranafile, a strong woman whose life was devoted to the service of others, who set her on the path to what many are now demanding, her canonization.

Mother Teresa was born into an Albanian family in 1910 at Skopje, in a largely Muslim area of what is now Macedonia. Her parents were both Albanian Roman Catholics. Her father Nikola was a merchant while her mother Dranafile was the pillar of the home. Mother Teresa's biographer recounts that while Nikola was away on business, Dranafile would busy herself about the house cooking, cleaning and mending. But as soon as Nikola returned all work stopped and her mother would put on a clean dress, comb her hair and ensure that the children were fresh and tidy to greet him.[1]

The youngest of three children, Mother Teresa was christened Agnes Gonxha (Rosebud) Bojaxhiu and had a very happy childhood. Her mother was devout and strict with her children, but was also wise, compassionate and understanding, believing it was better to teach by example than coercion. She told her children: "When you do good, do it unobtrusively, as if you were tossing a pebble into the sea." She took them with her to morning Mass whenever possible, taught them to say their prayers and to put faith into practice, by helping her to care for the less fortunate. When her mother went to take food and money to the poor and sick, Agnes went with her.

When Agnes was nine, her father died, perhaps murdered for his political activities (he was an Albanian patriot). The family lost almost everything. At first Agnes's mother was so grief-stricken that she left everything to her eldest daughter. But soon she set about building up a cloth and hand embroidery business. With this she not only provided for her family but also for the even less fortunate. Dranafile's dedication inspired Agnes to believe that the efforts of individuals could lessen adversity and poverty. She supported her daughter in her determination to became a nun, and there were no emotional appeals to remain close to home or imposed guilt to hold Agnes back. It is reported that Dranafile was in tears as the train left Zagreb taking her daughter out of her life, and perhaps this was the greatest sacrifice she could have made.

Mother Teresa transferred her love of her mother and the children she would never have to the cause of mothers and children in need. In 1981 a journalist asked Mother Teresa if she missed having her own child. She replied: "Naturally, naturally, of course. That is the sacrifice we make for God."

Mother Teresa is a shining example of selflessness, of the power of action rather than words, but her mother should not be forgotten, particularly for her unstinting sacrifice of her daughter and her daughter's unborn children. The hardest part for the mothers of the potentially great is to let them go, knowing that their love will be directed to humankind and there may be little time or energy for the mother who bore them. Is the sacrifice worth while to the mother? Do they never in the night wish their child was an ordinary person, not saint or conqueror? A good mother lets her child go, but women from Mary onwards must have wept as they lose to the world the child for whom they have sacrificed everything.

Florence Nightingale   Florence Nightingale, the Lady of the Lamp who was the heroine of the Crimean War and founded modern nursing, was certainly not inspired by her mother. She commented in 1867: "The whole occupation of my sister and Mamma was to lie on two sofas telling each other not to get tired putting flowers in water. It is a scene worthy of Molière when two people in tolerable and perfect health lie on the sofa all day, doing absolutely nothing, and persuade themselves and others that they are the victims of self-devotion for another who is dying of overwork."

She was born in Florence on 12 May 1820, the second child of William and Fanny Nightingale. Fanny loved socializing and wanted nothing more from her two daughters than that they should be successful socially and make good marriages. The family returned to England two years later and the girls were reared in a world of lavish entertaining and prosperity. The introspective William taught the girls Latin, Greek and mathematics and before long he and Florence would be closeted in the study with the books while her sister Parthe and Fanny would be in the drawing room practising more gracious arts.

Nevertheless both parents expected Florence to marry and to this end in September 1837 the family set off on a Grand Tour of

Europe. Fanny was delighted with her daughters' success at the operas, theatres and grand dances. Florence especially was greatly admired for her beauty, and when the family returned home Fanny was determined that Florence would make a first-rate marriage. When, instead, she announced her plan to become a nurse in December 1845 her mother resorted to hysteria and her father to anger. Nursing was not at the time a respectable profession. The only respectable nurses were nuns. It is hard to understand today that Fanny sincerely believed she was acting in her daughter's best interests. Many nurses had a reputation for being drunkards and women of low morals, at best doing little more than making their charges comfortable, knowing little of hygiene and often introducing infection that killed the patients they sought to cure. Charles Dickens's portrayal of Mrs Gamp in *Martin Chuzzlewit* did the profession no favours and certainly did not recommend it as a career for a respectable woman. How could it compare with a glittering marriage, prosperity, everything that Fanny saw as happiness and success for a woman?

Although she was twenty-five, Florence did not go against her family wishes. Matters deteriorated as Fanny's attitude hardened. Florence increasingly refused to mingle in society, attend parties and above all get married. When she turned down the man who had been proposing to her for seven years her mother felt that all hope was lost.

When Florence returned from the Crimea she felt her mother and her sister knew nothing of real suffering. For many years she cut herself off from them and would be seized by illness if they threatened to come near. Florence was nursed in her own illnesses by her Aunt Mai, whose own life and family were sacrificed to the needs of her niece. Only when her mother was old did Florence become reconciled to her, and she nursed both her and her sister who had married well. But to the end Florence resented her mother and sister for taking her from what she saw as her calling to the wider world and for draining her own sparse energies. Perhaps, in spite of all her numerous real achievements, part of her did resent the fact that her mother had not persuaded her into marriage.

It is a complex story, for Florence herself was a mixture of contradictions. Rude, aggressive and unreasonable towards those she saw as obstructing her mission, she was invariably loving and gentle to her "children", the wounded soldiers. "No one can feel for the army as I do," she declared. "These people who talk have all fed their children on the fat of the land. I have had to see my children dressed in a dirty blanket—and see them fed on raw salt meat—and 9000 of my children are dying from causes which might have been prevented . . . Oh, my poor men who endured so patiently. I feel I have been such a bad mother to you to come home and leave you in your Crimean graves. Seventy-three per cent dead in eight regiments. Who thinks of that now?"

Was she thinking of Fanny, the mother who had failed to understand Florence's real needs, which Florence herself had scarcely fathomed? Is it inevitable that those who make a significant mark on the world have to break away either physically or emotionally from the mother who bore them? Was Florence a good mother to "her children" but a bad daughter to her real mother?

Christy Brown   A powerful example of mother love triumphing over appalling odds and bringing a son to fame is found in the mother of Irish novelist Christy Brown. Her devotion helped him to overcome the horrendous disability of cerebral palsy to become one of Ireland's great writers, who could produce wonderful works like *Down All the Days* and *Wild Grow the Lilies* despite having to hold a pen with his left foot, the only part of his body over which he had total control.

In his autobiography[2] Christy Brown recounts how he was born in 1932, the tenth of twenty-two children of whom "only" thirteen survived. At twelve months Christy was still unable to sit up without a mountain of pillows supporting him; his hands were clenched nearly all of the time; his mouth was unable to grip the teat of the bottle. Doctors labelled him as an interesting but hopeless case. One called him mentally defective, not realizing the powerful intellect that lay trapped in the crippled body. His mother refused to accept the verdict of the doctors and even well-meaning family and friends who wanted her to write off her child. Christy Brown wrote in his autobiography: "In spite of all the doctors and specialists told her, she would not agree. I don't believe she knew why—she just knew, without feeling the smallest shade of doubt."

Although she had her other children to take care of she determined to bring up Christy no differently from the rest. As Christy records, she set out to prove that he was not an idiot, "not because of any rigid sense of duty but out of love". He could only lie helplessly, racked by wild, stiff, snakelike movement, his fingers and arms continually twisting and twitching. But she sat patiently for hours, reading to him, showing him pictures and laughing kindly with him. All seemed hopeless until one day, while watching his sister do her homework, he reached out and took the chalk from her hand—with his left foot. Realizing that the breakthrough she had prayed for had come, Mrs Brown set out to teach him to write with his foot, clutching a piece of chalk between his toes. Her labours and triumphs are recorded in *My Left Foot*, which is almost a hymn to a mother's devotion.

Dudley Moore   The British actor, musician, writer and comedian was also disabled as a child, also cared for by strong mother who forced him into the mainstream of life. In his official biography[3] he tells of his rejection by his mother Ada Francis Moore because he had a club foot and his left leg was withered. From his childhood she told him that she had wanted to kill him at birth because she felt so angry at herself and so badly about the pain that lay ahead for both of them.

Nevertheless, Dudley recounts that his mother was the driving force in his life. She fought for him to attended an ordinary school, spent hours massaging his leg, and was thrilled when he won a scholarship to Magdalen College, Oxford.

Life is incredibly hard for a mother of a disabled child. Ada Moore may have rejected Dudley initially at birth, but she was given little help by professionals or her family to come to terms with his problem. It is very tempting in later life to offload all one's complexes and failures on to one's mother's failure to love, a post-war trend in the West. Whatever Dudley's mother had done he might well have ended up feeling inferior and bitter because of his physical problems and small stature. As it is he has had a highly successful career, as a fine jazz pianist, a great comedian, and a Hollywood sex symbol.

Psychologists and family therapists invariably look at the mother's responsibility for a child's problems from bedwetting to joyriding. In fact, Ada was brought up under the baby-rearing methods of Truby King, the mental hygienist who produced such gems as: "Half the irritability and lack of moral control which spoil adult life originate in the first year of existence. The seeds of feebleness and irritability sown in infancy bear bitter fruit afterwards."[4] This was the age when experts were advising that a baby's arms should be splinted to avoid thumb-sucking and worse.

Freud   The behaviourist John Watson in 1928 advocated: "Let your behaviour always be objective and kindly firm; never hug and kiss your children, never let them sit on your lap—shake hands with them in the morning."[5] It is important to look at the context of any apparent neglect. Older women who were mothers at the time have revealed how they wept as their hungry babies cried because feeding was strictly by the clock. What then of the most formative mothers of all, the psychologists' mothers?

In fairness to Freud, he did not blame mothers for their children's shortcomings. He believed mothers were not capable of such conscious evil, as their egos were far too weak. Sigmund Freud had no doubts, however, about the mother's role in shaping the lives of great men, as a psychic field kitchen and cheerleader. As the first child of his father's second wife, Amalie Nathanson, Sigmund was certainly the favourite. From Sigmund's birth on 6 May 1856 until her old age, Amalie always referred to him as "My Golden Sigi" and told him he was destined to be a great man. Certainly Freud needed confidence to succeed in life. As a Jew in Imperial Vienna he faced anti-Semitism. His father's business was ruined and Sigmund had long struggles with money, finding himself at forty working relentlessly to support his wife and six children, his parents and his sisters while trying to promote his ideas of psychoanalysis.

Yet Freud won through to become the most influential psychologist of this century and a pioneer in the field of psychoanalysis. His views on motherhood were shaped by his own childhood impressions. Motherhood, Freud felt, was the goal of female development. He was convinced that all women wanted babies. It was part of the natural order of the world and their fulfilment came from raising them, as he was convinced his own mother had felt.

In terms of his own analytical processes it might be said that Freud idealized mothers as a defence against his ambivalence towards his own. He was acutely jealous when his brother Julius was born, and when the little boy died at fifteen months old Sigmund felt guilty that he had secretly killed him by his bad thoughts.

The Oedipus complex may be rooted in Freud's own early erotic memories. He admits to spying on his mother naked when he was four and years later remarked that the child, especially the male, "never gets over the pain of losing Mother's breast". Was the Oedipus complex also a projection on to his weak and ageing father of the admiration, mingled with fear, that Freud felt for his psychologically strong mother? If so, this effectively exonerated the mother from all negative feelings, and to the end of his days he refused to believe that there were cruel, rejecting or seductive mothers. This blind spot denied them any real will or intent.

On the surface Sigmund Freud and his mother remained devoted and he described the bond between mother and son as the "most perfect, the most free from ambivalence of all relationships".

But was he in denial, since it has been reported that other family members saw his mother as a possessive tyrant? Were the violent stomach cramps Freud suffered as an adult before his Sunday visits to his mother a result of swallowing his anger and resentment?

145

Jung A formative influence on the world of psychoanalysis, dreams and synchronicities, or meaningful coincidences, was the fey mother of Carl Gustav Jung, a former pupil of Freud. Jung had two abiding memories of his mother Emilie that encapsulated for him the two sides of motherhood: the virgin mother and mother earth that formed two of his main archetypes of ideal humanity. One early memory was of a slender young woman wearing a dress of black printed all over with green crescents, who could be happy and laughing but was subject to fits of depression.

The second from a later period recalled: "My mother was a very good mother. She had a great animal warmth, cooked wonderfully and was most companionable and pleasant. She had a decided literary gift as well as taste and depth. But this quality never emerged. It remained hidden beneath the semblance of a kindly fat woman, extremely hospitable and possessed of a great sense of humour."

The contrast between the inner and outer woman intrigued Jung. Indeed it could be said that his mother was his first in-depth case study into the complexities of humanity and the template for the anima, the feminine side of the personality we all possess.

While outwardly Emilie was conventional and overtly Christian, the essential woman was so different that Jung spoke of her later in life as being two people. An unconscious aspect of her personality would break through the conforming mother and reveal a power at variance with the compliant surface: "One personality was innocuous and human, the other uncanny. The second personality emerged rarely but each time the experience was unexpected and frightening. She would then speak as if talking to herself. But what she said was aimed at me and usually struck to the core of my being so that I was stunned to silence," Jung recalled in later life. So grew his personal vision of the power of the unconscious as the vehicle of speaking true, that went beyond his teacher Freud's concepts of instincts and drives.

Carl Gustav Jung was born in July 1875, the second son, the first having died a few hours after birth in 1873. His sister Johanna was born nine years after Jung and so for many years he was an only child. For the first few years of life his mother surrounded him with warmth and affection. Like Freud, he basked in the joy of being his mother's favourite. When Jung was three, he suffered from nervous eczema and later considered this to be linked to the sudden unexplained absence of his mother. Emilie was hospitalized for three months, possibly with some nervous illness.

The birth of his baby sister years later came as a total shock. His parents told him the stork had brought the baby which he did not believe, so he came to distrust his parents and become angry with his mother, an emotion he repressed. As his sister demanded more attention, Jung retreated to his attic bedroom. He found it hard to relate to his father, whom he blamed for his mother's desertion years before. After his father's death, during his medical studies, Jung's mother perceptively commented, perhaps to herself, "He died in time for you. You did not understand each other and he might have became a hindrance to you."

Jung's increasing fascination with the supernatural stemmed from his mother's psychic abilities, which he had witnessed since childhood. In 1902 a psychological investigation of spiritualistic phenomena formed part of his doctoral thesis.

On the night his mother died, in 1923, Jung had a dream of being trapped in a primeval forest with huge trees and rocks. A gigantic wolfhound appeared. To Jung, steeped in the belief that we all share in a common mythological heritage, the Wild Huntsman in the Sky had commanded the dog to carry away a human soul. Jung woke, calling out in fear, and the following morning he received the news of his mother's death.

Beethoven   "Whatever Beethoven missed in childhood he had the thing that means most in the formation of a boy's character—he had a good mother."[6]

Ludwig van Beethoven was not the sole object of his mother's devotion during his early years. There is little doubt she loved him, but was worn down with looking after her drunken husband and her two other children. In spite of this, Ludwig remained devoted to his mother throughout his life. It was, however, his drunken father Johann, a competent musician and himself son of a fine singer and musician, who pushed the boy along the path to music.

Johann had married a young widow Maria Magdalena Laym, a clever and industrious woman, and Ludwig was born in 1770.

During his early years Maria provided what physical comforts she could; in 1781, when Ludwig was eleven years old, his health was so poor that during a boat trip down the Rhine to Holland his feet would have been severely frostbitten had his mother not cradled them in her lap for most of the journey.

Ludwig was convinced his mother was the only person who understood him. In 1787, when he was seventeen, he was visiting Vienna—where he met and impressed Mozart—when he got word that his mother was seriously ill. He hurried home to Bonn and found his mother dying of consumption. Although she was only forty, she was exhausted by years of struggle.

For many years her grave was lost. It has now been rediscovered and a tombstone laid bearing her devoted son's words: "She was such a good and loving mother to me, my best friend."

Elvis Presley   The mother of Elvis Presley is the archetypal mother of the famous: strong, with a feckless husband and totally devoted to her only surviving son. Gladys was convinced that her son was destined for greatness from the day of his birth in Tupelo, Mississippi on 8 January 1935. His twin brother was stillborn and Gladys believed the hillbilly superstition that the twin who lives inherits the strength of the one who dies. From an early age Gladys told Elvis that he needed to fulfil this double destiny. She was constantly looking for portents that the hand of destiny was at work, and when on 5 April 1936 the Presley home survived a tornado which rushed through Tupelo killing 263 people, she explained to her son that he had been saved because he was chosen. As Freud said, the man who is his mother's undisputed favourite never loses the feeling of being a conqueror. But such favouritism also imposes a terrific responsibility to succeed on behalf of the parent.

Elvis spent his early childhood surrounded by song and inherited his mother's vocal abilities (Gladys was said to have the voice of an angel). As an infant, he was tied to his mother's back as she worked in the Mississippi cotton fields, singing the old songs as she worked. His father was put in prison when Elvis was young and so the major influence in his formative years was his adoring mother. In turn Elvis became protective of her, especially in the presence of strangers, and they developed their own special language of pet words that persisted in Elvis's vocabulary even after Gladys's death. Her encouragement of his musical talents helped him to fulfil the great destiny she had predicted for him, but success took him away from her physically and emotionally. She became distressed by his increasing fame, and at one performance she leaped on to the stage and dragged screaming fans off her son.

During 1956, as he became a star, Elvis went to see his mother only six times. A year later he moved his parents into his newly acquired Graceland mansion, but Gladys was not happy there. Her health became markedly worse and her only joy was to put on old clothes and go down to a shop in the vicinity where she could sit on the porch with a beer and bemoan life in a rich man's castle.

Elvis was on National Service in Germany when Gladys was admitted to hospital, desperately ill. He hurried to her bedside in Memphis, promising never to leave her again, but she died shortly afterwards.

What was her legacy? After he married Priscilla and she gave birth to their daughter, Lisa Marie, Elvis was unwilling to make love to her again, because she was a mother. Mothers could only be loved from afar.

The Legacy of Destruction

Sid Vicious   The bass player with the Sex Pistols was an object of horror to parents but an icon to the punk generation. To his mother,

Ann Beverley, he was her wonderful son Simon. But Ann Beverley was no ordinary mother. To the end of her days she carried in her arm the tip of a broken needle, the legacy of her own drug addiction. Sid died of a heroin overdose in a New York hotel on 2 February 1979. It is probable that his mother supplied him with the drug. When Vicious died he was on bail, facing a possible jail sentence in America. His girlfriend Nancy Spungen had been stabbed to death, it is alleged, by Vicious. Sid was also charged with an assault in a nightclub while on bail. He had been brutally treated by other convicts during his remand in prison. New York police believe that he and his mother knew what they were doing and that Sid chose death rather than jail.

Ann Beverley was born on 25 April 1932. She claimed to have been abandoned by her own single mother at the age of twelve, but some sources have suggested that she left home at the age of fifteen or sixteen. In either case she was still a child, in need of mothering herself.

Sid Vicious was born John Simon Ritchie on 10 May 1957, when Ann was twenty-five. She never married his father, who deserted her some three years later in Ibiza. While in Spain, she began taking drugs and let her baby son—whom she always called Simon—get drunk on the local brandy. When she returned to London she began taking heroin. She and her son began avoiding their creditors by moving from flat to flat. Ann married zoologist Christopher Beverley, a wealthy and well-educated man who died of cancer almost immediately. For nearly seven years Anne and Simon lived with Christopher's parents in Tunbridge Wells, Kent, but this period of settled life came abruptly to an end and the pair were soon moving from flat to flat again, one step ahead of the debt collectors.

In 1974 they were living in a council tower block in Dalston, north-east London. Simon was studying art at a local college when he met John Lydon, who became Johnny Rotten and who nick-named him Sid Vicious. The son had acquired his mother's taste for drugs and when a friend, seeing him boil a needle before injecting himself, asked Vicious where he had acquired it, Vicious replied: "From my mum."

Vicious played in other punk bands before replacing Glen Matlock as the bass player in the Sex Pistols in 1977. Matlock had been fired for being a "sissy". Vicious might not have been much of a bass player but his image was anything but sissy. He suffered injuries onstage, bled through performances, doggedly kept up his heroin habit, and, as one commentator put it, in general lived his life in a brutally demented haze.

The Sex Pistols broke up a year after Vicious joined, during a tour of the United States. Vicious was taken to hospital with a drug overdose but recovered and stayed in the States with his girlfriend. On 11 October 1978, he was arrested for Nancy's murder.

Ann Beverley arrived in New York to "take care of her son". When he decided to commit suicide Ann sat in another room, waiting for him to die. Was this an act of love, a final vigil for the son who had found no happiness in life? Or was it, as critics suggest, a cynical act to secure her own future? She left New York with five trunkloads of Sid and Nancy memorabilia and control of the Sid Vicious estate, which earned her £250,000 plus royalties in 1986 when the group's former manager, Malcom McLaren, settled a lawsuit brought by members of the Sex Pistols. She settled in a terrace house in Swadlincote, Derbyshire.

The house held mementos of her son: photographs and gold discs and, in a glass case on a velvet cushion, one of the locks and chains from his punk outfit. She spoke to few people, but was often seen walking her dogs with a can of strong lager in each pocket. She died on 6 September 1996 after taking a cocktail of tranquillizers, painkillers and vodka. Before her suicide she had neatly cut her credit cards in half, and bagged and labelled her most precious possessions. Why had she tidied everything? Was it an attempt to create some order out of the chaos or could she not bear to be found in a mess? Or is it a hint that, had Christopher Beverley lived, she might indeed have created a very different world for the son she ultimately destroyed.

The Monsters

Stalin   Ekaterina Djugashvili was a hardworking, resourceful woman who did her best to turn her son Joseph into a priest. Yet he did not go into the Church but changed his name to Stalin and became the murderous tyrant of the Soviet Union.

Stalin was born on 21 December 1879 at Gori in Georgia. Once rich in natural resources, Georgia had by the time of Stalin's birth become reduced to an area of great poverty in which three-quarters of the population were illiterate. His parents came from serf stock and had been freed only fifteen years before his birth. He was the third child to be born into the family, but the previous two had died in infancy and so Joseph was in effect the eldest. His father was a violent man, struggling to earn a living as a cobbler, who mistreated both wife and child. His mother, in common with the mothers of many famous men, proved herself a survivor. She was a loving mother, protecting Joseph from the worst of his father's wrath. She supported herself and Joseph after her husband moved to work forty miles away, and obtained a job as housekeeper in the house of an Orthodox priest. Joseph went with her, and with the priest's help Ekaterina enrolled her son in the Orthodox Church School. Even after his father returned when the boy was ten and took him away to work in the shoe factory, Ekaterina was determined Joseph should become a priest and persisted until he returned to complete his education at school and afterwards at the Russian Orthodox theological college in Tiflis (now Tbilisi). Scholarships and his mother's efforts ensured that Joseph was able to remain at the seminary until he was nineteen.

Although he became the most powerful man in Russia, Stalin's mother remained disappointed that he had not become a priest. In spite of all she had done for him, he saw his mother only a few times after he rose to fame. When she died in 1936, her beloved son did not attend her funeral, claiming pressing matters prevented him.

How can a loving mother produce an evil son? Abraham Lincoln, although not as brutally treated as Joseph, was also beaten by a father who discouraged his learning. Yet he rose to be a gentle, compassionate leader. The creation of a monster is a complex issue that delves into the nature of good and evil, of the interplay between genes and environment. Brutality alone is not the cause; the child Adolf Hitler was neither butalized nor deprived.

Hitler Adolf Hitler came from the Waldviertel, in Lower Austria, an area between the Danube and the Bohemian frontier. Although his ancestors were peasants, Adolf's father, Alois, rose through the ranks to become a customs officer. He was not a good father, more interested in his beehives than his family.

Adolf's mother, Klara, was Alois's third wife and twenty years younger than her husband. In time she accepted his selfishness and indifference, kept the home neat and was a good mother to both her own children and stepchildren by Alois's previous marriages.

Adolf was born an 20 April 1889. Following the pattern of many famous men, he was his mother's pride and joy and, until his brother was born when he was five years old, the undisputed favourite. The fact that he was not jealous of the new baby suggests that he was not replaced in his mother's affections. No great scholar, at secondary school Adolf showed only an aptitude for drawing and an early interest in war games. His father's death in 1901 removed what the boy saw as pressure to force him into the civil servant mould.

He was asked to leave school because of his lack of effort. His mother tried boarding school in the attempt to find the right place for her beloved son to blossom, but Adolf still proved, according to reports, to be lazy, stubborn and unwilling to accept any authority. During the summer of 1905 he became ill and pressed his mother to let him fulfil his true ambition to attend the Vienna Academy of Arts. However, he did not try for admission for two years because he was unsure whether he should apply his talents to painting, architecture or music. The matter was not urgent as his indulgent mother paid while Adolf fantasized.

Klara was not a weak woman, for she was managing alone and

making great efforts to persuade Adolf to plan his future career. To this end she sent him to spend four weeks in Vienna. Here he found the perfect setting for the lifestyle to which he aspired, using the legacy left by his father and the pension to which he was entitled as the son of a government official, both of which Klara controlled.

She was becoming frantic, for her life was running out. She was suffering from breast cancer and was anxious to see Adolf settled before she died. He failed the examination to enter the Academy but did not tell his mother, staying on in Vienna pursuing his "studies", which in fact meant his cultural and social milieu. However, when he learned his mother was dying he came home and nursed her until the end. When he came to power he changed Mother's Day to his mother's birthday, 12 August, and made it a national holiday. Mothers, after all, were the breeding machines of the Master Race.

Was it something in Adolf's mental makeup, triggered by his mother's indulgence, that led him to evil? Other over-indulged sons have risen to fame or remained in obscurity without perpetrating horrors. As one cynic has commented, motherhood is a lottery: you might end up with a saint or a serial killer, and whatever you do in the middle is, at best, akin to spinning a roulette wheel in the hope of getting a winner.

Mothers in Myth and Literature

There was a young man loved a maid,
Who taunted him. "Are you afraid,"
She asked, "to bring me today
Your mother's heart upon a tray?"

He went and slew his mother dead
Tore from her breast her heart so red
Then towards his lover he raced.
But tripped and fell in all his haste.

As her heart rolled on the ground
It gave forth a plaintive sound
And it spoke in accents mild,
"Did you hurt yourself, my child?"

Jean Richepin

The Perfect Mother in Myth

The nineteenth-century Icelandic poet Jonas Hallgrimsson encapsulates the ideal mother who will lay down her life for her infant in "*Modurast*" ("Mother Love"), a poem that has inspired artists and sculptors and has entered the folk tradition. Erla Hulda Halldorsdottir, head of Iceland's Library of Women's History, told me that the poem describes a young mother who is travelling between farms in a snowstorm with her small baby in her arms, wrapped in her brideclothes. She cannot see in the storm, becomes lost, sits down and shelters her baby with her own body. She begs God for mercy for her son. The next day she is found frozen to death, but the baby lives.

155

A similar myth comes from Japan about a shopkeeper who is visited late at night by a woman proffering money for candy which she says is for her baby. He sees it is shrine money, given in rituals to the dead, and hurries after her. He follows her into a shrine, and then she disappears. He looks around the shrine and finds the dead woman with a newborn baby in her arms, still just about alive. The grandparents knew nothing of his birth. Their only daughter had disappeared suddenly the day before and they had been seeking her frantically. She had gone alone to the shrine to give birth, unwilling to bring shame upon her family. When she died, her ghost had gone for help to save the baby's life.

The Husband/Child Dilemma

Another popular theme is the dilemma of a mother who must choose between her husband and her children. The theme is treated graphically in the Greek myths which recount how Uranus, the personification of heaven, lay with Gaia, the earth his mother, and fathered many children. However, he was so afraid that they might usurp his position that he refused Gaia time to give birth and they remained within the womb of the earth. At last Gaia gave her son Cronos (Time) a sickle with which to cut off his father's genitals, thus releasing the children and his mother from her agony.

However, Cronos did not turn into a loving father. He married Rhea, one of his sisters, who became Mother of the Gods. Like Uranus, he fathered many children. As each child was born, Cronos swallowed it whole, fearing that it might depose him as he had deposed his own father. At last Rhea hid her son Zeus and gave her husband a stone to swallow instead. She then gave Zeus a potion to administer to Cronos to make him vomit up the children he had swallowed. Cronos was banished and Zeus took control, marrying his sister Hera.

Chaucer, telling the story of patient Griselde in the Clerk's Tale, portrays a woman whose devotion to her husband rises high above that to her child. Griselde is the daughter of a humble peasant who marries the local lord. He wishes to test her sense of duty and heaps humiliations and cruelties upon her, all of which she meekly bears. Eventually a soldier comes to tell her that her husband has ordered him to kill her children.

> But even then her tears she did not spill
> And bowed down meekly to her husband's will.
> At last she found her voice and thus began
> And meekly to the sergeant then she prayed,
> That as he was a worthy gentleman
> That she might kiss her child before it died
> And on her breast this little child she laid,
> With sad face, and so kissed and lulled it.
> "But one thing will I pray you, of your grace,
> That, save my lord forbade you, at the least
> Bury this little body in some place,
> Where beasts nor birds will tear its limbs and face."

In fact there is no murder. The lord has hidden his children and they are restored to her after he is satisfied that she has endured her ordeal with becoming humility. To Chaucer and his audience, Fair Griselde was the model wife.

She is at the other end of the spectrum from another literary heroine, Mother Wolf in Rudyard Kipling's *The Jungle Book*, who adopts the human infant Mowgli. When Shere Khan the tiger comes to claim Mowgli, whom he sees as his lawful prey, Father Wolf is inclined to caution but Mother Wolf faces down the tiger, who realizes he is no match for a mother defending her cubs, who will fight to the death.

The Mother Who Changed America

Perhaps the most influential mother in literature was the young slave mother Eliza in *Uncle Tom's Cabin*, written by Harriet Beecher

Stowe. With its vivid descriptions of suffering and oppression, this book inflamed the people of the North against slavery, and thus became one of the factors that hastened the American Civil War.

Harriet Beecher was born on 14 June 1811, in Litchfield, Connecticut. Her father, Lyman Beecher, was a renowned preacher. Harriet was a student, and later a teacher, at Hartford Female Seminary. In 1832 the Beechers moved to Cincinnati, Ohio. Just across the Ohio River lay slave territory and Harriet's visits to plantations confirmed for her the horrors of slavery. In 1836 she married Calvin Ellis Stowe, a seminary professor, and they had seven children. It is often said that Harriet's own experience of motherhood enabled her to create the emotive figure of Eliza and strike a chord in the hearts of mothers throughout America. Soon after moving to Brunswick, Maine, in 1850, Harriet was challenged by her sister-in-law to "write something that would make this whole nation feel what an accursed thing slavery is".

Uncle Tom's Cabin appeared as a serial in 1851–2 in the *National Era*, an antislavery paper, and after publication in 1852 sold three million copies before the start of the American Civil War. Harriet died on 1 July 1896.

One of the most powerful scenes in the book is of Eliza's desperate attempt to cross the frozen Ohio with her small son to save him from being sold away from her to another master. Many women help Eliza, including a woman in a tavern who procures a ferry for her, and even the wife of a senator who defies her husband and gives clothes to mother and child. Indeed, Stowe addresses her book specifically to "You mothers of America" and invokes their pity for "those mothers who are constantly made motherless by the American slave trade".

In recent times the book has been parodied as racist, patronizing to women and overtly sentimental, but that is to ignore the climate in which it was written. Even today few can fail to be moved by the scene where Eliza makes up a little package of clothing for her son before their escape, and even in the terrors of that hour does not forget to include one or two of his favourite toys.

The Supreme Sacrifice

A mother's attempt to save her child from slavery is also the theme of Mark Twain's *Pudd'nhead Wilson*, but the course taken by Roxana, a slave in the Mississippi town of Dawson's Landing, is very different from Eliza's. Roxana is of mixed race, but the liberties taken by slave owners with their slaves over generations mean that she is only one-sixteenth part black. "To all intents and purposes Roxy was as white as anybody, but the one sixteenth of her which was black outvoted the other fifteen parts and made her a negro. She was a slave and saleable as such. Her child was thirty-one parts white, and he too was a slave and, by a fiction of law and custom, a negro."

Her son is born on the same day as a white child that she is given to nurse after his mother dies. Roxana is terrified by her master's threat to "sell her down the river"; the further south they went down the Mississippi, the worse slaves were treated. To try to save her son from this fate, she swaps the children. No one notices the exchange and the white boy grows up a slave and Roxana's own boy is his master.

But the true son is no credit to his noble-spirited mother. He is a spoiled wastrel, runs up gambling debts and is in danger of losing his inheritance. Roxana, who has been freed, makes the supreme sacrifice and allows him to sell her back into slavery to pay his debts. Despite his promise to find her a kind master and to buy her back in a year, her son sells her to a southern slave owner; he sells her down the river and gives the phrase the meaning it has today.

Dead and Never Called Me Mother

The theme of a mother who cannot acknowledge her real son is also at the heart of Mrs Henry Wood's novel *East Lynne*. The heroine is a runaway mother who returns as a governess to East Lynne, her former home, where she has to watch the lingering death of her son,

Little Willie, while unable to reveal her true identity. The phrase "Dead and never called me mother", which brought tears to Victorian eyes, was not written by Mrs Wood, however. It cropped up in one of the stage adaptations of her novel.

The Angel and the Demon

Sentiment thrived on both sides of the Atlantic. Expressing his dream of the perfect mother, Rudyard Kipling wrote:

> If I were hanged on the highest hill,
> Mother o' mine, O mother o' mine!
> I know whose love would follow me still.
> Mother o' mine, mother o' mine!

In fact his own mother, Alice, like many colonial parents, sent him back to England from his home in India to be reared and educated—in Kipling's case by the wicked witch.

Kipling was brought up in Bombay by his Indian *ayah* (nurse) and his bearer, whom he came to know and love more than his parents. As a young child, Kipling spoke Hindi. He and his sister would be presented at bedtime to their parents and reminded to "speak in English to Papa and Mama". This the children did with difficulty.

When Kipling was five years old, he was brought to England because of fears for his health. For six years he lived in a terrace house in Southsea, near Portsmouth, which he named the House of Desolation. His parents did not tell him that this would be his home for the rest of his childhood. He was entrusted to the care of an evangelical woman who instantly took a violent dislike to him and vowed to rid him of what she saw as his over-privileged mannerisms. From the beginning Kipling was regularly scalded, beaten, harangued and interrogated, and frequently shut in a dark cellar. His single plea "Help" can still be seen engraved in the cellar wall. When he was almost seventy, the writer described his childhood maltreatment as calculated torture. "I had never heard of Hell so I was introduced to all its tortures."

It was only when Rudyard's mother heard that his sight was failing that she came from India to rescue him. After being educated at the United Services College at Westward Ho, the sixteen-year-old Kipling went home to Lahore. So was Kipling's real mother o' mine neglectful? I spoke to another author who was a child of the British Empire. Elizabeth Watkins was brought up in Africa under colonial rule. She commented:

"When Kipling's mother came home and came upstairs to kiss him goodnight, he put up his arm to ward off the expected blow. I think that says it all.

"There was another problem for the children suddenly deprived of their mothers. The mental torture during teenage embarrassment was also great. My favourite story is of a schoolboy son who met his mother at the station. He put his hands on her shoulder and said, 'Mother, may I ask you something?'

" 'Yes, of course.'

"She was expecting a question concerning some family secret or sex. The question was what does antimacassar mean? The worry of making a social gaffe was enormous for colonial teenagers who were automatically considered inferior to the family on which they were parked.

"By my generation transport had improved sufficiently for few separations to last more than two years, but this was enough to shake a girl's self-confidence and happiness. After an awful school term you had nothing but trying to be polite and to fit into another household you also did not like. This made it more difficult to feel at home. The awfulness was exacerbated by the fact that girls were taught by poorly paid spinsters with little knowledge of the world or the problems we had to face. Many of the girls far outstripped the teachers in ability and as we grew up we were perceived to be heading for more glamorous lives, a fact that did not always tend to good relationships.

"As my mother left us for yet another long separation she used the chilling words, 'Don't cry, darlings. This is the price of Empire.'"

Peter Pan

The story of the boy who never grew up but stayed in Never Never Land fighting pirates and Red Indians is a children's classic. But *Peter Pan* has dark depths that echo the desperate attempts of its author, James M. Barrie, to win his mother's love. When he was seven James lost his thirteen-year-old brother David in a skating accident. James's mother took to her bed and remained isolated and in mourning for years, ignoring her younger son. On one occasion James entered her darkened room and his mother called out, "Oh David, is that you? Could that be you?" before saying, "Oh, it is only you, James."

James became driven by a desire to imitate his dead brother so well that she would not notice the difference. Wearing David's clothes, he would burst into his grieving mother's room and begin whistling in the special way his elder brother used to do.

But he could not replace David in his mother's affections. Worst of all, she told James many times that David died when he was still perfect, still a boy, never to be ruined by growing up and away from his mother. Barrie's obsession with trying to please his mother would last all his life. He once said of his own old age: "When the past comes sweeping back like the shades of night over the bare road of the present, it will not, I believe, be my youth I shall see but hers, not a boy clinging to his mother's skirts and crying 'Wait till I'm a man and you'll lie on feathers', but a little girl in a magenta frock and a white pinafore."

The curse lay on him all his life. He was barely five feet tall when an adult, and his case is often mentioned in textbooks on psychogenic dwarfism, a failure to grow for reasons of mind—including a lack of maternal affection—rather than body. Despite this he became one of the most popular playwrights and authors in Britain, although *Peter Pan* and *The Admirable Crichton* are the only two of his works that have successfully survived the test of time. He was never able to consummate his marriage. His own dilemma is expounded in *Peter Pan* when Peter repels Wendy's advances with the words: "But Wendy, you are our mother." When Wendy grows up and marries, Peter no longer recognizes her.

Sons and Mothers

David Herbert Lawrence, the son of an illiterate coal miner and a schoolteacher, was born in the Nottinghamshire village of Eastwood on 11 September 1885. With his mother's help he went to Nottingham High School and later to the University College in Nottingham. For several years he taught in London schools but when his first novel, *The White Peacock*, was published in 1911 he left teaching to concentrate on writing. In the same year, Lawrence met Frieda Weekley (born von Richthofen), an older married woman who left her husband and three children to live with him.

Lawrence waged a constant battle to free himself from the mother who had made him aware of the wider world beyond the narrow Nottinghamshire mining village. She gave him the tools to escape physically, yet he felt he could never be free from her emotional possession—even if he wanted to be. The clever wife/mother and the illiterate working husband/father were themes he probed again and again like a painful tooth. He was aware that a mother could be and frequently was ambivalent about her children, and that guilt and responsibility were a two-way lifeline and chain between mother and child until one died and beyond. His books are a warning of the darker side of mother/child love, and yet he conveys warmth and real understanding of bonds that link the soul.

PART FIVE

Breaking the Time Barrier

Pre-Birth Communication

Joseph and Mary were walking through the wood
They saw cherries and ripe berries as red as any blood.
Joseph and Mary walked through a garden green.
They saw cherries and ripe berries the finest ever seen.

Then up spoke Virgin Mary so meek and so mild
Saying: "Pluck me cherries Joseph for I am with child."
Then Joseph flew in anger in anger so wild,
Saying: "Let him pluck thee cherries who got thee with child."

Then up spake baby Jesus from within his mother's womb
Saying: "Bow down you cherry tree and give my mother some."
Then the cherry tree bowed down unto Mary's hand.
She said: "Joseph I have cherries unto my command."

The Cherry Tree Carol

Pre-Birth Influences upon the Unborn Child

In pregnancy and in some cases even before, quite a high proportion
of mothers believe they have been in contact with their unborn
children. Up to a point they have the support of Professor Peter
Hepper of the School of Psychology at the Queen's University of
Belfast who has studied pre-natal learning extensively. He found out
that babies whose mothers had regularly watched the television soap
opera *Neighbours* during pregnancy responded to the theme tune
after they were born.

Cathy from Essex told me: "During the last month of my second
pregnancy, I noticed how the baby inside me would react to familiar
TV signature tunes, kicking furiously and moving excitedly. Three

such tunes were *News at One*, *Neighbours* and *EastEnders*. After the birth of my daughter I was constantly amazed at her reactions almost from birth and for the next four or five months to hearing these familiar signature tunes. She would jerk her head towards the TV as soon as the tune started and stop feeding and turn her whole body towards the source of the sound. It was certainly evidence that babies hear and remember pre-birth sounds. I only wish I had introduced her to something a bit more classical!"

Professor Hepper has said: "Recognition is undoubtedly based on hearing and in all probability requires the storing of highly specific patterns of sound. Babies tested only responded to the *Neighbours* theme and not any other tune or the *Neighbours* tune played backwards. We have demonstrated learning as early as 24 weeks and other research has suggested that the *Neighbours* tune soothed foetuses as early as 12 weeks. It is unlikely to be psychic communication between mother and foetus, mainly because it is difficult to see how this would occur. There is undoubtedly, however, some communication between mother and baby. For example there is much evidence that the baby responds to the mother or anyone else pushing on the abdomen and will push back. Exactly what the foetus feels or gets from this is unknown, but this certainly stimulates the mother into action and believing she is interacting with her foetus."

One of his projects has also shown that babies just one hour old already prefer their mother's voice to that of another woman. Another project showed that newborns whose mothers had eaten garlic during the last weeks of pregnancy recognized the same smell on cotton wool.

Cathy's story is explicable in terms of known science. Does this inevitably rule out any possibility of a psychic connection? A more complex case is that of Raina who lives in Lancashire.

"Before the birth of my eldest son Saul in December 1983, my husband was very keen to have the baby listen to classical music in utero. After Saul was born, my husband continued to give him this input. He even made a note of the first music Saul heard after his birth.

"Two and a half years later, son number two was on the way, during 1986, World Cup year. We could not decide what to name this baby, should it be a boy. We spent a great deal of time at the end of the pregnancy watching football on the television and as a joke I declared we would give the baby the name of the player who scored the last goal in the World Cup Final. Two players called Karl and Heinz scored in that last match and so we called the baby Carl.

"Move forward in time to summer 1989. I was pregnant again. The baby was due at the end of June. I finished work five weeks before my due date and thought I had plenty of time for all my preparations. I was planning to do quite a bit of baking to stock the freezer, so that I would be prepared, should the baby be a boy, for the party that takes place after the circumcision ceremony when the baby is eight days old.

"Son number three had other ideas. He arrived three weeks early and the first words Ben heard his mother say were, 'Oh no, I haven't done any baking.'

"I now look at my sons and what do I see? Saul is a musician. He plays the violin and trombone and likes messing about picking out a tune on the guitar and piano.

"Carl is an ace footballer. He plays for two teams and has won a number of awards. He is a general all-round sportsman.

"Ben is a baker. He began helping me to cook at a very early age and by the age of seven was able to produce cakes and biscuits unaided, except for needing me to put things in and out of the oven."

Two-Way Communication

Many women talk and sing to their unborn children throughout pregnancy. Some believe that the communication is a two-way affair and will "see" or "hear" the infant in the womb. Felicity, who lives in the Home Counties of England, is now in her fifties with a daughter aged fifteen. Before her daughter was born, Felicity picked up information about the unborn child that even the most sophisticated scans today could not record. She used to talk to her unborn child, especially about the infant's father and older brother. "Gradually I realized the baby was returning the communication and was talking to me in my mind," Felicity said.

It was as if Felicity heard the baby's voice and conversations took place. "When I was about six months pregnant I asked the baby if she was healthy and she said she was. 'Any blemishes?' I asked her. It might seem strange to persist when the infant told me she was healthy but first-time mothers are especially anxious. 'Well,' the baby told me, 'I do have a birthmark on my heel that is shaped like an apple.' When the baby was born she was absolutely perfect except for an apple-shaped mark on one of her heels. There were no such marks in the history of our family."

For Diane from Dorset, a reassuring message she interpreted as coming from her child helped her through a difficult labour.

"I was in hospital as I started getting contractions eight weeks early. I was put on a drip to stop them. I became very weak and anxious about my baby, as I also had a fibroid growing in my womb. I had developed a chest infection and was treated with large doses of antibiotics. One evening just as I was falling asleep I 'saw' two large brown eyes looking at me calmly and happily telling me that everything was all right. I knew that it was my baby talking to me and I immediately felt relieved and calm.

"When my son was born six weeks prematurely, he was in good health except for a long-lasting jaundice and I felt a very strong bond with him though he stayed in an incubator for four weeks."

The link between a mother and her unborn child has been studied by counsellor Rosalie Denenfeld who lives in Michigan and is the mother of two children. Her thesis studying the relationship between first-time mothers and their unborn children was produced as part of her MA in humanistic and clinical psychology at the Center for Humanistic Studies in 1984. She writes: "A woman who is pregnant for the first time seems to experience her relationship with her unborn child as a catalyst for personal expansion and an increased capacity for love. Because of the uniquely intimate physical unity between the pregnant woman and her unborn child there may exist a peak potential for interaction and communication on physical, emotional and spiritual levels. For some women such interaction facilitates a growing attachment between mother and unborn child, paralleling the physical development of the child.

"As the mother's body expanded, so did her personhood stretch and expand. Such expansion included an awareness of time as both limited and infinite. What feeds and empowers the attachment is the love which develops between mother and unborn child." She discovered that as the attachment grows between mother and unborn child, so the fear of the unknown, that is greatest with the first birth, diminishes.

Rosalie worked with ten first-time mothers using such techniques as focusing to discover deep levels of awareness within the body through intuitive means, keeping a journal, interviewing, art and music. The women were well educated, middle-class and married, and were experiencing a minimal amount of internal, family and social conflicts due to their pregnancies. She comments that their "impressively clear verbal descriptions and artistic expressions provided a rich introduction to how pregnant women may experience relating to their unborn child".

On the spiritual level, Rosalie points out that "other than experiencing nine months in her own mother's womb, pregnancy is the only time a woman has the opportunity to experience a dramatic contrast with the separateness to which each of us is subject. Pregnancy is the ultimate intimacy possible between human beings. Pregnancy may be a vehicle meant to awaken love within women and bring more love into the world."

Some of the women Rosalie studied found their bodies picking up their unborn babies' feelings. Gail explained: "Every once in a while, I have a feeling but I don't know where it comes from. And then I realize that I am not the one having the feeling."

The first time Gail experienced it was during a thunderstorm.

171

"Where we live is on top of a hill, very open. Our bedroom has two huge windows and the trees are right outside the window, so it seems almost as if you are outside. And when there are storms, it feels as if they enter the room. One night I woke up feeling really afraid. There was lightning on the inside of the room and intense noise. There was so much noise from the thunder.

"I personally really love storms. I love to hear the thunder and I like to see the lightning. But I woke up and I was really afraid. I got out of bed and I walked around the house. I couldn't figure it out and suddenly I realized I wasn't the one who was afraid. It was the unborn baby. So I talked to the little one. I told the infant inside me that there was a storm and although the noise was disturbing, it was quite safe. The fear went away."

Several of the co-researchers experienced a sense of love coming from within the womb. Rosalie sees the most important implication of her work as helping mothers in disadvantaged circumstances, especially teenage mothers, to become aware of a pre-natal bond, not just physically but emotionally and spiritually, so they may be more willing to change a harmful lifestyle that can be threatening to the foetus and also perhaps break out of the cycle of abuse that was reflected in their own lives. If a mother can relate to the foetus as a tiny person with fears and feelings, Rosalie is convinced that she will be less likely to smoke heavily and take drugs or excessive alcohol. What is more, the mother who is bonded to her foetus is more likely to take care of him or her after birth.

One of Rosalie's main conclusions is: "The first-time pregnant woman needs to believe she is capable of communicating with and positively influencing her baby. That belief must be strong enough to replace the need for visual evidence of communication which is available post-natally. After birth the infant's signal responses of body and eye movements will provide her with such visual evidence that she is indeed communicating with her baby. But during pregnancy satisfaction must come from the willing investment in the less tangible yet personally significant beginnings of a bond with her baby."

Pre-Birth Prophetic Dreams

From my own research I have discovered a marked increase in significant dreaming among pregnant mothers. Dreams tend to be far more vivid than those experienced at any time since childhood and usually concern the unborn infant. Tracey, who lives in Redhead, Australia, wrote to me:

"My normal dreams in life have never come true, but the two concerning my unborn children did. With my first pregnancy I dreamed three times that my baby would be a boy, blond, born two months early and perfectly all right. I told myself not even to think about this as two-month premature babies aren't always perfectly all right. However, Simon was born at 33 weeks, blond and healthy.

"Before I knew I was pregnant the second time, I dreamed that I had twin girls called Jill and Sarah. Later in the pregnancy I was looking at some pottery 'babies' and kept being strongly drawn to the twins. At 14 weeks twins were diagnosed and I said they would be two girls. Sure enough we now have Beth and Sarah. My husband didn't like the name Jill."

Tracey's first dream prepared her for an early baby. Other women have told me they have "known" they would have an early baby, even when their other children have been full-term and hospital tests have given no indication. This seems to be some safety mechanism to insulate the mother from shock so she is ready to cope.

Although ancient cultures put great store on the importance of divining the future from dreams, Tracey found that only her dreams experienced during pregnancy proved prophetic. It seems probable, therefore, that the dreams are merely a part of the heightened intuition or sixth sense of a woman during pregnancy and childbirth. Those who are pregnant or in constant communion with small children find that dreams are just one aspect of psychic manifestation that can include visions, apparently random associations, unbidden

173

thoughts and feelings flowing between mother and foetus or mother and child. Freud called dreams the "royal road to the unconscious" but he did not study the maternal shortcut across fields still unexplored by science.

Karla from New Orleans in America had vivid dreams through all her pregnancies.

"When my first child was conceived I was living in Puerto Rico with my husband and had recurrent dreams that I had lost my baby in a grocery store. I could not speak enough Spanish to get anyone to help me. After these dreams, I can't really explain how but I knew that the baby would not be born. Many friends and family wanted to give me gifts for the child but I asked them to please wait till the baby was born. At 20 weeks I had an ultrasound scan. There we discovered that our little boy would not live.

"During our next pregnancy I knew again that this baby was not to be. I had had several dreams that she was a girl and that I lost her while swimming. Again I asked people to wait before bringing their gifts. My family and friends tried to tell me I was just anxious because I had lost the other baby, but I knew that I was just going through the motions. On 23 May 1989 I delivered a baby girl at 23 weeks. The child did not survive."

During her third pregnancy Karla wrote to me on 11 May 1991:

"At 6 weeks I had a dream that my doctor told me I was having twins. But when I told him soon afterwards I was expecting twins he just laughed. Later at my scheduled ultrasound test I told the technician about the dream. She smiled and left to go and get the radiologist who confirmed I was indeed having twins.

"Prior to my twentieth week, I had another of many dreams where I am with identical boys. When the doctor asked during another ultrasound test if I wanted to know what sex they were, I told him they were boys and I was right. My husband and I are in the process of divorce but I feel so good and so positive about this pregnancy. Everyone

wants to wait until the children are born to bring them gifts but I've been telling them it's OK this time.

"I have had a few bad feelings about the baby on the right side. In one dream I pick up his brother and tell him, 'Let's go save your brother.' I hope I am wrong. All the tests point to him being OK."

In June 1991 Karla wrote to me again enclosing a picture of two delightful babies: Richard who weighed 6 lbs 6 oz and Matthew who was just over 6 lbs. But her premonition was accurate. Matthew got into trouble during labour, so Karla had an emergency Caesarean. Now the babies are home and healthy.

The prophetic dreams of pregnancy helped another mother to reconcile herself to the birth of a boy which at first she did not really want. Karin was living in San Francisco when the dreams started.

"I had wanted to have a child all my life except during part of high school when I tried to persuade myself that I was programmed to want children because I was female. But things were never right enough and the older I became the less prepared I felt to embark on the responsibility. But by the time I was twenty-seven I felt so biologically ready that it seemed somehow everything would fall into place.

"While I had wanted a child, it had always been a girl I envisioned. A few months before I became pregnant my husband Rob and I discussed planning to try and conceive a child in a year or so. Rob asked what I would do if I had a boy and I realized I was not completely opened to the idea. I then started to have dreams, three of them about a month apart in which I had a boy child. He was newborn to age six. In each dream I loved my son very much and upon awakening felt there was no reason not to be joyful about having a boy. It did not matter at all.

"A month after the last dream I conceived a year ahead of schedule. I knew it was a boy and Rob felt it was a boy too. Once Rory was born I was delighted with him. I adore him. It seemed I had to be more open and realize I would love whomever I bore, then this Being came to us. Now it seems utterly silly that I ever had the reservations to begin with."

Since writing her experience, Karin has had many hardships to face, marital break-up, relocation and the need to work full-time outside her own field of holistic health. She spends less time than she would wish with her beloved son. But the bond forged before Rory was conceived has endured and she says: "My life is coming together again and I feel great."

Choosing a Name

I have come across many instances where an unborn infant has communicated his or her name pre-natally. In the case of Jane who lives in Oxford, England, her infant transmitted her wishes to both parents simultaneously.

"I knew I was carrying a baby girl from my scan. I had decided, together with my partner, on the name Aislinn. However, something was not quite right with that name. Perhaps certain names do not fit in with the parents' personality.

"One night I was in the bath and seven months pregnant. My tummy was merrily wriggling above the water surface when a name flashed into my mind. It was not a name I had previously considered. At that moment my husband Gabriel came into the bathroom. I said excitedly, 'I have the name.'

"He replied, 'Is it Ella or Ellie?'

"I nearly drowned with shock. We now have a beautiful ten-and-a-half-month-old Ella. I know she had a say in her name, communicating it to both of us simultaneously. It still gives me a little shiver to think about it. I am sure we have a bond with our unborn babies. I just wish I could have communicated with Ella more when she was inside. I always have woken in the night just before Ella needs me. I keep really still and quiet in case I influence her to go back to sleep, but it never works."

In my own case it was our fifth child, whom I "knew" to be a boy, whose name was troublesome. Not long before our son's birth in

1988, my husband and I were driving along in the car to a folk concert and had more or less settled on Michael James which seemed a good compromise. Halfway through the concert I was wriggling uncomfortably on the narrow wooden chairs, contemplating an early getaway, when our favourite singer Leon Rosselson began a stirring and highly melodic song called "News from Nowhere", about William Morris the Victorian philanthropist, socialist philosopher, designer of beautiful fabrics and furniture.

Instantly the baby inside me danced—I can only describe it as dancing—so enthusiastically that my heaving stomach nearly dislodged the person on the next chair. William Morris was instantly named and like his predecessor is sensitive, intelligent and sometimes very out of step with what he sees as an uncomprehending world.

Knowing the Sex of an Unborn Child

From time immemorial, pregnant women have held a needle on a thread over their stomachs to discover the sex of their unborn child. The needle will generally swing clockwise for a boy and anti-clockwise for a girl, or swing in one plane for a boy and in a circling movement for a girl. The mechanics vary, but this simple form of dowsing is invariably accurate if carried out by the expectant mother or her mother.

Most women instinctively "know" the sex of an unborn baby, whether the information appears suddenly in their heads or comes via a dream that may show the child as he or she will appear later in life. On occasions this has proved more accurate than even a scan at 20 weeks.

Maria Cadaxa, a midwife who works in Tucson, Arizona, wrote to me:

"As a midwife and mother of four, I have been intrigued by the definite super-sensory link between mothers and their children, especially infants.

177

Regarding pre-natal links I have yet to come across a mother totally surprised at the baby's gender. Nine out of ten had a definite knowing or a very strong suspicion. I believe this 'knowing' has a physical and spiritual component, the connection with the child's spirit and the mother's body knowing the new hormones controlling her body.

"Dreams are often prophetic as to both gender and appearance. To give one example from my own experience as a midwife: a mother thinking of an abortion has a very clear dream in which a child with dark, curly hair appears and asks to stay. She consents. The child who is subsequently born is a girl with dark, curly hair like the father's sister, a fact of which the woman who had the dream was unaware at the time."

A woman may know the gender of her child, but might not necessarily want to share this information, even with her closest family. Joan, who lives in New South Wales, told me:

"Jode is five months old. I guess I knew he was a boy about five months into my pregnancy. We both wanted a girl and I tried so hard to convince myself and my husband that it was. I always referred to the baby as she or her openly and I'd lie in bed with my husband at night, saying, 'I'm sure it's a girl.' Then before I went to sleep I'd laugh to myself and rub my belly because I knew he was male and I always privately referred to as him Jode.

"My labour was very short, thirty minutes after arriving at hospital, and all I could think of after the baby was born was, 'Thank God the pain's over.'

"Nobody told me Jode was a boy. They didn't have to. I already knew. I knew him the moment we met. I seemed to know exactly what he expected of me. We spent the first two days just staring at each other, getting into each other's minds. I came home four days later and it was as if we'd known each other for ever. It all felt so natural though he was my first child."

The Magic of Conception

Some women experience a very early pre-birth link. Rebecca from Ontario, whose connection with her son Alex was described in an earlier chapter, wrote: "About six months before I became pregnant, I had this very strong sense of a spirit 'hovering'. It wasn't negative or even an impatient feeling, rather a sense of someone near, waiting to be born.

"One day I decided to deeply meditate. I wasn't trying to meditate on anything specific but in my meditation a bright-light being came to me and introduced herself. She/he was androgynous but seemed more female than male. She told me she had been my daughter in a previous life and was getting ready to be born again. I asked when I'd become pregnant. My husband and I had planned to try in the New Year and she replied, 'January or February—you won't have any problem becoming pregnant.' Sure enough I became pregnant the first try, in January.

"I don't know if I imagined all this or what but the experience was so incredibly real and clear."

I have come across sufficient experiences akin to Rebecca's to take the phenomenon very seriously. Whether such occurrences are symbolic or actual, they provide a profound sense that the birth is part of a wider pattern and establish a connection on a deep, spiritual level.

Women are frequently attuned to the moment of conception. Regina of Staten Island, New York, knew that she had become pregnant, though doctors insisted the couldn't possibly tell at such an early stage.

"My husband and I had been trying to become pregnant for about two years. I had even started to take my temperature with a Basil thermometer to pinpoint ovulation. I wasn't worried, however. I knew when our baby was ready to come it would happen. One night we made love quite impulsively. The next night I dreamed I was pregnant with a

big rounded belly and friends surrounded me asking me how I felt. I told them I was elated.

"From that point on, I 'knew' I was pregnant, although it would be weeks before I could confirm it with a laboratory test. I went to be tested when my menstrual period was five days late and the doctor suggested this could be an hysterical pregnancy. I knew it was not because that dream had been so true for me and of course I was pregnant and had conceived the night before the dream."

The Inner Voice

The pre-birth connection can offer reassurance that all is well. However, occasionally a mother may feel that all is not well. All expectant mothers have natural fears and anxieties which in the vast majority of cases are groundless. However, the concerns Lisa felt were unmistakable and very different from the normal worries of pregnancy. By heeding them she saved the life of her daughter, one of the youngest heart-transplant children in Britain.

Lisa told me how she was convinced almost from the time Erica was conceived that there was something seriously wrong with her unborn child in spite of medical reassurances.

"Before Fiona, my eldest daughter, was born everything felt fine and I didn't worry at all, so I knew it wasn't an ordinary pregnancy anxiety I was experiencing about Erica. From early on in Erica's pregnancy I felt really bad about things. I kept having terrifying thoughts that the baby I was carrying had something dreadfully wrong with her, though I couldn't have told you what.

"As the pregnancy developed, I felt worse though clinically everything was OK. I had one of those urine tests and there was protein in it, so the doctors wondered if the baby had spina bifida. More detailed tests showed she was absolutely clear.

"I thought perhaps that was what was worrying me and for a couple of days I was fine. But then the feeling came back as bad as before. I was

even organizing in my mind how to bury the baby. I knew she would be born but knew I couldn't keep her. It was really strange. We had recently moved to a new area and I wanted to go back to my old home town for the funeral where all my friends and relations were. I used to think like this right up to the end of the pregnancy. I did not plan for this baby as I did with Fiona. I thought, 'I'll wait till later. What's the point in making any plans?'

"Then suddenly one day towards the end of the pregnancy, I had a burning desire to get Erica's room ready. I hadn't felt the same urgency with Fiona. The preparations had happened steadily throughout the pregnancy. But with Erica I had to get the room ready straight away, though I never thought she'd sleep in it. It was an ordinary natural labour and Erica weighed eight and three-quarter pounds. I said to Gerald, my husband, 'Is she all right?' and he assured me she was.

"Erica had a bit of trouble breathing at first but Gerald didn't tell me. I knew nothing about it till much later. When we were on the ward I inspected the baby and saw her feet were turned inwards. I pointed it out and the paediatrician said he'd get the consultant to have a look but not to worry. The next morning the consultant came and said Erica's feet were fine and that it was purely positional and that she would just need a bit of manipulation to put it right. I thought, 'OK. That's it sorted out. That was what was worrying me when I was pregnant.'

"Inside, however, I knew that was not my real concern. There was still something more. For the next three to three and a half weeks, the feeling continued. I was delighted with Erica and very happy but it was as if there was a big cloud hanging over her. I inspected Erica all over for any unusual signs. She was big and bonny but I commented to Gerald: 'Erica has a funny-shaped chest. She's pigeon-chested.'

"Gerald laughed at my anxiety: 'Fancy a little girl being pigeon-chested.'

"I was still dreadfully worried there was something very wrong. At four weeks, I started to pick up signs Erica was not healthy. I trotted off to the doctor on several occasions and he listened to her chest and said everything was fine and sent her home. The doctor thought I was fussing, but I hadn't fussed with Fiona.

181

"At the six-week check at the clinic, I said I thought Erica was having difficulty breathing. Erica had grown. The doctor thought he could hear something, but then reassured me it was all right. He said I could always see my GP if I was worried at any time. But I knew she wasn't right to me. On the Friday, Erica would not take her 2 p.m. feed. I told Gerald, 'If she doesn't take her 6 p.m. feed, I shall call the emergency doctor.'

"I was still breastfeeding Erica. She did refuse the next feed. I called the doctor and he came out and said she was fine. I was very upset because the baby wasn't feeding and I was worried she would get dehydrated. I insisted I wanted a chest X-ray because she was by now coughing.

" 'If it will make you feel better,' the emergency doctor told me, 'you can take your daughter for a chest X-ray at the local hospital to set your mind at rest.' I was conscious that the doctor thought I was being over-anxious. We had had a roast lamb dinner on the table. I left the dinner things uncleared and went straight to the hospital with Erica.

"When we got to Casualty the doctor realized something was wrong, gave Erica an X-ray and called a consultant. Erica was in severe heart failure and was sent straight up to the ward. On the ward she was put into an oxygen tent and was wired up to a heart monitor. Erica was six and a half weeks old and at eleven weeks was given a heart transplant. For a long time afterwards even when she was well, every day was a bonus. We didn't worry about the little things any more. I was too frightened to think we might be able to keep her. Only now, over two years later, can I feel more confident and accept she is mine."

Lisa's case is not a call to go against medical opinion, which would be very unwise. It is important, though very difficult, for expectant mothers to have the confidence to follow their inner voice or the "voice of the unborn child" and use this to express in their ante-natal care intuitions that can supplement medical knowledge. In extreme cases where there is no "right or wrong" a woman's gut feeling is ultimately perhaps the one to follow. Women do know their own child best, even before he or she is born. This knowledge can be used to mediate advice given by health professionals. Increasingly midwives and health visitors are accepting the expertise of the expectant mother.

When the mother's sixth sense combines with a professional medical training, then it can be the sixth sense which predominates. Rita Laws from Oklahoma told me of an experience concerning Andrea, a midwife friend.

"It was 1982 and the home birth of her fourth child, a boy. During her pregnancy Andrea became agitated about her unborn baby's health. Despite reassurances from a midwife and an obstetrician, Andrea, herself a midwife, continued to insist something was wrong. Her child was in grave danger. Even when a sonogram showed her baby to be healthy, her uneasiness persisted. The labour was long but normal and Andrea gave birth to a beautiful baby boy who was very much alive. The umbilical cord, however, had two true knots in it. Had they been tighter the baby would have been deprived of oxygen and probably stillborn.

"True knots are quite rare in umbilical cords. The child was born healthy but it was a condition no one could have foreseen, except that the mother did."

Saying Goodbye

More rarely, a mother may sense that she is not going to carry a baby to full term, and will lose the little one. Many women who have miscarried have had an acute sense that all will not be well. Again, this is very different from the normal fears of pregnancy in intensity and quality. Just as mothers are not sprinting home from the cinema every five minutes in case the house is on fire, so few women experience this certainty that they will lose the baby.

Why know if you cannot prevent the loss? In some cases, and I believe a woman only knows if it will be helpful for her to be forewarned, it can ease the sudden shock and allow mother and child to say goodbye. Helena is a midwife living in Fife and so was used to babies and knew that the overwhelming majority were healthy.

"My first pregnancy was a planned one and I always wanted a baby, but from very early in the pregnancy I knew I would not be having the child. I could never picture the infant. Another midwife was pregnant and I knew her baby would be fine. Colleagues tried to reassure me that I was suffering from first-time mother nerves, but I knew differently.

"When I had my eight-week scan, I saw the baby moving and quite formed. My husband was not there so I asked for a picture. The radiographer promised I could have one at the next scan, but I felt it would be too late. However, I did not say anything. I was the only one to see the baby.

"When I miscarried at 11 weeks I was upset but not shocked. I had gradually prepared myself to let go. I got pregnant the second time entirely unplanned, before I had finished grieving, and I was quite resentful at first. However, I knew that time from the start that everything was fine and I would have a healthy infant. I could sense and see this baby and now, nine years later, I am very glad I have the precious son I would not otherwise have conceived."

Heike, who lives in Reading in England, is a carrier of haemophilia and knew there was a 50 per cent chance that if she was carrying a boy he would be afflicted with the illness.

"Recently I had a profound experience that changed my outlook on life and my understanding of the connections between people and life forces. When I was five months pregnant with my second son Noah, we had a foetal blood-sampling test which revealed he had haemophilia. My first son Ben is not affected so we had hoped that this second baby might be lucky.

"The outcome of this was that I had a termination. Noah's birth and death took place in February 1997. When I was pregnant with Ben I was filled with inner confidence that he would be all right. The test at 21 weeks confirmed this and I was to have a wonderful pregnancy and birth. With Noah I felt a deep need to be as close to him as possible in the womb, to get to know him, to love him and to feel loved by him. With hindsight, I realize that this was because he would leave me. I saw a

therapist with whom I visualized contact with Noah. He appeared to me as a dolphin and he allowed me to see that he was a soul who had chosen this baby's body for a reason. He was very calm and loving and saw my suffering with compassion.

"I did not want to voice my fear that I was going to lose him, because I was scared of predicting a terrible loss. I still had hope that this baby, like Ben, would be all right. When we got the phone call that he was not, my husband and I were completely numb. Ben, who had been playing happily—he was eighteen months old at the time—suddenly threw a fit of crying and thrashing around. He would not calm down for a long time. He was expressing how we felt, he picked up the vibes that something terrible had happened.

"With Ben I had a waterbirth and he was born with his caul intact. When we went to the hospital to pick up the medication to soften my cervix in preparation for Noah's induction, we were given a note warning us that there was a water leak in the hospital. When I got home some of my water leaked into the bath, which had not happened before the drug. On the morning of the induction, water came gushing through our bedroom ceiling. Again this had not happened before or since. I took all these things as signs that my little dolphin was leaving me.

"After Noah's death and some time after his funeral I sensed that his soul was troubled. I tried to send him peace, and when I did that I felt warm pressure on my hands, as though someone was pressing the palms of their hands on to mine. At first this was quite frightening, and when I stopped concentrating the experience correspondingly stopped. When I started again, I felt the same connecting pressure.

"These may seem extreme experiences but the situation is extreme, when you are forced to show your child the greatest act of love you can ever show, to let him go, even to let him go into death. My brother has haemophilia and my cousin died from it recently at the age of sixteen, so I know what life as a haemophiliac means. I made this decision because I loved Noah and still love him very much.

"Ben slept in our bed until he was just under a year old and then he moved into his own cot in the same bedroom as us. Eventually when he

was fifteen months old we moved him into his own bedroom because every time we had sex he would wake up. This was not due to any noise. He would wake up just when we were drifting off to sleep afterwards and I am sure that he was picking up the vibes. Sometimes now when we create a bad atmosphere by arguing in bed, again quietly, he wakes up in his bedroom. When I go to bed and cannot sleep, listening for Ben to wake up, he is guaranteed to do so. If I go to sleep quickly, he doesn't wake up. If I wake up in the night, which doesn't happen often, and don't go back to sleep for a while, Ben wakes up too. I am not sure who is waking who up, but we affect each other that way.

"I have a strong connection also with my own mother. Sometimes when I ring her, instead of just answering hello she will say, 'Hello Heike.' I do not ring her at a certain time regularly.

"Recently I felt very faint, a feeling I never had before, and thought I would have to get the neighbour to look after Ben in case I did faint. I had to lie down. In that crisis my mother rang during the day. She does not usually phone at peak time from Germany."

The most intriguing piece of pre-birth communication or rather espionage by the unborn infant was sent to me by Ann who lives in British Columbia. She told me how an evening of passion turned out not to be the closely guarded secret she had imagined.

"My marriage ended in the midst of my pregnancy with my second child. Though the relationship had been ailing for a long time, mutual adultery dealt it the death blow. My lover had no aversion to sleeping with a woman who was seven months pregnant and one night we had intercourse in the cab of his truck. Though it may sound sleazy to some, this particular incident was a warm and happy memory for me, one where I felt adventurous but also close and friendly to the man involved.

"When my son (the baby in the belly at the time of this incident) was three years old, we passed a parked truck one day. 'That's a mummy truck,' my son announced. 'Are there daddy trucks too?' I asked, humouring him. Ignoring my question, he said, 'You were in a mummy truck. You had no clothes on.'

186

"Well, the only time I'd been in a truck with no clothes on was the incident just related. Maybe babies can project their astral bodies outside the womb and spy on what their mothers are doing, or it could be a case of telepathy. After all, when a baby is inside it is very intimately linked with your physical system and perhaps with your thoughts and emotions as well."

Mothers and Reincarnation

☙

Our Birth is but a sleep and a forgetting;
The Soul that rises with us, our life's Star,
Hath had elsewhere its setting,
And cometh from afar,
Not in entire forgetfulness
But trailing clouds of glory . . .
William Wordsworth, "Ode on the Intimations of Immortality" from
Recollections of Early Childhood

*W*ordsworth, one of the first of the Romantic poets, was reacting against the Age of Reason. The English philosopher, John Locke, wrote in his *Essay Concerning Human Understanding* (1690) that experience was the only source of knowledge and that the child was born as a *tabula rasa*, a blank slate on which parents wrote.

More than two centuries later John B. Watson, the American psychologist and expounder of behaviourism, stated that children were made, not born, and could be conditioned by reinforcement and repetition. Watson's work was largely based on studying the behaviour of rats, but nevertheless exerted a major influence when his conclusions were published.[1]

Yet the concept that when a child is born he or she may carry memories of an earlier existence still holds credence, not only in the Eastern world, but increasingly in Western Europe. Such a belief has profound implications for the traditional view of the early mother/ child relationship. If a child is born spiritually evolved, the child's soul is able to interact on a very deep level with the mother's. It also offers one explanation for the complex interaction before birth

188

between the unborn child and his or her mother. Mothers who believe this, usually because of strange comments their children have made when very young, emphasize the wisdom and spirituality of their children. But is it mere fancy? Bernadette is an international author and environmentalist. She is convinced that her daughter does have fleeting memories of a previous life and that the connection between mother and child has existed since before conception.

"When I conceived my baby I saw her in the act of love, and when she was born she was exactly the child I had visualized. While I was pregnant with my daughter, I had a vivid dream that she was standing in front of me, the size of a toddler, although she could speak. Yet my daughter did not look as if she was a toddler. She told me her name and I responded, 'Don't you think we should wait?'

" 'Oh no,' she replied, 'babies choose their own names and mine is Alexandria.'"

"I looked the name up in a dictionary and of course realized Alexandria was a place.

"When she was still tiny, Alex saw a picture of an angel. 'That's a glory angel,' she told me. 'They sing to you when you are a baby.'

"From when Alex was tiny she loved painting using brilliant colours and her pictures showed remarkable expertise in dimension and perspective for one so young. One day when she was about two and a half, Alex was painting in the kitchen and I remarked, 'You are very good at painting. Would you like to be a painter when you grow up?'

" 'Oh, no,' she replied, 'I've been that already. I had to paint the King and Queen at the court.'

"I tried to coax Alex to repeat her remark but she never said it again. At about the same age, it was a hot day and Alex was sitting on the banisters with her legs crossed, totally relaxed. 'It was like this on the beach in Brazil,' she told me.

"I had never been to Brazil and certainly never mentioned the place. However, two years before I conceived Alexandria, a clairvoy-

ant told me that I would have a daughter who had been a Brazilian princess. She had chosen to come back because she had great psychic abilities, but been spoiled and wasted her life in Brazil, so wanted to get it right with me. I had been channelling and suddenly had a vision of two children running across a playground, a girl with masses of dark hair and a boy who looked completely different from the girl. I asked the clairvoyant who they were and she told me they were my children waiting to be born. She also said that there would be a gap of seven or eight years between the children. I am now in the process of separating from my husband and Alex is four and a half, so I wonder what the future will bring.

"Alex has continued to paint. One day she cried out in frustration, 'I just cannot remember how to draw a chameleon.'

"When Alex was only two, I took her to the National Gallery in London. A friend who came along warned me Alex would be bored within five minutes, but was astounded as we were there for more than four hours. Alex was totally absorbed the whole time. She was especially fascinated by the paintings by Picasso and Monet. There was a lady painting a picture of a Monet and Alex sat down and drew the woman painting. It had all the right dimensions.

"Alex and I are very close. If she is with my mother, I will ring and know that she has asked to come home. My mother and I always phone at the same time too."

Dr Ian Stevenson, professor of psychiatry at the University of Virginia, has studied the phenomenon of reincarnation for more than thirty years. His book has become a classic in the field, based on exhaustive worldwide interviews and corroboration of facts.[2] His greatest successes have been with children who, he believes, lose the ability for spontaneous recall about the age of seven, a finding not very different from Wordsworth's own beliefs.

Dr Stevenson commented on his findings: "In studying cases of reincarnation I have to use the methods of the historian, lawyer and psychiatrist. Extrasensory perception cannot account for the fact that the subject has skills and talents not learned. Nor could it explain strange birthmarks, as in one instance where a boy, among twenty-six items recalled, claimed his throat had been slit by robbers. The boy was born in his present life with a scar around his neck."

Children have recalled precisely names and places that they have never visited, sometimes across the world, or have given historical details that contradicted accepted knowledge which later research has revealed to be accurate. Intriguingly, Bernadette's daughter gave her former name from her life as an artist/princess in Brazil, but Bernadette cannot find the paper she wrote it on.

Another Life, Another Mother

If reincarnation is a possibility, can the child choose the mother he or she wishes to bond with? It may be that Paul chose his present family in Scotland because he knew his mother would be kind to him. When Paul was about four years old, his mother was washing his face at tea-time when he pulled back suddenly and said: "Don't wash me there. That's where my mummy hit me."

Her immediate reaction was to say, "Come on now," because she was busy and children come out with all kinds of excuses to avoid the ordeal of soap and water. But she stopped and said: "Well, tell me about it then." He said in an abrupt manner as if she was stupid, "You know—that's where she hit me and I fell down the stairs and died. Not you, Mummy, but the mummy I had before. That's why this time I decided to come to a mummy who would love me."

Paul's mother could never get him to repeat his remarks. He had not previously expressed any objections to his mother rubbing his face and did not afterwards.

Often these remarks are one-off, uttered quite casually. If the mother questions the child, he or she may become defensive or simply have no recall. I have come across two or three cases where a young child will claim to have been killed in a road accident, in the

191

case of one boy using vocabulary that was totally beyond his normal range and a different, deeper voice. These are not the sorts of cases that will make the statutory eight-minute slot in a paranormal "investigation" on television and there are normally no witnesses apart from the mother. For this reason, as with many childhood psychic experiences, they pass unregarded by psychic researchers. Yet they are very common, and surely an indication that the child is far more than a *tabula rasa*.

Occasionally memories of the other life can persist for months or even years. Jo, who lives in Nottingham, England, accepted her daughter's "other family" without making undue fuss and so Hannah has been able to move away from the overlapping world in her own time.

"From the very first moment my daughter Hannah could form her own sentences, about the age of two until she started school, she regularly talked about her other mother and father. She always referred to this couple as Mother and Father, rarely Mum and Dad. Hannah has always called us by our first names, although we never encouraged her to do so, nor discouraged it.

"Hannah told me when she was about two and a half that her father had been killed by a gun. I was quite astounded at the time because of her having no interest in guns. She mentioned her 'other parents' in everyday conversation and it became a normal topic. Hannah has always talked about life and death from a very young age. She often used to say, 'When I was older than you and lived with my other mother and father.'

"Unfortunately as Hannah grew older and became aware of imaginary play the two became muddled and later became make-believe stories. For example: 'My other mother and father would let me have a kitten if I wanted one.'

"An amusing instance regarding Hannah's other mother and father occurred when Sharon, the mother of a friend of Hannah's, began helping out in the nursery class once a week. I had only met Sharon a few times and it was not until I knew her better that she told me she was very

confused about our family. Hannah had told her a few times about her other father and that she did not live with him any more and Andrew was her father now. As you can imagine Sharon assumed I had a partner before Andrew and that Andrew was not her real father."

Jo handled the situation with tact and common sense, allowing the other family to merge into fantasy and then disappear naturally. But in some cases there can be real distress. I met a woman whose son demanded to be taken to the white house where he used to live. His mother promised, to keep him quiet, but found that her son was very upset when she could not take him to see his other mummy and daddy.

The idea that our children may not be exclusively "ours" has many implications for the mother/child bond, not least that children are a gift that will unfold over the years and that mothers are caretakers of a repository of potential that may unfold in ways that are very different from our own aspirations. The positive side of a belief of reincarnation is that each child is unique and has goals, and lessons to learn that may only be partly rooted in the present family situation. For those modern psychologists who blame it all on the mother, the question has to be which one?

Coming Back as a Baby

There is a belief among many reincarnationists that people tend to return to the same group of souls throughout their evolution, albeit in different relationships. The strangest and most intriguing phenomenon is that of grandmothers and great-grandmothers who return as their granddaughters. Beth, who lives in South Africa, described her second daughter's other-worldly links.

"From a very young age Victoria was a strangely compassionate child who talked about concepts like guilt and blame even before she was at nursery school. I was studying for my finals in social work when I was

193

pregnant with her. Even more strangely, Victoria seemed at times to be someone else.

"Victoria would use words and make comments which just did not tie in with the fact that she was a child born in 1985. She would look at me lovingly and murmur, 'You were a beautiful baby.' When we drove past the house where I used to live when I was a teenager, she commented, 'I was so happy in that house. I loved living there.'

"Victoria talked about speaking another language when she was a child and not having had motorcars then. My Owma [Afrikaans for Granny], my paternal grandmother, had lived with my parents until her death in 1975. She had always worn her hair long and caught up in a bun and, a few years ago, the first time Victoria put up her hair for ballet, I asked her, 'Do you know how?'

"Victoria called back, 'Don't worry. I've done this billions of times.'

"I began wondering whether she might be the reincarnation of my beloved Owma, who was the only adult I ever loved. I was very close to my Owma who lived with us, because she only had one son who was my father and no daughters at all. She always doted on me, whereas being the eldest in a very 'boys are best' family I always felt that my parents would have preferred for me to be a boy. In fact my first word was 'Mama' addressed to Owma.

"Owma almost certainly spoke Hooghallands and drove in horse carriages as a child, and for as long as I knew her wore her long hair in a bun expertly pinned on her head. In spite of no previous interest in reincarnation, I began thinking Victoria and I had known each other before."

Beth's first daughter, Ellamay, had died in infancy before Victoria was born (see p. 334).

"Victoria's paintings and drawings done at play school almost always included a wispy, fey little waif in the background. When questioned she shyly admitted, 'That's Ellamay, my sister.'

"I said, 'But you've never seen her.'

" 'Oh yes, I have. I saw her before I was born.'

194

"Since then Victoria and I have talked on the subject. She is twelve going on sixty-five and she says that she believes too beyond the shadow of a doubt that she and I were meant to be together again.

"I think one explanation may be that we all carry inherited memories in our genes, so that a child can remember experiences not only of her mother/grandmother but much further back down the generations.

"About three years before Victoria was born, at the time the gynaecologists said I was infertile, a fortune teller told me she saw me having a baby. She was not sure what sex the baby was but described it as a strange, high and mighty spirit, probably a girl. Victoria looks exactly as I did as a child. I adore Victoria Beth, and I know that if Ellamay had not died I would not have had her at all and that would have been a great loss."

Rozanne, who lives in Delaware, believes her special mother-bond with her daughter Margaret started with the death of her husband Mark's grandmother, Margaret, on Mother's Day 1986. Two days later Rozanne and Mark went to view the body of Margaret, known as Nan to the family, at a hospital in Michigan.

"I knelt down to look and sensed a tingling that started at my shoulders and went down my spine. I knew she was standing behind me. At the funeral the next day I felt as though my heart would break. I had a physical throbbing that would not ease up. I wondered at myself. After all I did not know this woman well enough to be as troubled as I found myself to be. After the funeral we walked towards the middle of the town where her old house stood. As we walked I felt her presence beside us. My spirit reached towards hers to make a feeble attempt at comforting her in her loss.

"Over the next few months I discovered that our paths were fused together that day in a very special way. One evening when Mark and I went out to dinner, we drank a toast to Nan's memory and in doing so seemed to have invoked her presence with such force that we commented on it at the same time. Mark said, 'You know, I think that Nan will be

195

joining us soon. I know this sounds crazy but I think she wants to come back into physical form. In fact I think she wants to come in as our child.' I was aghast. After all we had never come this close to talking about having children, much less discussing the idea of conceiving an old relative.

"*Periodically I would check in to see if this Being we called Margaret was still around. There were still many doubts in my mind about the whole arrangement, but each time I would make an attempt to contact her I felt a strong sense of her presence and a soft smile growing inside of me.*

"*The day that we decided we were ready to begin trying to conceive this child I was both excited and scared to death. Mark was mostly scared to death. But as we talked we felt the sureness of our tune-in by the eager presence of the Being we were preparing a place for.*

"*The night before I used a pregnancy test, I dreamed I was standing with many people on the west side of the Hudson River. Tugging at my leg was a little girl. She looked dark-skinned like a Latin American. She had to leave and go through a door rather than take the bridge to get to the other side of the river. She said her name was Consuela and she said goodbye to me with her happy eyes. I made an attempt at remembering my high school Spanish and said, 'Poquito minuto.' What I meant was, 'I will see you in a very little while.'*

"*In the morning I took the test and it was absolutely positive. That weekend we visited St Patrick's Cathedral in New York with Mark's parents. At the shrine of St Margaret we started to talk about Nan. I asked Mark's mother what her communion name was and she told me Consuela, the same as her mother Margaret.*

"*There were times when the Being seemed far away and out of touch. I can only suppose in those moments she was busy with things I could not register in my own consciousness. Other times she made her presence known with a strong kick to my ribs.*

"*As the baby grew so did my worries. I decided to have an alpha-fetoprotein test at 16 weeks and a week later the results indicated a low reading. I was advised that because of this my chances of having a Down's Syndrome baby had doubled, and since my maternal age put me in the higher-risk group I was looking at some worrying statistics.*

"The next step was to have an amniocentesis. I was already experiencing the movement of the foetus and was strongly bonded in a way that meant I could never go through with a therapeutic abortion. Since I did have a few days to think about it, I cried and agonized and finally decided to forgo the amino. My instincts told me that my baby was already what it was going to be for whatever reason and that I would be able to cope with whatever that was as well."

When Rozanne went into labour it seemed to her as though the veil between the living and the dead dissolved.

"I could see and feel all my ancestors, friends and teachers who were on the Other Side. They were standing at the doorway assisting this Being into the world of form. This experience was as strong as the experience I had when I went to Mark's grandmother's funeral. It was a moment of undeniable power for me: a revelation of the relationship between life and death. I will never again fear death or birth because I know that I will not be alone.

"We named our daughter Margaret which means pearl and she was all of that and more. Her full head of hair was dark brown, and even her skin took on a bronze Native American colouring found way back on my side of the family. A beautiful Indian princess or perhaps 'un poquito minuto', Consuela my good friend.

"From Margaret I have gained deeper insight into what it means to teach. I have seen that her development will happen. All of the information is packed inside of her and comes out when she is ready. If I don't stand in the way but allow her to experience and express what she needs to do, she will automatically unfold into the little girl and then the woman she already is.

"I think that the inherent knowing of how to be a parent can be found within the heart and mind of every mother and father. I will often know better than any of the experts what my daughter needs. If I can trust my intuition then my learning how to be a parent will automatically unfold.

197

I am finding out more about who I am because this is the main legacy I will give to my daughter. Not what I have accomplished. Not the bestseller I haven't written but being who I am as honestly as I can. This is what I remember about Grandmother Margaret and this is what my daughter Margaret will remember about me."

If there is choice why would anyone return to a mother who made them unhappy in the first place? Liz Cornish, a rebirthing expert in London, explains: "The point of existence on earth is to overcome all problems. When we are reborn we choose the family we are born into because of some unfinished business in our previous existence, to fulfil some need. Why else would we choose what sometimes seem to be such appalling parents? Maybe we have been in different relationships with them in past life and this time are trying to get it right."

Sarah, who also lives in London, sees her problems with her mother as stemming from a past life when they were also mother and daughter. Sarah has had visions of a past life in which she lived in a slum with a mother who beat her and eventually abandoned her.

"I was extremely reluctant to be born again. I saw myself standing at the entrance to a long dark tunnel, protesting that I didn't want to go back. I am insisting 'I don't want to be born through that woman', meaning my present mother.

"I had to go down the tunnel. I think I hovered around my mother during the months before I was born, being unwilling to take up residence in the new body. At last I am being dragged out into the world before I am ready. Everything around me is hard, cold and white. The light is too bright and hurts my eyes.

"For as long as I can remember I have felt antagonism towards my mother, but my upbringing was normal and I cannot trace my feeling to anything in this life I can remember. I believe it was there already and that she was the same mother who had abandoned me before. Perhaps in her soul she wanted to make up for that. She may have had no choice in that earlier life and if she was harsh to me then it was because conditions were so hard in the slum.

"There is a parallel here with the statement of psychologists that people tend to repeat mistakes, placing themselves in similar situations again and again until they discover the root cause of the problems and can break the behaviour pattern. I am convinced we choose our parents either because there is a bond of love between us and we want to be together again or because of some lesson we have to work out with them."

The Mother as Seer

When my son walked in, it was as if he was covered in a
light, a glowing blue light all over. The thought came to me
as clear as anything I ever had come to mind, that the light all
over my son was death. I said: "Son, why can't you wear your
helmet? You are going to die today if you don't wear it."

Elise from Texas whose premonition saved her son's life

*H*ow can the mothering instinct break the time barrier and help a
mother to save a child from death? What made Michelle Bates
from Liverpool, England, break with her normal routine so that ten-
month-old daughter Demi was not crushed by a collapsing ceiling at
her local nursery? She told me:

*"I always left Demi in her pram if she was asleep at one end of the
nursery classroom while I went down the other end to hear my daughter
Samantha and her classmates sing or act rhymes. However, when we
went to the St Andrew's Day concert in November 1995, for the first
time I lifted Demi out of the pram and took her with me, although she
was in a deep sleep. It was an instinctive feeling, as if someone was
tapping me on the shoulder, telling me to lift Demi out of the pram and
hold her in my arms.*

*"Moments later the ceiling at the end of the classroom where the pram
was standing started to crack and a huge chunk of masonry crashed down
on to the pram. One of the teachers shouted, 'Where's the baby? Help the
baby!'*

*"Momentarily disorientated I looked and there was my baby in my
arms. I wondered whose baby they meant. I realized it should have been*

Demi under there and I started to sob. The other mothers and teachers too were crying with shock and relief.

"Demi hasn't slept since the ceiling collapsed and I can't bear to let her out of my sight. She has always been special. I lost two babies before Demi and had trouble in her pregnancy. I know now she is special and I was meant to keep her. I always knew when I went out with my husband if she was crying while we were away."

As far as Michelle is concerned trusting her instinct saved her child. Yet because such experiences cannot be repeated under laboratory conditions, they are frequently dismissed as anecdotal. Mothers who may have had no psychic experiences suddenly find that they can predict future dangers to a child. Jung saw this time-hopping ability, like synchronicity, as part of the mother/child link. For Jung, mother and child were a linked archetype, a root human relationship in all times and places. The accumulated power associated with all the feelings positive and negative inherent in this first and primary human relationship means that on a deep universal unconscious level of experience, time and space and even the laws of causality do not operate within the boundaries of the relationship. Hence mothers can link into their children's future dilemmas as naturally as they do immediate crises. The natural protective radar can leap ahead and, if trusted, can sometimes avert disasters.

Listening to the Warnings

The strangest phenomenon is when a mother acts in an unusual or seemingly illogical way, cancelling a visit or going home early, to avert a potential disaster that could not have been foreseen on a conscious level. Why should Michelle feel the urge to pick up a sleeping baby when she could have watched her daughter's concert unencumbered? Such experiences could be dismissed as coincidence, except that so many women do report a sudden prompting shortly before their child has an accident or faces unexpected danger. In

201

terms of survival value, these warnings seem to come from a protective radar around the child.

Alice, a journalist who comes from Holland and now lives in Britain, had no reason to return suddenly to her brother's house to see her daughter who was being well cared for.

"I have a fifteen-month-old daughter Isla to whom I am very close. About two weeks ago we went to Holland to stay with my brother and sister-in-law who have two young children of their own. After a few days my daughter was completely settled and, since I had to go to Amsterdam on business, Isla was quite happy to stay with our relations. After I had finished I met some friends with whom I was going out to dinner.

"However, I insisted on going home to see my daughter first, although it was out of the way and I knew there was no need to as my brother and sister-in-law are very experienced with small children and I had no worries about her. I just knew I needed to be there at that time. Five minutes after I arrived home, Isla suddenly managed to pull over a huge heavy mirror on top of herself. I was sitting very close to my daughter and managed to catch it in time and avert what would have been a horrible accident. No one else was near enough to catch it. My friend said that as I saw what was happening, I momentarily froze, took a deep breath and leaped forward.

"I am not deeply religious but I believe I had to go home to save my daughter."

It is often the timing of such warnings that makes them so remarkable. Elise from Dallas, Texas, had a vision that made her nag her son into taking the advice she had offered many times and which he had never heeded. However, she knew that on this occasion his life was in danger.

"My youngest son bought a motor cycle when he was eighteen. He lived about twenty-five miles from us and came by our house every afternoon when he finished work, staying between fifteen minutes and half an hour. I'd fuss at him for not wearing his crash helmet and every day he

came by without it again. There seemed no point in arguing with him. This one afternoon I was sitting at the dinner table looking outside and talking to my husband when my son drove up. When he walked in, it was as if he was covered in a light, a glowing blue light all over. The thought came to me as clear as anything I ever had come to mind, that the light all over my son was death. I knew it as well as anything I ever knew, a clear positive feeling. I looked at David and said, 'Son, why can't you wear your helmet? You are going to die today if you don't wear it.'

"Boys hate their mothers to try to make them do anything. They feel they are old enough to decide for themselves. But I knew I had to make him wear it this day or he would die. He got uptight for a minute and then yelled, 'All right, all right, if it will get you off my back, I'll wear my helmet.' He'd left one at our house and he went in and got it.

"Twenty minutes later and some miles on, a sixteen-year-old girl in a car turned left straight in front of my son. He had no time to do anything but hit the car. He was slammed into the windshield and cut his arm and shoulder really badly and went on and up over the car to the pavement several yards behind her. His helmet had a crack four inches long in the back. He was carried to the hospital in bad shape and was in intensive care for three days with internal injuries. I never saw that light around him after that but I know he would have died that day without his helmet. I've always been able to see the danger to my children before it happened and have, to my way of thinking, been able to counter it before it came to pass. I can't see these things where I'm concerned, though."

Years later, Elise had another premonition, this time warning of danger to her mother. Once again Elise trusted her promptings that were, as with maternal telepathy, very different from free-floating anxieties in both quality and intensity.

"I called my mother very early one morning to warn her not to go shopping to the sales with her friend. I had dreamed I saw her friend's car wrecked very badly and my mother was in it. In the dream they were both killed and I knew it would happen almost as soon as they set out.

Mom asked me if I'd been drinking. I never touch alcohol. I cried and made her promise me she'd wait until the next day to go to the sales. She agreed but said she thought I was mad.

"That morning at 9.10 her friend went on alone. A truck jumped a red light three blocks away from Mom's house and hit the car. Her friend was killed instantly. The truck hit the passenger side where my mom would have been sitting. Mom phoned me to ask me how I'd known but I couldn't explain."

Is there a scientific basis that might account for precognition? Dr Chet B. Snow theorizes that because our brains are in two parts, we either develop right-brain imaginational and prophetic systems to tell us what tomorrow will bring or we set up rational left-brain ways of collecting, organizing and comparing as much past and present sensory information as possible and try to predict from the data.[1]

Regarding maternal premonitions, could it be that since mothering involves loving, altruism and sensitivity, the right side of the brain is more active in the mother/child situation and so mothers have at their disposal this psychic predictive quality? I have discovered that fathers who have psychic links are often those who are closely involved in the daily caring of the child or who are very sensitive and empathic individuals.

Few of the accidents averted by mothers following premonitions could have been forecast for the specific time they occurred. The first time Elsie saw the blue light around her son's head was the day of his accident, although he frequently rode without a helmet on his motor cycle. So while her general anxiety could be explained as left-brain forecasting, the urgency of her prediction seems to have come from the right-brain psychic faculty. Her mother's car accident on the way to the shops was forecastable only in the general sense that any car trip may end in tragedy. That does not explain the panic of Elise on this particular day. Love between mother and child may be a powerful transmitter of this faculty.

Changing Fate

An even more intriguing concept is that a mother can change the future, not merely by warning the child of danger but by altering the vision or dream to give the predicted disaster a more positive outcome. Dolores lives in California and works for a police department. She believes that she saved her son's life by physically changing the situation she had seen by her own actions. This is a belief that has very ancient roots and is akin to the concept of being able to send strength psychically to a child in danger.

"When my son Greg was sixteen and a half, he begged his dad and myself for a moped. I did not want to buy him one but his dad gave in. One morning I warned Greg I had a very vivid dream that I saw him riding double with a male friend I did not know and that he had a fall. He laughed and said, 'Not one of your dreams, Mom,' though many had come true.

"Two weeks later I was at work, interviewing a woman on the phone, when I had a feeling of dread and it was almost as if a movie screen came in front of my face. I saw the accident I had seen previously in my dream. Greg fell off his moped and his head hit the cement. I could not see any blood and so I thought he was OK, although unconscious. Then I saw cars running over him.

"I did not know what to do but then I reasoned that if I could change the dream, if I could do anything, whistle, clap, sing, anything different from the dream ending, it would be all right. I put down the phone and got up and, strange though it sounds, started clapping to alter the tragic ending of the dream.

"Suddenly all the phones started ringing. There had been an accident in my home area. A young man was involved and I just knew it was Greg. The sergeant told me to relax as there were countless youths on mopeds. But I saw the vision again. This time I saw a van blocking the traffic keeping the vehicles from running over Greg.

"The news came through that it was Greg involved in the accident.

Greg was unconscious for twenty-five minutes. He had on heavy clothing which was ripped to shreds. A van had stopped inches from his head and shielded him from the traffic. The nurses at the hospital could not believe how lucky he was to escape alive."

Dolores believed she prevented a second dream of disaster becoming reality by taking her son's place and so changing the predicted outcome:

"I woke up one Tuesday morning sweating and yelling. My husband was next to me and asked what was wrong. I told him that in my dream Greg had been in an accident in my car. On Saturday Greg asked to borrow my car. I warned him he would have an accident if he did. I told him that the accident would happen at the East/South Street corner where the moped accident had occurred. Greg was very upset but this time listened to me and agreed to get a lift with a friend instead. I took my car and drove to work. When I was almost at the corner of East/South Street, I was thinking how I had changed the dream by not letting Greg take the car.

"Suddenly I had a very frightening feeling and intense cold. I looked up in time to see a car speeding into the road towards me. It was raining and I tried to turn left out of its way. However, it still hit me on the side and pushed my car on to the kerb against a concrete post. It would have been even worse if I had not diverted as the other car would have hit me head on. I could not open the door but I was able to lift the convertible top and get out. The car was ruined but I was spared. I believe that the crash was meant for Greg but I took it on myself."

The Unanswerable Question

Sometimes children or babies die. Their mothers and fathers are good, caring people but for some reason they are not given the chance to save their children, even though they love them. Stories such as Eileen's are deeply distressing but it is wrong to pretend that a psychic link takes away earthly pain. Eileen, who now lives on the Isle of Wight, lived in a part of the north of England where there was little traffic so her premonition did not make much sense to her.

"I was lying in bed one night next to my husband when I suddenly woke up. I wondered what had woken me. It wasn't the children, Geoffrey who was six or his little sister Pamela, crying. Then I heard a voice: 'Geoffrey's going to die.'

"It is strange to think now, but I just asked, 'How?' 'A bus,' the voice said, 'Geoffrey will be killed by a bus.'

"I was shaken. It was no use waking my husband. He would just have said I was dreaming. I wet my face in the bathroom and felt calmer. I tried to talk myself out of my fears. 'There are no buses round here,' I said aloud. 'The nearest bus is right down at the bottom of the main road and I always hold his hand. Geoffrey never goes anywhere where there is a lot of traffic.'

"Some time later, our young nephew came to stay and he and Geoffrey got on really well. My mother-in-law and sister-in-law came to collect the little boy. Out of the blue, my mother-in-law asked, 'Can Geoffrey come back and stay with us?' Geoffrey had never been away from me and I didn't want him to go. But Geoffrey really wanted to. He was a very brave little chap. I had always felt Geoffrey didn't belong to me. He was somehow different.

"Pamela was outgoing. But Geoffrey was always so sensitive. I just used to want to throw my arms round him and keep him safe. When Geoffrey was born and put into my arms, he started to suck his thumb. 'Isn't he beautiful!' everyone said and he was. He would lie in his little cot at the bottom of my bed with his eyes wide open as if he knew all the secrets of the world, and the nurse said he had been here before.

"I was frightened when my mother-in-law wanted him to go, because she lived in the town, but I couldn't explain about the bus. She would have thought I was mad. 'Go on,' said my mother-in-law to Geoffrey, 'say goodbye to your mother.'

"I didn't want him to say the words. I felt strange but I couldn't say anything except 'Cheerio'.

207

"Geoffrey went on the Sunday night. We weren't on the phone, nor was my mother-in-law. On the Thursday my husband said, 'Go and bring Geoffrey back. The house is like a morgue without him.' So I went. But Geoffrey was enjoying himself at his grandmother's and wanted to stay till Sunday, so I went home without him.

"On the Saturday Pam and I went to my mother-in-law's house. We were sitting at the table having lunch and Geoffrey was getting ready to go out with his grandma and my sister-in-law and nephew. I didn't know what to do as his grandmother was looking after him, but I didn't want him to go. I wanted to take him home safe. I had bought Geoffrey an Aertex T-shirt to wear, and put it on him. 'Let me fix it,' I said and he stood next to me quite quietly.

"Then they all went out. I was sitting in a chair by the fire. I thought, 'I mustn't look down the yard and watch him go,' because I suddenly remembered I'd seen a film where a woman watched someone go and they never came back. Then Pam and I went down to the shops to get some fruit to make pies when we got home. I said I'd come back on Sunday for Geoffrey.

"Geoffrey had asked for a cowboy outfit for his birthday in five weeks' time. I looked at a cowboy hat in a shop window. Should I get it? I stood for ages looking at the hat. But I decided not to buy it. I crossed over the road to where a man was selling goods on a piece of waste land. Should I get a couple of notebooks for the children? Again I hesitated for ages. I just couldn't buy anything for Geoffrey.

"As I passed the end of my mother-in-law's street, I saw a bus parked. 'Geoffrey, the bus,' I cried out. 'Oh, no.'

"Pam asked, 'Where's Geoffrey?' because she couldn't see him.

"I laughed it off. I wanted to go to my mother-in-law's house but I'd got no excuse. I wanted to know Geoffrey was all right but I knew she'd say I was fussing. It was the football season and buses brought people to the football ground so it wasn't strange to see one there, I reasoned.

"But I knew. I caught the bus home. There was nothing else to do."

Pam is now in her thirties. She was four and a half at the time. But she can still remember the incident. "We had been looking at colouring books in the market. Then, out of the blue, Mum cried out, 'Geoffrey, the bus.' Mum tried to laugh it off, but she went quite white."

"When I got home," Eileen told me, "I was cooking the dinner when my husband Bill, a policeman, arrived home.

"'Who was in the car with you?' I asked him.

"'Just a colleague,' he replied. Bill went up to the bathroom. I followed him. 'Geoffrey's had an accident,' he said, 'he was knocked down by a car.'

"'Is he dead?' I asked.

"'No,' replied my husband, 'but he's hurt his head.'

"'It wasn't a car,' I told Bill, 'it was a bus.'

"'How could you possibly know that?' he asked.

"'I saw the bus parked on the corner of your mother's road,' I replied.

"Bill hadn't wanted to tell me it was a bus because he thought it would frighten me even more. Geoffrey was such a little lad and buses are so big. My husband took me to the hospital ward. I knew Geoffrey would die. The voice had told me. I saw a child half sitting in bed. At first I thought it was Geoffrey and said to myself, 'It can't be that bad if he's sitting up. Maybe the voice was wrong.'

"Then I saw Geoffrey. He had tubes everywhere. 'Will he be all right?' I asked the doctor. But the doctor ignored me and spoke to my husband. 'You know what it's like. You see these things with head injuries.'

"She was so hard. After that I couldn't bear to stay. Bill said he would recover. But my husband didn't know what I knew. Geoffrey was going to die.

"My husband got the police car to take me home. It was four months since I had heard the voice. 'If Geoffrey regains consciousness,' Bill promised, 'I'll arrange for you to be brought back. If anything happens, I'll come home.'

"My brother-in-law who was a college student was waiting at home. 'Geoffrey's got a good skull,' he tried to reassure me. 'He'll come out of it.'

"I said nothing. They did not know what I knew. My sister phoned to say Geoffrey was a bit better. But they did not know what I knew.

"I was making toast when a car drew up. 'It's only Bill,' said my

brother-in-law, 'he'll be coming to tell us Geoffrey's on the mend.'

"The accident was at 3.45 in the afternoon. Geoffrey died at 11.30 in the evening. He never regained consciousness.

"I still can't understand the voice. People say it was God who spoke to me. But how do you know? I tried to sort it out in my mind. Was it something from my child's mind? Whose voice was it? Was it someone who had passed on trying to prepare me? If I hadn't stopped so long looking at the cowboy hat and the notebooks, I would have witnessed the accident. Was it planned that way? I looked down my mother-in-law's road at 4 p.m. The accident happened at 3.45 p.m. Was it all meant? I don't know."

In many cases, even when there is no definite warning the mother, especially of an unborn infant, senses quite intuitively something is wrong. Paula, who lives in Christchurch, New Zealand, wrote to me:

"In May 1989 after many months of trying my husband and I were delighted to learn that I was finally pregnant. Looking back, the pregnancy was fairly straightforward. I was twenty-seven, a non-smoker, in perfect health, physically fit and generally considered a classic low-risk patient. When I was eighteen weeks pregnant, my husband Ross and I went along for the regular routine ultrasound scan and suddenly reality hit. At last we were well on the way to beginning our much-wanted family.

"Around Christmas time, eight months into pregnancy, I became obsessed with the umbilical cord. At night I would seek affirmation from Ross that everything would be just fine. However, those reassuring words did not remove the doubt I held regarding the cord.

"Towards the end of the pregnancy I experienced a lot of severe back pain. But, not being one to complain and not having been pregnant before, I assumed that discomfort in the back was something that all pregnant mothers experienced.

"Finally my due date of 28 January arrived and went. Having been a schoolteacher, I am by nature an extremely organized person and yet there were still a number of tasks I would have expected to have

completed by this late in the pregnancy. For example, nappies had not been aired, bath towels not purchased. Little things that, when I look back, I wonder why? Had I known deep down something was wrong?

"As the month slipped into February, I told Ross the baby was waiting for Valentine's Day. Throughout the pregnancy Ross and I believed that our precious bundle was a boy and we lovingly referred to him as Lester. On 13 February before I went to bed I packed my bags and placed them by the front door, so sure was I that tonight was to be the night. The waters broke at 3.15 a.m. on 14 February 1990. The final chapter even after seven years causes me a lot of pain.

"Michael Ross was delivered by emergency Caesarean section in the early hours of 14 February Valentine's Day. He survived only twenty hours, twenty very precious hours. He never gained consciousness, never opened his eyes. He didn't even cry. He died so pure, so innocent, to us he was a true angel.

"What went wrong? After all this was the nineties. Michael was an undetected breech. That in itself would not have been a problem had he not been crouched in my pelvis. When the waters broke at home, along with the gush of water the cord prolapsed as well. From the moment the cord hit air it contracted and from that point poor Michael was fighting for life.

"The hours that followed his birth seem a complete blur. I awoke from the operation to a nightmare. My little boy was sick and fighting for his life. Because of the Caesarean it was several hours until I was finally able to see and touch my baby. Michael was cared for in the special ante-natal unit. Tubes, wires and monitors surrounded him in his incubator. I still remember the moment I stretched my finger through the clear plastic window of his incubator and into the palm of his little hand. I felt him give my finger a squeeze as though he knew his mummy was there for him.

"In the weeks that followed alone at home I would often hear a baby crying. I would sit for hours in Michael's room and tell him things or sing to him. There was such a feeling of loss. Life was not supposed to be like this after the birth of a baby.

"Now seven years down the track we have been blessed with two

211

beautiful daughters, Kate and Rebecca. Although both pregnancies were anxious times, I had a sense of peace about me. I knew that this time everything would be fine. A mother's intuition?

"Looking back now at my pregnancy with Michael there were lots of little signs that things were not as they should have been. I believe very strongly that a sixth sense was trying to tell me something or at least prepare me for what was to come.

"As it turned out the umbilical cord was to be a major factor in Michael's fate. Because Michael had been a very active foetus he managed to put two true knots in his umbilical cord. This caused the cord to become very weak so that when my membranes broke the cord was slack enough to prolapse along with the waters."

Shirley Firth, a British expert on Indian studies, told me of an Indian family for whom the child who died was seen as a gift they might otherwise not have had. The parents had had fertility problems and so considered they were blessed to have had a child even for a short time.

The experience concerns a two-and-a-half-year-old boy in Gujarat. The parents had taken the child to the market and bought him a little packet of fried rice nibbles. Suddenly a crow swooped down and snatched the packet from the little boy's hand. His father immediately offered to buy the little boy another packet but the child refused, saying, "I have no need of them, Father."

The father saw this as a sign the child would die. The child became ill soon afterwards. The father then had a dream that the Mother Goddess and another female deity were fighting the God of Death for the child's life. The parents had not been fertile and had prayed to the Mother Goddess for a child. They believed the child was given as a boon from her. Now even the Goddess could not save the child, the father believed, for he had only been given for a short time. Shortly after the boy died in his sleep from diphtheria.

A Chance to Say Goodbye

Since Geoffrey could not be saved, what was the point in knowing? his mother had asked me. For Norah, who lives in Bristol, England, the time leading up to her son Joel's death seemed, in retrospect, a time when he was leaving her gradually, precious hours that etched him on her consciousness for ever.

"My son Joel died in November totally unexpectedly from a cot death. Finding him dead shocked me to the core and yet looking back on his last week alive, it seems to me now that both he and I knew his life was about to end. When Joel died he was about six and a half months old. Though he was taking some solids, he was still breastfeeding. I loved feeding him and he never showed any signs that he was losing interest. Then one morning about five days before his death, he refused my milk.

"Joel wasn't unhappy or ill. He would take formula milk or even my milk so long as it was from a bottle. I was absolutely distraught.

"It felt as though Joel was rejecting me, leaving me, telling me our special time together was over. I said to my husband Doug, 'I feel as though I'm grieving' and that's how it was over the next few days. After Joel did die, I felt grateful to him for weaning himself like that. It seems clear to me that he was beginning to separate himself from me, preparing us both and especially me for his death. Having had to do some letting go of him that week definitely softened the wrench that I felt when he died, because by that time I had come to accept that I could not hold on to Joel as a baby for ever, that he would grow up and be replaced by a child and then an adult. On the morning of his funeral, I drained the last of my milk and poured it down the sink.

"On the day before Joel died I can see, looking back, that there were definite messages for me that it was going to be his last day. In the mornings, I usually got on with the household chores while Joel played in the same room. This normally seemed fine for both of us, but that day it kept coming to me again and again, like a voice in my head, that I should forget about the chores for that day and just enjoy being with Joel.

There was a softness around us both that day, I felt quite mesmerized by him and dreamy and spent more time than usual with him.

"Evening came and Joel was quite grubby, but I was behind with supper and getting ready to go out so I decided to leave him as he was and clean him up in the morning. While I was cooking I suddenly remembered a saying of my mum's that you should always go out in clean underwear in case you had an accident. Suddenly I felt compelled to clean Joel up. I laid him by the fire in the kitchen and bathed him from head to toe which he loved. As I dressed him in clean clothes I explained to him I wouldn't have wanted anyone to see him looking so dirty.

"There was no reason for me to suspect at the time that anyone would see him like that and yet again it was almost as if I knew.

"It may seem like a small detail, but it was a source of great relief to me that when we took Joel to the children's hospital the next day, he was looking clean and cared for. I was glad that I had given him that final wash, that he had not died dirty.

"After we'd had our supper, I gave Joel his last bottle. Often he would reach up with one hand and pull at my hair in quite a rough way, but on this night he was quite different. As he sucked earnestly on his bottle, he reached up with one hand and stroked the length of my face, running his fingers over my eyes, nose, mouth and hair in a very adult and loving way, very slowly and carefully, gently repeating the movement many times. I had a crick in my neck, because my head was bent for him to reach it, but I could not bring myself to move in case I interrupted this moment.

"Again there was a voice in my head reminding me to enjoy him for now. It was his touch and the way he looked at me that left me feeling that my absolute love for him was totally reciprocated. Recalling those moments now it also seems to me that he was reminding himself of my face, touching me one last time as though he knew he was saying goodbye to me.

"Later Doug was settling Joel down for the night when I had an overwhelming desire to have a cuddle with him. Part of me said to myself this was ridiculous, that I would unsettle him just as he was going off to

214

sleep. My urge was so strong that I stopped Doug from putting him down and picked Joel up for one last hug.

"Ever since Joel's birth he had been my alarm. The next morning we woke later than usual and there was silence. I said to Doug, 'What about Joel?' and even before Doug went into his room, I knew Joel was dead.

"For Joel's coffin, we had a cross made of white roses and carnations and after the funeral we brought it home and put it by the front door to our house. One day I came in and touched one of the roses as I passed the front door. As I did I thought of Joel. Suddenly something burst into life. It seemed to come into being from within me and around me at the same time and just kept expanding to fill the whole hallway. I felt full of joy and ran up the stairs to the room where Joel had died.

"I couldn't see anything, yet I sensed a warm and golden Presence. I 'knew' that it was Joel and remember being astonished because I had still thought of Joel as being a baby and realized that now he wasn't at all.

"There was a very strange quality to the days that followed Joel's death. On one level it was a nightmare too awful to be true. Yet the engulfing darkness of those early days was pierced somehow by a light, a feeling of grace in the house and around us. There were times we felt as if we were floating, even flying.

"We lost our baby, but we gained in knowledge. Finding Joel's body, collecting his ashes and seeing this plastic bag of charcoal that was all that was left of our beautiful son. And yet on another level, I knew beyond a tremor of a doubt that Joel's life was not at an end, but somehow a beginning. It is as though in dying, in making a transition from the physical to the spiritual, Joel opened up a door for me between these two realities.

"Though I remained in the physical world, for a while the spiritual remained more real to me. Joel passed from the visible into the invisible and there are times when I feel that actually these two worlds exist in the same space and if I knew how to cross the boundary between them, I could reach out and touch him."

PART SIX

When Two Become One

Birth and Beyond

We are taught to distrust our natural instincts and yet
they are the firmest indicator of the best course of action.
We leave our intuitions in the hospital car park when we
go to give birth.

Ruth, after the birth of her fourth son

G iving birth can be glorious or ghastly, sometimes both. Like any
journey it can be easy or hazardous, but it is always momentous.
Women give birth in many ways, in the back of taxis on the way
to hospital, surrounded by family and friends at home, in a room filled
with candles and crystals with soft music playing or in an operating
theatre with state-of-the-art technology. The sensations vary from
orgasmic to the fluttering of a butterfly's wing, from other-worldly
to physically agonizing.

Like the best-laid enterprises of mice and men, birth plans are
notorious for going awry. No woman can predict how her body will
react to the process of giving birth and this can vary not only from
woman to woman but from birth to birth. The most relaxed and
finely tuned muscles may unpredictably refuse to dilate or the baby
wedge him or herself into an awkward position.

At the end of the day bonding between mother and child depends
not on a perfect transition into the world, ideal though that may be,
but upon the following years of loving, guiding, getting the
relationship wrong, redefining, laughing and crying and hopefully
getting at last some of it right, often by pure chance. A thirty-year-
old will not recall that his mother overdosed on pain relief in labour
and declared that the midwife could place the squalling bundle down
the refuse chute. He or she will remember the hours a mother spent

when night terrors would not dissipate, washing dirty football kit for twenty, ripping down the curtains to make a costume for the school play the following day that the offspring just forgot to mention, pawning the family silver to buy a first work suit or set of wheels.

A Gentle Transition—From Womb to Water

In spite of some reservations that giving birth in water may not be suitable in certain cases, for many women the waterbirth at home or in hospital represents the ideal natural transition for a baby from the waters of the womb to the outside world.

Michel Odent, an internationally acclaimed obstetrician who runs a clinic at Pithviers, near Paris, is a follower and developer of Leboyer's "birth without violence" principle: that the newborn child must be received gently into the world. Odent first used a tank of water as a birthing bed for the mother because it eased labour in many cases. But he soon discovered it was an excellent way of providing a gentle door into this dimension for the child.

Igor Tjarkovsky, a Russian researcher, goes even further in his enthusiasm for the water tub than Odent. He believes that babies born in water are more clairvoyant than those delivered normally, and even has a parapsychologist in assistance at the birth.[1] He also believes that the mother and child communicate telepathically during the pre-birth period and that the newborn infant is open to psychic influences. Tjarkovsky claims that this increased clair-voyance and other paranormal abilities are natural brain functions that can be easily destroyed at birth. He says: "A gentle transition, both to the world of gravity and to a different way of breathing, opens up completely new possibilities for the human race."

All this accords with the evidence that gentleness, silence and acceptance are conducive to the mother/child psychic link. Cindy Bertrand-Brozdik, who now lives in Orange County in the United States, was in Ontario when she began working with the technique with other women after the waterbirth of her own son, Jonathan. It was this gentle transition that Cindy believes helped to foster the psychic link between mother and son: "We chose to have a waterbirth because it seemed the most gentle and natural way of birthing," she told me. "But before labour came there were lots of dreams, visions and feeling the presence of the new person's energy that led me to realize that my choice was the correct one.

"I began dreaming of dolphins. So vivid were these dreams I would wake and smell my hands to see if they smelled of the dolphins I was swimming with and touching. In one dream I was walking along a beach and all along the shoreline were baby dolphins but they had little children's faces and I wondered which one was mine. The last and littlest dolphin child looked me in the eye and I knew I was to care for this one. To my amazement when my son was one and a half years old and sleeping peacefully I looked at his little cherub face and it flashed in my mind that this was the face of the littlest dolphin in my dream.

"At our midwife's advice, my husband Rick and I told very few about our home waterbirth. It was still a relatively uncommon practice at the time. A few days before my son was born, my mother had a dream that she was picking up a baby out of the water and patting its back so it could breathe. My mother lives across the country and didn't know what we were planning."

Cindy's son Jonathan was born at home, among friends, and Jonathan slept his first night between his parents.

"We bought a tub, set it up in our dining room, filled it with water and waited and waited and waited, emptied the tub, cleaned it again, filled it up and waited some more. My due date came and went.

"Rick was not there when the first twinges came. A very powerful contraction had me yelling for Rick long-distance on the phone. I heard him say, 'Can you hold on, my wife is in labour and I have to go breathe with her.' We both laughed through that contraction.

"Time passes—it's time to get into the water. It's warm like my womb temperature. I feel relaxed, safe, secure. My midwife Catherine comes in

221

and sees everything is fine. Our girlfriends arrive and two other midwives, Mary and Jennifer. The energy is beautiful. Rick is behind me holding me while I squat in the tub. When the contractions get powerful, I pull his hair. He says he doesn't mind, that I'm doing a great job and that he loves me. I thank God. Another contraction—how many more of these? Catherine thinks between one and twenty-five but not to be concerned about it, just go with the flow.

"Four more pushes and out slid a perfect, beautiful, aware little boy. His eyes were open as he floated calmly in the water. Then he saw us and reached up; we took his face out of the water and held him close while Catherine gave him a squirt of oxygen because the cord was pinched. This was by far the most incredible moment of my life. Rick cut the cord, enthralled by its colour.

"We sat around a plate of fruit and shared our feelings: rainbows danced all over the room from crystals hanging in the window. Soft music played, we lit candles, held hands and thanked each other. The evening came and everyone left us. Bedtime came, we placed our newborn son between us and all drifted off to sleep. New parents were born.

"As our baby grew I could not help noticing the sense of a very old soul when looking into his eyes. Although on the outside he seems no different from any other child, he has something special. The few times I would leave him with someone I would jot the time when I felt messages or thoughts coming into my mind. When I returned home I would find that was indeed the time he needed Mama for nursing or comforting. Although Rick does not have feelings and premonitions as I do, he is still strongly connected with his son."

For Cindy the waterbirth strengthened an already intuitive bond with her son. As with breastfeeding, intuitive vibes flow more easily in an ideal situation. But the gentle way is not the only route to the bonding.

Trusting the Maternal Instinct

No one would advise a woman to ignore medical expertise, but there are times in the birth process when a mother will instinctively know that she must change her plans and take urgent action. In such cases, it is important for medical staff to take such promptings seriously. Like Cindy, Ruth, who lives in West Sussex, had experienced an ideal waterbirth and was determined that her next birth would be as memorable.

"When I was in labour with my fourth child, I knew something was wrong. I had been looking forward to having a waterbirth and taking my time pushing the baby out. During the previous labour, pushing the baby out had been wonderful. I had felt a sheer orgasmic rush as the baby was born underwater.

"The labour seemed to be going well and I was ready to begin to push, following the natural rhythms of my body to ensure the transition was as gentle and unhurried as possible for the infant. This birth was like the previous one, at home with midwives in attendance. Suddenly the feeling crystallized that the baby was in danger. I have never had such a clear awareness. I knew I had to push him out as fast as possible and not let nature take its course. I said to the midwives, 'I've got to get the baby out now.'

"I took over the momentum from my body and delivered my son within moments.

"As soon as Lawrence was born, I could see the cord was around his neck. He was grey, like putty, and lifeless. Had I not got him out so quickly, my son would have been dead. Lawrence was very ill for several days, and as I willed him to recover I discovered how very precious he was to me.

"One of the midwives remarked that God moves in mysterious ways. Lawrence had been one of twins. I had previously suffered miscarriages at 9 weeks and so was given a scan at 10 weeks in this pregnancy to check the babies were well. I discovered one of the twins, the little girl I so much wanted, had died. At 15 weeks I had bled and had resented the

surviving baby because illogically I felt he had pushed his sister out of the womb.

"Throughout the pregnancy I felt uneasy that I might resent the baby, but the feeling during labour was different, such a clear prompting that demanded urgent action. Nearly losing my little one showed me how much I treasured Lawrence, so perhaps it was part of some wider plan.

"I have learned and been taught by wise, supportive midwives to trust my own instincts what is right during birth and afterwards. We are taught to distrust our natural instincts and yet they are the firmest indicator of the best course. We leave our intuitions in the hospital car park when we go to give birth and indeed are encouraged to do so. It is only because I have been encouraged to listen to myself that Lawrence is with me today."

Louise was living in Yorkshire when she became pregnant with her second son Edmund. She believes that it was a message from her son in her womb that altered her carefully laid birth plans and probably saved Edmund's life.

"I had agreed with the midwife that I would give birth in a squatting position that felt most natural. Suddenly towards the end of labour I felt that I had lost the power to control my own actions. I felt the child within take over and knew that I had to lie prone. Tony my husband and the midwife tried to hold me up, so I could squat, but I felt I had no choice but to refuse. It is hard to explain. It had not been like that with the birth of my previous son.

"When Edmund was born the cord was tightly wound round his neck. The midwife told me that if I had given birth in any other position except lying flat, the baby would most probably have died."

Spiritual Births Under Less Than Ideal Circumstances

At the private Garden Hospital in London a mother is encouraged to consider all aspects of pregnancy, spiritual as well as physical.

Mothers-to-be take classes in yoga and hear lectures on the psychical aspects of birth. Nevertheless, Yehudi Gordon, an obstetrician there, believes that flexibility is essential, for the best birth plans can go wrong when Mother Nature refuses to cooperate. The most ardent natural birther may need anaesthetic and unnecessarily feel a failure as a result. He believes that the new methods are in danger of becoming as inflexible as the old-fashioned ways.

He has been quoted as saying that women coming into labour with a rigid birth plan, complete with all their friends, pillows, candles and pictures, can be just as misguided as the old unquestioning adherence to hospital protocol. "It is important," he has said, "to be able to go with the flow, without feeling a failure, even if a Caesarean is necessary."

Shawna, who lived in Oxford, had a hospital birth in which everything went wrong. But she believes it was the psychic dialogue which began while her daughter was still in the womb that enabled baby Mela to be born alive and healthy, although she was premature. This link also sustained Shawna and the baby through difficult weeks in special care.

"When I found I was pregnant with my third child I was thrilled. She was very much wanted. But throughout the pregnancy I had a feeling something was wrong. I had the normal blood tests and a scan. Everything seemed all right, but I couldn't disregard this feeling so I thought of some of the things that could be wrong with a baby and decided that, no matter what, this was my child and I'd love her. I also felt that whatever happened would be the right thing as good and not so good experiences are brought our way because they're what we need for a particular lesson. Anyway, this enabled me to let go of my fear and look forward to the birth of this baby as any other.

"I re-read books I'd enjoyed during my other pregnancies and a book about waterbirth which was the way I wanted to have my daughter. All through pregnancy however I pushed aside thoughts of 'be ready for something different' that tried to force their way in. One night when I was about twenty-two weeks pregnant I dreamed I'd had the baby in

hospital, not at home as I'd planned, but that this little baby born so early was healthy, even talking and sitting up. I woke from the dream feeling strangely relieved. I told my husband about it and said, 'But the baby in my dream was a boy and we're going to have a girl.' I thought the relief was a sign that there was nothing wrong and that was the end of the nagging feeling.

"A week and a half later just as I was going to bed I knew I wanted to order a baby's sheepskin and a tape of womb music. I pulled out the forms, and put them in stamped envelopes ready to post in the morning. That night I woke several times to go to the loo but kept leaking in between. I thought it was strange because I wasn't at all big—still able to wear my jeans—but I was tired so went back to sleep.

"In the morning I went to town with my husband and two boys. I felt fine at first but after getting off the bus started leaking a tiny bit. We went for coffee and when I sat down it dawned on me what was happening. I went straight home to pack a bag and call the doctor, leaving my husband to follow with the boys. When the doctor arrived, I told her I was leaking amniotic fluid and asked what I should do. She advised me to go straight to hospital and have it checked. I was right.

"I spent the next four days in hospital dying to go home and rest in my own bed with my children near, but also strangely confident and strong. I never doubted the baby would live even though the medical profession seemed to feel it their duty to disillusion me. I felt that my tiny baby was reassuring me, giving me strength.

"I was terribly worried about the psychological effects on a baby born early to be physically harassed and separated from her mother. But I had an inner calm voice that made me feel it was all right. I knew this little girl. She was courageous and sweet. She didn't need a frightened mother. When after four days in hospital I went into labour I knew my mental communication with my daughter was going to hold us both together.

"Through twelve hours of the strongest pains I've ever experienced I kept a communication going with her. I let her know I was all right and could cope and that she'd be fine. I was left alone in a large dark room.

"The nurse who couldn't examine me because of risk of infection had sent my husband away and told me I probably had an irritable uterus

and to go to sleep and it would probably all stop! I kindly told her that much as I'd like to agree, I'd been in labour before and just wanted her to make sure things were ready in case this twenty-four-week-old baby did arrive soon. To this the nurse replied that the baby wouldn't have much chance anyway and to think of myself.

"I calmed myself and mentally found a quiet place in my mind to rest with my daughter. I experienced the contractions with her from her perspective. It was unbelievable! I felt the way a squeezing contraction enabled my heart to pump the blood all around my body warm and fast and felt the surging adrenalin. Mela and I were together in the womb. I was massaging her. Then we were one, until I hit transition.

"I felt desperate panic for the first time, lost communication with Mela for a moment while I rang for the nurse, told her I couldn't take this any more because this baby was coming now! The nurse didn't believe me because I'd looked asleep to her while in an inner world with my daughter. She consented to examine me, and then she was panicking and I was fine—even happy.

"The nurses had not got anything ready for Mela, so after dashing down the corridors with me to the delivery room, they had to literally hold Mela back while a ventilator was hooked up. The nurse gave me words of encouragement and apologized for sending my husband away. But I felt relieved, strong and confident that all would be well. Once the nurses were ready I delivered Mela. I was shocked by her size and beauty. She was about the size of a Cindy doll, 1lb 4oz and bright pink, much pinker than my big babies. They whisked Mela over to incubate her before I could touch her. That's the only part I regret.

"So I delivered the placenta and walked over to watch them work on her. During the following months while Mela was in special care we shared hours of mental communication. It was painful being away from my new daughter, so I spent nearly all of my waking hours by her side. I sang to her, talked to her and stroked her and we thought together for much of the time each day. Many times I'd come in to be told they'd given Mela a slight sedative or she'd had lots of bradycardias, but while I was with her she didn't play up. Although her progress was slow, it was steady, with no major complications.

"When Mela was born her eyes were still sealed. The first time I held her she opened her eyes for the first time. She stared straight at me. I could hardly believe it was real.

"Mela is now a very healthy little girl and at three years old is happy, kind-hearted, thoughtful and wise beyond her years. She comforts and loves her big brothers when they're upset and takes endless delight in her little sister, Arwen, who was born at home in a birthing pool. I'm still learning from Mela and wonder if she'll ever remember any of what we went through. I've learned it's the soul of the person we should all communicate with. The body holds comparatively little relevance."

The Magic of Childbirth in Folk Traditions

To aid thee from the fays,
To guard thee from the host;
To aid thee from the gnome,
To shield thee from the spectre;
To keep thee for the Three,
To shield thee, to surround thee.

*A Gaelic birth ritual to endow the newborn
child with protection of air, sea and land*

From early times, a woman who had just given birth was regarded as special. In some traditions she was regarded as "unclean", but this in itself was an indication of the magic and spirituality with which she was imbued so that she could actually threaten the safety of those around her, especially her husband if he came too close. But sometimes the new mother was seen as little short of a shaman.

In Greenland it was believed until fairly recently that women who were in labour or had just given birth were able to control and calm a storm. They had only to go out of doors into the wind, fill their mouths with air, come back into the house and blow it out again. Witches were traditionally believed to control winds in several parts of the world and the new mother came to be regarded as equally potent.

In several parts of Europe a newly delivered mother was considered the symbol of fertility for other women and the land. It was believed that the first house she visited would also be blessed with a child. Straw from a childbed would be fed to cows who had ceased to give milk, and pregnant or nursing mothers were encouraged to be present at the planting of the crops. In various cultures these beliefs unconsciously or consciously link the new mother with the power and fertility of the Mother Goddess and the earth itself. For example, in parts of Bavaria and Austria it is said that a cherry tree will always be rich with fruit if a woman who has just given birth to her first child eats the first fruits.

Magic in Labour

Customs throughout the world invoke sympathetic magic to aid the act of giving birth. From Scotland to West Africa there are variations on a common belief that if knots are untied and locks opened, a birth will be easy. In some places, if the birth is delayed, animals will be set free, bottles uncorked, and windows and doors thrown open.

It is said that among the Hos in West Africa the witch doctor uses the same principle to aid a difficult birth. He looks at the labouring woman and says, "The child is bound in the womb and so cannot be delivered." At the pleading of female relatives, the witch doctor at last agrees to loose the bonds. The women fetch a tough creeper from the forest and with it the magic man ties the hands and feet of the expectant mother. He then takes a knife and, calling out the woman's name, cuts through the creeper, saying, "I cut through today thy bonds and thy child's bonds." The witch doctor then chops the creeper into small pieces and puts the strands into water with which he bathes the mother.

In some of the Slovakian regions, if a mother was experiencing a difficult labour, her husband would fetch a mouthful of water from a place where three little streams converged and bring it to her. This represented the power of flowing water, and if it failed to help he would shake her to release the blockages in the process.

No one understands fully the complex relationship between psychology and practices of sympathetic magic, but the fact that these methods have survived in different lands and ages, while it does not suggest that any woman can give birth easily given a bit of determination and belief, indicates that it may be possible to harness natural powers to make a difficult birth less painful.

Birth Customs in Different Cultures

Gaelic birth customs have become intermingled with early Christian beliefs, but can still be traced in modern ritual. The Christian baptism ceremony retains echoes of a much earlier Gaelic birth celebration at the magical transition of the infant's soul from the otherworld into this realm. Those most closely involved in the birth acted as the priests and priestesses and the ceremony took place immediately after the birth. The participants were the mother, the midwife and a nurse, plus the father who, it would seem, also shared the ritual of labour.

Immediately after the child was born, the midwife placed three drops of water on the infant's head (the first service the Celtic goddess Bride performed for the Christ Child). The baby was thus anointed with the power of sky, sea and land, and the verse quoted at the head of this chapter was recited.

The nurse would then administer the *baisteadh breith* or birth baptism, bathing the child for the first time in sacred Bride water in which gold and silver coins were placed to symbolize the powers of the sun and moon. Holding the child over the bath, the nurse would fill her palm with water nine times and rub it over the child while singing the incantation. Each handful of water would endow the child with an attribute rather like the good fairies in *The Sleeping Beauty*. These gifts included gentle speech, generosity of spirit, wealth, health and grace.

Then the child would be passed across a flame three times from the midwife to the father, invoking the power of the sun, and the father would carry the infant three times sunwise or clockwise around the fire. Finally it was the mother's turn to complete the ritual and make the connection with the womb of the earth in thanks. She would touch the child's forehead to the ground and recite another incantation.

A surviving superstition in the Western world, of carrying a newborn child upstairs or standing on a chair with him or her, dates from Celtic times. It would be the nurse's duty to perform the ceremony of lifting or carrying the child up a hill, so that he or she would become powerful in the world and gain riches and recognition.

The water ritual at birth has echoes in the Slovakian bathing rites that still prevail in remoter regions. When the baby was bathed by the midwife for the first time soon after the birth, tools and coins were placed in the water in the hope that the infant will become a handyman or craftsman—and rich. Sugar and salt were also added to the water in the expectation that the child would grow to be affable and healthy. In well-to-do families, a pen and pencil were given to the baby so that he or she would be scholarly.

After the bath, the midwife gave the child to members of the household and relatives to be kissed as a sign of welcome, after which the mother was given the baby to nurse. Once more the midwife is closely involved, not only in the birth but in ceremonies after the birth that can confirm for the mother that her child is special and unique. Some women today who have home births are able to celebrate the birth with friends and family immediately afterwards, but too often in hospitals in many parts of the world the personal celebration can be lost in the needs of the institution.

Romany women were regarded as *mochard*, unclean, in the ceremonial sense when giving birth and for a period afterwards. The labouring woman would leave the living wagon or tent so that it would not be defiled by the birth. It is recorded that until thirty or forty years ago, some New Forest Gypsy women used to go alone to a particular holly tree in a sheltered spot along Godshill Ridge to give birth.

More frequently, however, a special tent was set aside for the woman in labour and men were banished from the scene. The mother and child might remain here for up to two months, after which the birthing tent and everything the woman had used in it was burned.

The Gypsy mother had her own set of crockery and did not prepare food for several weeks before or after the birth of her child. The father would not hold the child until its christening, which would be according to the rites of the Church of the country in which the Gypsies were living. The modern Romany father is, however, more likely to be influenced by contemporary practices, especially if his wife gives birth in hospital.

In Bali, a small island midway along the Indonesian archipelago, the celebration of the birth is continued throughout the infant's first year of life. The first birth ceremony takes place even before the infant is born and another is held after the birth in which the afterbirth is ceremonially buried. Approximately halfway through the baby's first Balinese year (210 days), a major birth ceremony is held. Only eight first names are used in naming children, Wayan or Putu for the eldest child, Made or Kadek for the second, Nyoman or Komang for the third. Thereafter, the fourth child is Ketut and the fifth child is Wayan.

The Cajun people were formerly French Canadians driven from Nova Scotia by the English colonists during the eighteenth century. They settled in south-west Louisiana but retained the language and customs of their forebears. It has long been the custom in the extended family favoured by the settlers for any older relative or neighbour to be *tante* (aunt) or *oncle* (uncle). The titles Marraine or Parrain, godmother and father, were reserved for the baptism at which the chosen adults would promise to be responsible not only for the spiritual but also for the material welfare of the new infant. In earlier times, where illness might strike and the child might be orphaned, this pledge might well need to be honoured.

Another relic of these earlier, harsher times was the fact that the baptism was carried out almost immediately after the birth, since it was believed that an unbaptized child who died would become a *feu follet* (will-o'-the-wisp).

For the modern mother, the act of giving birth has lost much of its former ritual. Yet she may still find that she touches the other dimensions seen by women in earlier times and becomes truly magical.

The Magic of Birth in the Modern World

> I have definitely seen golden light surround the emerging
> baby on several occasions. I have not established a pattern
> of who or why except that those children were coming to
> loving parents. Born in the Light of Love? It is quite an
> awesome happening to see this light and perceive the
> beauty and sacredness of birth. It is like seeing through
> the door into another world.
>
> *Maria Cadaxa, midwife*

*I*n the course of my research I have come across a strange
phenomenon which I have called the Near Birth Experience
(NBE) in which a women during labour has an experience akin to
the Near Death Experience (NDE). People who have undergone an
NDE when they have technically "died" for a short period during an
operation or accident have reported leaving their bodies and looking
down upon the scene below. Sometimes they fall down a tube of light
and meet deceased family members before returning to life.

Women have reported such experiences during labour, the only
difference being that their lives need not be in danger. The woman
in labour may rise out of her body and see visions of beautiful places
or converse with shining forms.

My own hypothesis is that when a new life comes forth and the
infant's psyche begins to form a separate existence along with the
body, psychic energies are triggered that can for a brief period part
the veil between alternative realities. These experiences more than
any other suggest that the bond between mother and child is not

rooted entirely in the physical or even in the psychological, but in the dimension of the spirit.

Karen's labour was traumatic, though not life-threatening. It soon became obvious that everything was not going as it should and the baby was in great difficulty.

"I was turned on to my front with a gas-and-air mask over my face. As I lay in this position, I can remember saying 'Please help me, God', and then I felt myself rising out of my body. I found myself in a dark place, almost like being in space.

"My mother's face then came towards me out of the dark and said, 'You can't stay here. You have to move on.'

"I asked, 'To where?'

"There was no answer and then her face left and my father's face appeared and said the same thing, and then my husband. It was so real. I was aware I had to get back into my body and said or thought, 'I'm not ready for this yet. I want to go back.'

"As I started to draw down to my body, I had a flash, almost like a picture of the world. I opened my eyes and said to the nurses, 'I have just died.' They laughed at me. 'You just fainted,' they insisted. I then said to myself, 'Well I wouldn't have believed it either if it hadn't happened to me.'

"The point I can't understand is that my husband and mother and father are still alive and yet they were there. I would just like to add that my baby was born safely and is now a healthy two-year-old boy."

Karen's experience was remarkably similar to a child's NDE, where researchers report that children tend to see living rather than dead relatives. Could it be that Karen was sharing the experience with her child and so viewed his transition into this world through a child's eyes?

The nurses laughed. Sometimes it is difficult for professionals to cope with the unusual, unless they possess great sensitivity and confidence in themselves as people behind the mask of professionalism, for their competence depends on their being "in control". I have however come across a considerable number of psychic mid-wives and nurses. I have a theory that the same qualities necessary to be a good, caring nurse are those that make people receptive to experiences beyond the accepted range of senses. Also, perhaps, because they are constantly working on the extremes of experience, birth and death may make them more aware of the outer limits of human existence.

Physical or psychic, it was a very significant moment for Karen. It is perhaps easier for some to accept that Karen's experience was the effect of the gas-and-air, although countless women using this form of pain relief have not reported such experiences.

British doctors Andrew and Penny Stanway point out: "Birth being the astonishing and wonderful process it is, it is hardly surprising that it is sometimes associated with the supernatural. Many people see birth as a time when a woman is especially vulnerable to disease or death. Some even interpret the otherworld-liness of labour as women 'hanging between life and death'."[1]

Even when the woman's life is in danger, what separates an NBE from an NDE is that it is the bond with the newborn baby that calls the mother back to the everyday world. The story of Pauline's birth during the Second World War was told to her many times by her mother.

"My mother suffered a very prolonged and complicated delivery at home, supervised by a young and very inexperienced midwife. As a result my mother was in a state of shock and her heart was failing by the time the family doctor had arrived. The doctor had to resuscitate her in the old-fashioned way by heart massage when my mother went into cardiac arrest. At that point my mother said she felt only a wonderful sense of relaxation and total freedom from pain. She had a sense of floating through a pale blue mist, smelling the perfume of innumerable flowers, hearing music and singing sweeter than anything she had ever heard in this world. She felt the presence of warm and friendly people and was convinced that soon she would emerge from the mist and be able to identify the unseen presences. At that moment my mother heard me cry

237

and a voice saying, 'You have a baby now—you must take care of it.' She decided to return to her body and found herself back in the world."

Pauline's mother often said her greatest fear was that she might be unable to return to the place she had visited in her vision.

For Alison it was the bond with her first child as well as the newborn infant that, she believes, gave her the desire to return to life. She recalled:

"Everything happened very quickly. I left home at ten past five in the morning and my second son was born at ten to six and that's when it happened. I haemorrhaged just after the birth and all I remember was the two midwives present saying, 'Quick, get a doctor.' I never had any gas-and-air or injection and by the time the doctor arrived I remember them slapping my face and saying, 'Don't go to sleep.'

"After a few minutes I felt myself rising away from my body, floating above myself, and I came to a place where I saw streams and beautiful gardens and I wanted to carry on. I also saw my whole self lying on the bed. I could see my whole body below, although I floated upwards, and suddenly I thought of my oldest son who was only two. I gripped the sides of the bed and pulled myself down. I couldn't have gripped very hard because I was so weak. It gave me a terrific fright."

Although this happened nine years ago Alison still remembers the terror of it. However, she also remembers the joy and says: "If that's death then I reckon nobody need be afraid of it."

Dr Peter Fenwick is consultant neuropsychiatrist at the Maudsley Hospital in London, and also president of IANDS (International Association for Near Death Studies) UK. When I asked him about women's NBEs, he said: "I believe your idea that NBEs could possibly be related to the bonding process—a viewpoint I have not heard discussed before—raises interesting implications. I would suggest that one argument against it would be that as NBEs are extremely rare it will only make a small difference to the bonding process and thus is unlikely to have a survival value. However, I think we need more data before we can come to that viewpoint. From the point of view of physiology, NBEs are very similar to NDEs and these are thought to be a disorder of brain function. There are really severe difficulties attributing subjective experience totally to brain function as we as yet have no scientific models of this."

In a paper written by Dr Fenwick and David Lorimer, the chairman of Medical and Scientific Network,[2] they point out: "We know that we live in a world where love, beauty, meaning and value are part of our daily lives, indeed are the most important aspects of our world. This subjective experience is what we call consciousness and even if the physicists have no place for it, it has still to be reckoned with."

Jane, who lives in Oxford, England, told me of her mother's strange experiences during and just after birth.

"My own mother suffered a series of miscarriages and the death of a baby boy when she was seven months pregnant with him.

"When Michael was born, his lungs were not fully developed and my mother had severe pre-eclampsia. She was very ill and unfortunately Michael died. My mother is extremely well balanced, quiet and intelligent, but insists that she saw a white light pass her bed and hospital window and knew before the sister told her that Michael had died. I believe my mother but then I know her.

"A similar situation occurred when I was born. Mum had been in hospital with raised blood pressure on and off for the whole of her pregnancy. The doctors were determined my mother should have a healthy baby and booked her in for a Caesarean. Pre-eclampsia struck again, and when her vision started to blur the doctors decided it was time for me to make an urgent appearance. My mother recalls that during the operation she and I were in a long line of people, some going one way and others another. She said to me, 'When it's our turn, scream "We're alive!"' '

"I suppose I must have done because I was born healthy. My mother suffered a collapsed lung and was again very ill, in intensive care for a

few days. She found out later how close to death she had come. In her dream I was a girl. Prior to this she had only chosen boys' names as she was certain I was a boy."

Lights are often seen around a dying person. The phenomenon is especially powerful when an infant dies. Sally, who is now in her seventies, described how, the night her young daughter died in hospital, a light flickered around the bedroom of Sally's home, witnessed also by Sally's husband. One theory is that it is the astral or spirit body leaving the physical one, another that, just as in birth, death also triggers psychic energies that are perceived in this way. Moving towards a point of light down a dark tunnel is an integral part of many classic NDEs.

Bess's NBE took place after her baby was born, when her own life was not in danger and she was not under the influence of analgesics. Bess saw the light as part of her post-partum experience.

"I was only twenty when I gave birth to my first child. I found myself feeling very lonely and frightened during labour, which was excruciatingly painful. I remember praying to God for the pain to end and to die.

"I had a daughter and was placed in a three-bedded room of which I was the only occupant. I dropped off into an uneasy sleep and awoke to find my nose one or two inches from the ceiling. I looked down on myself and thought I was looking at my twin sister. I realized it was myself.

"Momentarily I felt frightened but found myself drifting peacefully and naturally down a dark tunnel with a bright light at the end. This seemed to happen very quickly. I arrived at the end and a person on the other side spoke to me. I could hear a voice but not see any form, as the light was so bright. The voice knew who I was and seemed kind and loving. He asked me, 'Who would look after the baby if you died?'

"We went through the possibilities and I agreed I would have to go back to care for my daughter. Instantly, I was back in my body and in pain."

Although such experiences may last only minutes or even seconds, their effect is usually more long-reaching. A woman may feel especially close to her infant and have a sense that there is more to life than the immediate. Several mothers whose experiences I have documented have expressed a feeling that they no longer fear death.

However, as with conventional NDEs, not all NBEs are positive. Where mother and child are involved, the other-worldly encounter may reflect underlying doubts about the forthcoming baby. If sensitively handled, the experience can provide an opportunity for the new mother to discuss and resolve these fears with family or sympathetic professionals. Too often, however, the mother is disbelieved and so, in the case of a negative vision, feels even more isolated than before. Jennifer, who almost died during childbirth, is convinced that her baby shared her experience:

"I was nine months pregnant and started to bleed heavily. The doctor put an oxygen mask over my face. Next I was in a dark, dark tunnel which branched in two. I was travelling down the dark tunnel to the junction. I had to choose which road to take. One was jagged and bumpy and very dark. The other was smooth as silk, a pure cylinder with white light at the end.

"Every ounce of power that was in me pulled me towards the easy route. I screamed inside at the thought of the jagged one. Suddenly an unbelievable surge of strength which can only be described as a dam breaking forced me down the terrible, endless, dark, jagged tunnel, down and down. There was no escape. A voice echoed over and over in my head, 'Who cares anyway? Who cares anyway? Who cares?'

"I floated up to the ceiling and watched the nurse tell me I had a baby boy. I could see the clock on the wall. I watched myself smile, but it was not me. I floated down again. When I woke up the doctor told me I was lucky to be alive. He called my son a miracle baby. He had nearly died too.

"Sadly I did not feel any bond with my baby. My husband says when my son was born, he screamed and screamed. He had never heard a baby cry like that before. I feel certain the baby had a similar experience to my own and that he too would have gone down the smooth artery if that

force had not pulled us both. I suppose I will never know.

"Recently, however, my son fell downstairs and for a few seconds he hugged me tenderly and I hugged him."

Tanya from Oxfordshire had an NBE that connected her not only with her unborn daughter, but also with her late mother. She saw her experience as touching the collective wisdom of all mothers and the Great Mother, an association that other women have expressed.

"I had my third child in a nursing home twenty-two years ago. I was in labour when I got to the home at 11.30 p.m. The midwife would not believe me and did not even examine me. She insisted I had a sleeping pill. I refused. My husband was there, but would not intervene on my behalf. The nurse told me to stop being a nuisance and added that if I was in labour the pill would make absolutely no difference. 'If not we'll all be able to get some sleep,' she added impatiently.

"My waters broke suddenly and the midwife started to panic. My doctor had promised to be present at the birth, but the midwife refused to call him. Even my husband was not allowed to stay. After five hours of very bad pain, I asked for something to relieve it. The midwife again refused. I was exhausted. 'Why not?' I asked.

"The midwife replied: 'You had a sleeping pill. You're on your own.'

"I realized I was in trouble. I went very light-headed. A feeling of dying came over me. I became calm at the inevitability. I very nearly drowned as a child. Now I had the same sensation. At this point, a voice in my head cut across my thoughts, saying: 'You must ask for help.'

"I started to argue, 'I have already asked for help, but the nurse won't give me any.'

"The reply came: 'Ask the Mother for help.'

"My father, who was a doctor, had been at my delivery. He told me that during labour my mother cried out for her own mother in her pain and my father had been very contemptuous of what he saw as weakness. When the voice said, 'Ask the Mother for help' I had not wanted to ask for my mother, as she had done at my birth, because my father had told me such behaviour was silly and childish in a woman during a natural

242

process. Now I had a blinding realization whom I must ask for help.

"*I still resisted and said aloud 'I am not a believer', then, eventually, I cried out, 'Mama mia, help me.' But the racking pain continued and I waited at the end of the contraction for peace. Another contraction started straight away. I was angry. I had done what I was asked to do and had been convinced help would come. At the peak of the pain, it stopped. One moment, it was so intense, knife-like, and instantly it cut out. 'Thank God, thank God,' I cried out in overwhelming gratitude over and over again.*

"*My eyes were closed. I heard the midwife say, 'Tanya, move your leg. Come on, move your leg. We have to get the baby.'*

" *'I have moved my leg,' I replied.*

"*There was a slapping sound, but I could not feel anything. 'I think we have lost her,' the midwife called out to someone I could not see.*

" *'No, I'm fine,' I answered and I was. I opened my eyes and could not understand what was happening. Someone had lowered the ceiling to a couple of feet above my face. I looked towards my feet. There was a light on a wire. I was disorientated. I looked round and found myself staring on to the head of the midwife. Another nurse wheeled in a huge cream machine. There was a parting in the midwife's hair. She had dyed hair and I could see the different colour of her hair growing through. To the left was a hospital screen near where I was lying. I could see over the top and a nurse ran behind the screen and was frantically dialling from the phone that was attached to the wall. I discovered later the phone was not visible from my bed. Then I tried to work out what was happening. I asked myself, 'Have I got a body, have I got a leg to move?'*

"*I was convinced I had as I could sense the outline of my body, just as you can when you shut your eyes when you are awake. I could hear, I could see, I could talk, but no one could hear me, I realized.*

"*I was absolutely at peace, altogether, complete. That 'me' was, however, no longer attached to my body. Then I heard the voice, the same firm male voice who had told me I must ask for help, telling me, 'You must go back.'*

" *'No, I am not going back,' I answered.*

"*Then the voice asked, 'What about your baby?'*

"I had totally forgotten. Then I was reminded of my other two children. 'Yes, of course,' I said. 'I have two other children and a husband.' Eventually I agreed, 'Yes, I suppose I have to go back.'

"As soon as the thought formed, everything went black. I was conscious of a heaviness like weights, like sacks of flour all over me. It was very unclear. The midwife was saying, 'Thank goodness, she's coming round.' In a different tone, she spoke to me, 'Now, Tanya, try and move your leg.' I tried but it was like a ton of bricks. 'Now push.'

"The baby was born. Apparently I had haemorrhaged before the birth and had lost a pint and a half of blood. The placenta had ripped before delivery.

"My experience changed my life. I had no idea until then I had a soul or spirit. I was left with a tremendous yearning and motivation to do something worthwhile with my life. I eventually did a theology degree, though I had three children at the time. I also later took a course in counselling. I felt in need of counselling myself. I vowed to talk about my vision and use it for the benefit of others."

Shared Experiences

Some African tribes calculate a child's birthdate from the day the child was a thought in its mother's mind. The woman sits under a tree and listens to the song of her child. While making love, she and her husband sing the child's song to invite the baby into the world. While pregnant, the woman teaches the song to the midwives, so they can sing the song to welcome the child. Over the years, whenever the child is hurt, the song is sung to comfort her or him. When the child does something wonderful, the song is sung in celebration.

Theresa M. Danna, American author

*I*n the developed world, mothers look nostalgically to a more natural style of mothering when the baby was constantly carried with the mother and was fed at the first stirrings. Studies into so-called primitive mothering were common in the 1960s and 1970s, where babies and young children among the few remaining remote tribes in Central and South America were compared with Caucasian infants in North America.

One study was carried out by T. Berry Brazelton among a tribe of American Indians, the Zinacantecos in south-eastern Mexico.[1] Immediately after birth the baby was placed naked by the fire while protective rituals were performed, and then the infant would be swaddled in the mother's arms in heavy clothing for the first month. Thereafter the baby was carried in a sling on the mother's or another woman's back for the first year, neither being propped up or put on the ground to explore. The baby's face was covered during feeding for the first three months to avert the "evil eye".

The mothers rarely talked or interacted with their children or even made eye contact. Yet the children were blissfully content. During the early weeks these Mexican infants did not have prolonged fits of crying and were generally calm, with fluid transitions between the sleeping and waking states.

The swaddled infants had not practised motor skills spontaneously nor been encouraged by parents in motor skills or experimental play. They were unfamiliar with balls, rattles, cups, spoons and cubes. Nevertheless, when tested the Zinacanteco infants were found to be no more than a month behind American children who had been stimulated since birth. This gap in performance did not widen. By a year old the Zinacanteco children had shown normal mental and physical development in the same stages and in the same order as the American children, although they lagged slightly behind. What was noticeable in all these studies was the lack of anxiety among the Zinacanteco children, except the normal fear of strangers at about nine months. What the children in these studies lacked in curiosity and independence was more than compensated for by their serenity. Even as toddlers they began to assume responsibility for chores and the care of younger siblings. Most remarkable was the total lack of the tearful bedtimes with angry parents and hyperactive, exhausted children seen in some nuclear families in the developed West.

Primitive mothering sounds idyllic, but the fast-disappearing world of the isolated tribes has limited horizons. The passive offspring of the Zinacantecos would not survive in a technological society where a child must be articulate and clued up. The best qualities, the calm feeding times and quiet sleep with the mother intuitively in tune with the child's needs, are found among mothers throughout the developed world in homes where serenity is the predominant quality.

Brazelton also found that the Zinacanteco mothers lactated before the babies cried. This phenomenon also occurs in industrialized societies. In Newcastle upon Tyne in the north-east of England, Rachel underwent a similar experience to that of the

Mexican tribal mothers with her son Jacob, who was born on 2 January 1991.

"Jacob has very irregular night feeds but I find I always wake, leaking milk, just before he begins to stir. This has only happened for the last three weeks. I used to only wake when he was crying. Now he never even whimpers before he is fed.

"At first I leaked milk from both breasts. Now I find I only leak milk from the breast that is due to be used. I only feed from one breast at a time."

Breast Milk and the Psychic Link

Rita Laws from Oklahoma breastfed her three birthchildren and some of her adopted six, so for her the breast-link is of immense importance. Her link was so sensitive that she even produced milk when a child began crying a block away.

"My second birthchild, Eddie, was born in 1982 and was totally breastfed until he was seven months old and did not wean for several years. I returned to my job teaching fifth-grade students when Eddie was eight weeks old and expressed milk at work to give the babysitter. Eddie would cry at irregular intervals during the working day, but intervals which always coincided with my let-down reflexes at work a block away.

"I was a leader in the La Leche League [an international organization set up to promote and support breastfeeding] for four years and have sat in on many meetings when this breast-link was discussed and have heard many women tell similar stories to mine. It is common for many women to admit to having many more psychic experiences while pregnant or nursing. I have heard midwives say that the woman in labour is the most psychic of all people. As her body opens to birth, her sixth sense opens too.

"I remember once I was writing multiplication problems on the

247

blackboard at school when I felt the familiar, let-down tingle in my breasts. Moments later the milk had soaked through. Quickly I gathered the sweater kept on the back of my chair for just such occurrences.

"It was only 10 a.m., minutes after I had expressed several ounces of milk for my three-month-old son. So I was puzzled. I hadn't been thinking about him, hadn't heard him cry, so why the let-down reflex? At noon I raced to the sitter's home, anxious to nurse and cuddle my infant.

"But as I settled down to feeding, the sitter, an elderly woman who thought I was silly to go on nursing, began to complain, 'Your baby cries too much. He wants to be held all the time. Just this morning at ten o'clock he had a crying fit the likes of which I've never seen before.' Now I understood. The baby had needed me and I had responded."

To be certain, Rita decided on an experiment.

"For the next few days, the sitter and I recorded the times of the unexpected let-downs and the inconsolable crying fits. The crying always preceded the gush of milk by five minutes or so.

"I always knew when my babies were about to wake from a nap five minutes before it happened even though the babies napped at different times every day and for varying lengths of times. My doubting husband became convinced after several correct predictions in a row. I found I was no longer able to make any predictions about wake times once the infants grew older, about seven months of age. But until then I was unerringly correct."

Working mothers in other societies share the problem. They respond to the baby's cry for food though they may be miles away and there is no chance of feeding the infant. Odani lives in Sagada, an Igorot village in the mountain region of northern Luzon in the Philippines.

Talking about the birth of her first child, Odani described how, in common with most other Igorot women who farmed, she had to go back to the fields when her son was two months old, leaving the child with his grandmother. She described how sometimes when she was in the fields her breasts would tingle as the ejection reflex occurred. Igorot mothers, she said, believe that this is a sign that miles away in the village the baby is hungry and crying, so, if they possibly can, they hurry home.[2]

As Rita found, the flow had nothing to do with regular feeding times. Vicky, a maths lecturer in Southampton, England, would put her baby to nap in the pram at the end of her long garden during the day. Suddenly Vicky would find that her sweater was wet and she would know the baby was crying though the infant had no regular feed times during the day. Several times when her mother was present, Vicky would be in another room, completely out of sight or earshot of the garden, see her wet sweater and say "The baby is awake", though the baby might have been awake only an hour before. Vicky's mother would not believe her daughter and would creep down the garden to prove the baby was still asleep. But to Grandmother's annoyance as soon as she was within sight of the pram, she would see the baby's mouth opening and closing in rage.

Many mothers do discover that while they are breastfeeding they are exquisitely in tune with an absent infant's needs. Maria, who lives in Victoria, Australia, and knew when Alex was about to swallow a handful of needles (see p. 12), left her baby with a loving grandmother, plus a bottle of breast milk and a dummy. But this was not enough to placate the little fellow.

"When Alex was only a few weeks old, my husband and I decided to go the movies for an outing at night. I was breastfeeding and I expressed milk into a bottle for my mother-in-law to give Alex should he need it. He always took a dummy and so I thought he would accept the bottle. The whole time I was out, about three hours, I felt agitated, restless and totally fidgety. I just wanted to get back to Alex. I didn't know why.

"On our return Alex was beetroot. He had continually screamed. My mother-in-law said he didn't want the bottle and refused his dummy

and just wouldn't settle. As soon as I picked him up he nuzzled into me and wanted a feed. As I fed him and he gave delightful little burps of contentment, it occurred to me that I had literally dumped him and run. So the next time I had to leave him, even though he was only six weeks old, I would 'tell' him what I was doing and where I was going. I'd spend a few minutes holding him and giving him comforting thoughts along the lines of 'Grandma will hold you warm and cosy and loving. Mummy will be back soon. Not long. Mummy loves you.' It worked every time. My mother-in-law couldn't believe it. The monster had turned into an angel.

"Alex and I have such a special relationship, it's just beautiful. He only says about three words (he's sixteen months old) but just knowing I can communicate with him without them is wonderful."

Incidents such as these are not uncommon among mothers and fathers too, says Rita Laws, though she has found mothers reluctant to discuss such incidents openly for fear of ridicule or disbelief. "We as a society should celebrate—not hide—the psychic link which exists between parents and their children of all ages. These invisible bonds are just one more indication of how special the love is between mothers, fathers and their sons and daughters." Rita recalled a similar incident in her own life.

"I was at a rock concert by Hall and Oates in 1985. It was the first time I had ever left my third birthchild, Greg, who was born in the previous September. I was uneasy leaving him but my aunt lived very near to the concert auditorium. I expressed some milk for a bottle and when we left him he was very happy. I had every reason to believe he was fine. I spent the whole concert wanting to phone my aunt but I forced myself not to. I was trying to be practical.

"For two hours I sat on the edge of my seat unable to relax at all and didn't know why. All my senses were on edge but my hearing seemed particularly acute. In fact the music seemed so loud, it was painful. Placing tissue in my ears finally allowed me a little comfort. Then suddenly every muscle in my body relaxed simultaneously. I fell back in

my chair feeling sleepy, removed the tissue from my ears and at last began to enjoy the concert. The last part of the concert was great.

"When my husband arrived and I went to pick up our son, he was sleeping peacefully but my aunt and uncle looked haggard. The baby had screamed for two hours and screamed so loudly it hurt their ears. He had refused the bottle of breastmilk and all of his favourite toys. Then, exhausted, he had fallen into a deep sleep. Mother and son had been linked all along."

It was Rita's third child so it was not simply a question of a new mother's anxiety at leaving her first child for the first time.

Maria Cadaxa, a midwife in Tucson, Arizona, commented: "Regarding nursing, the let-down connection between the nursing pair seems to be universal. I have yet to encounter a mother who has not experienced it at least once. The most common happening is the milk coming in just seconds before the baby's first squeal of hunger, often after a long nap. The timing is so coincidentally precise it can't be just be the interval between feedings causing the let-down as the occurrences span a wide range of time, the milk coming in precisely before the child's waking. Another curious reflex is a mother letting down milk when any child cries, if her own child is not present."

Although breastfeeding seems to strengthen the bond, it is not the only way. Dana Raphael, director of the Human Lactation Center in Westport, Connecticut, who has spent more than thirty-five years observing thousands of mothers and babies, warns against trying to simplify the issues of bonding to a breast vs bottlefeeding dichotomy.

"We are not chickens or goats where, I admit, patterns of relationships seem to depend somewhat on early mother/infant behaviour. We are human beings, not bound by instinct, and appear to be able to fall in love—or bond—even at the age of ninety. I know of mothers who breastfed (promoted these days as a kind of bonding) yet hated their kids and others who bottlefed and had loving relationships—and yet others

who breastfed and hated it but did it and still love the creature that made those early days so unpleasant.

"I know fathers—who do not breastfeed—who were unable to see their child for the first several months yet adore them. And ditto for all the mothers and fathers and children in the less developed countries except they have a harder time because so often mothers must choose which child is to get the little bit of extra food and live and which they must break their hearts over and bury.

"All parents love their children, so how dare we say that village women who breastfeed are any better (at bonding) than the inner city mother who struggles as well?"

From my own work in this field, I have come to the conclusion that it is not necessarily the breast milk per se that facilitates the link. Many of the psychic bonds described in this book occurred with bottlefed babies. The answer may be that breast milk is instant and available so that, given the mother's ability to wake before the infant, the baby suffers no anxiety or frustration in waiting for food to be prepared. Tranquillity at feeding times promotes the quiet connection that encourages psychic communication.

Shared Dreams

A phenomenon of relationships between mother and child where there is a quiet mutual acceptance is in the area of shared dreams or nocturnal telepathy. It can persist for several years, especially occurring if mother or child is experiencing strong emotion. Julia, who lives in Gouting, in South Africa, sent me this passage from her journal dated 23 April 1996. Her daughter became four years old in March 1997.

"I had a dream on Saturday night/Sunday morning that I had left Justine with a babysitter. For some reason I was terribly delayed and knew I just had to get back to Justine. At the moment I woke, Justine

woke. The first thing she said was, 'Mummy, you must not leave me with that babysitter again.'

"After the incident I had to wonder if we have to ability to somehow share thoughts. I suppose it is possible."

Naomi, who lives in north London, saw the world through her infant daughter's eyes in a dream and as a result adapted to the infant's natural rhythms.

"When my daughter was about three weeks old, we both collapsed with sleep on the bed one afternoon. I woke up after a nightmarish dream. In the dream I was being carried around the bedroom so quickly that everything seemed to whirl before my eyes and I felt unbearably dizzy.

"I told my husband who is a psychotherapist and used to talking about dreams. He commented, 'I expect that is what a baby feels like when he or she is carried quickly.'

"I was so shocked that from then on I carried my daughter extremely slowly. I noticed that she and her brother as babies were really happy to be carried slowly and I used to sing songs with slow rhythms to help me remember. Later I became a breastfeeding counsellor, first for the National Childbirth Trust and then the Active Birth Centre and the La Leche League in the UK, so I have a chance to pass on what I have learned whenever it seems relevant.

"When my daughter was about eighteen months old, I was continuing to breastfeed her and we were very close. We spent our days together and I managed to combine nearly everything with her friendly companionship. She was lying asleep and I was in the same room, feeling regretful that it was so long since I had visited Fenton House, a museum of historical keyboards in Hampstead. I had been visiting it since my childhood. My mother's cousin was a professional harpischordist so I used to be allowed to play. I felt myself ache for the sound of the music when suddenly my daughter called out, apparently in her sleep, 'Harpsichord.'

"Even if she had heard me use the word on a previous occasion, it was

way beyond her vocabulary of everyday words at the time. I am sure she did not even know what a harpsichord was. I can only think that some kind of telepathy must have operated between us. When she was nine, my daughter took up the study of the classical harp, was accepted at one of the few music schools in Britain and eventually read twentieth-century music at the University of Sussex."

Some mothers share their children's daytime visions. Vivien Greene, the widow of the late novelist Graham Greene, is herself a woman of great insight and sensitivity. She told me the following story at her home in Oxfordshire, where she has among other treasures a renowned collection of Victorian doll's houses. Vivien's house is a delight. She has placed crystals in the windows so that they catch the light and throughout the year throw rainbow patterns across the floor.

"When my son Francis was between three and four years old, we were living in Oxford. Francis slept in a bed with dropside cot rails on either side. One evening I was putting him to sleep when he suddenly became distressed and told me, 'I don't like the little man at the bottom of my bed.'"

"I saw momentarily what my son was seeing, the top half of an elf or gnome with a malevolent spiteful face, standing there. Then, as quickly, the creature was gone and there was just a pile of brown blankets at the end of the bed. I moved them. 'See, darling, it was just the blankets frightening you,' I reassured the child.

"He never mentioned the little man again, but for that flash I had shared my son's terrifying vision."

In a reversal of this situation, the fears of Donata from Ohio were transmitted to her daughter Hope so strongly that the child conjured them up. Donata described how Hope shared not only Donata's feelings but the contents of an adult book, of which Donata had not spoken, long before she could read.

"I was reading a novel about a black slave woman forced to kill one of her own children to save the baby from a worse fate at the hands of the slave traders. The child's ghost haunts the mother's heart and home. I only read a few chapters that night before I felt too much sympathy for the woman. Agitated, I went upstairs to lie down with Hope. I wanted to be close to her, to feel the safety of her presence while I remembered other mothers throughout history who sacrificed their precious children in the name of love.

"The next morning Hope was very agitated about a ghost in the house. She checked all the cupboards and chatted endlessly about it. I realized my preoccupation with the novel's theme had been transmitted to my little girl.

"We quickly read a benign story about a friendly little ghost who eventually finds just the right home. This defused the ghost issue in our house and I learned a valuable lesson about Hope's perceptive abilities."

Beatrice, a member of the La Leche League in Düssnang in Switzerland, had a similar experience with her daughter Annika, her third child. When Annika was four and a half years old in early 1991 she was still being breastfed twice a day. One evening Beatrice broke her usual habit and watched a TV film about a mass murderer. Before long she was quite upset by it and went to bed. The next morning she and Annika were silently breast-feeding, a ritual they used to tune themselves in to the new day. "But my thoughts were bleak as they ran over last night's film and I began wondering if the front door was locked," said Beatrice. "A wave of fear began to spread over me. Suddenly Annika let go of the breast and with wide eyes said: 'Mami, I am terribly afraid. Let's go down in the kitchen.' I wonder how much of my feelings were transmitted directly through the act of breastfeeding?"

255

Natural Parenting

Some parents deliberately strive to emulate natural "primitive" mothering practices. In one case, although both parents provided an unhurried environment, it was the mother's mind that young Holly seemed able to read. Her father Tom, who lives in British Columbia, has studied both Native North American and Mexican birth and child-rearing practices. He and his wife wholeheartedly endorse the relaxed approach which he says should start right from the time of birth.

"It's amazing what one can learn simply from not meddling in natural functions. The birth of my daughter Kitty was so quick, easy and wonderful and Kitty herself was such an amazing creature, everything I thought I knew about birth and about babies had to be discarded. I've since had many opportunities to confirm that what I observed and experienced was in no way abnormal; quite the contrary. My daughter Holly's birth and childhood, though much different from Kitty's, further enhanced my understanding of what is normal and what isn't.

"Medical professionals and most parents just look at me strangely if I mention that my children didn't cry at birth, that they had only breast milk for the first six months, that they never tasted 'babyfood', that they never fussed, threw tantrums or otherwise misbehaved, that there was never a time to eat or go to bed and that we never owned a crib, a buggy, a walker or a stroller.

"I clearly remember how both Kitty and Holly responded to thoughts from me when they were still tiny babies and I especially remember when Holly's mother told me of something astonishing that occurred one evening.

"Holly must have been between one and two; she had her own little sleeping space then, near to her mum but separated by a partition. She had gone to bed and was singing to herself as she often did, while her mum picked up a book to read. The book was about Switzerland. Holly

stopped singing, then quietly but very clearly said 'Switzerland'. For several minutes, Holly continued to pronounce words that her mother came across as she turned the pages. Then Holly apparently fell asleep and that was the end of it.

"I've always wondered how common it might be, perhaps only occurring where bonding has not been compromised or perhaps occurring but not noticed where bonding is poor. Scientifically dismissible, I expect, until such time as 'hard evidence' is produced."

PART SEVEN

Maternal Sacrifice

Mothers Who Risk Their Lives for Their Children

I do think mothers have this special strength in times of danger. The power of the maternal instinct is incredible.
Julie from Yorkshire, who saved her baby from beneath the wheels of a lorry

Mothers show incredible courage and altruism when their young are threatened, and find seemingly superhuman strength to protect their children. Is this an automatic gut reaction or is there a moment when the mother consciously decides "my life for my child's"?

I faced this decision quite suddenly with my youngest son. Not long after he started school, I had taken Bill and his elder sister Miranda to a paddling pool across the road from the beach so that they could try out their new small inflatable boat. The children took turns at sitting and pulling the boat along on its rope. After a while they wanted ice creams, and we went over to the beach to eat them. I told them that when they had finished they could paddle and make sandcastles at the water's edge, but that they must not play in the boat as they had on the paddling pool, because it could easily be carried out to sea.

The tiny boat was on the shore not far from where we were sitting. I had a really bad headache and, confident that the children were safe, I closed my eyes just for a minute. How often accidents happen in that single minute of inattention. The beach was quiet in the early evening. I opened my eyes two or three minutes later to see Miranda running up the beach towards me, crying. The children had taken the boat to the edge of the water and decided to tow it with them through the shallows as they paddled. Bill had climbed in to retrieve their spade, which was in the boat, and at that moment a gust of wind had carried the boat away from the shore.

Swept by the tide, the boat was fast floating out to sea. Bill was not panicking as he did not realize the danger. I looked around but there was no one on the beach. I am a very poor swimmer and am afraid of water. I knew that I had no chance of swimming out to the boat and getting it back to shore against the current. Then, too, there was the risk that Miranda would follow me and drown, and probably Bill also. Equally I knew quite calmly that there was no choice and that I could not leave my son alone while I ran for help, because at any moment a wave could turn the boat over, or he could try to climb out as he was carried further out to sea.

I told Miranda to run for help and, taking off my shoes, began to wade into the waves. The sea was very cold. I fixed my eyes on Bill and carried on wading. I was above my waist in water when I turned for signs of Miranda returning and saw a teenager and his father on the beach. The teenager saw the boat, swam out and pulled Bill to shore. If he had not come to the rescue, if he had not been a strong swimmer, would I have continued to walk to my death? Should I have left the other children motherless when I could not save Bill? Could I have lived with myself if I had not tried?

Julie, who lives in Yorkshire, showed incredible strength and courage in saving her son Reece's life. And there was no instant happy ending. Julie not only endured great physical suffering after saving fourteen-month-old Reece from being crushed by the wheels of a juggernaut, but was temporarily rejected by the very child for whom she almost died.

Julie was trapped by her skirt under the wheel of a lorry as it suddenly pulled away from the kerb. Reece would also have been crushed had Julie not held the pushchair away from the wheels as she was being dragged along. Throughout her agony, Julie's thoughts were for Reece and her first question as she was dragged, crushed and semi-conscious, from beneath the lorry was: "Is Reece all right?"

Julie told me: "All I felt was that I wanted to get Reece out of the way of the lorry. I suppose I did have a special strength that day I don't normally have. I wasn't bothered about myself. All I thought was I'd got to save Reece and all I thought about even afterwards through all the pain was my baby. I do think mothers have this special strength in times of danger. The power of the maternal instinct is incredible."

It was not until Julie was at the hospital and had been shown her son well and unscratched that she could allow herself to face her own dreadful injuries and the fear she might lose her leg. It took five months of painful treatment to save the limb but, Julie explained, her suffering was worthwhile. "Reece was a very special baby, my first child and very much wanted. It must have been that. I just couldn't have lost him. It's surprising what you can do if your child's life is threatened. If it's your child, I don't know what it is but something comes out of you and you just do what you have to do. To save my son from what I've been through, I'd do it again tomorrow."

But Reece had been frightened at the sight of his mother swathed in bandages while she was in hospital. His last memories of her were of the day of the accident, of blood, noise, fear and her apparent desertion of him. He was too young to understand his mother's sacrifice.

Julie's mother looked after Reece while her daughter was in hospital. When Julie hobbled back through the front door for what she hoped was to be the happy re-union, Reece clung, screaming, to his grandmother. It was not until some weeks later after endless tantrums and tears that Reece climbed on to her lap and cuddled her for the fist time since the accident.

Conny, a thirty-three-year-old mother from Schilde, Belgium, also displayed seemingly superhuman strength in saving her six-year-old daughter Lindsy from almost certain death in 1997. Mother and daughter were on the chairlift that links the French alpine skiing resorts of Auris-en-Oisans and Alpe-d'Huez. As the chairlift set off, Lindsy slipped from her seat. In that split second, Conny caught hold of a piece of Lindsy's ski-suit. She knew that if she let go or moved, her daughter would plunge to the rocky ground thirty feet below. She kept her precarious grip on the four-stone child, who was weighed down with heavy boots and skis, but she did not have the strength to pull Lindsy back to safety.

The ski-lift stopped 150 yards from the start, but no one could reach the child. Conny tried to reassure her terrified daughter, but she could feel her own strength ebbing away. Below her she could see the rough terrain where people were frantically placing blankets and anoraks to cushion Lindsy's fall.

Conny heard shouts of "Hold on, the helicopter is coming", but could feel her daughter's hand becoming limp. "Hold on," she begged the child. "Help is almost here." Conny knew Lindsy was slipping from her grasp.

"Mummy, I'm tired," Lindsy whispered. "I'm going to fall. Goodbye, Mummy."

These words gave Conny almost superhuman strength, making her forget the agonizing cramp in her arms. The ski-lift attendant scaled a pylon and worked his way along the cable to the mother and child. There he managed to attach himself underneath the chair with safety ropes and helped Conny to support her daughter until help came.

Afterwards Conny commented: "Luckily I was slightly wedged in place by the safety bar. But when the lift operator arrived it was just in time as my own strength was exhausted. I heard the sound of the helicopter but I didn't dare look up. I didn't dare move. Then I saw a man dangling from a rope and in an instant I found myself sitting free of strain with Lindsy safe and sound beside me."

The ordeal had lasted ten minutes. It seemed like a lifetime to Lindsy and Conny.

From where do mothers get this extra strength and courage? Biological surges of adrenalin are partly responsible for the immediacy and intensity of response, but in such cases something beyond

264

the physical would seem to be involved. Julie says that she believes she was given special power to save Reece.

Marie Osmond, the American singer, saved her children from almost certain death on a singing tour and is convinced that her guardian angel helped her. Marie and her children were travelling overnight on the tour bus and had settled into their bunks and fallen asleep. Suddenly Marie was aware of something trying to wake her and thought it was one of her children. But they were still asleep. She then heard the voice telling her to go to the front of the bus at once. There she found the driver slumped across the wheel and the bus about to leave the road and crash into a huge snowdrift.

With strength inexplicable in physical terms for such a small woman, Marie managed to drag the driver, who had lapsed into diabetic insulin shock, away from the wheel on to the floor, and bring the huge vehicle back on to the road. All this she did in seconds. Marie attributes the warning and her strength to her guardian angel who she believes protects her family.

It may be that people are interpreting the same power in terms that are meaningful to themselves. Mother love and protectiveness exist on many levels, although most often they manifest themselves in physical terms. Whether it is due to an external or internal impetus or both, it is the mother who places herself between her child and sometimes overwhelming danger. Perhaps it is not too fanciful to imagine that when a mother calls for help to any deity or angel her plea is heard, since she asks not for herself but for her child.

In Texas, two mothers between them defied the power of a tornado to protect their young. On 27 May 1997, the tornado killed twenty-eight people and tore houses from their foundations in Jarrell, Texas. They and their six children were the only ones in their immediate vicinity to survive.

Twenty-nine-year-old Maria had only seconds to save her children at 3 p.m. when she saw a half-mile-long black mass hurtling towards her home. Gabriel, her husband, who had built a storm shelter under the kitchen, was at work. Maria seized her small children Gabriel, Jimmy and baby Mariel just as her neighbour Rosa and her three young daughters also came rushing into the house to seek refuge because they did not have a storm shelter.

Maria pulled the door off the storm cellar underneath the house and helped everyone inside. She then pulled the door across.

As she did so, the tornado hit her home, ripping the house apart. Dust and debris poured through the cracks between the boards of the door, so that the women and their children were choking. Worse still, the door to the cellar was torn open by the force and slammed shut. This happened four or five times.

Maria realized that if the door was ripped off, they would all be sucked into oblivion. She screamed to Rosa and the two women perched on the swaying ladder, trying with all their might to hold the door shut against the force of the tornado. They did so, it seems, by their overwhelming will to protect their terrified children. At last the mothers fell back, holding the children, and the door remained shut, wedged by debris. They were rescued when the storm had passed.

Dying for a Child

In the cases described above the mother's decision to save was almost instantaneous, prompted by an immediate external threat, invoking some deep primeval protective instinct. But what if the sacrifice involves deliberation, so that the mother has to live with the consequences of her altruism over months or even years, knowing that death will eventually claim her as the price for sparing her child?

Gertrude lived with her mother on the eastern borders of Germany during the Second World War. With the prospect of an Allied victory came the news that the Russians were advancing, bringing the threat of a ruthless occupation. There was a car leaving the village for the west and only one vacant seat. Gertrude did not want to leave her mother behind to an uncertain fate, perhaps even death. She wanted them to face the future together and if necessary share their last moments.

However, her mother insisted that her daughter go while there was still a chance of freedom and a new life. She told Gertrude: "I am old and I have lived my life. Now it is your turn. So go with my blessing."

Gertrude did reach freedom, but could get no news of her mother in the occupied territory. At last she heard that her mother had died. Gertrude felt great guilt that she had left her mother behind, which did not lessen as she built a successful life for herself in the US.

Many years later, Gertrude's mother came to her in a dream, embraced her daughter and told her, "It's all right". Though the words were simple, Gertrude said that they were the blessing she needed on her life. She no longer felt guilty because she now knew that her mother approved of what she had made of her opportunities.

Anita, who lives in south-east England, postponed cancer treatment in 1995 to give birth to her baby, knowing her action was potentially fatal. She was seventeen weeks pregnant with Hannah when tests confirmed she had cervical cancer. A consultant advised Anita to terminate the pregnancy and have a hysterectomy, but was unable to guarantee that this would destroy the cancer.

Anita was determined to continue with the pregnancy. She said: "I had heard Hannah's heart beat and seen it move on the screen. If the doctors had told me that I was going to die the day after giving birth to Hannah, I would still have gone ahead with the pregnancy."

She gave birth by Caesarean and afterwards had a hysterectomy. A week after Hannah's birth Anita started chemotherapy and radiotherapy and the treatment appeared to be successful. But as the family was preparing to celebrate Hannah's first birthday in August 1996, a biopsy showed an aggressive malignant tumour. Anita was told her body could not take any further treatment and she had about two years to live.

Anita described her emotions: "At first I just screamed. I am thirty-two years old and have two children. I asked God, 'What have I done to deserve this?' But I really do believe now that I gave my own life for Hannah. If somebody had told me two years ago this was what was going to happen, I would not have done it any differently. I have given my partner his baby and my other daughter the sister she always wanted. I still get days when I sit and cry that I am not going to be with my baby when she goes to school. But I do believe that there's a God and that when I die I am going to heaven and will be able to see my daughters grow up."

The Little Lights of Japan

Atushi, my friend who lives near Tokyo, sent an account of the "little lights of the future" who were protected by their mothers from Japan's worst earthquake since the Second World War. The earthquake, which struck Kobe city and the surrounding area on 17 January 1995, registered 7.2 on the Richter scale and left 6,309 people dead, 43,177 injured and more than 234,000 homeless. But in January 1995 one newspaper described how "In the chaos, new lives are being born one after the other."

It cited the case of Kazuko Miyoshi, who was living at Hiramtsu-cho in the Hyogo prefecture. Mrs Miyoshi, who was eight months pregnant, was warming herself in the apartment block and chatting with her family and a friend. Suddenly the quake struck. There was a rumbling of the earth and violent shaking. The woman threw herself forward, instinctively lying down and bending over to protect the child in her stomach from the blast.

Miraculously, it seems, she was unhurt although her friend who remained seated on the floor was seriously injured and four people close by were killed. Afterwards she said: "It may be the baby in my womb that saved my life. The reason I instinctively lay down at that moment was to protect the baby in my belly." That action saved her life. The ceiling came down and she lay in the darkness unable to move until neighbours made a hole and rescued her three hours later.

Hiroko Kakinomoto believes that, had she not been late in giving birth to her child, her tiny son might not have survived the earthquake. Mrs Kakinomoto had been at her parents' home in preparation for giving birth. The ground floor of the two-storeyed house collapsed. Mrs Kakinomoto, who was sleeping on the first floor, immediately crept on to the bedding to protect herself from falling objects. Her husband who had been sleeping by her side covered and shielded her.

Since she was four days beyond the expected date of her confinement, she was taken to the obstetric and gynaecological clinic near Nishinomiya Station for safety. At 10.30 on the night of 17 January, the day of the earthquake, the labour pains started. Two hours later she gave birth to a baby boy. In her hospital room, Mrs Kakinomoto, holding the newly born baby in her arms, smiled calmly and commented to reporters: "It was a good thing that he was born past the expected date. Otherwise I could not have had the confidence to protect this little life safe and sound."

These births were taken as symbols of hope in the midst of despair. The mothers instinctively protected their infants in the womb in a quiet way, offering stillness and shelter amidst the shaking world. I can understand why they are regarded as heroines and their infants as little lights of the future.

Whether remaining quiet and calm in the epicentre of an earthquake, preventing a child from falling when every muscle is screaming to let go, holding back a tornado or watching a beloved child take the last passage to freedom, human mothers, like Kipling's Mother Wolf, will go to the brink and beyond to preserve the life they brought into the world.

Devoted Mothers

I shall never forget my mother. She implanted in me and nurtured the first seed of good. She opened my soul to the lessons of Nature. She aroused my interest and enlarged my ideas. What she taught me has had an everlasting and blessed influence on my life.

Immanuel Kant

Mother Love in Times of Social and Economic Hardship

Until after the Second World War and the establishment of more formal systems of welfare benefits in the industrialized world, many mothers struggled, especially during periods of high unemployment in the 1920s and 1930s, to keep families fed and clothed. I have spoken to several women who are now in their seventies and eighties who can recall the hardships endured by their mothers. Such accounts are not sentimental but reflect that what is called now "quality mothering" came second to more practical considerations. However, in times of crisis, many mothers would give up everything for their children. Vera, who lives in Essex, described how her mother refused to give up, even when the doctors said there was no hope of Vera's recovery.

"My mother is responsible for my life in more ways than one. When I was two years of age, I was in the London Hospital with corneal ulcers in both eyes. I was in there for six weeks, with my eyes bandaged. Children were not allowed visitors but my mother was told that if she came during

the evenings, if I was asleep, she would be allowed to look at me. On only one occasion was I asleep and my mother was very shocked to see my eyes bandaged. She continued to visit every night, even though there was little hope she would be admitted.

"After six weeks I was sent home as I cried so much for my mother. Nurse called twice daily to administer drops. My mother nursed me all that time, not letting me cry as this would have counteracted the effect of the drops.

"Several weeks after that Mother had to take me every day to the London Hospital for a special mercury vapour lamp treatment that was only obtainable from that hospital. We had a bus ride, about twenty minutes each way, and a long wait at the hospital, all for one minute a day, increasing to five by the end of the year. Money was very scarce, so my mother went without food to pay the fares. She was told that the treatment was vital for my whole nervous system, as corneal ulcers are caused by a virus. She saved my sight.

"But my troubles were not over, nor was her infinite patience exhausted. Five years later, following chicken pox, I was completely paralyzed, unable to do anything at all for six months, could only speak in a whisper. I also went blind in one eye. Doctors at the time had never seen anything like my symptoms and thought it was either meningitis, cerebral palsy, poliomyelitis or polioneuritis. Only a few months ago, when I was referred to a neurologist as the aches and pains I have suffered since childhood are now getting worse with age, it was finally diagnosed as inflammation of the brain following chicken pox. I was told this is extremely rare and that I am lucky to be alive as people almost invariably used to die with this condition.

"After spending six months in hospital, I was sent home and the doctors did not expect me ever to walk again. My mother rubbed me all over every night with warm oil and bought me a skipping rope, hoping it would encourage me to get my feet off the ground. It worked and after I had been home a year the hospital sent to see whether I was still alive. Three doctors examined me and said it was a miracle. They could not understand how I could walk. I did. It was my mother's love made me better. I can remember all of it, including *standing in my cot, shaking the bars and screaming for my mother.*

"When I was nine years old, my mother thought I should have a piano, although I never asked for one or showed any signs of wanting to learn. She had no money to buy me a piano but gave her new blue leather three-piece suite with six matching dining chairs in exchange. After the first lesson my parents could not keep me away from the instrument, but they took a great risk and gave away all they had of value for that piano.

"My mother passed on last year aged ninety and since then her sisters have told me the reason she wanted me to have a piano was because she had been afraid I would never walk again. She hoped that if I could learn to play and teach, I could earn a living.

"I have been a teacher of music for over forty years and had my first pupil when I was only fourteen. Recently I held a musical soirée at my local theatre."

Vera's mother left a letter, revealing that Vera's success had made her own dreams come true.

"When I was a little girl, I always wanted to learn to play the piano and used to peep into people's parlours. If I saw a piano, I thought they must be rich because we were very poor and I knew we could never own one.

"After I grew up and went to work, I remember having a dream. When I looked in the dream book I possessed to find the interpretation, it was that a child would be born to me who would live by brain work. I made a joke about it and said to my friend that it would not happen to me.

"As the years went by, I married and had a baby daughter. When Vera was one year old, my mother bought a piano, hoping my sisters, who were then working, would learn to play. They did not have the inclination or patience to practise so my mother wanted to sell it.

"By this time my daughter was about eight years old and I thought it would be a dream come true for me if Vera could learn to play the piano. I did not have any money to pay for the instrument, so I asked my mother if she would take my front room furniture, which I had only just finished

paying for, in exchange for the piano. My mother was delighted.

"I was so happy to know that I was going to possess a piano at last, especially to have my young daughter play it. Vera started lessons as soon as we could arrange them and I never needed to tell her to practise. She loved the piano from the start.

"After only a few months war came and my daughter missed her lessons during the war years, but she carried on practising and taught herself. After the war ended, Vera found a school of music and paid for her own lessons. She passed exams and won certificates for playing in music festivals. Vera is now a teacher of music and I am very proud of her achievements after years of hard brain work. So you see my dream really did come true."

Pat, who lives on the Isle of Wight, is now eighty years old herself. Her mother Flo, like many women living around the turn of the century, rarely showed any physical affection towards her family, a legacy that left Pat with a fierce determination to demonstrate her love in kisses and cuddles to her own children and grandchildren. Flo's life, however, was devoted to her family and it was through duty and hard work that she expressed the love that could not be spoken.

Pat told me about her early life:

"I was born on 21 April 1917 in Southall, Middlesex. During the 1920s things were hard and my dad would walk for miles, searching for work, sometimes earning just a couple of shillings labouring on a building site, which he would bring home to Mum.

"Mum worked cleaning for a lady. One dinner hour when I was eight or nine, the lady of the house was giving my mother a box of Quaker Oats. 'Oh good,' I said, 'now we can have porridge because we haven't anything for dinner, have we, Mum?'

"My mother was furious and when we were going home, turned on me quite fiercely. 'Don't you ever tell people we haven't got anything for dinner. That's our business. We don't want anyone feeling sorry for us.'

"Mum had been one of nine children. My maternal grandmother

died when she was thirty-four in Lambeth. There were eight girls and one boy. He was called up in the war when he was seventeen and was dead in six months. When their mother died, my mother was only nine years old and the children were farmed out among the relatives. If the family had not taken the children in, the children would have been put in the orphanage or workhouse. It was considered a terrible thing to see your relatives in an orphanage. All the cousins and aunts took a child.

"After she was nine, Mum rarely went to school as she had to look after the little children in her new home and do the chores. Mum was treated like a little skivvy. They were hard times, but she was grateful even for the little she had. 'The family was very good to take us in. We were extra mouths to feed. If we had not been cared for, we would have been beaten and not given enough to eat in the Poor House,' she said.

"Many of the mothers of my own mother's generation, the late Victorian and early Edwardian period, were stoical and self-sacrificing, but their hard lives meant there was little energy or inclination for loving children in a physical way. There were no retirement pensions. People worked until they died. I can remember when my aunt Lizzie had a stroke when she was seventy-five, her sisters were upset that she would never be able to work again. Until her stroke she scrubbed the steps at Whitehall every morning.

"When my mother was fourteen, she and her elder sister Elsie were sent back to live with her father. Elsie went out to work but my mother had to take care of the house. My grandfather was a very harsh man and kept my mother working day and night. Once when she was fourteen she was given a penny to buy a bloater for her father's tea. She cooked it and was keeping it warm on a covered plate by the fire. It smelled so good and she was so hungry she took a little bit to eat. When her father discovered what she had done, he beat her black and blue with a broomstick. When Mum's sister came home and saw the bruises, she threatened to report him if he touched Flo again. Mum defended her father's actions in later life and said, 'He was hungry too.'

"Before they were married, my father came to take Mum out one Saturday night and was told that she could not come as she had to scrub the downstairs and the back passage. 'I'll help you, mate,' my father *replied. He tied a piece of sacking round his waist and scrubbed with her until it was done. My mother and father always called each other mate, although they showed no physical affection towards each other in front of us.*

"We children never kissed our parents good night. I never sat on my mother's knee even when I was very small. I recall standing behind my mother as a child when she sat in a low chair and creeping as close to her as I could. My mother would smile at me, but would never put her arm around me. I can still remember the ache of wanting her to hold me, especially one occasion when I was three or four years old. I was sitting on a low chair by the iron bars of the grate. I got up and stood behind Mum as close as possible, willing her to turn round and cuddle me. Dad was sitting in his chair and she winked at Dad, making fun of me. My injured pride leaped into action. I stepped away.

"Being a good mother—which she was—meant for her bringing in enough money so that we children would have enough food, decent clothes, and that we were respectable. I think she and my father simply did not know how to show love. They had been brought up in a harsh, cruel world where survival was of the fittest and in their consuming struggle to bring up their family and put on a front to the world, they did what they saw as right.

"I can still vividly feel the pain of my mother going to work and having to leave me when I was about three years old. A friend of hers used to take care of me. I can still recall one afternoon standing on a chair while my mother was dressing me and telling my mother that I did not want to go because the two girls at the house had smacked me. Mum promised me that she would sort it out but she deposited me at the gate as usual and did not even kiss me goodbye. I was only three years old.

"Once I was old enough to go to school Mum had to go to work at eight o'clock and my sister and I made bread and dripping before school. In the evening, if we were lucky there were scraps of meat to make a potato pie that was heated up in the neighbour's oven for when my brother got home, because Mum was still out working. If not we made penny Oxo gravy to dip in bread for dinner.

"One great trauma has remained in my mind from those early years,

although I know my mother did not act out of malice. Every Sunday afternoon, my mother would get bread and margarine ready for our tea. She and my father would then go down to the Labour Hall for a drink and not get back until about ten o'clock at night. This would happen winter and summer. On Sunday afternoon I would look at the clock and watch Mum crimping her hair with curling tongs and I would start to cry because I dreaded being left. 'Now don't you start,' she would say to my sister and myself and then the door would close and the house fall silent. I can still picture us two little girls. My sister would sit at the top of the stairs and I would sit at the bottom, rocking myself and feeling utterly lonely and deserted. I felt it when I was five and I still felt it when I was ten when they went out of that door Sunday after Sunday.

"When we were younger, my sister and I did not have a close relationship. My sister would leave me a few minutes after my parents had gone out and go to her friend's house for tea. My brother would be off with his friends. I would wander round the recreation ground and go to the bandstand. I would see the other mums and dads with their children. I was on my own. Always on my own. Even today, although I am eighty, on Sundays I still feel lonely about 5 p.m. and try to spend the time with someone. Even today hearing a band playing in a bandstand fills me with sorrow and loneliness. How could my mother have left me at five years old? Sunday was their only day off, their only time together and they loved going for long walks alone.

"Mum and Dad would light the gas in the kitchen summer and winter so I could put on the lights when it was dark. I would come into the downstairs flat where we lived. One autumn Sunday when I was not very old, my sister was supposed to be in by seven o'clock. It was dark and Mum and Dad had forgotten to light the gas. I sat by the stove in the darkness and sobbed. In those days people kept themselves to themselves. Eventually my mother and father came home and said they were sorry for not lighting the gas. The neighbours came down to tell them that I had been crying in the dark. Mum made me a cup of cocoa, to make it up to me.

"With the birth of my young brother Billy, however, the most incredible change came over my parents. I was ten when Billy was

born. My mother had a good job and there was more money. We children were told nothing, but we could see Mum getting bigger. Mum was sweeping the floor in the kitchen. Suddenly she bent double with pain. 'Let me do that,' Dad said and tried to take the broom. Mum snatched it back in anger and insisted on finishing the cleaning. Everything had to be nice.

"My sister, brother and myself were sent out for the day. When we got home the neighbours were all in the house admiring the new baby. Suddenly we saw a different side to Mum. Baby Billy had a bath every night with his own special soap that was expensive and we were not allowed to use. And there was my father too drying the baby in a towel. They both cuddled and fussed over Billy in a way they never did with the rest of us. Only the best was good enough for Billy. The rest of us had a bath once a week in the tin bath, my brother, then my sister and then me, so by the time it got to me the water was pretty dirty. What is amazing is that we felt no resentment towards Billy and he turned out a lovely person. When Billy was born, my mother gave up work to be with him. Billy had grapenuts cereal which was very expensive, like children in well-off families. We were pleased for him.

"My mother adored the boys and we girls always had to take the back seat. But it never occurred to us to feel deprived. It was the way the world was. However, Reg, the eldest, never got cuddled by Mum, though he could have anything he wanted.

"It is hard for people in the modern world to understand but my mother was devoted to us. She once saved up for three weeks so I could have a birthday party. We had bread with real butter and jelly and custard. The local children had never tasted butter before. I only ever had one party but I have never forgotten it. She and my dad were also very proud of anything we did. Once they made me a special costume for the school play. I was sick for a rehearsal and had the part taken off me. My mother wrote to the school and insisted I was given my part back. It was unheard of to question a teacher but I was in the play and Mum and Dad came and clapped and cheered. Mum was so proud of me.

"When I was fourteen, my mum took me down to the local factory where I got a job making sausages. I didn't like it but I hadn't expected to. When you were fourteen you said goodbye to childhood and grew up overnight. I was there for four weeks. One day I came home with my skirt stained with salty water which had dried on me. Before I could change Dad came home and shouted at my mum, 'What are you doing, letting her work up there? You go up there in the morning and get her wages. She's not going back.'

"That was the first of many jobs, mainly in factories. When I was fifteen, I had a chance to be a telephone operator but I would receive no pay for thirteen weeks while I was training. My mother said I could not take the job and I understood. There was no way she could manage without my money. My dad said nothing, but walked out of the room. He felt he had let me down.

"My mother was a natural fighter and had no time for the finer feelings of life, but she taught me courage and endurance under hardship and never to complain if life was less than perfect. Dad died first and my mum moved to a little bedsitter in Southall in London.

"When I first went to see Mum's new home, I was appalled that she was reduced to a single room, but she was desperate to the end to keep her independence and not live with her children or become a burden. Mum had her 'bits of furniture' as she called them and kept everything neat and shiny. She was happy there. She used to come and see me for three weeks at Christmas, Easter and the summer. Every day, on her doctor's orders, she walked two miles, a mile along Southall High Street to the Black Dog public house for a Guinness and then home for another one. Mum would regularly have her Darts Club night.

"At Christmas, my mother cut herself on a plant pot just before coming down to stay with me. She had a bad cut and I took her to the doctor. The next day Mum developed a sore throat and became very ill. She was admitted to hospital with tetanus. I went to see her and she told me that she was content because she had had a really good life.

"I could not believe my ears. 'Mum, how can you say that after all you have endured?' I protested.

" 'I had a husband who was one of the best. I lost my boy in the war but I have had a good life, good children and cannot complain.'

"My heart went out to her because she had tried so hard and had so

278

little reward from life. I held her hand. 'Don't feel lonely, Mum. I'll visit you tomorrow and you'll soon be home. Before you go to sleep, sing "Lord, Keep Us Safe this Night".' This was a hymn we used to sing at church. 'No,' she replied, 'I'll sing "Gracious Spirit of thy Goodness" instead.'

"The next morning, I woke at five o'clock and could not get back to sleep. I felt restless and uneasy and went downstairs to make a cup of tea. I was not surprised when the police came at 6 a.m. to inform me Mum had died at five o'clock.

"When I went to the hospital, the sister of the ward told me that my mother had a lovely death. In the early hours of the morning Mum had told one of the nurses that she was thirsty. By the time the nurse returned with a drink, my mother had died of a heart attack. Her death had been instantaneous. She deserved that at least.

"We had arranged the funeral for the Wednesday. On the Tuesday evening the funeral director told us that it could not go ahead as there had to be an inquest. Everyone was coming, the flowers had been ordered, so I asked the pastor if we could have a memorial service instead and leave the flowers in the church as it would have been such a waste. Flowers came from people we had never heard of, including wreaths from several public houses near Mum's home. The following week there were only three of us at the funeral. We took flowers and to our great pleasure more flowers arrived from the hostelries.

"When I went to London after the funeral I visited the Black Dog and was told what a lovely lady my mother was. At closing time in the afternoon she would gather the ash trays and wipe down the tables. Old habits die hard.

"Since Mum's death I have detected her presence. We used to run a social club next to our house. When Mum came to stay, she would sit on the high stool at the far end of the bar. Once everyone had gone home, we would have a quiet drink, myself on the other side of the bar and my husband and mother on the stools. A little while after her death, my husband Bill was on his usual stool when Mum's stool, which was next to his, started rocking furiously. 'Our mum's here,' he told me and we knew she had joined us as usual."

What moved me particularly about Pat's story was the very human qualities her mother displayed, strengths such as altruism and dedication marred by physical coldness. Flo was a woman who, Pat said, made sure that the family never went hungry but left her young daughter alone Sunday after Sunday. It is perhaps significant that when family finances improved, Flo felt able to cuddle and express physical love for baby Billy.

No other human office, not even the priesthood, is expected to display such high ideals in the real world as that of motherhood. Society past and present is quick to condemn any deviation from perfection by mothers, yet may offer little in terms of practical support, especially to those who are of lower economic status. The neighbours heard young Pat crying alone in the dark flat, but did not come to help her, nor did they offer Pat's exhausted mother a few hours' relief while they watched the children. Some modern neighbours are more likely to phone the social services to report the mother than to offer support when the situation reaches crisis point.

Pat considers her mother a good one and Pat herself became a warm, empathic person, a successful mother and grandmother. If child abuse and delinquency are on the increase in the West despite the plethora of psychiatrists, social workers and parenting experts it may be that the qualities of patience, hard work and stoicism of women such as Flo were worthy of admiration.

Devoted Mothers Today

Has there been a decline in devoted mothers, caring for sick or disabled children or struggling to make ends meet on meagre benefits? Caring, self-sacrificing mothers are still numerous, but they rarely make the headlines, the women who scrimp and save so that their child can go on a school trip, who take night jobs out of economic necessity so that they can be with a young child during the day. Career women may be passed over for promotion because they insist on staying at home with a sick child and having time off to see their children in school plays. They may give up a lucrative job since they are unwilling to hand over the daily care of their child to outsiders. There is no doubt that child abuse and neglect are given more prominence as more newsworthy than good child care. However, occasionally a dedicated mother does make the front page. Atushi, who is in his seventies and lives near Tokyo, sent me the following account of a mother who donated part of her own body in an attempt to save her son's life. In May 1996 a newspaper reported that the first intestinal transplant from a living donor in Japan was conducted on 17 May at the National Kyoto University Hospital. The mother, aged thirty-one, had one metre of her small intestine, almost a quarter of its length, removed and given to her young son. Most of the boy's small intestine had been removed earlier because of necrosis which meant he could not obtain nourishment from meals. Although the boy may not live long after the operation, his mother was prepared to sacrifice part of her own body for the chance he might survive. The mother was with her son the whole time he was hospitalized until the night before their operation, when she had to be confined to her own room.

On the morning of the operation, the mother visited her son and played with him, encouraging him and saying to him, "Be brave, show your nerve." The transplant was successful, although the mother was warned that she might need another operation because of possible intestinal obstruction. Only seven successful such operations have been carried out throughout the world.

Linda, who lives in Llandudno Junction in Wales, and is in her early fifties, donated a kidney to her daughter Emma who is twenty-five. Emma explained how her mother made a normal life possible: "I became ill when I was seventeen and kidney failure was diagnosed. I went on home dialysis four times a day for sixteen months. I could hardly go out. Then my mother offered to donate a kidney."

The transplant in 1993 gave Emma the chance to try for a baby. Such a decision posed a dilemma, since there was a risk that the pregnancy could mean the loss of both the baby and the kidney. The

North Wales transplant co-ordinator Averil Bentley, who works from Gwynedd Hospital in Bangor, explained that a third of women who had kidney transplants and subsequently became pregnant did lose the transplanted kidney. She told reporters: "I asked Emma which she would prefer—to have the child and risk ending up on dialysis again and back on the transplant list or to stay as she was. She said she would be happiest having tried, in spite of the risks."

Liam John was born in March 1997, a healthy baby, and Emma is also well.

Emma's mother commented: "To see my daughter holding her baby makes it all worthwhile. I lost a kidney and became a grandmother."

Sometimes a mother cannot give up one of her own organs to save a sick child because it is not the right match. British mother Shirley Nolan found that her own bone marrow could not help her desperately ill son Anthony. Rather than give up, Shirley turned all her energies in a race against time to find a suitable donor, tackling officialdom and raising money by using skills she did not even know she possessed, prepared if necessary to widen her search worldwide.

Anthony was born in 1971 suffering from Wiscott-Aldrich Syndrome, a rare bone marrow disease which left his immune system unable to fight infection. His illness was diagnosed as incurable. In 1973 the first successful bone marrow transplant using a non-related donor was performed and Shirley realized that Anthony had a chance of life if a matching donor could be found.

She brought him to London and the search began for a suitable donor. Shirley soon discovered to her horror that there was no major donor register nor any facilities for establishing one. Many people would have given up at that point, especially with a sick child to care for. However, Shirley began an appeal for bone marrow donors in 1974, realizing that thousands of donors needed to be found because of the high odds against matching donor and patient.

Anthony was a patient at Westminster Children's Hospital where Shirley met Dr David James, a consultant pathologist who was responsible for the existing very limited donor testing programme for bone marrow transplants. He was eager to increase the volume of tests but told Shirley that a major problem would be funding the tests needed to match the tissues. A laboratory technician working full-time could manage only five of the complex tests each day and in 1974 £3,000 per year was needed to fund such a technician.

Again Shirley was not deterred, vowing to raise the money by any means once a register of donors was established. Her local paper in Thanet, Kent first published her story and offers of help began to come in from individuals and charitable organizations, especially local Round Tables from Ramsgate, Margate and Broadstairs. They began fund-raising and established the first donor clinic at Margate Hospital. Television helped to publicize Anthony's story and several stars from the world of entertainment offered their support.

The money was found for a technician and a small space in the basement of Westminster Hospital with a large broom cupboard served as an office. Dr James, the technician and Shirley started the first register of volunteer bone marrow donors from there. She divided her time between Anthony and her increasingly desperate quest. By 1978, six people were working on the register but the accommodation was proving increasingly awkward. No government grant was available and many bureaucrats and members of the medical profession saw little value in the project. In 1979 Anthony died before a successful match could be found.

Shirley did not give up. She vowed that, if it was humanly possible, no other child would suffer a similar fate through lack of a suitable donor.

The National Round Tables of Great Britain and Ireland and many other organizations and individuals supported her venture, and the culmination of their efforts was the permanent Anthony Nolan Research Centre, completed in August 1990 at the Royal Free Hospital in Hampstead.

Now the Anthony Nolan Bone Marrow Trust manages the world's first and largest fully independent register of non-related bone marrow donors. Shirley believed that by helping children with similar illnesses to her own son's, she was keeping Anthony's memory alive.

Mothers and fathers who lose children through an illness with a high mortality rate are sometimes motivated to channel their grief and loss into promoting research projects to save other children, a transference of parental devotion. None would say that the success of such a project offers consolation but it does have very positive results. What is more, it reveals an altruism and nobility of spirit in mothers such as Shirley who respond to personal tragedy by devoting their energy to saving other parents from the pain of losing a child.

Mothers Who Do Not Lose Hope

Equally devoted are those women who care for a sick or disabled child for years in their homes, in some cases for as long as mother or child lives. Some of the children do go on to an independent life, thanks to their mothers' constant efforts, and there are certainly great rewards in such relationships. As Sue who lost two sons and now cares for her profoundly disabled teenage son Tony said: "Tony is my driving force." Even the most severely handicapped people can offer inspiration and bring joy to those who care for them.

Mothers might care for a severely disabled child at home because there is no suitable local care, or because they are unwilling to send a beloved child perhaps hundreds of miles away to be brought up by strangers, however kind. Too often, they discover that their other children and their marriage suffer and that their personal freedom is curtailed, their health ruined by years without sleep. Yet for the cost of a residential place, help could be given to these mothers at home, technological aids provided to alleviate some of the practical problems caused by disability. Relief care could be offered, and financial resources provided. I have known many women who find that while counselling and sympathy abound practical relief is in short measure.

There are no rights and wrongs and some mothers cannot or do not wish to care for severely disabled children. They should not be condemned. As medical care prolongs the lives of children who even twenty years ago would have died in infancy, so society needs to rethink the way it can offer such children a good quality of life and enable the mother also to look forward to a future in which her own needs will be met. The care of disabled children still, in spite of government papers and recommendations, depends to a great extent on the goodwill of mothers.

It can be heartbreaking and frustrating when a child looks entirely healthy but is suffering from a disorder that makes his or her behaviour seem strange or threatening to the outside world. Inevitably it is the mother who bears the burden of a child who does not respond to love. Rachel, who lives in Hampshire, told me of her struggle to get help for Ben, her autistic son.

"Ben was born on 1 July 1981. It was a very quick labour of two hours and was completely painless. Everyone in the hospital was very taken with Ben, as he was so small and beautiful, and one of the nurses remarked he was one of the 'special babies'.

"When we got home, everything turned sour. Ben would cry nearly all day and wouldn't be comforted by a cuddle. He refused to feed and slept for about two hours a night. At about the time when babies would begin to interact with their mothers and show interest in things, Ben would totally ignore me or scream. Nothing could get through to him.

"At eighteen months old, Ben was not even attempting to speak, and I was told it was because I didn't talk to him or stimulate him. I knew something was wrong but no one would listen. Ben looked so normal and beautiful the doctors thought I was being neurotic.

"In desperation I read all the books I could find on different handicaps and eventually found a syndrome which seemed to fit in with Ben's behaviour. This was autism. All the various doctors, psychiatrists and paediatricians told me I was wrong and that Ben was just slightly delayed and that he would soon catch up.

"Things went from bad to worse. Ben got bigger and violent. Five times his baby brother David had wounds that required stitching because

of Ben's aggression. Ben would attack me and pull my hair and scratch. He would bang his head on the walls or walk round and round the room aimlessly. He would break every toy and was more interested in the paper it was wrapped in and how it would tear. He would tear the wallpaper and smash the light bulbs. He would throw violent tantrums in shops and refuse to walk or be carried. Ben was completely incontinent until he was nine years old.

"When Ben was four, he was put in a special unit attached to mainstream school. This catered for all different handicaps. Ben was the most normal-looking child there and I was told it was his treatment at home that was causing him to be delayed, and that with proper instruction Ben would show himself to be 'normal'. They even put him into a mainstream class to prove they were right, but Ben went berserk and locked himself in a cupboard.

"Eventually I was so frustrated trying to get everyone to believe that Ben was handicapped that I contacted the main specialist for autism, Dr Lorna Wing. She agreed to see Ben and assess him and finally diagnosed him as having classic autism. Nowadays, people diagnose autism all the time, but fifteen years ago it was not so well known and specialists were reluctant to label children as autistic as it carried such a bad prognosis.

"As soon as Ben was officially diagnosed, all the doctors who had been dealing with my family admitted that they had thought Ben was autistic but they hadn't wanted to upset me.

"When Ben was seven years old, he was admitted to Portfield School which specializes in autism and he hasn't looked back. Portfield says that if Ben had got the proper help earlier, he might have been able to talk properly. As it is, Ben makes sounds and uses sign language to make himself understood. Most people connected with him can now understand him so his frustration has lessened and with that his aggression.

"Ben has a very special quality about him. All the staff at school described him as a breath of fresh air and some of them even have him to stay at weekends. Ben is very able at sports and can compete against normal children of the same age. He has got his canoeing badges,

swimming awards and is halfway through the BTA trampolining awards. He may represent England in the Paralympics if he continues progressing so well, according to his coach.

"When things look really black and you feel there is never going to be any improvement, when the prognosis is so lacking in optimism that everything looks hopeless—never give up. If you keep trying, there is always hope. Ben is such a pleasure to have that I am almost thankful that he is handicapped. We have learned so much together and I feel I am a nicer, more patient person because of Ben. We can now share jokes and also have similar interest such as archaeology and fossil collecting.

"On 1 November 1995, Ben went into hospital. It was a relatively minor operation but it was expected to be quite painful for a few days. He was fourteen at the time and it was difficult because of his autism to make him understand what was going to happen. I tried to explain and he was fairly calm when he eventually went to the operating theatre. I was told that he would be in theatre for about an hour.

"By the time Ben came back to the ward, after nearly three hours, I was getting worried, but he seemed fine and recovered quickly from the operation. We came home the same evening and although I was told Ben would be very sore and possibly very sick, he slept well all night with only a little discomfort.

"The next day Ben was watching television when he suddenly started talking about 'being a ghost'. He can use only limited vocabulary and uses a mixture of speech and sign language. I asked Ben what he meant and he explained that when he was asleep during the operation he had become a ghost. He said that he was looking down from the ceiling and saw himself lying on the table as the doctors operated on him. He said the doctors were wearing masks and green gowns and he was lying with his eyes closed.

"Then Ben described going through the wall to a place like a big cloud. There he saw Sai Baba, the Indian holy man who a large number of people believe is God incarnate, who welcomed Ben. Baba materialized vibhuti [sacred healing ash] which he then sprinkled over the site of Ben's operation. Ben described his grandmother's dog, also called Ben, who had been put to sleep eighteen months previously. Ben said the dog was now new and was jumping up so excitedly at Baba that Baba told him to sit. The dog had been quite old when he had passed over.

"Ben also saw the 'taxi lady'. She had been the escort for the school taxi and had died very suddenly just before Christmas last year. Ben said she was very happy and hugged him and told him to be a good boy. Ben mentioned another lady with eyeglasses who turned out to be his great-aunt Annie who had died two years earlier.

"My son next recalled the doctor tapping him on the arm, telling him to wake up. Ben went quickly back into his body and woke up. Ben does not usually display any emotions but as he was telling me about his experience, he kept wiping tears from his eyes.

"Four days later the nurse came to our home to remove Ben's dressing. She was amazed that the incision had healed so completely that Ben no longer required a bandage. He has recovered very well from the operation and has experienced very little pain.

"Since Ben had his out-of-body experience, he has been very calm and has a very spiritual air about him. He has a very special relationship with one of the autistic girls at school and is the only person who can reach her and calm her down. Ben is very caring and thoughtful and shows more understanding about other people's feelings.

"Ben is still very autistic and has no pretend play, imagination or proper communication skills which is why his account of his out-of-body experience was so extraordinary. He could not have read anything similar and could not have made it up. He enjoyed it so much that he wants to know if he can have another operation so he can see everyone again.

"Ben's main difficulties lie now in his communication skills. He cannot talk clearly, so people who do not know him well find it difficult to understand him. He also has a deep love of books and his weekly treat at school is to go to the library. Unfortunately he cannot read either but spends hours just looking at the pictures.

"Being unable to read causes Ben great sadness, so he wrote a letter to Sai Baba asking him to help him talk and read. Ben's grandmother was due to go on a pilgrimage to see Sai Baba and took Ben's letter with her and was able to leave the letter in Baba's interview room. A short time *after the letter was written, I went to a meeting in Blandford and there I met an American lady called Pat Theisen. She has devised a unique programme which has enabled handicapped people to talk and read and is also very helpful to dyslexic people. Ben is also dyslexic and this lady thought she might well be able to help Ben both talk and read. We saw Pat when she came to Britain and the progress Ben made in the short time we saw her has given us great hope for the future."*

The Mothers of Plaza de Mayo

Can mothers make any difference to the situation beyond their own homes? Few mothers have suffered as much as the Argentinian mothers who lost their children and sometimes their grandchildren in the military coups of the 1970s. Risking imprisonment and possible death, many of them protested in the only way they knew how, by peaceful demonstration, facing not only harassment by the authorities but seeming indifference from fellow countrymen and women. I am indebted to Debra Guzman, the international journalist and human rights campaigner, for the background to this story.

Debra has written several articles highlighting the plight and courage of these mothers. She described how on Friday 28 December, 1979, General Leonardo Fortunato Galtieri was installed as the third Army commander-in-chief since the military coup in 1976. The Mothers of Plaza de Mayo tried to hold a march on the same day and were chased by the police around Buenos Aires while frightened passers-by ignored the blatant harassment.

The aim of the group of about two hundred mothers and relatives of missing people was simply to lay flowers at the foot of the San Martín monument on Plaza San Martín in memory of their missing children and grandchildren. However, the police blocked the mothers' path a number of times as they tried to walk down Florida Street towards the Metropolitan Cathedral on Plaza de Mayo, and managed to break up their demonstration.

Debra wrote: "The mothers, most of them carrying flowers, met next to the San Martín monument at about 5 p.m. Uniformed and plainclothes policemen arrived shortly afterwards ordering the mothers to move on and at one point threatening to arrest them."

Passers-by watched a display of folk-dancing as screeching police cars continued in efforts to break up the peaceful march. The mothers were menaced by police using patrol cars to block their path or drive wedges through the marchers to disperse them.

However, the mothers continued their march in spite of police harassment. Debra reports they attracted "a little more attention to themselves by producing little placards with the names of their missing ones, or simply stating 'I am the mother of a missing person.'"

One woman, when she realized who the mothers were, said: "They should have taken better care of their children before they disappeared."

One child asked his mother, who was shopping: "What are these people queuing for?"

"They're the mothers of missing people," she answered.

"What are missing people?" the puzzled child asked back.

The Mothers of Plazo de Mayo have continued over the years to support anyone who has missing relatives and to campaign for information as to the whereabouts of their lost loved ones. From 1995 onwards, several former military officials have talked about the past, admitting to horrific torture sessions and murders. Debra points out that it took twenty years before those people began to say what the mothers and others had been saying for a long time. This confession is partly due to the Mothers of Plaza de Mayo who are still walking around the square.

"In what was intended as a gesture of reconciliation, the government recently gave out more names of 'disappeared' people; but the mothers and other human rights organizations are asking questions about what happened to these people and who is responsible for these acts."

Although some of the mothers are now quite old, they continue to march on the anniversaries of the dates when relatives were seized and wherever support is needed. They have vowed not to rest until the fate of all missing loved ones is revealed and those responsible for the atrocities are brought to justice. "Because of their work," Debra says, "their solidarity, their spirit, memory is still alive."

The Soldiers' Mothers' Organization of St Petersburg

Nikolay N. Semenov, Assistant of SMO, very kindly sent me information about the work of the Soldiers' Mothers' Organization of St Petersburg and I have based the following section on some of these reports. These Russian mothers have banded together to try to save their half-trained sons from the military. The teenagers face not only injury and death in battle hundreds of miles from home, but brutality at the hands of their own officers.

Ella Polyakova, Co-chair of SMO, writes:

"Human security is an abstract notion in Russia, and up until recently this issue could not even be discussed in a candid manner. Formally, all the attributes of state power that are supposed to ensure the security of each individual are present in Russia. Yet still in real life illustrious public figures, journalists, businessmen both from Russia and other nations have been assassinated in the light of the day while the killers are typically not to be found.

"I represent the civil rights organization Soldiers' Mothers of St Petersburg. Our purposes include developing practical procedures (legal and medical) aimed at defending the rights and natural interests of draftees, servicemen and their family members. Our organization has been working since autumn 1991, and over 65,000 people have resorted to us for aid over this time. Today, an average of 400 to 450 people apply to us every week. Through our help, 57,000 draftees have asserted their legitimate right not to serve in the army, and over 3500 servicemen have defended their life and health and have been demobilized from the military service on the grounds of their health.

"However, the notion of human rights is perceived with a much

greater difficulty by officials since most them are still unable to break away from their totalitarian past. Members of our organization, myself included, have been more than once to the Chechen Republic to search for and free prisoners of war. I, personally, took part in the search for the newspaper men from St Petersburg who had disappeared in Chechnya and acted as an observer at the presidential election there.

"It was for the first time in our history that parents of soldiers and sailors were not afraid to prevent their children from taking part in the infamous war. Many parents went to the combat area and took their children away. It is our belief that the war crimes in Chechnya should be condemned by the International Tribunal; this is why we have collected and presented to the UN Human Rights Commission documentary evidence of the violation of the fundamental human right to life with regard to peaceful inhabitants of Chechnya, journalists, soldiers and their parents.

"The people who were killed, missing in action or hurt are not known, not only by name but even in terms of their number. It is shameful to be aware of the fact that more precise statistics are available abroad.

"Our organization has enough evidence to claim that humiliation, beatings, tortures and even killings of young soldiers by officers and senior team-mates are widespread in the Russian Army. Beatings of soldiers have become everyday practice for many units. The statements of servicemen and their relatives describe beatings with hands, legs and different objects (chains, belts, etc.). As a consequence of inhuman treatment by their commanding officers and senior team-mates, young soldiers have been suffering ill-health and sometimes dying. The massive appeals of the draftees' parents to the soldiers' mothers' organizations throughout Russia have been caused by their concern about the health, life, honour and dignity of their offspring.

"We have been involved in defending the rights of Serviceman Dima. After numerous beatings, tortures and humiliation Dima was delivered unconscious to the Vyborg Military Hospital with a diagnosis of dystrophy, broken nose and multiple bruises all over the body.

"It took the military doctors twenty days to save his life. His mother, Lidya, said that when she saw her son on 18 November 1995 he looked *just like a corpse from a Nazi concentration camp. She testifies that her son was repeatedly denied either lunch or dinner having no breakfast whatsoever and then was battered for allegedly slow work.*

"According to her evidence, Dima was brought to the extreme state of exhaustion, the ultimate indignity being forced to eat from a dog's bowl.

"Sergey served on a ship He was beaten and humiliated by his crewmates. They pounded him with sticks on the head and feet, kept him in a pressure chamber for several days and then made him write a farewell letter home to the effect that nobody was to be blamed for his death and that he was quitting life because he was tired of living. On 7 August 1996, his chums were 'educating' him by hanging him repeatedly by the neck to a beam rope. Today Sergey is a disabled person, unable to walk on his own and getting a minimal pension.

"It should be noted that the only thing that we've been managing to achieve so far with respect to the victims of tortures and inhuman treatment has been their release from the military service on health grounds. Those people who had mutilated Seaman Sergey were lightly reprimanded by the court and were denied the right to promotion for twelve months."

The Russian mothers, like those in Argentina, face a seemingly impossible task: to change centuries of oppression. But they are standing against the might of a ruthless system and showing by their quiet courage that mother love can overcome brutality and change society at last.

Mothers Falsely Accused

Our car was wrecked, paint daubed everywhere, excreta
left on the step, daubed on the walls and pushed through
the letter box. It was like living under siege for the
children. Throughout our ordeal, I was trying to keep the
children's spirits up. If the mother goes under, then
everyone does. The mother carries everything.

Alison, falsely accused of ritual satanic abuse

"There's no smoke without fire," the saying goes. But in some
areas of Britain less than 5 per cent of child abuse investigations
produce any real suggestion of anything wrong within the investigated
family. It is offered as justification that such raids are in the interests of
the children who are abused. Yet it is hard to think of another area
where extreme measures with a failure rate of 95 per cent would be
considered acceptable.

No one would wish to diminish the terrible effects on children of
physical or sexual abuse, and this chapter is not to deny the suffering
of abused children or the need to apprehend the perpetrators of such
evil. But this area has rightly received so much publicity that some
psychiatrists and social workers regard all families as potential
abusers and see any signs of emotional and sometimes physical
distress in a child as evidence of abuse. This attitude creates untold
misery for good, loving parents and yet is rarely acknowledged. At
one time doctors and social workers who received an anonymous
accusation against a family would tread carefully. Now all too often
is there a knock at the front door that can shatter the lives of an
innocent family.

Names, areas and minor details in all the cases in this chapter have been changed to protect innocent families who have suffered enough.

Those who have experienced false accusations, especially the mothers, say that it strikes into the very heart of family life. If child and mother are separated while investigations are carried out, then the family may never recover.

The Knock-Knock Monster

Pam, the mother of five-year-old Julie, works from home as a proof-reader for a large publishing company. The family lives in a small village in the south of England. When Julie was four, she attended the local playgroup three mornings a week. Pam told me how their lives were suddenly turned upside down.

"It was one of those mornings. Julie had wet the bed which was not a problem, as she only had the odd accident at night. However, the washing machine had broken down. I had a rush job to finish. My husband was away on business for two days. I had stayed up until the early hours working on the proof-reading and, bleary-eyed, I took Julie to playgroup. About noon, I bundled up the final papers and caught the post just before it was time to pick up Julie.

"On the way back, Julie was very quiet, but when she got home she brightened up and asked for rice, eggs and peas for her dinner, the current favourite. As we got lunch Julie sang the new song she had been learning at playgroup that morning, 'The Wheels on the Bus', with lots of waving and stamping. One way and another there was more rice on the work surface than in the saucepan as she stirred the egg into the rice and watched it make yellow trails. I would have to have a frantic clear up later, but first I promised myself a sit down and a coffee, while Julie watched the cartoons.

"Then she dropped her little bombshell. 'A lady at playgroup said if you or Daddy hurt me or hit me, I can tell her and she will tell social services and they will take you away,' she remarked casually.

"*The usual playgroup leader had been away ill for some weeks and a group of local mothers seemed to have taken over the group. One had commented disparagingly that morning that Julie had wet socks—it had started to rain on the way and Julie had been splashed by a car. We were new to the area and most of the mothers had gone to school with one another. It was very cliquey and parochial. But I was not having any of them saying stupid things like that to Julie. They found it hard to understand my life was not just gossip and sewing. Because of the high unemployment in the area, most of them stayed at home and spent the day in and out of each other's houses. I had tried to be friendly but they did not really want to know.*

"*'Let me carry my dinner,' Julie broke into my thoughts. 'Can I eat it in front of the television and watch the cartoons?'*

"*Had my daughter asked to eat her dinner standing on her head, I would have agreed. I just longed to sit in the chair and close my eyes. My head was starting to ache. I remembered the sheets that I had just dumped in the bath. They must be reeking to high heaven. Yesterday's dinner and the breakfast things were still in the sink, the breakfast cereal on the table. But at least the work was off in the post and the resulting cheque would pay off most of the overdraft which had been getting alarmingly high.*

"*At that moment, Julie accidentally tipped her plate and most of the rice, peas and eggs went all over the carpet. 'What the heck,' I thought. Ten minutes' sleep and I would be ready to tackle Everest. I gave my daughter an apple and some cheese. Julie trotted back to the television.*

"*I sat down again and there was a knock on the door. Not double glazing salesmen again. We had been plagued with them recently. The place looked more in need of demolition than new windows. I opened the door, the joking words on my lips. Two unsmiling strangers, a young man and a middle-aged woman, stood there. 'We're from the Child Protection Team. We have reason to believe that your child may be in danger.'*

"*They glanced towards the chaos and their expressions darkened. They pushed past me and the woman went over to Julie who was laughing at* the cartoons. 'That's not the child we were told about,' the woman said accusingly as Julie turned and smiled at them. 'We were told she was half dead. We've got a paediatrician on stand-by at the hospital. Let me see the bruises.'

" 'There's been a mistake,' I stammered. My mind was not functioning. Amazingly I smiled at them, although I could feel my body shaking.

"The man opened his notebook and reeled off our names. 'We have reason to believe the child is in danger and we have a car waiting outside to take you both to the hospital.'

"Julie looked alarmed, as the woman started removing her clothes roughly until she was in her underwear. I was totally frozen, tears coursing down my cheeks. Then I was running to and fro, trying to protect Julie from the woman who was examining every tiny scratch while my daughter attempted to pull away. I was frantically thumbing through the telephone book to find someone, anyone who would make these people go away. I dialled the playgroup leader, then remembered she had gone away. I tried the local doctor but it was his half-day.

"Julie was screaming with fear. It was like a dream in slow motion. When I later read the report the woman had commented on my disjointed behaviour. 'Who told you that Julie was hurt?' I sobbed.

" 'Someone from the playgroup phoned social services to inform us that your daughter's life was in danger, that her socks were wet. We are unable to tell you more. We must protect the confidentiality of our informants. We would like you to come with us.'

"I wanted to laugh. They sounded like robots. I realized I was talking nonsense, burbling, and the man was recording it all, drawing diagrams of my position, Julie's position, the furniture. They were gathering evidence. 'Not a mark.' The woman sounded disappointed. 'Are there any other children?'

" 'No.' I was handling it all so badly, not keeping calm. I was so cold, although the heating was on. But I was not going anywhere with them. Nor was Julie.

" 'We have to check.'

"The social workers, for so I assumed they were, went round the house. I remembered the wet sheets in the bathroom. I sank on to the futon in the sitting room. Julie fetched me a blanket because I was shivering. She was comforting me, patting me, cuddling close, offering to make me tea. She brought me a chive sandwich she had made.

"The couple returned. 'Nothing,' the man said. He seemed puzzled. The woman scraped a squashed pea off her shoe.

" 'What now?' I asked

" 'You're lucky this time,' said the man who I found out later was a plain-clothes police officer although he failed in his obligation to tell me, 'but we'll keep you on file for next time. There always is a next time.'

"Then they were gone. On the way out the woman noticed I had two copies of a book on child care and asked if she might take my spare copy.

"It was all a mistake. They had broken every rule in the book. They were a new team on their first job who totally mishandled the situation, who should never have been operating unsupervised. 'Learning on the job' was how their role was later described to our solicitor. Yet though it was all a mistake, records were written and kept at the County Social Services Department, about the dirty house, the urine-sodden sheets, the fact there was a bed in the lounge. The woman had obviously never seen a futon and assumed the room was used as a bedroom. There was a Van Gogh print on the wall. The woman asked me if I had painted it myself and what I called it. ' "Starry Night",' I replied.

"Once they were gone, I cleaned the house obsessively, scrubbing every surface, washed myself and Julie, washed our clothes, but I could not wash away the feeling of having been raped. If I could not protect my daughter in our home, where could I protect her? I should not have let them in, should have insisted on a solicitor being present, stayed calm. But it was so totally unexpected.

" 'Knock-knock Monster gone,' Julie said. 'We'll get Daddy to fix a new lock. It's safe now, Mummy.'

"But six months on, every time someone knocks at the door, she hides. Every time she goes to bed she says, 'You won't let the Knock-Knock Monster in again, will you, Mummy?' and might after night she wakes screaming about the Knock-Knock Monster taking her away.

"Although I was innocent, the identity of the informant was protected, while mine was gossiped round the neighbourhood. All I *know is that she is a mother at the playgroup and when I go to collect Julie at school she is there also, watching. I hear the mothers talking and Julie is no longer asked to tea. I am paranoid about matching socks, about never shouting.*

"I am on trial by a hidden judge and by the community. The vindictive talk and back-biting in the village has been unbelievable. 'No smoke without fire,' they say, and Julie is aware of it all. Children would ask her what her mummy and daddy did that made the police come, would provoke her and exclude her from their games. I do not blame the children. They hear their mothers talking. It is a small community with few contacts with the wider world.

"Julie's behaviour deteriorated after the raid and there have been several incidents where she has hit children quite hard. She is always getting involved in fights, for which she gets blamed. Several mothers have demanded I keep my child under control, although I have seen their children fighting and swearing when Julie is not with them. Julie will not allow anyone to take off even her cardigan, and pinched a helper who tried to change her knickers when she wet herself, which she now does in the day as well as at night.

"Julie could not remember which mother it was who told her about social services, the playgroup leader was unable to find out who it was and everyone tells us we must put the matter behind us, because we were not charged.

"My daughter recently started school. The head teacher would only take her with a helper because of the constant wetting, and the educational psychologist who has visited Julie says she may be suffering from hyperactivity or Attention Deficit Disorder, because of her suppressed fury that breaks out in temper tantrums at the bullying of the village children and her aggressiveness towards adults in authority. He even suggested she might be better in a residential school.

"Because my husband in particular has become very angry at the way officialdom has blocked us as we struggle to get Julie a fair assessment and proper help, we are considered a problem family and have been offered appointments with a psychiatrist who is known locally for her obsession with child abuse.

"If my husband Phil or I tell Julie she cannot have a new toy or must go to bed, she threatens to tell social services and they will take us away. It is a Pandora's box that has been opened and I am afraid what she might say that might be misinterpreted. The experts tell us that there is no way one visit from the Child Protection Team could have made Julie the way she is. I know the bright, happy, loving child she was before, who was doing well at playgroup and was never aggressive.

"It took several months and several hundred pounds in legal fees to get a written apology, twelve months before the file of the unsubstantiated views of various officials has finally been shredded. In our area there is no longer a policy of keeping detailed files on the innocent, although our name remains on social service records and a note that we were investigated but no abuse found.

"Worst of all, we met the social worker who raided us five months later and she could not even remember who we were. 'There are so many cases,' she said. She has now left the area and the head of the Children's Service assured us that the department had learned from the mistakes it had made with us and so we had helped other parents. But the Knock-Knock Monster remains."

Families Torn Apart

Alison lives in the south-west of England. Her life and those of her children were torn apart by accusations so bizarre that even the prosecutor's own doctors dismissed them. But that was not sufficient to prevent the witch hunt.

"We have lived in the same small street in a market town for twelve years. Two years ago, a series of false allegations were made against us that we were guilty of ritual satanic abuse and we were forced to abandon our home and leave our four children in the care of eighty-year-old grandparents.

"The nightmare began when our youngest daughter was only thirteen and our eldest sons were at university. Several new families moved into

300

the street from different places. Some of the children had been experimenting sexually and were caught by their parents. They panicked and accused the young teenage boy who lived next door to us of interfering with them. The parents attacked the boy and his family. The people next door had young children as well as the teenager. They and the adolescent lad were arrested and their young children who had never slept away from home were taken into care. Then the families of the children who had been experimenting with sex accused us and our thirteen-year-old daughter.

"My daughter was pulled out of school in the middle of the day by police and social services and accused of drugging the younger children across the road. She was taken to the police station and we were not told. Our solicitor raised Cain and she was released.

"My husband and I were arrested and bailed to live at an address not within a mile of our home. I always felt that the local police were on our side. The families who accused us went to the county police. The county police and social services worked together and used my young daughter to try to implicate our whole family, as she was the youngest and most vulnerable.

"These carers abused her horrendously. At the age of thirteen from a sheltered background she was asked whether her parents had digitally penetrated her and had she had oral sex with us? She did not even know what the terms meant. The social workers had to explain to her. The Child Protection Services abused my daughter by their questioning but there is no redress. There was and is tremendous anger in my daughter that I as her mother could not protect her, that I failed her and let her down in some way. Will it ever heal? How could I have protected her from the so-called child protectors?

"While we were away vigilante neighbours attacked our home and terrorized our helpless teenage children and their elderly grandparents. Our windows were broken. Our trees cut down. While it was all going on, at Christmas I saw a television programme about life in Sarajevo during the war. There was a mother in a bomb shelter, living behind a broken window, in a street in Sarajevo, trying to live a normal life. I felt like her, under horrendous attack but trying to get on with life. Our street was like that street, our car wrecked, paint daubed everywhere, excreta left on the step, daubed on the walls and pushed through the letter box. It was like living under siege for the children. Like that mother on the television, throughout our ordeal, I was trying to keep the children's spirits up. If the mother goes under, then everyone does. The mother carries everything.

"I was suspended from my job as a Special Needs teacher. My husband suffered greatly, but at least he could go to work and was not left at home to think and worry. As the mother you bear the pain with and for the children and you are so helpless.

"Because our children insisted that we had not abused them, social services were not able to deny us access. We were able to visit them, but they could never visit us. The teenagers were so angry that no one would believe them.

"The allegations made against us were bizarre: that we used fishhooks and knives in the children's genitals. One mother maintained this had carried on for three or four years. Yet she had apparently noticed nothing and there was no medical evidence of abuse. The case was pursued to justify the misjudgement.

"There was nothing to substantiate the accusations apart from what the children had done to each other. When my thirteen-year-old insisted that we had never abused her, social workers insisted she was in denial. Yet the eleven- and twelve-year-olds who said they had been mutilated by rats and fishhooks were believed. It became a witch-hunt and went on for a year. The culminating factor was the case conference with those most involved. The doctor who had been engaged by the Crown Prosecution Service said that there was no medical evidence of abuse and at the outcome they all had to conclude we were not an abusing family. But the children were still not allowed home until the Crown Prosecutor went to London to say that he was prepared to take the case to court, but that the Chief Prosecutor would have to take the responsibility for its failure.

"My husband and I would have preferred it to go to court so that our name could be vindicated, but we could not bear to live apart from our children any longer. We wanted it over, but we also wanted to be *acquitted publicly. When we returned home, it was quite dreadful. My daughter's rabbit was in the garden. It was the first fine days of spring and she went out playing with it. She was seen by the vigilantes and the next morning we found the rabbit with its head chopped off.*

"The effect on the children was totally devastating. My daughter says she would not take a dog to social services. When we got the evidence back we discovered that mothers who accused us had themselves been abused as children and were striking back at society. Many social workers themselves were abused as children and have a hidden agenda.

"I still work as a Special Needs teacher and have to maintain a façade of normality, especially as I have to work alongside the Child Protection Agency. My son went to a case conference when he was sixteen and told them that he would take legal action if they did not take his name off the register. I still cannot get my children's names erased from the register. It is only two years down the line that the full impact is beginning to hit us. It hit one of our sons so badly he had to take a year out of his studies and so lost his peer group. The head of my daughter's school says that my daughter has no respect whatsoever for authority now, although before the experience she was a happy, willing child. Every time my daughter sees the subject in the newspapers or on television programmes about the police, she becomes very upset. You cannot avoid the issue for the rest of your life, but any mention always reopens the wounds. You meet people and they are horrified by our experience but some think, 'There's no smoke without fire.'

"I feel I am sitting on a time bomb with my children and that any time it could explode."

In June 1994, a report commissioned by Virginia Bottomley, then the British Health Secretary, said that evangelical Christians campaigning against new religious movements had been "a powerful influence encouraging the identification of Satanic abuse". They were joined by psychologists and childcare workers who engineered the hysteria which led to children being taken from their parents in Rochdale, Nottingham, and Orkney. Of eighty-four cases examined in detail by the researchers, no evidence was found to justify any allegation of Satanic abuse and only three claims of ritual abuse were substantiated. Professor Jean La Fontaine, the report's author, said that even these three cases did not merit the description of ritual abuse as the desire for sex was more important than the element of ritual. "I think the evangelicals created the climate in which people could believe this sort of thing was happening," she said.

Professor La Fontaine said claims that the children themselves alleged Satanic and ritual abuse were false. "The fact is that the small children didn't actually say these things. They said bits and pieces that were picked up by the adults." Once allegations had been made, Professor La Fontaine found that interviews with children were badly conducted, with frequent and aggressive questioning. "What is defended as 'what children say' may be nothing of the sort," the report said. The report was welcomed by Mrs Bottomley, who said there had been "speculating and scaremongering" for years.

Unless you are articulate and know your way through the system, "the child protection" machine will roll over you. Many people have said to me that such things do not happen in a free world. But the fact is that innocent parents are accused of hurting their children physically and sexually.

On the Other Side of the Divide

Even those connected with the caring services are not exempt from false accusation. Susan is a respected foster and adoptive mother living in the south of England. She often took small babies at short notice if a young mother decided that she could not to keep her infant, and fostered children who were considered at risk. Susan and her husband Alan had two adopted children, eight-year-old twins, Ray and Don, whom they had cared for almost from birth. They had been unable to have children of their own and had been very carefully vetted for adoption by social services.

Ray had suffered a lack of oxygen that left him partially sighted and with very poor speech and coordination. With Susan's constant care, Ray had learned to speak and to walk for short distances, and was in mainstream school with a helper.

Just after Christmas in 1994, Susan received a frantic phone call from her local social services department, saying that a teenage girl had just brought a small baby into their offices, saying that her boyfriend had turned up unexpectedly and she was going to London to start a new life. Susan was already fostering a girl of two whose mother was unable to care for her, but after persuasion she agreed to take the child, David, at least until more permanent arrangements could be made.

New Year's Eve was spent pacing up and down with David who was a sickly baby, always crying, and seemed to hate being touched. Susan took David to the doctor several times and mentioned to the case worker who visited that David seemed distressed. Both told her that David's troubles would be put right with plenty of cuddles and attention.

At the beginning of February, Ray was lifting the baby out of his cot when David started to scream. Susan noticed that the infant's arm was stiff and discoloured. She comforted Ray who was upset he had hurt the baby unintentionally, although he was always gentle as a lamb with the tiniest infant. Susan drove David to casualty as it was quite late in the evening, his screams rending the air. David's arm was found to be broken, for which she could offer no real explanation. David had not been dropped, nor had he fallen from a height which would explain such a bad fracture. There were also two small fractures in the other arm which had healed

To her horror, Susan realized that the doctor and nurse were conferring, and she was left in a room while the doctor phoned social services to see if there was any record of the family. Susan became angry. "You think I've harmed the baby. Don't be ridiculous. Of course I have a record with social services. I take care of children who have been hurt by their parents. I work for social services."

Susan heard her voice rising shrilly and she was becoming hysterical. The baby's arm was splinted and she was allowed to go home. Next morning at precisely nine o'clock the health visitor was on the doorstep. Susan had known Elaine for years and laughed: "I suppose you've come because you've heard I'm baby battering."

Elaine smiled nervously, refused coffee and asked a lot of questions: if Susan was finding things a strain with the baby and Ray, if she was sleeping properly, was becoming irritable, how Alan was and if Ray was jealous of the baby. Susan replied flippantly, but noticed her friend was taking notes. "Come on, Elaine, you can't seriously think I hurt the baby."

Elaine's reply was non-committal. Suddenly Susan discovered she was on the other side of the them-and-us divide and her excellent record of child care stood for very little. Elaine explained that foster mothers could suffer from a kind of post-natal depression and there was no shame in admitting that you could not cope.

Susan found that meetings at the Family Centre changed and that, from being the fount of all wisdom, she was being treated even by her friends as though she were guilty. Senior social workers avoided her eyes and remembered urgent appointments if she tried to talk to them. One foster mother even refused to let Susan hold the new baby.

"What do you think I am going to do, kill it?" she screamed and the room went silent. After that Susan began to avoid contact, although visits from the care worker increased. The care worker seemed to be "just passing" almost every day and decided to pop in for a chat.

Susan found she was for the first time nervous of handling the baby, holding him awkwardly as if he was made of cut glass. She was sleeping badly and aware that the house was becoming a mess as she grew quite obsessive about watching the baby for harm and shouting at the children if they went near. David continued to scream night and day and she found herself shouting at him too, something she had never done with a child.

She was even watching her husband surreptitiously, wondering whether Alan had secretly hurt the baby. Then she felt guilty and blamed her own tension for disturbing David. Fostering, her joy, was becoming a nightmare.

Three weeks later, Susan was changing the baby on his little mat on the floor. The phone rang, and as she spoke into it she heard a blood-curdling scream like a wounded animal. Dropping the phone, she ran to the baby who had rolled off the mat and banged his head on the leg of the coffee table. A huge bruise was coming up. Waking the toddler from her nap, Susan drove as fast as she could to the hospital. X-rays showed David's skull was fractured, as was one of his legs. Susan began to cry and as she heard her stuttering words about the mat on the floor and the coffee table they sounded ridiculous even to herself, the words of a guilty woman.

David was taken away and she was not allowed to see him. The toddler was also taken away. Alan arrived at the hospital white-faced and shaking. The police had picked him up from work. The next few hours passed like a nightmare, the twins being taken past to an examination room, a policeman and social worker interviewing her with question after question until she felt prepared to admit anything. Worst of all, Susan wondered if she had hurt the baby and not remembered.

She insisted on speaking to the head of fostering whom she knew well, but suddenly her phone calls could not be put through. Her care worker arrived and, looking at the floor, explained that the two-year-old was being taken to another foster home "while matters are cleared up".

The policeman told Susan that for now she was not being charged, but the twins were being taken into care while they were examined more fully. When pressed the care worker said that Ray's bowel incontinence—which had always been regarded as part of his condition—now needed investigating in the light of the new situation.

Susan was not even allowed to say goodbye to her foster daughter or the twins. Don understood everything and she could hear him crying, "My mum would never hurt us. She loves us." Ray was saying "Mum, Mum" over and over again.

Alan returned home hours later from the police station, haggard and sick. He refused to tell Susan what had been said. Their solicitor was sympathetic. Had it not been for his efforts it is doubtful that tests on David to discover the cause of his fractures would have been carried out.

Time passed in a total blur as she and Alan doubted each other, blamed each other and then clung together like drowning children. The care worker came to collect the children's things. Susan cried as she packed their favourite toys. She was not allowed to see them as it might upset them. Ray kept crying was all she was told. Susan did not press for access, as she knew she could not have left the children once she had seen them.

The doorbell rang. It was a senior social worker Susan had never met. He explained that the baby had brittle bone disease; the slightest pressure was enough to cause a fracture. But there was no apology. The baby would not be returned to the family as it was felt that she and Alan needed a rest from fostering. The twins were returned but Ray was devastated and became clinging and lost much of his speech. The gossip at the school gate affected Susan so much she started to take tranquillizers, and the marriage was seriously shaken by the harsh things she and Alan had said in their confusion.

Susan was never offered any more foster children. Not that she would take them. She commented:

"Judge and jury may declare you totally innocent, but once these people have their mark on you, there is no way it is ever removed. As far as they are concerned not proven is the only verdict. It made us very wary with the boys, unwilling to touch them to cuddle them. If I raised my voice in public when they were naughty, I felt as if people were spying on me, waiting to report me.

"Alan's life is more or less back to normal, but it is the mother who bears the question mark of bad parent at the school gate, in the local shops. If you are not careful you take it into your soul. These people whom I helped, worked for, admired, trusted as colleagues and friends, have ruined my family life, but they do not even have the decency to apologize, to admit they were wrong. Such arrogance is terrible. I wonder, did I ever take in a child who was removed unfairly? I am

ashamed to have been one of them. It is not very nice on the other side of the fence."

Such stories as Alison's and Susan's seem incredible in a so-called democratic world. It is unbelievable until it happens to you.

Although Susan's story happened a few years ago, things do not seem to have improved. In March 1997, newspapers on both sides of the Atlantic reported the case of an American doctor who left her two young daughters asleep in her car for less than a minute while she went to a shop. Many parents must have acted similarly. No others that I know have had to spend £10,000 clearing their names of child abuse because of this innocent action.

Dr Bobbie Sweitzer left Sheridan, then aged one, and Sydney, four, in her Porsche while she dropped off a roll of film for processing at a camera shop in the Boston suburb where she and her husband live. The girls were sleeping soundly so Dr Sweitzer parked the car, partially opened a window even though it was a cool day, turned on the car's burglar alarm and locked the doors. According to Dr Sweitzer, the children were out of her sight for thirty seconds at the most but during that time a passing shopper called police.

"It never entered my mind that I was doing something wrong," Dr Sweitzer said. But she was contacted at her home by police later that day and told by Massachusetts Department of Social Service that there was sufficient evidence to justify a charge of child neglect.

"I was horrified and angry," she said. "As a physician I am well aware that hot cars can cause brain damage and dehydration. But this was never the case here. Yet I was treated as if I were a sixteen-year-old drug-addicted mother who hadn't thought twice about her children's safety."

The Sweitzers hired a lawyer and although the social services department finally decided against a criminal charge, it recorded that the mother posed a "moderate to severe" risk to her children. Unless this was challenged, the allegations would remain on file until the youngest child reached eighteen.

"I don't think I would go to doctor who has been accused of child abuse," Dr Swietzer said. "I was willing to do anything to clear my name."

The Sweitzers called on a psychologist and several character witnesses to provide affidavits on their behalf to a hearing in January. Finally the social services department conceded that Dr Sweitzer's actions did not rise to the threshold of neglect and agreed to remove the incident from the records.

Robert Sherman, the Sweitzers' lawyer, said the family might well have remained on the child abuse register for seventeen years if they had not had the time and resources to fight a stubborn system. "Unless you are willing to spend thousands of dollars to fight it, you get lost and chewed up by the system," he said.

A social services spokesman said: "We always walk that fine line between the need to protect children and the unwarranted state intervention into families."

But in the cases I have recorded and others I have not, the carers crashed through that fine line with what can be described only as a total lack of sensitivity for the feelings of mother and child. I can only hope that the examples above remind them that there is such a thing as mother love.

PART EIGHT

Deaths of Mothers and Children

The Pain of Parting

At the end, Mom was so afraid. She hated being
anywhere on her own and we were with her, holding her
hands as she slipped away.
Marian from Birmingham, England, on her mother's death

*M*others are always there, it seems, cajoling, nagging, scold-
ing, fussing, comforting, whether the child is just starting
school or becoming a grandparent. When a mother dies, she leaves an
aching emptiness in her children's lives. The thoughts come—"I must
tell Mum . . . I must ask Mum . . . Mum will laugh when I tell her"—
and then the aching memory of loss returns. Each remembering is
another little death.

Marian was in her mid-forties when her mother died after
struggling with a long and painful illness. At that stage in her life
Marian was a successful teacher, happily married and with children
of her own. But she found, as many men and women do at such
times, that the focal point of her world was suddenly gone, along
with her certainties.

*"At the beginning of the end, Mom saw the four of us—myself, my dad
and my brother Malcolm—as a magic circle. If we all held on tight, we'd
beat death and we tried. We were in turns ecstatic when something good
happened, distraught when the tables turned. We laughed and joked
endlessly—but then we always have.*

*"When we brought Mom home for the last time, I pushed Malcolm in
a wheelchair to the ward. Dad followed scolding, with a jar of sweets for
the staff. A bit of a bump and my brother was propelled from the chair*

like a Jack-in-a-box. We were laughing and silly, overjoyed to be taking my mother home. Although we knew we had so little time, all we could see was that we were taking our Mom where she belonged.

"We never left her. She wanted dad with her twenty-four hours a day and he was there, no grumbles. At the end, Mom was so afraid. She hated being anywhere on her own and though we were with her, holding her hands as she slipped away, I knew she was alone. I got so far. It was dark and I was so afraid. There were shadows and whisperings but I could not see past that. I didn't have the words then and I don't now.

"The funeral was sparkling, a shining sort of day, bright sun, masses of colours in the flowers and monumental figures in black, in shiny black cars with gleaming chrome. We arrived at the church, Dad and I. My brother, husband and two cousins were to bear the coffin. No one else was going to carry our mom. At the end of a tunnel of trees, the vicar appeared and drew us into the day. We followed the coffin up to the old lych-gate, which was shoulder high. Four six-footers and a lot of flowers was too high.

" 'Bend the knees a little, gentlemen, please.' Bearing solid oak with mahogany veneers and lots of brass (nothing too good for our mother), the coffin bearers faltered. Suddenly it was as if she was there. That bubble of mirth rose inside as I caught her eye and we homed in together on four pairs of strapping knees trembling in unison as they limboed under that gate. I wanted to laugh but of course I didn't. The vicar finished the service by saying, 'She was such a lovely lady' and truly she was."

I was only nineteen when my own mother died. She had lung cancer and a secondary tumour on the brain. I was nineteen and a student teacher. I looked after her with some help from my aunt, because there was no good reason why I should not.

I was struggling to lift her for her wash when she died. I remember thinking it was true about the death rattle. Her voice faded away in mid-sentence and seemed to echo further and further away until it was gone. She was very white and her jaw was loose.

The nurse arrived and asked if I would mind helping to lay my mother out. We put pennies in her eyes and tied a scarf round her jaw. A locum doctor came and certified her dead. I rang the undertaker to take the body away and tidied the room, leaving everything as it had been, as my mother had taught me. It was a relief to leave the front room and go out into the fresh air.

At first hand, death had proved very ordinary, not enriching, no glimpses into eternity.

Its significance was simply that it was the last thing my mother and I did together. I did not speak her name for two years and no one held me close.

Dr LaVonne Harper Stiffler described a woman separated from her birthmother at birth who, with no knowledge of her identity or whereabouts, not only "knew" her birthmother was ill and felt distressed on the date she later discovered her birthmother was diagnosed with cancer, but experienced deep sorrow during the month of her mother's death. The birth family confirmed these dates.[1]

Another woman wrote in her journal years before she traced her birth family, "I feel someone close to me has died." It was the date of her birthmother's death. Stiffler quotes John Gribbin who has a doctorate in astrophysics: "Particles that were once together in an interaction remain in some sense parts of a single system which responds together in future interactions."

In other words, love once activated never dies. This would suggest that the mother and child will maintain their bond throughout life—and maybe in death. The connection would be strongest when intense emotion is felt by one of the participants, which would explain how mothers can know when daughters are in labour or at the point of death, even if mother and child are hundreds of miles apart. Helen, who lives in London, had been concerned about her mother's health, but her mother was in no immediate danger.

"My mother aged eighty-four was in hospital. For several months she had been losing weight but there was apparently no physical or psychological

reason for this. She had a very strong Christian faith and an equally strong spirit of independence. I had been caring for her for seven months in her home and finally in hospital and it was obvious that she would never return to living on her own.

"Mother refused to come to us and tensions were high as she was equally determined not to go into residential care. She told me that she was praying that God would either take her or make her well enough to return to her own home. The doctors alternately marvelled at or were exasperated by her determination and her will to live.

"My husband and I were part of a group due to visit the Czech Republic, a ten-day trip that had been planned for some months, and the geriatric consultant persuaded me to go as my mother was not deteriorating rapidly and she thought I needed a break. A decision over my mother's future would have to be made on my return. When we said goodbye to Mother on our way to Dover she seemed brighter and happier than I had seen her for some time and she was looking forward to hearing all about the trip.

"Eleven out of the group of sixteen succumbed to a gastric flu virus immediately on their return home. We were travelling home by car, visiting friends in the former East Germany en route. We arrived in Gera and were persuaded to stay with night with a Baptist pastor and his wife whom we had met in Budapest in 1989 at the European Baptist Federation Rally. I became ill during the night and the following day was delirious and needed medical attention. The second night I was drifting in and out of conscious-ness and was very aware of my mother. I could see her face clearly and I began praying for her. At some time during the night I began to thank God for her and for her influence on my life and, although I do not remember this, my husband said that I woke him in the early hours and told him my mother had died during the night.

"We tried to ring our eldest son at 7 a.m. and got no reply. I gave my husband the hospital number and he was told by the ward sister that my mother had died at 11.45 the previous night. One comforting thought, amidst the feelings of desolation and guilt I experienced, was that my *mother had felt me as close to her as I had felt her close to me in her last moments.*

"I was her only child, named after her beloved sister who died in childbirth while my mother was in Hong Kong. My mother had been aware of her death even before the telegram arrived from England."

Mothers Who Return after Death

&

> The only ghosts, I believe, who creep into this world, are
> dead young mothers returning to see how their children
> fare. There is no other inducement great enough to bring
> the dead back.
>
> <div align="right">The Little White Bird, <i>J.M. Barrie</i></div>

Comforting a Child

The death of a mother leaves a child feeling totally bereft, even if
other relations try to compensate by being extra loving. Anthony, a
teacher and doctor who lives in Wiltshire, believes like Barrie that
mother love is so strong that it can transcend even death. He is sure
his own mother returned to comfort him after her death when he
was still quite young.

*"In the last year of the Second World War, I was living in a large family
house in the Midlands with my father. My mother had died a month
earlier after a long painful illness. This particular night I lay awake, not
thinking of my mother, when I was aware of two puffs of air on my face
from above. The head of my bed pointed to the door and in the past my
mother had often looked in on her way to bed to check if I was awake.
She did this by blowing on my face lightly. I would respond, if I was
awake, with a 'Goodnight, Mum,' and so on.*

*"I was really startled by this familiar happening. I sat up and looked
around the darkened room. Then I got out of bed and went to my father's
room across the landing. He was lying awake, in the dark, smoking his
pipe. I told him what had happened. He thought a moment and said,*

'Obviously your mother looked in to see how you are—you know how she worries about you. Not scared, are you?'

"Denials from myself. Father said, 'Get back to bed, then. Your mother won't want you wandering around at this hour.' I went back to bed quite relaxed and quite sure that my mother had looked in on me."

The response of Anthony's father helped to confirm the experience as a positive one for the boy. Too often, the shocked replies of adults when a child tells them he has seen a dead parent can make the child feel stupid or, worse still, wicked. Whether the mother does survive death and can communicate with her children in a recognizable form, or whether the bond remains less tangibly of the mother/ child love created in her lifetime, the experience can be enriching.

For Anthony, the validity of the incident was apparently confirmed when his own son appeared to know the grandmother who had died so long before he was even born.

"Thirty years after my mother died, I was sitting with my young son looking through family photographs. To my surprise there was an old photograph of my mother taken in 1941. I had only seen it a few times, a small fading photograph of a dark-haired woman of forty-five. My son had never seen it before. On an impulse I asked, 'Who is this?'

"Quite casually my son said, 'It's Gran.'

"Thinking it a guess I pointed out, 'But Gran [my wife's mother] has white hair and no glasses.'

"My son looked at me as if I was slightly retarded. 'It's my other Gran,' he said.

" 'Of course, of course,' I said and left it there. My wife confirmed that she had not shown him the photo previously or any other photos of my mother and neither had anyone else. He recognized immediately, from among pictures of other middle-aged ladies, his grandmother who had died long before he was born."

Visions of Comfort

For older people too, the loss of a mother can leave a sense of desolation. From the hundreds of letters I have received, it seems that a particularly vivid dream or vision of the deceased mother is an important part of the grieving process, although some psychologists argue that such an experience is blocking the acceptance that the person has died and will not return.

Joyce, who is now living in a nursing home in Hampshire, remembers thirty years later the immense consolation of seeing her mother after her death.

"I was forty-seven and my mother eighty-two when she had her second stroke in 1967 and died. I was alone with her when she died. She was unconscious so all was silent. Suddenly like a stroke of lightning I felt as devastatingly alone as if I was cut off from the whole world. Next minute her breathing just stopped, the colour drained out of her face.

"Three weeks later I woke in the middle of the night and saw my mother coming across the room in a gentle blue and white glow. I was aware of two worlds at once. My mother looked so proud of herself. She had done it. She had survived death and come back to comfort me. She took me in her arms. We were quite solid to each other and as never before I sensed her personality. Then her Mother Love rose in a great tidal wave and swamped me. I had never felt it function so strongly in all my years with her. Then she vanished."

When a mother has deteriorated or died in painful circumstances, seeing her in a dream or vision healthy and well again can help the grieving child to move on. Paula, who lives in North London, was desperate to know that her late mother was safe and well, especially as she believes she shared her mother's experience of death.

"In 1988 my mother was ill. However, we were not expecting her to die. One night I woke suddenly at about 5 a.m. and felt so sick. I also felt

that my stomach was being churned round and round like a washing machine. I felt breathless and woke up my husband, saying to him, 'Help me! I feel as if I am dying.'

"It was a feeling I had never experienced before: intense sickness and a deep churning feeling. I finally fell asleep, feeling exhausted. Next morning I was woken by a phone call. My sister was ringing to tell me that my mother had died at about 8 a.m. I immediately thought this was why I had those terrible feelings. I suppose I felt the spiritual umbilical cord separating. However, I am still mystified why I felt this a few hours before Mum died. The only thing I can think of is that it was my mother's last energy going.

"About four months after her death, my sister and I decided to go to the Spiritualist Association of Great Britain for a sitting with a medium as we were both still grieving. The sitting was very disappointing and even though we both kept open minds and tried not to just focus on Mum, we got little to help.

"We went our separate ways feeling dejected. That night I prayed really hard. I am not a religious person as such, but I do believe in the spirit world and the power of thought. I remember saying. 'Oh Mum, we really miss you.' I cried and went to bed, feeling generally emotional.

"During the night, I suddenly realized that I was awake in my sleep. It was different from dreaming. I really was awake. Out of a mist, I saw my mother. She looked about ten years younger than when she had died, but tired. Behind her I could see shapes, figures with lights around— about four of them—and I felt they were helping my mum to come and see me, because she was still very weak. I rushed over and hugged my mother and said, 'Oh, Mum, is it really you?'

"She felt so real. She replied, 'Yes, darling, of course it's me.'

"I then said, 'I love you, Mum,' and she replied, 'I love you too, darling.'

"I knew then it was time for her to go. It was a huge effort for her to be with me but she had come to help me over my grief.

"The figures returned and I felt my mother being guided away. Strangely, I felt no sadness, but uplifted and happy for her. I woke suddenly and found I had tears of joy streaming down my cheeks. I went *to phone my sister but as it was 4 a.m. I did not. I wish I had because I was ecstatic and had such a feeling of pure joy and love. Since then I have never felt so sad about my mother as I know she is well and happy."*

The Reverend Jean Wadsworth wrote: "A lot of people feel the presence of a deceased person. A great friend of mine, a priest who was very close to his mother, says that he felt her presence very strongly at his ordination. If we say that we believe in the communion of saints, we should not be surprised at this. I am sure my friend's mother was praying for him and rejoicing with him, as she had longed before her death for her son to become a priest. This belief only becomes unhealthy when the bereaved spend all their time trying to contact the dead. I always want to say, 'Leave them in peace.'"

Reconciliation in the Afterlife

The words "too late" are terrible when they are spoken where a mother has died with resentment or anger towards her child. Kim from Arizona wrote:

"In 1981, my grandmother and my great-grandmother exchanged some harsh words just before my great-grandmother's death. They were two very strong and ardent Hispanic women and the pillars of our family. The argument pretty much revealed a lot of ill feelings that had taken a lifetime to accumulate. The two did not speak for weeks.

"Three months later, my great-grandmother passed away. My grandmother, wrought with guilt, underwent a tremendous emotional change that had its effects at home where my mom, my sister and I were living with her. Grandmother was constantly crying and was generally a wreck. We were very worried about her until one day, at breakfast, she told us that all was well and that we shouldn't have to worry about my great-grandmother any more. After this declaration, my grandmother went back to normal, yet we never asked why—until 1991, that is,

when I asked her about the sudden change and the events that led up to it.

"With some reluctance, my grandmother explained that one night about six months after Nana's death, she woke up to get a drink of water. It was summer and we left all the windows open in the house to cool us down because of the hot Arizona summers. She was drinking some water from the kitchen tap when she heard someone call her name from the backyard.

"It was a moonlit night and an uncharacteristically windy chilling August evening. She went outside to our back patio and saw Nana sitting on her favourite lounge chair rocking back and forth. Nana reached her hands out to my grandmother and she knelt beside her for what seemed like hours but actually lasted only a few seconds according to my grandmother.

"Nana didn't utter a word but my grandmother remarked that her peaceful expression washed away the guilt, fear, and anger the two may have been holding in her last days. After a few moments, she found herself alone on the cement patio and stood up. She looked towards the far end of our yard and, just beyond a swing set, she saw Nana standing at the far end of the yard. After a few moments, my grandmother said goodbye and the image faded. She remarked that the next thing she knew it was morning and she woke up in her bed. She felt very much at peace and smiled at a photo of Nana on her dresser and thanked her for her 'dream'. Moments later, she remembered, she looked at her legs and noticed the dents of small rocks and concrete bits at her knees.

"My grandmother passed away in August of 1992. There still remain some things left unresolved between us as well. So far, I haven't heard her call my name."

Sending a Sign

Often a deceased mother will intervene at times she would have done in life, offering help and advice. Christine wrote to me from the English Midlands, telling me how her late mother helped her finish her daughter's wedding dress. In her letter Christine enclosed a piece of the lace from the wedding dress which I will always treasure.

"I had many psychic contacts with my mother while she was alive that continued after her death. While she was alive we became so much on the same beam that on several occasions I found myself standing next to her in a shop or crossing the road in the city to meet her on the pavement, though no mention of the proposed visit was made. My parents lived ten miles from the city in one direction and I came from the other.

"My daughter's wedding dress had been cut out, pinned, tacked, fitted and stitched, the lining and hems adjusted. It was all ready for trimming and I was baffled. Yards of cream lawn with a fine white stripe hung over the cream lining. The problem was where could I get lace and braid to finish the garment in time? I was standing pondering and looking vainly into my bedroom cupboard knowing there was no time for an excursion into the city, and the local shops had been unable to help. Then I heard, and there was no mistaking my mother's voice, 'Go to the linen cupboard and look in the left-hand corner of the third shelf at the very back.' A typically worded instruction, loving, precise and to be instantly obeyed.

"My mother had died a year previously and we had moved to a large bungalow where my father could have his own domain and yet have familiar objects around the property. So we had brought with us many things from both homes, some of my mother's sewing things among them.

"Very puzzled I went to the linen cupboard. I had no recollection of anything other than sheets, pillow cases and towels therein. Moving the front pile of sheets I cautiously felt behind it and right at the very back there was a parcel. Pulling it out I found that it was covered by the grey and while paper of a draper's shop from a distant town where my parents had lived many years previously. Opening the parcel I found a chocolate box and on it in Mother's fine writing, 'Twelve yards braid, ecru.' It was the perfect trimming for my daughter's wedding dress and a generous quantity too.

"With fervent thanks I darted back to the bedroom and laid a length of the braid across the dress. It looked awful. I could not believe that this *was all so I went about my duties and waited for a solution. Hours later the next instruction came. 'Try bleaching a little of the lace, dear.'*

"*In a few minutes a short length of braid from the bottom of the box was in a little bowl, gradually changing colour from coffee to cream. When it was rinsed and dried it was a perfect match. The braid was made in double strand with the diagonal pattern arranged for left and right, the beautiful raised motifs about an inch apart. When I came to stitch it on to the dress, in all the positions the patterns fitted perfectly as though they had been bought specially for the dress, so there were no complicated manipulations to be overcome. It was wonderful.*

"*This all took place almost fourteen years ago and the bubble of joy at the memory of the whole event never ceases to explode inwardly.*

"*My daughter told me much later that she too had been aware of her grandmother's presence. Her joy and radiance on the day, her dress and old-fashioned dropper necklace (also my mother's which came to light in a similar fashion) made the wedding a memorable day for everyone.*"

Christine recounted similar incidents in which her mother helped over practical issues. Often her presence was heralded by the scent of her mother's favourite perfume which would suddenly appear in the air. Fragrance is a frequently reported sign of both mothers and grandmothers and can range from perfume to lavender furniture polish, the scent of roses or even home-baked bread. However, the sign may be more subtle, for example in the unexpected appearance of an article imbued with emotion, perhaps on the anniversary of a mother's death or another significant date. The following experience was contributed by Mark Fraser, editor of the *Haunted Scotland* journal.

"*Mary's mother died in April. When Mary's birthday occurred in the following October, during the quiet of the evening, Mary began to cry because she realized this was the first birthday she had not received a letter from her mother. She went into the kitchen to make a cup of tea. As she passed the sideboard she noticed something sticking out of one of the drawers: the birthday card which her mother had sent the previous year.*

The card had certainly not been there during the day. Mary was comforted that her mother had sent a card on her birthday after all."

Such signs only have meaning to the people concerned and can breach the gulf between dead and living as the bereaved child recalls through the symbol her loving mother. At any other time the card would have been a pleasant memento. But appearing "out of the blue" on Mary's birthday, it assuaged her grief.

Another instance was recorded by the writer and journalist Christopher Booker not long after his mother's death. "For as long as I can remember, every year on my birthday, which falls in October, my dear mother has recalled that, at the moment before I entered the world at 6.30 in the morning, she heard a blackbird singing in the garden outside. Every year for at least thirty years I have respectfully informed her that it could not have been a blackbird singing in October. It must have been a robin. Two weeks ago, my mother died, and on Wednesday last, in a Dorset country churchyard, I had the sad task of placing her ashes in the earth. At that moment, a few yards from her grave, two birds began to sing very loudly. One was a robin, the other was a blackbird. I hope she was able to share the joke. Perhaps she arranged it."

Was this an example of psychic communication? I asked him. He replied: "Keenly aware though I am of 'sixth sense' experiences and of the 'hidden web' of significance surrounding our lives, and often involving nature, I cannot say that I had any special bond of this kind with my mother, although her mother was a very strong intuitive and had many extra-sensory experiences. I did have a teasing relationship with my mother, based on her rather dogmatic acceptance of what she was told—for example by weather forecasters in the media which I would counter with intuitive common sense that weather forecasters were usually wrong, as a look out of the window might indicate! The ongoing badinage about the blackbird was an example of this. My mother had established an *idée fixe* which I knew to be wrong, but nothing could talk her out of it. That is why, as I lowered the ashes into the ground and heard both robin and blackbird striking up together, I had a smile on my face.'

Kristina from Atlanta, Georgia, described the sign that for her indicated the presence of her late mother.

"In 1992, my now husband and I were about four weeks away from getting married. We were living in a condo in Atlanta. One afternoon, we were doing laundry when I noticed that the washing machine had stopped. I went to check and the lid was up. I figured that my husband, who always added things to a load after it started, had simply forgotten to put the lid down. When I questioned him, he said he thought he had, but couldn't really remember. We didn't think any more about it until it happened again about a week or so later. I thought that perhaps the load was unbalanced and the machine simply stopped automatically. So I checked the manual—no mention. I also called the manufacturer who told me that my model didn't have that option.

"Still I didn't think very much about it until the day before we were to leave to drive to DC where we were going to be married. I was home by myself and did a quick load of laundry. I was standing in my kitchen where I had a very clear view of the machine. Suddenly the machine stopped. I looked and saw the lid open. I felt chills running up and down my back.

"I walked to the machine and said in a somewhat calm voice, 'I'm sorry, Mom, that I am doing a mixed load—I know it isn't the correct way to do laundry but I'll try not to do it in the future.'

"I closed the machine and finished the load I was doing. I figured that it was my mother who had died twenty odd years ago, making sure that everything went smoothly. During the next year that we lived there, we never again had trouble with the washer, but then I never did another mixed load in the washer."

Vendettas in the Afterlife

Occasionally there are instances where a deceased mother tries to interfere in her son or daughter's life and the results can be destructive if heeded. Thelma, a widow in her seventies who lives on the Isle of Wight, told me how in 1917 her father was persuaded to attend a large Spiritualist meeting in Detroit. He was very reluctant to go and only went so that he would not offend his hostess. His worst suspicions were confirmed as he gazed at the rapt audience and he stood up to leave. At that moment the medium came on to the platform and said, "I have a message for the gentleman by the door. 'Oh, Willy, I did miss you.'"

"My father burst into tears because that was what his deceased mother used to say to him when he came home late as a little boy. She never scolded him but by telling him she had missed him she made him feel guilty and kept him under her thumb."

Thelma told me that her father was so eager to hear his mother's voice again that he went out and bought all the paraphernalia, and then desperately tried to persuade friends to hold seances with him. But he never heard his mother's voice again and his obsession caused difficulties with his wife.

No truly loving mother would have returned in that way. When a relationship has been destructive in life, a mother may return in a dream or vision and try to put things right. This can be very healing or in a few cases it can mark the closing of a chapter, so that the bereaved person can bury the past.

The mistake was not that Willy went to the meeting, but that he let the message influence his future behaviour. Had Willy's mother been alive it would have been equally destructive to allow her to affect his actions so drastically.

It is not always a question of angels and demons, but can be a matter of personalities. A mother may clash temperamentally with one daughter or son or have a favourite grandchild. The same person can react entirely differently with various members of the family. Occasionally these differences can manifest themselves after death so that a ghost can appear both as an angry mother and devoted grandma.

Tracey, who lives in Berkshire, told me about her deceased grandmother who had always disliked her eldest daughter Jan and continued the quarrel almost to her last breath. The old lady vowed on her deathbed that she would come back to haunt her daughter and never give her a minute's peace. For her part, Jan, tired of her mother's haranguing, said, "I'll be glad when you are dead."

After the death of her mother, Jan regretted her words and was thinking lovingly of her mother at the funeral tea which she had prepared. Suddenly glasses started flying off the sideboard. At every subsequent family gathering organized by Jan crockery smashed as though hurled by an invisible hand and things inexplicably tipped over. Jan inherited her mother's house and what had been a quiet home seemed to take on a life of its own. Doors banged and windows rattled even when there was no wind.

Tracey was only thirteen when her grandma died. She used to sit with the old lady while she was ill and tidy the house. In contrast with Jan's, Tracey's experiences of her grandmother after her death, like those during her lifetime, were entirely positive.

"About two weeks after the funeral I was tidying my bedroom and I could suddenly smell Gran's scent. Gran used to get me to pick roses for her in the summer and she would make rose petal water to dab on her wrists. The sudden smell of rose water heralding Gran's presence went on for years and once when I got in my boyfriend's car I told him, 'Gran's here' because the perfume in the car was so strong.

"It was as if she had walked straight through me, and we watched our step that evening knowing Gran was watching. I was always very close to Gran, as she had brought me up for much of the time. The last time I sensed her around me was when I was just eighteen. She had a beautiful sixty-year-old ring she always said I would have on my eighteenth birthday. Now I have been given the ring, I hardly ever smell Gran's perfume. It's as if now I have the ring, I don't need to be reminded of her."

The old lady's most recent appearance was at Tracey's eighteenth birthday party, organized by her Aunt Jan. Once again glasses went flying around.

Perhaps if any conclusion can be drawn from the last two experiences it is not that we should fear the hauntings of the deceased but that we should try to resolve earthly resentments while we have the chance. Whether we accept the existence of ghosts or not, we can be haunted by old resentments and guilts that are better laid to rest by the living.

Closing a Door

Where a mother has died with anger or indifference towards her child, the unfinished business may linger if there is no reconciliation. Ironically this can be more painful even than a vendetta. It was Barbara's husband Geoffrey, who lives in Lancashire, who told me the background to the following story, although Barbara described her dream of her deceased mother. Barbara herself died recently. Geoffrey explained:

"Barbara's mother put great store on being a nice lady, but she was a hopeless mother. Everything was subordinate to her own picture of herself. She reduced her husband to a cypher and he had a long nervous breakdown in late middle life. He could talk freely to me only when his wife was not present and he was a most intelligent and amiable man.

"Barbara was always very intuitive and very musical, but her mother would never recognize either her gift or her needs, as they competed with her own self-image. No adequate steps were taken to encourage Barbara's music. Her mother insisted on secretarial training instead.

"In the last three years of her life, Barbara's mother refused any help, insisted on running a large house she could not manage and had a crisis about every three months. We would collect her, nurse her back to health in a week or two and she would at once refuse to be a burden to us, insist on going home, until another crisis occurred a few weeks later. She died in a geriatric hospital, quite insane after a series of falls. She would never accept that Barbara wanted to look after her. Barbara's memories of her mother were very painful."

Barbara herself told me: "My mother always hated me, due, I am sure, to a particularly difficult birth and to the fact that I had a vague memory of life before coming to earth, light and love. All through my life until her death eight years ago, she was always ready to think the worst of me. I was never taken into her confidence. However, several months ago, after my mother's death, I had a dream in which I saw my mother surrounded by shadowy figures who were close to her, but unknown to me. She was smiling and genuinely pleased to see me. I was glad to see my mother so well and happy, but we both knew that we really had nothing to do with each other. Since this dream I have not been so distressed."

For Barbara the dream was the closing of a chapter and the resolution of unfinished business. For me experiences such as Barbara's are convincing proof of an after-life where there is free will, where people are still essentially the same and where sometimes contact is not sought or welcomed by either side.

The Death of a Child

The death of a child knows no words we can say that
will ever comfort a parent. It can only be compared to
Our Lady losing her child Jesus.
Father Sean MacAulay, parish priest of Mrs Frances Shand Kydd,
speaking after the death of Diana, Princess of Wales

*T*he death of a child, especially in early childhood, is so tragic a
loss that many of us find it hard even to contemplate. It is now so
far from the norm in the Western world for parents to be predeceased
by a child that people outside the bereaved family do not know how to
react.

But even in those parts of the world where child deaths are still a
frequent occurrence, for the parents, and especially the mother who
carried the child in her body for nine months, the pain remains acute
for ten, even twenty years; perhaps for life. The memory of the lost
child, whether he or she lived two minutes or thirty years, is one that
never fades. Women whose children died young still recall the
tragedy when they themselves are old, and visualize the child as
untouched by the years.

Suffer the Little Children

Alison, who lives in Brisbane, Australia, lost her third child at birth.
She is convinced that her infant not only comforted her after the
death, but came to her husband to help him accept the loss. She has
had five children, with all of whom she has had strong links while
they were in the womb.

"*Probably for me the most conclusive evidence of a link between the unborn baby and myself was the absolute certainty of the sex of each child and the vivid dreams and visions of exactly how each would look which were 100 per cent correct in every case.*

"*This pre-natal communication was particularly valuable for me in the case of my third baby, Janet, who did not survive her birth. I was knocked out by general anaesthetic as the doctor tried to 'save' her by ripping her out of me with forceps—even though everyone except myself knew it was too late. As a result of the terrible injury to my cervix and perineum, I spent two and a half hours unconscious while being repaired and did not officially 'know' that my baby had left her body. However, as soon as I woke and without anyone telling me, I was aware that Janet was dead. I remember looking round the recovery room to find her as I felt she was waiting there for me.*

"*To this day I know Janet was there, looking down on her shocked and suffering mother with compassion, waiting for half an hour or so until she was sure I had grasped the reality of the situation. Janet then left me and I have never 'sensed her presence' again.*

"*I believe she has not been back in touch with me because I have largely come to terms with her loss and am back on track again, although one never gets over a baby's death. The same cannot be said for Arthur, my husband. In the two years following her birth and death he was a rock for me and my closest ally, but did not pay enough attention to his own grieving process. Arthur is not particularly psychic, nor is he as sure about eternal life or reincarnation as I am. Yet it was he who has received messages from Janet. Nothing dramatic, but the two years following Janet's death, whenever Arthur was feeling really sad and hopeless, he felt a tug on his trouser-leg or a touch on the lower back exactly where a tiny child could reach. Arthur has felt these touches a number of times and we have interpreted them as Janet saying, 'Pay attention, Dad. Learn what needs to be learned.'*

"*Arthur was never frightened by this contact but happy and sad at the same time, and the touches are fewer and further apart nowadays. Perhaps he doesn't need to be reminded so often.*

"*I recalled while writing this that Janet actually waved goodbye to me*

333

in utero. *The last movement before her heart faltered and I was put under was a rippling sort of salute which filled me with great sorrow though I did not know why until much later."*

Beth, who lives in Rondebosch in South Africa, lost her baby daughter, not at birth but not long afterwards in a cot death. Like many mothers in similar circumstances, Beth wonders whether she could have done anything to prevent this and tries to find meaning in the seemingly senseless tragedy.

"Ellamay, who was my second child, was so reluctant to be born that she was finally induced on a Friday, three weeks after her due date. Her head crowned a full two minutes before the rest of her, screaming loudly. I said, 'She doesn't want to be born,' and the doctor replied, 'Well, too late now.'

"Another very ominous note was that the wayside pulpit message at her baptism was 'Die now and get it over with'. This seemed tasteless at the time and even worse seven weeks later when Ellamay died.

"Ellamay was an exquisitely elfin creature. I used to carry her everywhere I went in a pouch on my chest, and when she caught her first cold I knew intuitively that she was dying. I kept pestering our GP and the clinic sisters to have her hospitalized but everyone said I was being silly until on the Monday morning I found her dead in her basinette.

"An amazing series of synchronicities surrounded her death after which I realized that my younger sister, also a second child, had also died in August, possibly even on the same day of the week.

"Ellamay was three months and two days old when she died. In retrospect it was as if she was very slowly withdrawing from me, almost like a rehearsal for when she would not be there any more. I was not at all angry when she died, just so shocked and numb with guilt.

"It was called Sudden Infant Death Syndrome (cot death) on the death certificate, but no autopsy was ever done and years later I pieced information together. I surmised that Ellamay had been one of those babies who had inexplicably been born without an effective immune

system. My own immune system has not worked since then. I blamed myself because I did not breastfeed. As an over-reaction I breastfed my second daughter Victoria for nineteen months until one day she said 'Oh, yuk' and refused to nurse any more.

"I also felt guilty because I was twenty-eight and did not have the confidence to march into the nearest children's hospital and demand that they hospitalized Ellamay until she perked up a bit.

"For years I roamed from gynaecologist to gynaecologist in a state of shock requesting fertility treatment so I could have another little girl, only to be told after extensive tests that I was no longer ovulating. Finally encouraged by a recurring dream of a plump little moppet and a fortune teller who foresaw another female baby in my future, I went for acupuncture and became pregnant on our thirteenth wedding anniversary.

"One month short of four years after Ella's birth, also on a Friday, I gave birth to a little girl so plump and moppety my husband and I called her Victoria after seeing photographs of Queen Victoria as a baby. After I got Victoria safely through the first few years, I did start getting angry that I had so little support both before Ellamay's death and after. I had a great many people saying truly terrible things to me, such as 'I know how you feel because my cat has died.'

"Depending on my mood, I sometimes now think I could have saved her life if I had been more assertive, but mainly I believe she was not meant to be here any longer.

"Had she lived, Ella would now have turned nineteen. But I still miss her fragility and elusive charm. I count myself extremely blessed to have been her mother even for a short time."

Although there is rarely anything the mother could have done to prevent the death of her infant, the helplessness and the feeling that she has failed her child by missing a sign or not insisting on medical intervention is inevitable and hard to deal with. As Beth discovered, outsiders in an attempt to reassure the grieving mother make well-meaning but quite inappropriate remarks. One woman was told after her baby's death to go out and buy a new hat; another was told that she should have another baby as soon as possible to replace the one she had lost.

The Reverend Jean Wadsworth, vicar of the parish of Holy Trinity, Rotherhithe, in London, said:

"At one point I worked in an area of very high infant mortality. I can imagine no loss greater than that of a parent losing a child, because it cuts across the norm and undermines our hope for the future. Over the years I have realized that it is best to say as little as possible, to concentrate on helping couples to reflect and to find their own comfort and meaning in life.

"I feel strongly that the Church should not collude with those who want to pretend that the tragedy has not happened, that the baby, however premature, never lived. As a Christian minister I think that it is important that I emphasize that the baby was God's creation and that she or he had real value, although their life was short, and that that life continues and develops in a way that we cannot understand. I have found that the family will often give instances of the way in which the baby's life has had positive effect, for example healing family rifts. The dignity and worth of that life is terribly important."

When an Older Child Dies

One woman who had lost her only son when in his thirties said to me: "I mourn my son that he will never again come through the door. I grieve also for the grandchildren I will never see and perhaps also their children I might also have known. In a single night my family present and future was wiped out and I cry for them all."

When an older child dies, the pain is no less than that of losing an infant. When a child dies in mysterious circumstances, or by taking his or her own life, the natural pain is compounded by unanswered and unanswerable questions. Sue, who lives in Kent, lost two sons, one in infancy and one when he was eighteen.

"*My son Daniel was eighteen. He went out saying 'I will see you this evening' and never came back. Later he was found hanged. I have often thought that perhaps I could have said something, detected unhappiness in his eyes, that might have saved him. But there was no sign that he was distressed. The enormity of it is not hearing the key in the door at night and knowing he is safe, knowing I will not hear that sound again and his feet and his laughter. I never expected to lose a child on the brink of his life.*

"*Serious threats had been received in the period prior to Daniel's death. I told the coroner and a police investigation was opened, but nothing was found which made it all so much worse. Was there any connection? I do not know. The coroner recorded an open verdict.*

"*I have had to be strong for everyone. Mothers do. After my husband died in 1990 I had to be everything for the children. Daniel and I together had found my husband dead. Daniel would not talk about it and I feel so guilty now. The worst thing is not knowing why Daniel died. I have searched and searched his bedroom and the house for a note, but there is nothing. I want to hold him, to ask him why.*

"*I have a severely disabled son Tony who is fourteen and has taken it all very badly. Over the last few years, he has lost his grandparents, his father and now his brother. I carry everyone's grief. The week before Daniel died, my mother died unexpectedly of a heart attack. Her funeral was on the Monday and on the Tuesday Daniel died. Had I not been preoccupied with grief and burdens, could I have listened?*

"*Daniel loved old cars and driving about in them. The night he died the police came to the door and I wondered if he was involved in some teenage trouble. I was watching tennis on the television when the police knocked. They asked what time I had last seen Daniel and again I thought it was just some scrape. Then the police asked if they could come in and said they had bad news. It was as if they were talking about someone else's son. I switched off and watched the scene as if from a distance. It could not be happening. A couple of times Daniel was involved in bad crashes in the car. That was how I always feared he would go, but not like this.*

"*I would hate Daniel to be somewhere not at peace. My fear is that*

Daniel may not have gone to heaven because of the way he died. I want him to know how much I love him and for him to be with his father and grandparents and his brother Dominic who died as a baby. I went to see a medium, not long after Daniel's death. She told me that Daniel was still in a state of shock and he seemed to be in some sort of intensive care ward. Those caring for him had given him his favourite music. She assured me that my mother was there and was well. My mum had suffered from senile dementia before she died. I said if Daniel was playing his loud rock music, Lord help the angels. But I would love to hear it again resounding through the house.

"I lost my first son Dominic when he was a baby when I was twenty years old. Dominic was born with an abnormal stomach. I saw my son being born in the early hours of the morning and then he was whisked away. The doctors kept telling me that Dominic was ill and was getting worse, but they would not let me see him or tell me what was going on. I became angry, and the nurse offered me a cup of tea instead of my baby. 'Just give me the baby,' I was crying.

"A doctor rang my husband John and told him that I had a baby. When John asked about the baby he was told, 'Your guess is as good as ours.'

"At only twenty-two years of age, John was expected to break the bad news to me that our baby had died. I screamed at him. John's parents refused to talk about the baby I had lost and told me to get rid of the baby stuff and go on holiday. I remember asking my father-in-law if I had a little girl or boy and he replied, 'What does it matter? It's dead.'

"It was as if Dominic had never existed. My husband did not tell me about the funeral. I do not even know if he went. People would tell me I should forget Dominic and that I could have another child to replace him, but he is always there. I was not allowed to talk about my loss. Eventually I found his grave but it was not until after Daniel died that I was able to talk about Dominic's death. I have put Dominic's name on a plaque on an obelisk dedicated to other babies who died and it helps so much.

"I have dreams about Daniel since his death, that he is a baby, that I cannot reach him and save him. Then I have dreamed of him older, but

still screaming and shouting for help, and I still cannot reach him.

"*I miss him so much. I have become so depressed, even suicidal, and wondered why it was not me and why I cannot be with him. On the night before he died, I had a bad headache and the back of my neck hurt. I was in the bath the next morning and had a searing pain in my throat about the time he was hanging. Was I picking up his pain?*

"*My love is overwhelming and has not stopped with Daniel's death. Everybody loved him. He was larger than life. He would bound in the front door and into the kitchen to get food and fill every available space with his presence and his music. At the funeral all Daniel's friends came. I used to think they were awful, with their ears and noses pierced and peculiar names, but they all thought so much of him.*

"*Daniel was so much like Dominic. He is still inside me. The pain never goes away, first Dominic and then Daniel. It hurts that out of four children, I only have two children left. The only thing that keeps me going is the thought of Tony. Who would get him out of bed if I were not here? Tony is my driving force, my reason for living. Tony was adopted when he was eleven weeks old. He is brain-damaged and was only given a few years to live, but he has outlived all expectations. Tony has no speech, no eyesight and no balance, but he has a brilliant brain and smile and is now working for his GCSEs. I remember when Tony was very small we went to the Isle of Wight on holiday and he had bad convulsions. I took him to a doctor who commented, 'He doesn't do much, does he?' The doctor then told me that there were nice homes on the Isle of Wight where I could leave Tony. I told my consultant when I returned home who said that the doctor had a point and Tony had the intellect of a fly. Now Tony is determined to pass his GCSEs and uses a stick on his head to tap out the words. He is so full of determination and I am overwhelmed by admiration and love for him.*"

Even when a child is expected to die, a long illness over weeks or months and the gradual deterioration bring a different but equally pernicious sorrow. The most recent memory is not of a strong healthy child, but of a body and sometimes a mind racked with illness. In such a case dreams, visions and synchronistic symbols linking mother and child can be doubly precious as a reminder of the essential lovely, loving child.

Anne, who lives in Cheshire, wrote to me about the death of her sixteen-year-old daughter.

"My youngest daughter Sarah passed away on 18 February 1994, having being seriously ill for eighteen months. However, I felt the loss of Sarah some twelve months before she showed signs of her illness. I was not able to understand what I was feeling at that time because it did not seem rational.

"Often I would be sitting at home in the evening. Sarah would be in her bedroom where she loved to be, with her computer games, television and video films, and I would have the feeling of her going away from us. This is the only way I can describe it. I mentioned this a few times to my husband Barry but he could make no sense of it. Sarah was a lively, outgoing girl and she was extremely healthy. She was thirteen years old and we were not experiencing the problems we had with our other daughters who were older than Sarah. Sarah was a joy to have around, but still these thoughts would nag at me.

"A year later, like a bolt out of the blue, Sarah contracted a very rare disease of the central nervous system. Now the feelings became much stronger but because the disease was so rare, the medical staff treating Sarah were unwilling to give us a definite prognosis. Throughout her illness she had good times and bad. I would always know weeks before she had a relapse because I would get a sickening feeling deep inside and become quite ill myself. This was very distressing because at times when Sarah appeared to be getting better, I knew from my soul that she was not.

"On Sarah's sixteenth birthday, I woke in the morning and all I could feel around me was death, such a feeling that I never want to experience again. I can only describe it as drowning in an ocean of black tears and unbearable pain. This was 20 November 1993.

"After Sarah left this life in the following February I believe she has contacted me many times.

"One of the first experiences I had after Sarah's death was when I was

in her bedroom about three weeks after her death. I had sprayed some of
her favourite perfume on to her quilt cover on the bed and put my head
on it, stroking the cover with my eyes closed so that I could visualize her
by her smell. When I opened my eyes, her tall mirror in the corner of her
room tipped forward so that I was the image in the mirror and then it
tipped back to its normal position. I went over to the mirror and touched
it, stamped on the floor but I could not get it to tip forward or backward
as it had done at that moment.

"Another morning I got up to find all the clocks in the house were
exactly an hour slow, the manual clocks as well as the clock for the central
heating and the oven timer clock. A week or so later, my wrist watch on
two occasions was exactly an hour slow.

"I have sensed Sarah's presence in the house many times. Sometimes
she has been in the room and at other times she feels as if she is draped
over me like a warm comforting cloak. I have never seen Sarah while I
have been awake but she has come to me in dreams. The quality of
dreams is very different from the normal dream state and I have woken
with an incredible sense of peace. Sarah has let me know through the
dreams that she is well again and is the beautiful vivacious girl she was
before the illness.

"One morning as I lay in bed awake but with my eyes closed, I felt
Sarah's hand on top of my hand and then, on top of Sarah's, my father's
hand holding both of us. My father passed away seven years earlier.
Sarah was his favourite and I know he is with her. When my father died
Sarah was nine years old.

"I was not sure about an afterlife but I believed that if there was one
my father would let me know. A week after he had died, I was woken
early in the morning by Sarah's voice at my side saying loudly and
clearly, 'Granddad is moving around.' I thought Sarah had come into
my bedroom but when I checked on her she was fast asleep in her own
bed. This message was confirmation for me that my dad was with me
and had used Sarah to convey the message.

"One day after Sarah's death, I was driving to work. I put a tape in
the cassette player. I was not really listening to it as I was getting very
upset about what my friend Angela had just told me about Sarah. I had

known Angela for years and her daughter was Sarah's lifelong friend. Because of Sarah's illness, my daughter knew she would never be able to have children and I know this had upset her very much. We never talked about it but I discovered that Sarah had discussed the matter with Angela. I felt I had let Sarah down. Suddenly the tape switched off and the radio came on. The first line of an advert was 'Do you have a pregnant teenage daughter?'

"I thought at the time that the tape had come to an end, although it never had before automatically switched over to the radio. I was in the work car park by this time and switched the radio off. After work I put the stereo on and the the tape which had been playing continued. It had not reached the end at all.

"On New Year's Day 1995, in the morning before getting up, I lay in bed in a distressed state. It was the first New Year without Sarah and that February would be the first anniversary of Sarah's death. I felt at that point that I could not go on and at that moment a musical teddy bear that I had bought for Sarah when she was a baby and kept on a sofa in my bedroom started to play its tune. At first I did not realize what it was and then Barry, my husband, asked, 'Is that Sarah?'

"I told him it was and assured Sarah how much I loved her. Sarah gave me the strength to get up that day. This was a special day for Barry because he had not experienced Sarah in this way. Try as we might we could not get that teddy bear to play its tune again.

"My other daughter Shelly was extremely close to her sister and has been aware of Sarah's presence many times since Sarah's death. Shelly has felt her sister sit on the end of her bed when she has turned out the light. As first Shelly was disturbed by this, but now accepts that Sarah wants to be near her. One morning when Shelly was in her bedroom drying her hair she had her television on. Suddenly the clock radio came on, playing the song Sarah *by Thin Lizzy, a song we had played at Sarah's funeral. When Shelly checked her radio, she discovered it had been switched to the off position when the music was heard."*

The signs between a deceased child and living relations are not those that stand up to scientific scrutiny. Clocks slowing, a mirror tipping, are not in themselves phenomena verifiable as objective proof of an afterlife. But emotions are not objective, they are linked with meaning, a significant song suddenly on the radio of a grieving sister, a much-loved musical teddy that plays to a mother who feels she cannot go on without her lost child. They are endowed with the power of shared love, manifesting themselves at moments when the pain is too much to endure.

PART NINE

Bonds of Blood or Love?

Adoptive Links

Psychic phenomena during and after the adoption process are a valuable source of confirmation of a bond. We feel more secure in our roles as parents when we can point to an unexplainable event, an impossible coincidence, that somehow validates the match.

Rita Laws, adoptive mother and
expert on parent/child intuition

Linda had a classic pre-birth dream: it correctly predicted the sex and looks of her child. But there was a vital difference. Her son Ivan was adopted. I met Linda and Dick, who come from Oklahoma, when I went to Los Angeles to make a programme on maternal instinct in NBC's *Unsolved Mysteries* series. Linda told me about a vivid dream that was more than a dream, almost an out of body experience, in which she was in a labour ward.

"It was so real I could almost touch the woman, a blonde, fair-skinned woman. I watched the baby being delivered, a dark-skinned, dark-haired boy. The moment was incredibly moving and I was convinced I was witnessing an actual birth. Then I was in my bedroom, wide awake. I noted down the date and the time, although I thought I had somehow witnessed the birth of the child of a neighbour who was pregnant at the time. However, my neighbour had not given birth.

"I told Dick, my husband, about the dream and we discussed what it might mean. When we were given Ivan, our adoptive child, he was indeed the child whose face I had seen so clearly that night. The date and time of his birth exactly coincided with my dream. I knew that I had witnessed his birth for a reason, to confirm the rightness of the adoption.

"Sadly, Ivan's mother died and I was sent some photographs from her family for Ivan. She was the fair-skinned, blonde-haired woman in my dream and I felt very close and loving towards her as we had shared such a precious moment."

Dick said that for him his wife's dream drove away any doubts he might have harboured about the adoption and he knew that Ivan was meant to be theirs. He felt this bonding helped him through the daily problems of bringing up any child. Most wonderful, the closeness of the bond is not all-exclusive, for Linda and Dick have encouraged Ivan to see his birthfather and I was shown photographs of them together.

Linda's experience would suggest that intuitive links are not based in biology alone, but in the more intangible quality of love, that can exist even before the child is born. Conventional wisdom lacks the tools to explain this phenomenon. We can only speculate about why Linda's dream was so uncannily accurate. Did she somehow telepathically tune in to her prospective adoptive son, as one might suddenly come across a distant and unfamiliar radio station? Or was the source of dream the boy himself? In the end the explanation is not so important as the fact that it helped Dick and Linda to bond with their new son.

This is not an isolated case. Dr Lauren Bradway is an adoptive mother from Oklahoma who has extensively studied the adoptive bond and works for the United Methodist Counselling Services. She too felt a strong pre-adoptive link with her daughter: "I had a dream one night my daughter was born and was reassuring me she was on the way. Exactly sixteen months later we received a call from the agency where we had applied to adopt saying that they had a little girl for us. Then they told me her birthdate—it was the night of my dream."

As children grow, many adoptive mothers maintain close tele-pathic links with their adopted children. Sheila, who lives in California, adopted two girls, Hilde and Davida.

348

"Hilde and Davida are my two little miracles. I nearly died twice when I had two tubular pregnancies within five months. I did not know until I recovered from each surgery that the pregnancies were life-threatening. After the second surgery I awoke to find my entire family surrounding my bed. They were there because they were told I was dying. I almost smiled because I did not feel as though I was dying. At that time I only wished to die because I knew I would never be able to have children. Three years later Larry and I adopted Hilde and three years after that we adopted Davida and brought her home. I felt my life was complete.

"When my husband Larry and I first saw Hilde in the adoption agency our hearts melted. For me it was love at first sight. Although we did not specify gender, I wanted a girl so badly I could think of nothing else. When we adopted Davida we had decided we wanted another daughter.

"Once Davida went on a ski trip with a group from school. At about noon that day I felt a sudden thud on my forehead. I knew something had happened but could do nothing. I could hardly wait for Davida to come home. When she finally arrived home she had a huge lump on her forehead. After hugging and kissing her I just asked, 'What time?' She told me that her foot had slipped out of the ski, which had come up and hit her on the forehead, at noon.

"Hilde must have been about eleven years old and I was working part-time. While at work, I was aware that all was not right. I was hyperventilating and worried. I left my desk and tried to relax. I got a somewhat distorted vision of Hilde. I called the school to hear that Hilde was suffering an asthma attack. I had to leave work at once and pick her up.

"When Hilde was a young adult, she worked as an emergency medical technician on the night shift and did not usually get home until about 6 a.m. I was asleep when I sensed a smooth black stone falling with great speed on my pillow and I heard a whoosh as it hit. I fell back asleep and then I felt as if someone or something had kicked me in the small of the back and nearly knocked me out of bed. I sat up, looked at the clock and saw that it was 1.30 a.m. I neither heard nor saw anything.

"I went back to sleep but woke with a jolt. I thought we were having an earthquake. My heart was racing and I sat up in bed and realized

that nothing was moving or shaking but me. I tried to go to sleep again, and as I closed my eyes a distorted vision of Hilde's face appeared to me. I sat up and knew then that something was going on with Hilde, only I did not know what or where. I just had to wait. At about 4.30 a.m. Hilde came home and I asked her if everything was OK and why she was home so early. She said she must have a sudden fever. She had gone to an emergency room because her heart was beating so rapidly and she was shaking. I asked her what time this happened and she said it was about 1.30 a.m.

"When Davida was eighteen, she went to Ireland. She rented a room and worked in a pub for several months. One day I had an overwhelming feeling I needed to contact her. I tried several times without success. When we finally connected she wasn't feeling well and was in need of some sympathy and mothering. She had been trying to reach me but could not get through. We chatted for a while and she felt much better by the time I hung up.

"When I met Hilde's birthmother, I felt I had known her all my life. She is a lovely woman. I feel her pain but am grateful to her. She provided me with Hilde. I was never opposed to my girls searching for their birthparents. My feeling has always been that everyone has a right to his/her own identity."

Rita Laws from Oklahoma, who described how she shared psychic toothaches with her own son and her adopted child at the same time (see p. 36), sees the psychic link between parents and children as very important in aiding the bonding process between adoptive parents and their new offspring. She told me:

"Adoptive parents tend to be, understandably, a bit more insecure about their role, at least at first. Psychic phenomena during and after the adoption process are a valuable source of confirmation of a bond between them. We feel a bit more secure in our roles as parents when we can point to an unexplainable event, an impossible coincidence, that somehow validates the match. Eventually this insecurity fades entirely, helped along in part by the continuing and growing psychic link. Just like

biological parents, adoptive parents find themselves waking up moments before the baby does and jumping when the child, playing in the next room, hurts himself. Even though this link grows more slowly than it does for birthparents, in the end it is just as strong. The bonding catches up to the parent and child if they are patient and loving with one another.

"Our first adopted son was born in February 1984. Our third birthchild was born exactly seven and a half months later. When he was seven and a half months old, I joked to my husband that it was time for another baby, but even as I joked, I had an overwhelming sense that we would have three sons born exactly seven and a half months apart. We then applied to adopt a girl but were offered a son instead. Jesse, adopted in July 1985, was born in May 1985, exactly seven and a half months after Joaquin.

"I was able to breastfeed Tony and Jesse even though they were not born to me. Jesse and I had every bit as close a linkage as I had with any of my other children. And when it came to sleeping we were the closest. For the first five years of his life, Jesse always woke when I did. He slept with me till he was three but even in a different bedroom he would wake up within five minutes of me. I used to think this was because of the breastfeeding but he did this even after weaning. It is only recently that he has begun, sometimes, to sleep later than I do."

If children unborn do choose their parents Jesse must be one of the most tenacious. Rita explained.

"When we were ready to adopt in 1985, we contacted my tribe, the Choctaw Indians of Oklahoma, the Native American Adoption Resource Exchange in Pennsylvania (NAARE), a private agency and the state adoption agency. We asked for a girl, preferably younger than our eldest child, who was five, and we were open to disabilities. We were firm about not wanting another boy, as our daughter wanted a sister, and about not wanting another infant. We already had two. The tribe called in March and described Jesse who was not even going to be born for two months as half-Black, half-Choctaw, gender unknown and paternity unknown. We sadly declined because, male or female, this was an

351

infant. We couldn't see it was fair depriving another couple of an infant when we had already had that pleasure.

"In May, NAARE called. They had matched us to a newborn Oklahoma baby, half-Black, half-Choctaw—the same one the tribe had called us about.

"Again we declined reluctantly. In June, the private agency called and offered us the same baby! In July, we called the tribe and asked for the child, convinced by now that he was meant to be our son. But the tribe no longer had custody of Jesse. They had turned him over to the state which was now trying to find him a family. I called the state and asked for a social worker who had known us for several years. She immediately said she had been going to phone us that day to offer us a child. When I described the child to her she was amazed. 'How did you know?' she asked over and over.

"Three days later Jesse was home. Later we found out he was born in Shawnee, Oklahoma, just like our second child, Tim. Jesse had also been delivered by the same doctor who delivered Tim. A year later I obtained a photograph of Jesse's birthmother and was surprised to see she was wearing the exact same wristwatch I have. One more thing, Jesse's initials before adoption were LAW—similar to my last name."

A series of coincidences or something more profound which we cannot understand? Whatever the reason, the experience helped to create a link between Rita and Jesse which, as she has said, was every bit as close as any of her other children. Rita says:

"Several of my friends have, like me, adopted both infants and older kids as well as having given birth. We tend to agree that eventually, the frequency of psychic events and the intensity of bonding is no different between adopted and biological infants, and also that omens and signs are a very important part of this bonding process. However, the bonding between older adopted child and parent is unique and different in that you are friends first and then you become parent and the psychic link is still there, growing stronger over time. But because the child is older the frequency of happenings may be much less."

In the case of Rita's latest adopted son, the instinctive call helped her to connect him to her in circumstances that might have proved traumatic for both the foster mother, Rita herself, and the child.

"Our last child, Jamie, was two years and eleven months old when we adopted him and, though very delayed in development, he was old enough to be very attached to his foster mother—the only mom he had ever known. For some reason I had tacked up his photo on the wall, though he wasn't the only child nor necessarily the most likely child we would end up with. There were several others.

"When the social worker telephoned to inform us that Jamie would become our son, I was looking at his photocopied picture on the wall. I was delighted, but very worried he wouldn't want to leave his foster mother and come with us. Then I had a dream in which Jamie came with us willingly because his foster mother gave him verbal permission to love us. Strange as it sounds I decided to try that approach because I believed the dream was giving me an answer to a potentially very distressing situation when logic couldn't.

"On 1 June last year, I flew to the big and totally unfamiliar city of Baltimore and attempted to drive across a couple of counties to meet my son. My husband was to meet me the next day. In spite of excellent directions, I became hopelessly lost in my rented car, time and time again. Finally, late in the afternoon, I called the social worker from a phone booth at the height of rush-hour traffic with tears of frustration streaming down my cheeks.

"In spite of my pleas, she refused to come and get me and instead told me to calm down and 'come meet your son'. I did calm down and concentrated on homing in on Jamie, deciding to go where my heart led me. As I approached different highway interchanges and exits, I consulted my map, but also relied on my inner radar. I arrived quickly at my destination in spite of construction detours without any further problems. Jamie stuck close to his foster mom and pretty well ignored me during that visit, but I loved him deeply immediately.

"I returned with Amado, my husband, the next day and we helped the foster mom pack Jamie's things. At this point he figured out he had to go

with us and he began crying and screaming and clinging to his foster mom, a very common scenario. I asked her to speak to Jamie in our presence, even though he probably wouldn't understand much, and explain that it was all right for him to go with us. I tried to explain to Jamie's foster mother, I 'knew' Jamie would understand in his heart, even if her words seemed incomprehensible. But she refused and fighting back tears demanded that we just go, take him and go. She had not been able to adopt him herself due to health problems. I picked up Jamie and we got as far as the front door when he began kicking and screaming hysterically. My heart was heavy because I knew this was the worst possible way to begin the adoption.

"As I stepped outside, the foster mom suddenly changed her mind, called us back in and took Jamie from me. She sat down on the sofa, put Jamie in her lap and smiled at him. Then she told him it was OK to love us, because we loved him as much as she did. She promised to always love him and to be his grandma and write him letters. Then she told him to go with us and not to worry about anything. It happened just as I had seen in my dream. Jamie immediately stopped crying and looked at me as if he was seeing me for the very first time. He held out his arms to me and said, 'Go bye-bye now.' He left with us quite happily, racing us out to the car, and did not cry, not one little bit. In fact he did not cry for two weeks after the adoption and then only because he fell off the swing in the yard and bumped his knee.

"To this day he looks at photos of his foster mom, calls her Grandma and seems perfectly content. I always feel like I saw a miracle that day. I believe the psychic bond to be of a protective nature. My maternal heart, knowing that Jamie could be potentially traumatized by the adoption, found a way to protect him and conveyed one possible solution to me via a dream. I wonder if Jamie had dreamed a similar dream, making the real-life event familiar to him as a déjà vu experience."

The experiences of Rita and the others with their adopted children seem to suggest that the psychic bond of motherhood can develop with anyone who occupies a positive mothering role for the child. I believe the link does not depend entirely on genetics and is not exclusive to birthmothers. The strangest thing is, however, that although separated by perhaps thousands of miles and twenty years or more, sometimes a child can still hear a call from the mother who first gave him or her life.

Although adoptive mothers and indeed fathers do bond closely, there can be potential conflict where a birthmother appears on the scene or a beloved child searches for his or her "real mother". Given wisdom and understanding on all sides, the adoptive relationship can actually become stronger when a child finds early roots and there can be warm feeling between the mothers.

Dr Marlou Russell, who lives in Santa Monica, California, is a clinical psychologist and an adoptee who has been reunited with her birthmother and two brothers. She counsels and runs workshops for adoptees and birth families and has extensively explored what she calls the lifelong impact of adoption. Her innovative work has done much to help a more open and empathic view of the adoptive process. She explained:

"The adoption triangle or triad has three members, the adoptive parents or parent, the birth parents and the adoptee. All members are necessary and all members depend on each other, as in any triangle.

"There have been many changes in adoption over the years. It was thought that all the triad members would get their needs met by adoption. The records were amended, sealed and closed through legal proceedings and the triad members were expected never to see one another again. It was discovered, however, that there were problems with the arrangement of closed adoption.

"Some birthparents began having trouble forgetting that they had a child and were having difficulties getting on with their lives as suggested by those around them. There were adoptees who wanted to know more about their biological roots and had questions about their genetic history. Some adoptive parents too were having difficulties raising their adopted children and were being confronted with parenting issues that no one had told them about.

"Clinicians and psychotherapists became involved because more and

more adopted children were being brought in for psychotherapy and being seen in juvenile detention facilities, in-patient treatment centres and special schools. Questions began to be raised about the impact and process of closed adoption.

"From these questions it became clear that there are new basic tenets in adoption. One is that adoption is a second choice for all triad members. For example people don't usually imagine that they will grow up, get married and adopt children. They expect to grow up, get married and have children of their own. People also don't expect to get pregnant and give their child to strangers to raise.

"A second basic tenet of adoption is that it involves loss to all involved. A birthparent loses a child. The adoptee loses biological connections and the adoptive parent often loses the hope for biological children. The birthparents' parents lose a grandchild while the siblings of the birthparent lose a niece or nephew.

"Since loss is such a major part of adoption, grieving is a necessary and important process. For triad members grief holds a special significance. They may not even be aware that they are grieving or mourning their loss. Adoption can create a situation where grieving is delayed or denied. Because adoption has been seen as such a positive solution it may be difficult for a triad member to feel that it is OK to grieve when everything is working out for the best. There are no real rituals or ceremonies for the loss of adoption.

"Some triad members resolve their grief issues by trying to find the person they are grieving for. Search and reunion offers triad members the opportunity to address the basic and natural curiosity that all people have in their inheritance and roots. The missing pieces can be put in the puzzle and lifelong questions can be answered. In addition there is an empowering aspect to search and reunion and an internal sense of timing that brings with it a sense of being in control and touching one's own judgement. For most people who search, knowing, even if they find uncomfortable information, is better than not knowing.

"Whether someone genuinely actively searches or not there is usually some part of the person that is internally searching. A common experience among adoptees and birthparents is searching in crowds for someone who

could be their parent or child. What holds many triad members back from searching is the fear of hurting other triad members. Adoptees may worry about hurting their adoptive parents' feelings and appearing ungrateful while birthparents may worry that their child was not told of the adoption or that their birthchild might reject them.

"Reunion between triad members is the beginning of a previous relationship. It is where fantasy meets reality. Reunion relationships impact on all triad members and those close to them. As with all relationships there needs to be nurturing, attention and a respect for people's boundaries and needs. Reunion relationships show us that adoption was not just a simple solution but indeed a process with lifelong impact."

The Homing Instinct

The migratory and homing behaviours of animals have been admired, yet mysterious to mankind of all generations. Should there be any less marvellous program for an adoptee's homing instinct than that designed for the Alaskan salmon?

Dr LaVonne Harper Stiffler on birthmothers
and their separated children

*F*or Sophie, who lives in Edinburgh, the homing instinct took her thousands of miles to be reunited with her birthmother Patricia who lives in Western Australia. Patricia described for me the "synchronicities" that brought her lost daughter back.

"Having recently been reunited with my daughter Sophie in circumstances that can only be described as fate, I have subsequently discovered coincidence after coincidence in our lives.

"Fate is a word I have used repeatedly in the last months, describing the events that led up to a reunion with my daughter. With the laws as they were in 1971 when we were parted, I thought I would never see her again. I followed the changes in the law with interest and began to see a glimmer of hope. Just before her eighteenth birthday I wrote to the Adoption Society, giving permission for all my identifying details to be revealed and indicating my desire for a reunion. I also enrolled on NORCAP [National Organization for Counselling Adoptees and Parents] and the National Adoption Register in the UK where I had given birth.

"Late last year Sophie resigned from her job and decided to take an overseas holiday before starting work with her new employer. She went to London from her home in Edinburgh for a couple of days before she was

due to leave and made arrangements to meet friends while she was there. At the last minute Sophie's friends were unable to meet her so she made a spur-of-the-moment decision to visit the Adoption Society. This was the first attempt she had made to trace her birthmother and had not been part of her plans for the short stay in London at all.

"Sophie attended the initial interview expecting it to be the beginning of a long and difficult search or perhaps to lead nowhere. When her file was opened everyone was stunned when they realized I had written from Australia, her destination the next day.

"I received the absolutely stunning news from the NORCAP counsellor that my daughter was trying to trace me. The counsellor was very careful to reveal only minimal details at that stage because, from her point of view, there was a possibility that either or both of us would get 'cold feet'. Before learning anything specific, I somehow knew that everything would work out well from the following non-identifying information that I received over the period of three days before we actually spoke together.

"The connection was made so quickly because I had written to the Adoption Society when Sophie became eighteen in 1989, so my letter was already on file. My other daughter, Katherine, had been diagnosed with childhood cancer when she was six years old, three years earlier. It was so advanced that she was given a 5 per cent chance of survival and there was every chance that we would lose her. That really brought home the fact that I had effectively lost one daughter already and I determined to do everything in my power to help my daughter find me in the future.

"I decided not to try to trace my daughter. I still feel that a birthmother giving a child up for adoption has to accept that it is for ever and it is up to the child to decide if he or she wants a reunion. You can't expect to 'have your cake and eat it', although I know that open adoption is becoming fashionable, particularly in the States.

"Although I knew that it was statistically probable that Sophie would never seek me out, I never gave up hope of a reunion. It was based not only on a gut feeling, but on a quite uncharacteristically irrational belief that I have subconsciously held for twenty-two years. Just before I migrated to Australia from Bristol in 1975, the Scottish husband of an

ex-flatmate asked me if he could tell my fortune. I was extremely sceptical, but his wife assured me that he was rarely moved to use what he believed was inherited second sight and felt strongly that he had something to tell me. Neither he nor his wife had any knowledge of Sophie's birth in London some four years before I moved back to Bristol, and yet the gist of his predictions could be applied to no other circumstance than a reunion with my daughter. I made no comment at the time, but was very shaken! I wrote to the couple soon after my reunion with Sophie and told them the whole story. Alex wrote back immediately to say that he had never forgotten the strong but inexplicable feelings he had had twenty-two years ago and was pleased to have them clarified.

"My rational mind says that my reaction to the predictions was wishful thinking, but I find it hard to explain why Alex also remembered the occasion so vividly after such a long time.

"Sophie had come to Australia on her own, for a holiday. I've spent my whole life on the move and it seemed auspicious that she also had the travel bug and was thoroughly independent. She was taking a six-week diving course in Airlie Beach, Queensland. This is the other side of Australia from my home—six and a half hours' flying time from Perth. In European terms this is probably the equivalent distance of London to Siberia. However, the Australian perspective is quite different and it is no distance at all.

"We had previously lived in the Eastern States and spent a family holiday in Airlie Beach in 1986, as soon as Katherine had miraculously responded to her initial cancer treatment, so we knew it well. In addition, my husband was currently working in Queensland, relatively near Airlie Beach in Australian terms. That seemed an extraordinary coincidence.

"When we finally spoke on the phone after three days of using the NORCAP counsellor as an intermediary, it seemed to be the most normal conversation in the world, although I think my Australian accent fazed her at first! Katherine, fully recovered from cancer and quite wonderful, came home from university while we were still speaking and chatted to her new sister quite naturally, too.

"Once we had spoken on the telephone we then had an opportunity to exchange letters and photographs until previous commitments on both sides allowed us to actually meet. The perceived coincidences came thick and fast during this time.

"After I sent over photos of myself to Sophie in Queensland, she said that she thought she looked a lot like me, and enclosed a photo in return. I picked the photograph up from the Post Office Box on my way to deliver Meals on Wheels one morning and was so struck by the resemblance which could have been me twenty-five years ago that I couldn't resist showing it to June, my delivery partner, and asking, 'Who do you think this is?'

"She immediately said, 'That's you when you were younger, of course.' I had to tell her the whole story. We had already found by chance that we had much in common. June's husband is a geologist and my husband is a mining engineer, so we had a shared experience of being mining widows with husbands always away. Later in our friendship I'd discovered that she'd also had a child who suffered from childhood cancer. Sadly, her son died at sixteen. As soon as I explained that the photo was of my long-lost daughter and not of me, she told me that she had had a similar experience some years previously. The daughter she had given up for adoption thirty years ago had contacted her out of the blue just before she was getting married. June and her husband actually financed a honeymoon in Australia so she could meet her daughter. How's that for coincidence?

"I discovered that Sophie had read maths at Oxford. Both my parents graduated from London University in physics, with maths subsidiary. My main course at college was maths. There's obviously a genetic bias there, but neither of my other two children has more than a general aptitude for maths, despite my background and the fact that their father is an engineer.

"Although my parents did not study at Oxford, my father spent the greater part of World War Two before I was born doing technical research on behalf of the RAF at an Oxford college.

"Sophie's adoptive mother, Evelyn, was a translator. She died when Sophie was eighteen. Her adoptive father, Martin, read geography at

Oxford and is an accomplished and practising musician in piano and singing.

"My eldest sister is named Evelyn. She read geography at London University and is very much involved in the Bedfordshire musical scene as a singer, having, in her youth, gained an LRAM in piano.

"Sophie spent a year at the Abbey School in Reading before being sent to boarding school. The two eldest daughters of an old college friend of mine whose husband is an Oxford maths graduate were at the Abbey School at the same time—one in the same year as Sophie!

"Although her mother and stepfather moved to Lancashire during her teenage years, Sophie was sent to a boarding school in Hertfordshire. This school is only a few miles from my mother's home in Southgate in North London and my second sister's home in Harpenden, Hertfordshire, so Sophie is very familiar with my home patch.

"Whilst at Oxford, Sophie played mixed seven-a-side rugby and rowed with the women's crew. Jim, my son (now twenty), was a champion rower at school and a State representative at rugby. This might seem a tenuous connection, but it would surely have been more obvious for her to have played tennis or netball.

"My husband, Joe, actually met Sophie before I did because he was able to arrange a meeting in Queensland before she came over to Perth. He hadn't been home to see her photo or read her letters, so he had no preconceived ideas about her. He reported that he felt that he could have been talking to me twenty-five years ago. It wasn't just the result of the physical similarities, but the fact that her mannerisms and personality seemed to be so like mine. This is extraordinary when you consider that Katherine resembles her father in almost every respect. She has something of me in her, but it isn't immediately obvious, and my son Jim is a mixture of both of us. Why are Sophie and I so alike?

"When she actually arrived in Perth I was relieved that she was so much her own person or she would have felt she'd lost her identity! Everyone who met her was overwhelmed by the similarities between us. As only one small example, the whole family thought we were quite mad to spend the extremely hot days standing in the pool under the shade of an umbrella doing advanced logic problems together. My eldest sister is the *only other person in the world who would understand the fascination.*

"Our common travel bug led to two coincidences. I taught in Canada for a couple of years during my early career and Sophie's natural father still lives in Montreal. I feel it is fairly extraordinary that Sophie has actually spent some time in Montreal in the course of her travels. I also think that the fact that I've visited Chattanooga, Tennessee, where Sophie spent a year as an exchange student, is worthy of notice, too. As far as most people are concerned, familiarity with the same city in the UK might have been enough evidence of an unusual connection. With such a huge world out there, it's amazing that we have taken so many similar routes.

"When Sophie returned to Edinburgh at the end of January to take up her new job, she finally found time to thoroughly digest the file that had been handed to her by the Adoption Society. She discovered an incredible coincidence in some correspondence dating from 1971. Soon after 'Elizabeth's' birth I finalized all the adoption formalities in London and returned to Bristol where I had lived before my two-year stint in Canada, to take up a teaching position. I was really looking forward to returning to a normal life after a fairly traumatic few months. I had left Canada because my father had died suddenly. I had no idea that I was pregnant when I returned home to help my mother sort things out and my reasons for not going back to Montreal to marry Sophie's father are completely irrelevant right now. Suffice it to say, I made a wise decision, despite the consequences!

"Having settled back into life in Bristol, it's impossible to describe how I felt when I received a letter from the Adoption Society some months later to say that all the paperwork had been mislaid and I would have to go through all the legal procedures again. It was very tempting to say that I had changed my mind and would take my baby back! I engaged in correspondence with a social worker from Buckinghamshire County Council which had been responsible for the adoption until matters were sorted out. Until Sophie read her file in detail, I hadn't realized that the social worker who I had dealt with in 1971 was the same NORCAP counsellor who helped to reunite us in 1996. When I wrote to ask the counsellor if she remembered the incident, she replied that it was

indelibly etched on her memory as one of the worst moments in her career. That really is a coincidence."

Are such shared experiences between separated mother and child coincidence or the call of love? Many birthmothers and adoptees responded to a single appeal I made to NORCAP and to more general appeals throughout the world, intrigued that the synchronicities that they had observed during these reunions, and indeed the years apart, were not unique, but part of a general pattern.

Indeed, the magnetic homing instinct from a child separated from his or her birthmother can be so strong, it seems, that it can survive even death.

Wayne, who lives in Leicestershire, told me of his wife's experience:

"My wife Jenny was an adopted child and longed to know about her real parents. We visited a Spiritualist church in Kettering where Jenny was given a message that there was a lady in Spirit whose name was Peggy watching over her. The medium told Jenny that the lady was showing the tip of her ring finger on her left hand and saying that the tip of the finger was missing. Peggy had passed over quite recently with an internal complaint. Jenny could not identify this person but the experience remained with her.

"About twelve months later, new laws were passed allowing adult adopted children to obtain information about their parents. Jenny and I went along to the Record Office in Northampton and, after filling in various forms, were given Jenny's birth certificate. From it we discovered that Jenny had been born in Kettering to an unmarried mother named Peggy. After careful thought, Jenny decided to call at the address where she had been born to try to locate her mother.

"The door was opened by a woman who was Jenny's aunt and had been hoping that Jenny would call. They became good friends, and Jenny gained a half-brother and several cousins. Jenny's mother Peggy had died three years before Jenny's visit, suffering from cancer of the liver. Peggy had worked in a shoe factory in the next street and some years previously a ring on her finger had become trapped in the machine she was

operating and had cut off the tip of her finger to the first joint. No mind-reading on the part of the medium could have been involved since Jenny had no knowledge of her mother at the time of the meeting with the medium."

However, the majority of intuitive communication between a birthmother and the child from whom she is parted takes place in the everyday world, although the links can be equally inexplicable in rational terms. The connection frequently manifests itself in subtle but unmistakable ways. For instance, one American couple, Barbara and Dave, commented that their adopted daughter Darlene, now aged five, does not know that she was originally named Louise, but she has named every doll she has ever had Louise.

Dr LaVonne Harper Stiffler has carried out extensive research on the intuitive links between adopted children and the natural parents from whom they were separated at birth. "This memory of a name the child never knew is particularly significant," says Dr Stiffler. "Whether or not the birthmother officially named her baby, each mother knows the name by which she will remember this life and carries it with her in unspoken prayer, bringing it to her conscious mind on the birthday, anniversary or other occasions."

One adult adoptee told Dr Stiffler: "When I was a little girl and all though my teenage years I always wanted to be called Maggie. Not for any particular reason. I just always wanted that name. When I located my original name in the state's birth register, I found that it was Margaret. So I really was a Maggie all along."

The name-bond can also work in reverse, as one mother recalled. "I had sent for and received records from the hospital where I had given birth to my son twenty-five years before. Also enclosed were a copy of his footprints. The footprints were what really got to me emotionally. I wrote a poem about him that day and superimposed copies of his little footprints on the poem. I thumbtacked it to the wall just inside my bedroom door. A few months later, I walked into my bedroom to get ready for bed. I glanced at the tiny footprints again. At that moment the name Bryan appeared in my thoughts out of nowhere. I felt somewhat shaken. I decided it had to be the name given to him by his adoptive parents and when we were reunited I discovered his name was indeed Bryan."

Dr Stiffler's work for her doctorate from the Oxford Graduate School in Dayton, Tennessee, is unique in that previously parent/child intuition had only been studied in relation to children who were raised with their families. She studied sixty-four sets of parents and their children who had been separated by the social and legal practice of secret, stranger adoption and who had been reunited in adulthood after a lengthy search. Most of them were residents of the United States and were studied between May 1990 and May 1991.

In many cases, after a reunion, Dr Stiffler discovered that, as the mother/child pair begin to piece together the years of their separation, as well as mutual physical characteristics and personal mannerisms "are incidents of intuition and synchronicity, suggesting a continuance of the pre-natal bond".

Dr Stiffler sees this link as beyond our current understanding of genetics. "The memory of a lullaby may have originated pre-natally. But whence come the vivid dreams, the naming of an imaginary playmate or the strange drawing towards a particular location?"

The search of birthmother and child is also an area where primitive "homing" instincts seem to operate. Dr Stiffler comments: "The migratory and homing behaviours of animals have been admired, yet mysterious to mankind of all generations. Should there be any less marvellous program for an adoptee's homing instinct than that designed for the Alaskan salmon?"

Ann said: "I had been searching for my mother for a year and getting nowhere. One day at work a co-worker asked if I was having any luck. Another woman who worked there overheard us and asked, 'Luck about what?' I took out my birth certificate and the woman said, 'I might know someone who can help.' She asked me for a baby picture and took it home to compare with one she had. She was my mother. She had been trying to find me for nearly twenty years, always running into dead ends. It is a large city of around 230,000 people and I had started working at this store just a few days before she did. The other girl we worked with was raised by my birthfather. She knew exactly where he was. So, all in one day, I found my mother and knew where my father was too. And in that city for nearly three years I had been living just three blocks away from my mother."

Dr Stiffler also discovered that in times of crisis mother and child, though they had been separated shortly after birth, responded to each other's distress. Said one: "I kept a diary before our reunion and I wrote in it about the time my daughter was fifteen that I felt unusually upset about our separation. When we were reunited, she told me she had run away and had tried to find me at the age of fifteen, to no avail."

Another birthmother told Dr Stiffler: "When my daughter was thirteen years old, I found myself thinking about her constantly. I felt that if I was with her things would be different. That is the year I decided that someday, somehow I would find her. I later found out that was the year she lost her virginity to an older man and was having great problems with her family."

Was it an early memory of the few months mother and child were together or intuition that prepared one adopted daughter to meet her mother many years later? She told LaVonne:

"I always felt a piece of the puzzle was missing. It took me a long time to begin my search and it wasn't until it was over that I understood I had been guided all along. Throughout my life I was always interested in sign language and I learned it from friends and people in my church. When I finally located her Mom and I exchanged letters and pictures. In one letter, Mom wrote, 'For a long time I cried for you. I prayed you were safe. I hoped I would find you again.'

"Then she came to visit me and we met at the airport. I raised my hands in front of me in a gesture God had been preparing me for without my knowing why. Mom was deaf. We came closer. Carefully my hands signed the one word beautiful word I'd longed to speak, 'Mother'."

Just as separated twins have unexplained links in their lives, so, according to Dr Stiffler, do mothers and children who have been apart. "My daughter and I were both in bike accidents in 1971," one mother remembered. "She fell off her bike and broke her front tooth and I went flying over my bike and broke my front tooth. When she told me she had a cap on her front tooth, I said, 'So do I'."

Another mother said: "One year I absolutely had to buy a particular short dark green corduroy jacket with a hood. It also came in burgundy. I have learned that my daughter in the same year insisted that she must have the same burgundy jacket even though her folks were poor. We both had acted entirely out of our normal patterns, with a frantic desire to have the coat. After our reunion when I was giving my daughter some of my old clothes, she squealed to see the same jacket."

Dr Stiffler's work demonstrates that birthmothers do seem to keep links with their children even though they were separated from them at birth and may have no idea where they are. This should come as no surprise, for we never forget the children we lose, whether by adoption or death. They are always a part of us.

Daphne, who lives on the Isle of Wight, was reunited on Saturday 12 April, 1997 when she met her only child Caroline for the first time since putting her up for adoption thirty-six years earlier.

"It was a total bolt out of the blue, but it was the most wonderful thing that has ever happened to me. My life has completely changed. I have always lived in hope this day would come but I never really expected it. I had tried to get in touch with my daughter but the adoption people wouldn't let me know who or where she was so I gave up," said Daphne who is sixty-three and became an instant grandmother on the reunion.

"My husband and I had been away and my sister left a message that someone wanted to get in touch with me and could I ring her urgently. As luck would have it I had lost my sister's phone number. She was ex-directory and I had to wait a frantic two days before my sister got the letter I wrote and rang me. 'Your daughter has been in touch,' she told me.

"My husband was eating dinner and I stood there crying. He realized at once what it was and came and put his arm around me. There are so many similarities between Caroline and myself, in small but significant ways. For example when I first went to see Caroline in mid-Wales, she had an unusual wind chime exactly like the one I had. She loves plates decorated with pictures and I have a large collection. I met Caroline's adoptive mother and father and we were all like one happy family. I was especially worried about upsetting Caroline's mother who had brought her up for thirty-five years but we are all friends. It has completed my life.

"Losing Caroline broke my heart. Though I had always loved and wanted children, because of an internal problem I did not think I could have them. I was thrilled when I knew I was pregnant, but worried about what my boyfriend George would say. He just said 'Oh' and went completely quiet. He then insisted I should have the baby adopted as there was no way he would stay with me and support us. My mother who had disapproved of the relationship refused to help me and I had no money.

"Throughout the pregnancy I still hoped I could keep the baby, but George still showed no interest, not even asking me how I got on at ante-natal clinic. I knitted piles of baby clothes that I sent with the baby when she was taken away. When Caroline was born she was so beautiful. I have never seen such a lovely baby. Her skin was so clear. I cradled her in my arms. George saw her in the nursery but said nothing. One word from him or my mother and she could have stayed with me.

"It was all arranged that Caroline would be taken from the hospital. I did not see her go or say goodbye. I could not have endured it. All the other mothers in the ward sat nursing their babies. They were going to take their babies home. I knew I could not. It hurt so much.

"When I left hospital there was no one to meet me. I have never felt so alone without my baby. George was out with another woman. Whenever I saw a baby I thought of mine. I never thought of her as older, only as that lovely baby.

"Every birthday I would recall her. When I married my present husband, I decided to find Caroline. I left my name and my address in *case she tried to contact me, but the letter was never handed on to her when she tried to get in touch. This Mother's Day for the first time a card and flowers arrived. I sat and cried with pure joy.*

"The strange thing is that Caroline went to school in Guildford while I was living there. We could have passed in the street as strangers. Would I have known her? I like to think so."

In the case of Daphne, Caroline's adoptive mother was supportive of the reunion. Daphne feels that perhaps she did not represent a threat, since she always was careful not to try to take the adoptive mother's place but to treat Caroline as a much-loved friend. Where there is resentment from adoptive parents who can feel betrayed, an understandable emotion, the adopted child can feel guilty at wanting to find his or her birthmother. However, especially when the child has children of his or her own, and is asked about family history, the desire to discover roots can suddenly be overwhelming.

Angela from Swindon, England, was given away at birth. Once she had children herself, Angela felt that she needed to find out about her natural mother.

"When I had my own children people would say, 'Oh, he's like your husband's mum.' I did not know what my mum was like. During my pregnancy, if I was asked about family illnesses, I could not answer. It was as if part of me was not there.

"I contacted the Record Office to obtain my original birth certificate and was offered an interview at St Catherine's House in London. I went with my husband. I was asked why I wanted to contact my mother. I said I just wanted to assure her I was well and happy, even if she did not want to meet me, and to thank her for giving me life, even if it was not intentional. The officer gave me a piece of paper with my date of birth, my original name and my mother's name. I at last knew who I was and where I came from. I was Jane and my mother was Susan Jane.

"I then wrote to the Record Office of the area where I was born— Bangor in Wales—and was given the address where I was born and found out that my dad had been an Australian. Gradually the jigsaw of

my past was taking shape. But I became nervous and I left it for three years.

"I might never have carried on, but I had a really bad argument with my adoptive mother and decided to try to find my real mother. I went through the telephone directories for the area of my birth and found nine numbers with the right name. I tried five numbers and the fifth like the others said that Susan was not there, but the woman was sure she had seen the name in an old directory. She rang back with a number that was not one on my list. I tried it and the woman said that her sister-in-law was called Susan. I made up an excuse that I was trying to arrange a school reunion and she asked my name.

"I made one up and was given the phone number of my mother. I rang but there was no answer. Meanwhile my adopted mother had phoned and we had made up our quarrel and I decided not to go through with the contact. However, my real mother's phone registered the last number as call back and about 10.45 the same evening the phone rang and a voice said, 'Who has been ringing my number?' I said, 'I'm Angela.'

"The voice replied, 'I'm Susan.' The connection was like an electric charge and I found myself saying to this woman who all those years ago had been my mother. 'This may be a shock for you but I think I'm your daughter Jane.'

"My mother started to cry. 'Oh, my baby Jane? Is it really you after all these years?'

"Soon we were both crying and the years melted away. Then my mother's sister rang and my younger brother and soon I had a whole new family. The strange thing was that the daughter next down in age from me had told my mother only a few days before that she should try to trace me. I went with my husband to see my mum and the new family and it was as if we had never been apart. They love my children, who are now spoilt by a new Grandma, aunts and uncles. The amazing thing was the similarities between us. Now I feel that all the missing pieces are together and for the first time I know who I really am. My mother and I like the same foods and dress alike. There is a picture of my mother at a wedding wearing a black and red outfit. I have an identical one. I am so happy.

371

Even on the phone there is a closeness and naturalness between us.

"The only sorrow is that the reunion has upset my adopted mother. When I first told her she would not talk to me for three weeks and told me I had been deceitful and gone behind her back. I do understand her feelings but I had to find the lost part of myself. Now I have roots and so have the children. I owed it to them."

Many adopted children who as adults find their birthmothers say that it makes them complete. Especially if a child has felt different from the adoptive family, finding a birthmother can explain what seem oddities as family traits, and can confirm that a child's path which is strange to the adoptive family is the same as that of the birthmother.

Mandy, who lives in Surrey, was regarded as the unconventional member of her adoptive family.

"I am almost thirty-five. I was adopted as a baby and had very loving parents, although there is a big generation gap. But I knew I was always different from the rest of the family. I was fascinated by the psychic and spiritual and drawn to Native American culture. About twelve years ago I decided to search for my natural mother. But I could not find her.

"Almost three years ago I knew the time was right and that my mother was close to me. When I discovered my mother she told me that she had known at that time I was coming and that the family had toasted me at Christmas. My birthmother Jo is a spiritual healer, a path I have also been taking recently. Jo is also a psychic and my grandfather was the son of a Sioux Indian. The connections were amazing. We were both nurses. I used to feel strangely drawn to a particular house near the hospital. It turned out to be the house where I was born.

"However, I hated the nurses' home, a gloomy Gothic building, could not settle there and eventually moved out. It was the building where my mother had convalesced when she could not keep me.

"When my mother and I met for the first time, it was like coming home. We were wearing the same black, hippy clothes, the same silver jewellery. We talk in the same way and use the same gestures. It is like

looking in a mirror. I had heard her voice in my head many times as a child and when she spoke I would have known her anywhere. Strangely her other children do not share her mannerisms, nor dress like her. Neither does anyone in my adoptive family dress like me.

"We both get the desire to travel in the spring and autumn—the times the Sioux would be on the move—and we love the outdoors. I had never understood my yearnings. Now they made sense and my mother reflected my actions and attitudes. It was an affirmation of who I was at core, that I was on the right track, although different from my adoptive family.

"From childhood I had felt connected with my natural grandfather. A palmist once told me that he was always with me, which I knew especially late at night when I could sense his presence. Another psychic told me that March and the number four were important. I met my mother on 4 March.

"Esther, one of my grandfather's last living relations, died just before I met her. I rang Jo one night because I could not settle and said that something was wrong with Esther. My mother said she was fine but then news came that she had died at the moment I had been thinking of her. I belong to a whole interconnectedness of people I sensed as shadows who now have form. My life makes sense. I know who I am and I can see in my son Fred the sallow yellow skin of his native roots.

"I can understand why my mother could not keep me. Jo fell in love with my father who was a Hungarian. Her father was a Hungarian Jew and they came to England as refugees. My father was tall, dark and loved poetry. Jo knew the second she had conceived me on Guy Fawkes Night. My father gave her his grandmother's ring and his family were very excited about me. But my mother woke up one morning. She was only nineteen and knew she could not go through with marriage and bringing me up.

"Her family, who were very wealthy, were angry when they found out she was pregnant and sent her away to London for the birth. After my birth, she could not stay at home without me, left her family and eventually fell in love with a poacher. They lived as Romanies for several years and had three children. We recognized each other instantly—

strange though it sounds we smelled right to each other. She is a registered shaman and now I understand why I too have always heard voices and known things. I have come home."

Sadly, some reunions can end badly, although few regret having made the contact. On the whole it is better to know than not to know, though in some cases pain can outweigh joy. Where failures occur it is often not through lack of good intentions or love, but because the intervening years have made the gap too great to breach. Christina, who lives in Christchurch, New Zealand, wrote to me, describing how her initial joy has changed to sadness.

"I am a birth mother who relinquished my daughter in 1966 most reluctantly with reasons that at the time seemed urgent and optionless. As time passed, once the pain had eased, I discovered that I did have options and certainly had the qualities necessary to bring up a child alone. However, the main overriding reason that I succumbed to the pressure to give up my daughter was the overpowering fear of hurting my parents, who I thought were vulnerable and innocent and would possibly be destroyed by my keeping the baby.

"The one and only request I made to the social worker when I was parted from my child was not respected. Repercussions from this omission have sadly affected the happy reunion I might have had with my lovely daughter nine years ago. I had asked via the social worker that it would be explained to my daughter as gently and kindly as possible, as soon as she was able to understand, that she had another mother who loved her, but could not keep her.

"Not knowing my request, her adoptive parents had resolved right from the start not to tell my daughter that she was adopted. For twenty-three years I had believed them to be the most wonderful people, taking the best care of my precious and cherished baby, until one day I could be with her again. I did not discover this omission until the social welfare officer told me what had happened when I made my first tentative enquiries for contact.

"After a difficult start in our relationship, stemming from my

daughter's early shock, despair and horror at discovering she was adopted, I was deluged with questions and interest. I gave my new daughter everything she asked for and more. I would have just about sacrificed everything for her. My twin sons, who are eight years younger, immediately took to her. We all met. She was overwhelmed by the similarities that we shared. I told her my background, my nature, likes and dislikes. I wrote letters of twenty pages to her each time, filling in the missing years.

"But as suddenly as the closeness began, my daughter informed me that it was all impossible, that her loyalty and obligation to her adoptive parents must come first and that she could not promise to keep in touch with me. We had fused together, I know, on a deep level. However, she had mentioned earlier a large legacy that was due on her twenty-fifth birthday. I can only speculate that her adoptive parents wrongly thought that they would lose her, that I would take her away, and so demanded she returned to the fold.

"All I can do is wait and be patient and understanding. I know adoption was supposed to be an ideal solution for all those concerned. I believed I did the right thing for many years. But personally from my corner I feel it served no one. I used to silently communicate with my baby before she was born, assuring her that I would always love and want her. So many thoughts I shared with her, and the expression when we met reflected she felt the same bond. Now there is nothing, except my love, to carry us over the second parting."

The Second Rejection

There are circumstances that make close bonds with a child conceived many years earlier difficult to kindle or rekindle, especially if the birth has been kept secret from the birthmother's present partner and subsequent children.

However, women like Patricia, who lives in Cheshire, believe that they have a right to know the identity of the women who bore them. For Patricia, the separation was particularly cruel as she was given away while her older sister was kept at home. When she rediscovered her birthmother, she expected her at least to show some pleasure in discovering her long-lost daughter. Instead she suffered a second rejection.

"My natural sister is also named Patricia. I was named Anne by my birthmother but by coincidence my adoptive parents named me Patricia. They did not know my natural mother or who she was. My sister is three years older than me. I was adopted. She was not. We both have three children and have been married twice.

"I believe that I was one of the first people to be given my original birth certificate, soon after the law was changed in the 1970s. I had only a two-minute conversation with a social worker and was given no advice.

"My birth certificate had my mother's address at the time. It was only about forty miles from where I was living. I picked the local telephone directory and found someone living in the same road with the same name, quite an unusual name.

"Not wanting to cause my mother any embarrassment, I decided to be careful whom I approached. In the end I went to see the local vicar. I explained my situation and asked him if he could find out if the people were related to my mother. I asked the vicar not to disclose who I was to anyone except my mother and if he could not speak directly to my mother, to say nothing at all.

"The vicar came back to me with the news that the people living at the address I had given him were my grandparents and my mother's brother and his wife. I was very excited by this. However, he had related the whole story to my mother's sister-in-law without asking me first. I felt my confidence had been betrayed. It turned out that my mother and her sister-in-law had never been on good terms. The vicar also informed me that my mother was living abroad and that my aunt would ask my mother to see the vicar next time she was home. She was expected back shortly after the meeting.

"A few weeks later, the vicar asked me to see him as he had spoken to my mother. When I arrived I discovered to my disappointment that he

had not contacted me while my mother had been home. She had been to see the vicar, had promised to visit him again, but had not and had subsequently returned abroad.

"I was also upset because the vicar had prevented me from making my own approach to her. He did, however, have the news that my mother was married, her husband did not know about me and that she had two other children.

"Eventually I contacted my aunt and uncle and built up a relationship with them. They visited me quite often. This went on for a few years without my mother ever being mentioned. She did not want to see me, so I felt guilty asking about her. Was this a throwback from never feeling I could ask my adoptive mother anything? I later found out that my mother had been back to this country again and my aunt and uncle had not told me. Once again my mother had made no attempt to contact me.

"After this I realized I would not make any progress without telling lies. I had learned that I had a sister called Patricia who had married a local farmer. I rang another aunt who I knew existed and extracted my sister's married name by telling a lie. By a circuitous route I finally located my sister who was no longer married to the farmer and eventually was able to ring her. I asked if I could come and see her. I did not say who I was in case she refused to see me. I wanted to meet my sister, if only once.

"When I arrived I found out that my sister knew nothing of my existence, but she later told me she knew what I was going to say when I walked into the room. My sister was cool but not hostile. She readily gave me her mother's phone number. My mother was now living in the UK but had still not contacted me.

"It has taken twelve years for my relationship with my sister to become like that of sisters. However, we got there in the end and now her daughter sometimes comes to stay with me.

"When I rang my mother I gave her no warning and neither did my sister. I did not feel emotional. After all she could have contacted me for quite a few years and had made no attempt to do so. I said, 'Hello, Mother, it's your daughter Patricia, the other one.'

"*I felt jubilant. I had achieved this despite all the obstacles in my way: the parish council who had suggested the adoption to my mother, the state which had taken my identity, my adoptive parents who had told me nothing and withheld information from me, the 1953 floods which destroyed my adoption records, the local vicar who withheld information which my mother later told me she had given him, my aunt and uncle who also omitted to give me information and above all my mother herself.*

"*I am still not very close to my mother. However, the relationship has improved slightly over the years. By this I mean that she now asks about the welfare of my children. I have only met her once. She came to see me soon after I contacted her. Our relationship is conducted over the telephone. This is her choice, not mine. Her husband still does not know anything about me. I do not believe she would want a close relationship with me even if that was not the case. I have never received a Christmas or birthday card from her.*

"*I telephone my mother every few months. She has only ever telephoned me once in twelve years and that was when she found an unfamiliar number on her answering machine and rang back to see who it was. I had been calling her from work. I do not think she is in line for the Mother of the Decade award. The relationship exists only because I am persistent and always hope it will improve. My existence is an inconvenience to her. She says that I am a reminder to her of a very hurtful and unhappy period in her life. This I can understand and try not to disrupt her life too much. Despite this I do need to have contact with her, even knowing that it is unwelcome.*

"*Because she is my mother I feel I understand her, even though I do not know her very well. It took me about a year to extract from my mother who my father is. This caused some animosity. After my mother gave me this information she admitted that she should have told me as soon as I asked.*

"*My natural father had been married at the time and his wife was also expecting a baby. I went to see my father and he denied all knowledge. This was a bitter disappointment. It had never entered my head that anyone could do this to his own flesh and blood. He was very*

378

hostile. I understand that he was protecting what was important to him, his wife and the family he has brought up. A few years later after a great deal of persistence on my part, he half admitted that he was my father and asked me what I wanted. I replied, 'Five minutes of your time now and again.'

"*Since then my father has tolerated my phone calls. Recently I asked him about some family history and he became very annoyed. 'Your five minutes are up,' he informed me curtly.*

"*I would swap my father for anyone who had been pleased to see me, even if they had been on Death Row.*

"*I believe very strongly that I am the daughter of my natural parents, despite having a very happy upbringing in a stable family home with my adoptive parents. Even though it is said that the adoption took place as the best thing for the child, I have to say that my adoption came about also as a convenience for all the other parties concerned. I do not believe that the state had any right to take my identity away. After all, I was never asked. I also believe that information about me belongs to me and that I have a right to it.*"

Can a woman who gives away her child at birth for whatever reason then close the chapter for ever? Some do. But can giving birth be regarded as a mistake to be forgotten? What if the adopted child craves to find his or her identity? Some argue that long-term fostering rather than adoption is the answer, but I know experienced foster mothers who talk of the disruption and heartbreak for their long-term foster children who may be let down time and time again by natural mothers, leaving the foster mother to pick up the pieces. Could it not be a burden of a different kind for a child to know details about parents whom he sees as abandoning him? After all, can a teenage girl who gets pregnant and has her child adopted be expected to have lifelong maternal feelings for a child whom she sees as ruining her life?

On balance, I believe that it is crucial for the adopted child to know about his or her birthmother to establish identity, but I have no real answers.

Suzanna, who lives in Dublin, described her double rejection:

"My story does not have a happy ending, but it is reality and maybe others could learn from it. I was born in Ireland in January 1961. My birthmother was a sixteen-year-old high school student from the west coast of the USA. She came to Ireland with her mother and younger sister when they found out she was pregnant. My grandmother had been widowed a few years before my mother's pregnancy. Her husband shot himself accidentally while out hunting.

"I was adopted by a loving Irish couple who were unable to have children of their own. My birthmother never saw me and was instructed to pretend the birth had never happened. She returned to the USA a few months after my birth never to return to Ireland again. She married two years later, but not my father, and had two children, a boy and a girl.

"I grew up in a protected, loving environment and my parents adopted another daughter in 1964. We were sent to private schools and had the very best of everything. I always knew I was adopted. My mother told me that my parents had been killed in a car crash and that she and my father had chosen me specially. I always had the feeling I was not Irish. Deep down I knew I was American, although I could never explain this to anyone. My father died when I was ten. That was the end of the happy, secure childhood. I was sent to boarding school and my sister stayed at home with my mother. I felt unwanted and out of place in Ireland.

"When I went to secondary school I heard other girls talking about unmarried mothers and unplanned pregnancies. I asked my mother if this had been the case with my birthmother and she admitted it had.

"My birth grandmother had always kept an eye on me when I was growing up. She sent a priest to visit us on many occasions and I later discovered that he reported back to her. When my adoptive father died, she offered my mother money through the priest. My adoptive mother was very upset and did not accept the money.

"When I was seventeen, I decided I wanted a baby to replace the

birthmother who had given me away. I had been working and studying in Spain and Germany. When I returned to Ireland in 1979 I became pregnant with my son. I was thrilled when he was born.

"When my birth grandmother died, I was expecting my son. The priest came to visit me and told me that my grandmother had died. I could not understand this, as to me my grandmother was the lady who lived down the road with my granddad. The priest then admitted to knowing my birth family very well. He had been paid to keep an eye on me and was very angry when I said I was going to search for my birthmother. A year later I married someone I had met only once. It was a mistake but I stayed in the marriage for twelve years, returning to Ireland for good in 1993.

"I started looking for my birthmother in 1987. The nun at the adoption agency had told my adoptive parents that my mother was from a wealthy professional family and that her name was Suzanna. They discovered this after they had named me. When I was eighteen I became a member of the Anglican Church. I always knew deep down that I was not Catholic. My natural grandparents were, I discovered much later, Episcopalian.

"I located my birthmother easily because she is very well known and lives in a tiny village. Initially she did not want any contact, but finally agreed to one meeting which took place in Antwerp, Belgium, in the fall of 1988. We met in a hotel room. Her husband came with her and my son came with me.

"My mother and I are very alike in many ways. I felt I had known her all my life. She made so many promises which she did not keep. That was the one and only time we met. It was a happy reunion. I felt so much better about myself afterwards. I knew who I was. So much was explained. We kept in touch every Christmas. She used to write and send gifts, but all contact stopped when my marriage broke up, and when I was very ill earlier this year I received a letter from my birthmother saying that she never wanted to see me again. This was very difficult for me to come to terms with. It seemed so cruel when I was so ill. She begged me not to come to America or to visit her. I still have not come to terms with this. I deal with it one day at a time and the pain is still very acute.

I realize that I am very fortunate to have met my birthmother and to have all my questions answered. I have a wonderful son and a very supportive family, a lovely little house and two adorable cats.

"I have a half-brother and sister that I will never know. This is very sad. I firmly believe that my birthmother is a very selfish person to have rejected her child, not once but twice. She has to live with that."

Christine's Story

A towel was put over your face or a pillow on your chest
at the time of birth, so that you could not see your baby
being born. If you were quick you could get a look at
the baby before he was taken away. I remember willing
my baby very strongly, 'Please remember me, I love you.'
Christine, a seventeen-year-old unmarried mother in 1965

*I*n 1965, Christine, a New Zealander, became pregnant. She was
only seventeen and unmarried. She was given no choice in the
matter by her parents or the system: her son Anthony had to be given
away against her will. "It was six months before my infant was
adopted," she told me, "so Anthony had to be placed in a foster
home until his adoption. My parents had forbidden me to bring my son
home in any circumstances.

*"My parents were furious with me when I told them of my pregnancy,
but seemed more concerned at the loss of the family good name and what
others would say when my predicament was known than with me. I
immediately became a lost cause in their eyes, shop-soiled, dirty and
someone no decent man would ever want.*

*"Marriage to Anthony's father Des was not a possibility. I already
knew that marrying him would be a disaster. To avoid being forced into
marriage, I refused to confirm his name to my parents. In view of their
attitude, it seems surprising that they did not insist. Des had been the
only young man in my life. My parents' immediate solution to the
problem was to confine me to my bedroom so that I should not be seen.
Within a fortnight, I was sent to Auckland to a young mother and baby
institution. Before I left it was firmly drummed into me that the baby*

was never, never to come home and if I came back with 'it' I should not be welcome either.

"The institution was not a bad place. The people who ran the home were kind and while we had to work fairly hard, the material and medical needs of all the girls were met. It was made clear to me what my parents' instructions were regarding the baby. On arrival I was given a paper to sign. At the time I believed, because the other girls told me, that it was the adoption paper and that once signed there was no going back. Our babies were given away and nothing we could say or do could ever change things. It was no wonder we delayed signing and returning that paper as long as we could.

"Last year I obtained a copy of that paper to find that it simply gives physical and educational details of myself and the father. It was not a consent to adoption at all. I do now believe that the institution was aware of our thoughts, but chose to keep us misinformed about the true purpose of that paper, which was, I feel sure now, to match a baby with prospective parents in advance.

"I remember how I initially tried to convince myself that it would not be too difficult to give my baby up. But as time went on my heart told me what I knew deep down, that it was going to be heartbreaking. I had seen girls returning to the home absolutely desolate after the birth of their babies.

"All the same I was almost ignorant and absolutely terrified of giving birth. The little information that we girls gleaned and shared together was all we knew. One thing we did learn from girls returning from giving birth was that a towel was put over your face or a pillow on your chest at the time of birth, so that you could not see your baby being born. We knew that if you were quick you could get a look at the baby before he or she was taken away. In my readings about adoption practices, I have discovered that the towel/pillow practice was not uncommon at the time, the so-called Swinging Sixties.

"In that last stage of labour I kept waiting for the towel or pillow but to my amazement it did not happen. I still feel a sense of wonder and joy that I was spared though my friends in the home were not. Words seem so inadequate to describe the wonderful feelings I had after the birth, *happiness, elation, pride and above all love for this little baby boy. When the blue-eyed midwife wrapped him in a towel and gave him to me to hold, I was totally fascinated by his huge navy blue eyes that seemed fixed on my face. His face, his fingers, body, his hands and feet, were so perfect. That was when I gave him his name Anthony David and, for the first time, willed him to remember me. I have heard it said that a first-born child has a special place in a mother's heart and for me it is true.*

"However, during that hour in which I lay holding him, I had to face the awful fact that I would probably never see him again, because unmarried mothers would be given another unmarried mother's child to care for in the hospital, rather than their own.

"Eventually a nurse took the baby from me and I cried as if there was no tomorrow. Another nurse, trying to be kind, told me to rest and that I would see my baby in the morning. I did not believe her and I did not sleep. None of them seemed to know that I was unmarried.

"To my delight the next morning, Anthony was brought to me to be fed. I had my own beautiful son. Two nurses tried to get me to breastfeed. I was horrified and could not see how this would work. Something had gone wrong. They did not understand that I was not married and not allowed to keep my baby, certainly not breastfeed him. In the end I was able to bottlefeed Anthony and later the next morning I was taught how to bath him and change nappies.

"During the night I would go and sit by his bassinet. Some of the night staff did not like me doing this and got cross with me. In fact I was in trouble with the staff for much of the time because during the day I used to take Anthony out of his bassinet, wrap him up and sit on my bed with the baby in my arms. Some days I slept with Anthony. All I wanted to do was to love my baby boy. Each day was so precious, joy and misery together. Each day brought closer the one when I would have to leave him.

"On the last day, even though I had already bathed and fed him earlier, I placed Anthony on my bed, undressed him and touched him all over his little body. 'Please remember me, baby. Please remember me. I love you,' I said.

"I left Anthony at the hospital, knowing that there was no home,

adoptive or foster, for him. I was devastated. I had no permanent job nor home nor money and there were no state benefits for single women with children. Although a stranger in Auckland, I knew that I had to find a job and somewhere to live as it was my responsibility to support my son when he was put into foster care.

"It still hurts me to know that my son's birth was completely unacknowledged by my parents. In fact for the whole time I was in the mother and baby home, my mother, who wrote weekly, never once mentioned my pregnancy. During the foster care period, never once was any mention made of her grandson. It was just as if Anthony never existed. I was never asked if I needed money. In fact my parents were told about Anthony's new home before I was, but did not pass the information on to me.

"I was contacted by the mother and child home two weeks after leaving hospital and told what I had to supply for my son in foster care as there was no permanent home for him. I was not allowed to know where my son was but I was relieved at least Anthony was no longer in hospital. A few weeks later Jean, Anthony's foster mother, contacted me, and invited me to 'come around and see the wee man'.

"I visited every Saturday and Sunday and occasionally midweek, although the bus journey was long and complicated. At first Jean let me bath and feed Anthony. I would often just sit in the garden with him on my knee and sometimes we would go out for a walk. His foster parents were very kind and although I hated leaving, I knew that my son was well cared for. Jean told me that the baby would cry when I left. She put a lot of pressure on me to keep Anthony.

"I really liked cooking and sewing and made most of Anthony's clothes. There was immense happiness when my grown-up son came to visit me in 1996 with those little bits and pieces I had made that his adoptive mother had carefully wrapped and put aside for me.

"I went back home that first Christmas and hated every minute of it. My family behaved as if I had never been away, as if nothing had ever happened. I missed my son dreadfully and cut short my holiday. My life was in Auckland. But there came a time after New Year that Jean let me do less and less for the baby and started to criticize the way I handled

him. I felt threatened that she was trying to steal my son, although in retrospect I can see that Jean had become very attached to him and loved him as her own.

"I did not know what to do and this was a dreadful time in my life. Then in early March things started to happened fast. I 'knew' that a home had been found. The first confirmation was when Jean phoned my workplace in a distraught state to say that Anthony was going to his new family in New Plymouth that very afternoon. There was nothing more I could do. It was beyond my control and I could not even say goodbye. I really thought my life was not worth living. I could not eat or sleep and worst of all could not even cry. Day after day was black, when I could not see my way through the next hour because of the black haze of despair.

"Five or six days later I received official notice, giving me no option except to be at a place at a given time to sign the appropriate papers. The solicitor was a sour man. The only words I can still recall are: 'You must give your word never to see this child again, never to contact the child. It [not he] is not yours.'

"I started to cry. He told me: 'Pull yourself together. You have no rights in respect of this child. Sign here and stop wasting my time.'

"After the adoption, I kept in touch with my son on a deep, intuitive level although I had no knowledge of his whereabouts or his life. I was aware instinctively for more than a year after the adoption that my son was very unhappy and there was nothing I could do to change things and make them better. I was heartbroken at this time and spent what was the most miserable period of my life as one black day ran into another, although I became master at putting a mask on for the world."

At this point there came a break in Christine's letter to me. Later she wrote:

"I could not go any further yesterday. I was so upset when I read what I had written. I must have needed a good cry. It is all so painful still. In time I hope that I will heal and the pain will soften around the edges. Meeting my son many years later has been a wonderful experience but never in my dreams did I imagine I would have such difficulty in coping

387

with the feelings and memories of so long ago. Nothing was forgotten, just put away in my box and stored for a later date.

"My son remarked that his adoptive mother told him that he cried dreadfully and was a very unhappy baby when he came to them, but that the crying gradually lessened during the year. I also discovered that the foster mother continued to visit the family during the year. His new parents thought that the crying was associated with these visits and eventually his father told the foster mother not to come any more. It has been hard to come to terms with the fact that his foster mother had been able to locate him easily and continue visiting him, while I, the mother, was forbidden by law to do so. Is it any wonder everyone was so unhappy?

"After this I closed off that part of my life and as my life took on a new direction I more or less settled down. I returned home only years later to marry Dave who had helped me through the difficult years and then went back to Auckland. In all the thirty years we were apart my son was never far from my thoughts. Even though I felt sure that my boy was well cared for and was in a loving, happy home it was always as though there was something missing. Birthdays were the hardest. It was only, however, when my son reached his teens that I started having thoughts and feelings that all was not well with him.

"When Anthony was around thirteen I was startled by the thought that something terrible had happened in his life. When we did talk about his growing-up years, my son told me that his best friend had been killed by jumping off a bridge at this time. I had vague concerns when he was seventeen, at the time he left home and became an electrician.

"From that time on I found myself having times of concern when my son came very strongly into my thoughts. These continued until he was twenty-two when I was suddenly more at peace. The worst time was when my son was twenty-one and I felt all was not well in his life. At twenty-two Anthony met a young lady whom he was eventually to marry and his life took a new direction.

"I had an instinctive awareness early in 1993 that he had married. He and his young lady in fact married on 13 February 1993. I was concerned with his health when he was about twenty-five, 1990, and thought that an accident or serious illness had befallen him. His wife told *me that in 1990 he had a really bad time with malaria, having worked overseas. My son in turn worried about me later in the same year. My husband was diagnosed with a brain tumour. October until December was a very traumatic time for us.*

"By mid-1995 I had a very strong sense of despair that I was missing out on his life, and a sense of urgency. My husband Dave was also very concerned for me and was urging me not to leave my search too late. On my son's thirtieth birthday, Dave said, 'He's looking for you, I know.'

"1995 was the time my son started his search which eventually led him to me. My son later told me he was at that time also getting quite desperate about seeing me before he went overseas in 1996. When he located me it was his last shot before going away. He had drawn blank after blank and it was the last try when he succeeded in contacting a cousin of mine who phoned my mother and so the family secret was out.

"My mother rang me in a great state. She told me, 'I'm in this terrible dilemma. And I don't know what to do.'

"At last she explained, 'You know that boy, that child you had all those years ago? He's looking for you. What do you want to do?'

"All I could do was cry. I was blown away and my mother started to panic. I told her: 'Tell my cousin to assure him more than anything in the world I would love to hear from him.'

"The same evening my son rang. 'I'm sorry for bursting into your life like this.'

"It was so beautiful and wonderful, hearing his voice. After the phone call when I went to tell Dave, all I could do was cry. On the day I signed the adoption consent papers, the first piece of music I heard on the radio was 'Mission Bell' by P. J. Proby. The night on which my son telephoned, the first piece of music I heard on the radio was 'Mission Bell' by P. J. Proby, thirty years later.

"In his first letter to me, he wrote, 'After our phone call, I had this incredible feeling of belonging and also a deep-down relief of not being rejected. Over the years, even though my adoptive family loves me, I have felt quite distant because I look and act so differently.'

"I also have a sense of wholeness, of being complete. I call my son Bill now, a name he chose for himself as he was uncomfortable with his

adoptive name. Initially I felt really uncomfortable about this because in my heart he will always be Anthony. When I sat in a family group with Bill, the younger ones were talking about birth times and weights. I was suddenly acutely aware that Bill had missed out and did not know important facts about his early life.

"Bill was 7 lbs 4 oz, born shortly after midnight and the first baby born in the hospital that day. That night I dreamed and relived his birth and it brought it all back, the long walk down the hospital corridor having strong contractions. No one had come to my aid when I had rung the bell, so I went in search of a nurse. I was sent back to my bed, told to stop making a fuss, then when someone did attend to me there was a rush to the delivery theatre. The birth was easy. I saw again the black-framed clock with my son's birth time, 12.18 a.m. The blue-eyed midwife told me his weight and that he was twenty-one inches long.

"Sitting in a café with my husband, new son and his wife, we heard the song 'Bill Bailey Won't You Please Come Home?' Bill's adoptive surname is Bailey, so we fell about laughing and considered it a good omen.

"I have one little photograph, thanks to Bill's foster mother, taken when he was twelve weeks old. The only photograph my son has ever seen of himself as a baby was identical to mine.

"On my son's thirty-first birthday, the first we could share, he wrote to me from Bali, 'Today is a special day, it's my birthday,' and I wrote from New Zealand, 'Today is a special day, it's your birthday.'

"We both write in a right-sloping rather large style with similar sayings and ways of expressing ourselves. Both of us do little illustrations, decorations, in our letters which came as something of a surprise. We are both keen on gardening and garden design. He has completed his horticultural certificate and I began mine in early 1996. Our gardens both feature French and English lavenders. I also love roses. Indeed, we both arrived on our first meeting carrying flowers for the other. Mine are all planted for somebody. My son's rose, planted on his twenty-first birthday, is Deep Secret.

"While I love my mother and enjoy many things with her, I find that I am unable to talk to her about Bill. She does not understand that I love *my first son and always have. To her, he will always be 'that boy'. I am sad about this as she is Bill's only living grandparent, but she is an old lady and I cannot expect her to change now. For Bill and myself, I have a really good feeling about the future and know that all will be well. My story has a very happy ending after all."*

Marlou's Story

I have two mothers. Each mother did what the other
mother could not. I feel differently about each mother
and feel very strongly that there is a distinct place and a
necessity for both mothers in my life.

Dr Marlou Russell

*M*arlou's story is the other side of the coin from Christine's.
She is an adopted child who searched for her mother. She is
also the clinical psychologist who counsels adoptees and their families.
Her own background as an adoptive child has enabled her to empathize
closely with her clients. Marlou has recently sent me an account of her
personal struggle to come to terms with her own loss of her birthmother
and their subsequent reunion.

"*My interest in the connections between a mother and her baby has
expanded. I gave birth to a beautiful baby girl last June and have become
a full-time mom and a part-time therapist. I'm in my office two half-
days a week and still do my seminars on the lifelong impact of adoptions.
The rest of the time I spend with Katie. She's a delightful, happy, sweet,
amazing little person. I never knew being a mother could be so great! I
know I had been resisting the idea of being a mother for so many years
because of my pain about being adopted. I didn't want to have to re-
experience the old feelings again. Luckily, I had some experiences that
gently led me to considering having a baby. It feels like it all went
according to some well-guided plan in terms of emotional readiness.*

"*Like every adoptee, I have two mothers. Each mother did what the
other mother could not. I feel differently about each mother and feel very
strongly that there is a distinct place and a necessity for both mothers in*

my life. I need them both just as they needed each other. My wish is that my mothers would meet and talk about what they have both contributed to mothering me.

"When I found my birthmother I felt grounded for the first time. I found my place in the world. I was connected to more than me. My ancestry and genetic roots finally had faces. I stopped searching the crowd for someone who looked like me. I could relax my watchfulness for anyone who might be a close or distant relative. I found someone who looked like me and had my hazel eyes. I found someone who was tall like me, who liked to sleep late and who hated fish. We had a lot in common. Our cadence and flow are the same pace. It is comfortable to be with her. She is my mother in a way that no one else can or should be.

"I met my mother for the first time when I was thirty-five years old. She was nothing like I imagined. When I was a child I was sure she was a movie star, hopelessly in love with the leading man but unable to be with him for some obscure but romantic reason.

"When I was a teenager I thought she was probably a drug addict living on the streets. Why had she not come back to claim me or at least enquire about my well-being?

"I was adopted as an infant in what is called a closed or conditional adoption. I was not supposed to meet my birthmother. She was supposed to forget me and get on with her life. We were supposed to ignore the fact that something out of the ordinary had taken place.

"I found out I was adopted when I was seven years old. My mother told me that she and my father had wanted to have babies of their own but couldn't have any although they had tried for many years. Then one day a doctor said that there was a baby available and did they want it? They had already adopted the child who became my older sister and decided to adopt me as well. My adoptive mother said that my other mother loved me and wanted me to have a good home. They had never met her but had heard she was a nice girl.

"I recall hearing what my mother was saying but not being able to take it in. I felt numb. She said I was special and that she and my father were really glad to have me and my sister. I felt sad. My mother never brought up the subject of adoption again.

393

"*Losing the mother who gave you life is traumatic. I wanted to keep a part of her in my soul and I thought about her a lot. My fantasy life about my birthmother was rich since I did not have a lot of facts to counteract what I imagined. I wanted to believe that if my birthmother and I were in the same place at the same time we would immediately recognize each other. For years I peered at faces in crowds—was she there? I was always looking, in the grocery store, in movie lines and later even in bars. I wondered if she ever thought of me. Did she remember my birthday? I had lots of questions I wanted to ask her. I wanted to see her. I wondered if I looked like her.*

"*I was the tallest member of my family. People would ask how I got so tall. I didn't know. I grew up with short people. They had blue eyes. I had brown eyes. They were brunette. I was blonde. I wanted to look like someone who looked like me. Whose eyes were those in mine?*

"*Adoption was one of our family secrets. My sister and I were told not to reveal to anyone that we were adopted because they wouldn't understand and besides it was none of their business. Keeping the secret created some problems. One year my sister and I were on the camp bus on the way to a new summer camp. Some of the kids on the bus would not believe we were sisters. When we got to camp, they took us in separate rooms and asked us our home address to check our stories. It didn't occur to me to say that we were adopted. That would break the family taboo.*

"*I did, however, tell some people that I was adopted. There would come a time in our relationship where, if I trusted a person, I would confess to my status of being adopted. Usually it was no big deal to the person concerned but to me it was a turning point in the relationship. Would they accept or reject me? Could they understand what it means to me to be adopted?*

"*I began to search for my birthmother when I was twenty-three. I joined support groups and wrote letters which would help me to locate her. When I visited my adoptive parents I would ask questions about my background to try to get any piece of information that might help in my search. My adoptive mother cried and my father got angry. They did not understand my need to know. I told them I felt as if a piece of me was* missing. *They became offended and asked why they couldn't fill those needs. They weren't able to see that it wasn't something about them—it was about my beginnings.*

"*It is not an accident that I became more active in my search after my adoptive father's death. I didn't want to face his hurt and anger and I didn't want to search behind his back. My search took many routes and I finally ended up with her phone number. I dialled, the call was transferred and my birthmother was on the other end. In one long, rushed, tearful sentence I stated my birth date, my home town and that I thought she might be my birthmother.*

"*A moment of silence, then sobs. Yes, she was my birthmother. And how was I? Was I OK? More sobs from both of us. Yes, I was OK. For me, I feel I have come home. I feel connected and centred. I know who I look like. I now have a place in the world.*

"*Meeting my birthfather while I was pregnant with my first child has completed the search for my roots. I have met his parents, various aunts, uncles, and cousins. It gives me joy to know that my daughter will know her relatives and not have to wonder. We have filled in the missing pieces. My birthfather's parents were thrilled to meet me and to meet their new great-granddaughter. They asked if I would accept them as my grandparents in their first letter to me. Nothing has given me more pleasure. They are the grandparents I had always wanted since I had grown up with none. Seeing my grandmother hold my newborn daughter was wonderful and sad. I wish she had been able to hold me at that age. I wish I had been able to have known them all.*

"*Next week I will be going to visit my birthmother and my new relatives. She is planning a party so everyone can meet my daughter for the first time. She gave me a baby shower when I was pregnant and is very excited about being a grandmother. It is bittersweet to visit my birthmother and to attend the parties. I enjoy meeting my relatives and getting to know them better each trip. I feel welcomed by all of them and I know they are truly pleased that I searched and found my birthmother. It is exciting and sweet that my mother goes out of her way to plan the parties and do all that she does.*

"*It is also very sad. I become sad in a very primal way when I visit my birthmother. Seeing her reminds me of what could have been. The baby shower could have been for her when she was pregnant with me. I could have grown up knowing people I am related to and shared in the stories they tell.*

"I am not sure the sadness will ever go away. I am not sure if I ever want the sadness to go away. It has been with me all my life. It is what I know when I think about my beginnings. It inspires me to continue to talk about adoption.

"Birthparents must bear the pain of their decision for the rest of their lives. What can be more difficult than giving away your child to strangers to raise? The birthmothers that I have known and worked with have never forgotten their children or stopped loving them. Despite being told by social workers and their families they should forget the experience and get on with their lives, these mothers have remained mothers in their souls and hearts. There is much grieving and forgiving that birthmothers need to do. For birthparents too a reunion is bittersweet. It is amazing to see your child again and sad that you missed so much of their growing up. Present experiences can become fond memories but the past remains a painful loss."

PART TEN

A Grandmother's Love

Maternal Instinct in the Third Generation

There still lives a remembrance of old grandmother, with the loving, gentle eyes that always looked young. Eyes can never die. The eyes, those mild, saintly eyes, are the same.

Hans Christian Andersen

"*G*randmother is very old, her face is wrinkled, and her hair is quite white; but her eyes are like two stars, and they have a mild, gentle expression in them when they look at you, which does you good. She wears a dress of heavy, rich silk, with large flowers worked on it; and it rustles when she moves. And then she can tell the most wonderful stories. Grandmother knows a great deal, for she was alive before Father and Mother—that's quite certain."

So wrote Hans Christian Andersen in one of his lesser-known tales entitled *Grandmother*, based on his own recollections. Grandmothers have a good image both historically and mythically. On the whole, grandchildren have close relationships with their grandmothers. This is perhaps partly because, at a generation's distance, grandmas are removed from the direct conflicts of everyday upbringing. What is more, with the wisdom of experience, they have learned what is of importance and when to keep silent. Grandmothers are traditionally the dispensers of family wisdom, the repository of home remedies for everything from sciatica to a broken heart. Modern grandmothers may be jet-setters rather than watching life from their rocking chairs, but in many cases the bond with grandchildren remains strong and they will drop everything to answer a call from a distressed child, whether received psychically or on their mobile phone.

Grandmothers Who Detect Danger

Occasionally a grandmother will pick up on a child's distress hundreds or even thousands of miles away. Jenny was living in Essex while her daughter and grandson were in Barbados. One day Jenny woke with a terrible feeling that her grandchild was in danger and she insisted on flying out there the next day. Jenny did not know what the problem was but knew that a telephone call would not help. When she arrived her young grandson was listless but otherwise not ill. But Jenny knew something was wrong and noticed an old gas heater on the wall. She insisted it was checked and it was discovered to be leaking lethal carbon monoxide fumes which had built up to a dangerous level.

"I just knew that my presence was needed to avert the disaster and so flying halfway across the world was a small price to pay," she told me.

Carole, who lives in Hampshire, was also far away from her grandchild when she detected all was not well.

"Our eldest son was in the army and posted to Germany. His wife was expecting our first grandchild and we were very excited. When the baby was born, my daughter-in-law wrote telling us the general details of his weight and birth and that they were calling him Paul. My husband and I could not go to Germany and had to wait to see the baby until my son came on leave with the family to England.

"One night I had sudden sharp pains in my ankles and feet. I woke my husband and told him, 'There's something wrong with Paul. I know it's to do with Paul's feet.' He replied that Paul was only a baby and that our son would tell us if anything was wrong. I was not convinced and wrote to my son and daughter-in law asking if Paul was all right.

"They told us then that Paul had been born with both feet turned

*inwards almost touching his legs and had a plaster cast put on both feet
and ankles in an effort to straighten them. They hadn't told us as they
thought we might worry too much. Paul is now twenty-one years old and
six feet tall."*

Strangely, Carole's psychic link did not operate in the case of three
children that she lost.

*"I had no premonitions about their deaths although I had a special,
intense love with all of them. The last one, when he was a baby, looked at
me in a way that was far too wise and soul-searching.*

*"Linda, the second little girl we lost, died in Singapore on an army
posting. One day I heard my daughter Tricia outside chattering and
laughing, but she was on her own. I asked to whom she was talking and
she told me, 'Linda's come to play with me.'*

*"I told her that Linda could not talk that much as she had only been a
year and a half old when she died. 'Well, she can now,' and 'She's telling
me in my head,' she replied."*

Peggy, an antiques dealer who lives in Wiltshire, is another
modern grandmother who has lived up to the traditional image.
She had a very bad relationship with her own mother who rejected
her from an early age. Perhaps this is why Peggy has fostered warm,
close links with her own children that have continued into the third
generation. In these relationships, telepathic communication is so
routine that, as Peggy told me, it is only when the other party replies
out loud to an unspoken conversation that it becomes surprising.

*"My granddaughter Charlotte was coming to stay at my house. About
two hours before they were due to arrive, I got a towel from the airing
cupboard and was twisting it around the handles of the lavatory door.
My daughter Jo asked me what on earth I was doing. 'I must tie up this
door so that it can't shut or Charlotte will get her hand caught in it,' I
remember replying.*

"Just at that moment the telephone rang. Jo answered it and it

was Charlotte's mother saying, 'We'll be at least an hour late. Charlotte has just shut her hand in the lavatory door and has no skin on her fingers.'

"That happened in Kent, more than a hundred miles away."

A Grandmother's Instincts

Peggy has very strong views on children and her sensitive, totally unsentimental and empathic approach towards them is perhaps the key to her close bonding with her grandchildren. "Don't talk to children, listen to them," Peggy told me.

"Children are highly evolved beings showing spiritual instincts. Parents rapidly set about despiritualizing them to create mercenary humanized creatures in their own image. At the age of about three and a half, children tend to shed their spiritual aura almost like a snake shedding its skin. It is perhaps when a child is three and a half that some parents win the battle. The terrible twos is probably the last effort of the child to cling to its own image before surrendering to parent power.

"I always bonded with my grandchild Charlotte. From when Charlotte was about five months old, I would read to her and talk to her and she would respond, holding my fingers and working them as I spoke. I remember when Charlotte was ten months old, she was sitting in her high chair and we were chatting away as usual. We had such fun. My son-in-law, bemused, asked me, 'How do you know what she is saying? I can't understand a word.'

"But of course I did. Charlotte and I always had wonderful conversations and naturally we can read each other's thoughts. It has always happened with my own daughters so there is nothing strange in it—it is part of an incredibly close and mutually supportive relationship. But usually it shows up in simple ways. For example, once, when she was about five, Charlotte was staying with me and we were driving along in the car. I was wondering what we could have for dinner that evening. I thought, 'There's a chicken in the freezer.' At that moment Charlotte

piped in 'And I'm going to stuff it with tarragon because I always stuff chickens with tarragon at Gran's.'"

So why is Peggy able to maintain the kind of everyday close links usually reserved for the maternal link? Because she gives to her grandchildren not continuous but close, accepting care when she is with them. Peggy recalled for me just one of numerous telepathic incidents spanning her own children's adolescent and grown-up years. "When my daughter Penny was sixteen we were going shopping and as we were going out of the door she said, 'I could do with one too.' 'What do you mean?' I asked. 'A Guinness when we've finished the shopping.' Then she stopped. 'Wasn't that what you said?' Well of course I hadn't said anything out loud but that was what I was thinking."

It is the timing that makes these incidents so remarkable. Penny just carried on her mother's unspoken communication without a break, a continuity that can so often supplement or replace spoken words in close relationships, parapsychologist Joe Cooper's "soul-flow".

Anne, who lives in Christchurch in New Zealand, has close intuitive bonds into the fourth generation.

"I am a great-grandmother and very fond of my granddaughter. When her first baby was nearly due, she and her husband were dining with me one evening and suddenly I felt an overwhelming love and warmth for that little life sitting beside me and soon to be with us. I just knew that it was a little girl reaching out to me. All I could say was, 'Oh, I am looking forward to this baby.'

"That feeling has never left me and a very real and strong bond exists between me and the little girl Melanie who is five now and in her first year at school. She brings her drawings and first books to see me regularly and enjoys cuddles with her eighty-one-year-old Little Grandma, as she calls me. When little Melanie was about four, she rang me up on a toy telephone from her home to say, 'Little Grandma, your lamp is falling down.'

*"My granddaughter told me about this 'pretend conversation' later.
However, Melanie had been right. At about that time my reading lamp
had indeed overstrained its screws and fallen over my shoulders."*

Grandmothers Who Return

Grandmothers are naturally concerned with the welfare of their
grandchildren and many people have told me that when they are
sick or worried they have detected a deceased grandmother's
perfume or sensed her presence. In human, if not scientific,
terms such contact would seem quite explicable. In the absence
of any real tools for assessing psychic experience the main criterion
is often whether the encounter has purpose and above all meaning
to those involved. Helen, who lives in Southampton, England,
believes that her grandmother's ghost returned to save Helen's
own life.

*"I was born in the north-east of Scotland, the land of the Picts. My
beloved grandmother died when I was eight. We had always been very
close. Years later I married a US serviceman. My daughter was born in
England, six days after my twenty-first birthday, a breech birth. It was a
long labour and a four-hour delivery. The baby was not breathing when
she was born, but she was resuscitated. Twenty months later my son
was born, a straightforward birth, but this time I suffered post-natal
depression. My husband was a womanizer and violent. My mother
visited every day to find fault and criticize my husband but they were
sweetness and light to each other. I was worn out between them.*

*"One evening, I was sitting at the table. The children were asleep and
my husband was out yet again with another woman. I had just had a
particularly unpleasant visit from my mother. I poured a tumbler of
whisky, emptied a bottle of anti-depressants and a bottle of paracetamol
on to the table, put my head in my arms and wept.*

*"I felt a tweed skirt touch my face, an arm went round me and I was
held close to the skirt. I do not know how long I was held but a wonderful*

peace filled me. I knew it was my grandmother, although I did not look up.

"I realized then I could not leave my children to be raised by my mother or my husband. My grandmother gently placed my head back on my arms and I sat contentedly for a while before flushing the whisky and the anti-depressants down the toilet. The paracetamol went into the cupboard."

Such an experience is not unique. I have met a woman whose deceased grandmother had saved her from being crushed by a horse and a grandmother who saved her grandson during interrogation when he was a prisoner of war. However, the most common paranormal experience occurs when a grandchild links into his or her grandmother's death. What is fascinating is that Ingrid, a senior advertising executive, did not consider her experience as a psychic one.

Ingrid's grandmother lived in Prague. In old age, she became ill and could not communicate with her family. Ingrid was working in England but was going home for Christmas. She asked her sister what she could buy her grandmother, although the old lady seemed too ill to appreciate anything. Ingrid's sister suggested a big bunch of flowers to place next to the old lady's bed.

Not long before Ingrid was due to return home, she had a vivid dream in which her grandmother was sitting up in bed, smiling and talking. The old lady looked really well. She told Ingrid that she felt fine and that her granddaughter must not worry about her any more. Ingrid woke at 5 a.m. and the phone was ringing. It was her father and Ingrid knew before he spoke that her grandmother had died during the night, about the time of her dream.

It would be possible to dismiss such an experience as coincidence, except that so many people have reported similar experiences at times when the grandparent or parent was not even known to be ill. If one accepts that any loving grandmother might be thinking strongly about her family at the point of her death, it is not surprising that this telepathic link occurs. It may also be that the great psychic energy created at death, paralleled only by that of the act of giving birth, enables the dying person to move in her astral body to visit a loved child or grandchild. So little is known about the process of dying, and nothing of what lies beyond. Ingrid still questions the nature of her experience, but nevertheless she finds it very positive and reassuring.

Perhaps the most remarkable phenomenon I have come across is where deceased mothers and grandmothers turn up at the birth of their grandchildren and great-grandchildren. My own theory is that the intense energies released at birth make the mother giving birth especially spiritual and able to contact other dimensions, while the woman linked by birth is attracted by the same energy.

Elspeth, an accountant living on the south coast of England, told me that while she was in labour with her son twenty years ago a beautiful tiny grey-haired nurse in a grey dress and no apron kept popping in and out of the hospital ward to see her.

"She was lovely, chatting to me and holding my hand. She had a beautiful circular brooch with brilliant pearls, emeralds, diamonds and rubies. I remember thinking she was the only one in the room wearing jewellery apart from the other nurses' clip-on watches. The old nurse told me I was having a boy. All the way through my labour, she kept encouraging me. It was wonderful.

"The doctor at last told me I had a little boy, which I knew anyway because the old nurse had informed me earlier. I had a sleep and woke up starving, demanding my breakfast. They told me it was dinner time. I asked if I could talk to the older nurse with the beautiful brooch. I wanted to thank her for being so kind to me. But nobody knew her. I said, 'But she was there,' and they started talking about childbirth fever and seeing a psychiatrist. So I did not mention my grey lady again until I got home. But I was very puzzled. I told my father and he asked me for details of her. 'You daft ha'p'orth,' he told me, 'it was your grandma come to see you were all right.'

"Then he realized she had died when I was only eighteen months old so it was not surprising I hadn't recognized her. He produced a picture I

had never seen before. It was his mum and there she was in the photograph, the kindly older nurse, and she was wearing the brooch. I can picture her now. She wasn't insubstantial. She looked as real as you or I and she held my hand all the way through labour. I told Mum and she said, 'Oh, Dad's filling you with his weird ideas again.' But I knew better."

People frequently say when hearing such experiences that the person involved had seen the photograph earlier in life and forgotten. Before the Second World War, photographs were not that common. I myself have only ever seen one photograph of my grandmothers, who died years before I was born, and indeed only have three photographs of my own mother who died in 1967. What is more, I have come across several instances where children have been visited in the night by a lady who says she is Great-grand-mother. When ancient family photos have been retrieved, the child will pick out "Great-granny" from rows of faded sepia figures, who elderly relatives will confirm is indeed "granddad's mummy". I even came across an account of a boy who saw his great-grandmother for the first time in a Near Death Experience and years later identified her as "the lady who sent me back".

In the case of Sadie who lives in Yorkshire, her son formed a bond with a great-grandma who had seen him only twice as an infant before she died. Young Lewis had not seen any photographs.

"My newborn son Lewis yawned as his great-grandma held him and commented on what a bonny baby he was. My husband Glen, who is twenty-four, and I had taken the baby to show Glen's grandparents Jayne and David for the first time. Jayne only saw Lewis once more before she died.

"We continued to visit Glen's grandfather regularly. One Sunday when Lewis was four we went round. Lewis was playing on the living room floor. 'Where's that lady gone?' he asked suddenly. 'There was a lady with dark hair sitting there.'

"He was staring at the chair where Glen's grandmother always sat.

When we got home, we asked him about the lady. 'She had dark curly hair, big glasses and a mark on her neck,' he told us. Jayne had worn big glasses, had dark curly hair and a very noticeable dark mole on her neck. 'She had her hands out like this,' said Lewis, putting out his hands in the way his great-grandmother had cradled him as an infant. Lewis had never seen a photograph of Jayne. Those that existed were in family albums he had never been shown.

"*That Christmas we went to see Glen's grandfather. His Aunt Sylvia came with us. We did not say anything at the time but afterwards asked Lewis if he had seen the lady in the chair. 'Yes,' he said, 'but she was upstairs watching Aunty Sylvia was doing things properly.' Sylvia was the eldest daughter. Her mother had been very houseproud.*

"*Our young daughter has seen nothing on the visits.*"

Grandmothers seem remarkably adept at overcoming the time barrier and I am convinced that the power of family love is one of the most powerful forces of all.

Grandmotherly Devotion

The destination of this journey
is the same for each:
time to let go,
mother no more.

How different we feel,
distanced,
as if watching the lives around us
from afar.
In our heart the love is there,
just as always,
yet changed somehow.

Anne Johnson, "Grandmother Spider's Corner"

Surrogate Grandmothers

One of the strongest examples of a grandmother's love is the modern phenomenon of the surrogate grandmother. In this case the surrogate is motivated by pure love: the desire to give a daughter who is unable to conceive the chance to be a mother herself. This is not an easy choice. The surrogate mother faces the possible dangers of having a baby late in life, the paradox of being at the same time mother and grandmother, and the uncertainty of not knowing how mother, grandmother and grandchild/child will react fifteen or twenty years after the birth.

The British surrogate grandmother Edith who gave birth in 1996 has suffered from unexpected post-natal depression. She has complained of feeling empty with apparently nothing to show for her nine months of pregnancy. She said several months after the birth: "I tried to get around this problem during pregnancy by constantly telling myself and other people the child I was carrying was not mine. Nevertheless it is still very hard to come to terms with when it is all over. But at least I'm still lucky because I can see Caitlin whenever I want and I know how happy she has made Suzanne and Chris.'

Every surrogacy involves loss as well as gain for the birthmother and the mother who could not carry her own child in her womb. There is a possibility that in such a case as this, where the surrogate mother continues to have close contact with the child to whom she gave birth, ambivalent feelings may occasionally surface, especially where there are differences of opinion regarding the child's upbringing. However, at its best this unique three-generation link can offer a deep bond of love between the women and children involved.

The first surrogate grandmother gave birth to triplets in South Africa in 1987, and ten years later, at the time of writing this book, the relationship seems to be thriving. Pat was forty-eight years old when she agreed to act as surrogate for her twenty-five-year-old daughter Karen. The family live in the small town of Tzaneed and mother, daughter and grandchildren remain firmly bonded.

Pat still maintains: "A mother will do anything to make her child happy."

The children are not worried, explaining to anyone who asks, "Granny gave birth to us because Mummy had no room in her tummy."

Karen was fertile, but after the birth of her son in 1984 her uterus was irrevocably damaged. She and her husband were devastated as they had hoped for a large family. Karen became progressively more depressed, as she longed for a daughter. Pat offered to act as a surrogate and was implanted with embryos from the couple. On Pat's birthday in February 1987, the family discovered that she was expecting triplets.

Pat wanted to keep her surrogacy private, but decided that this might lead to problems when the news did eventually break. To her amazement she became a worldwide celebrity overnight and the response was mainly totally supportive of her decision. "We were besieged," Pat said. "I had to wear a blonde wig when I visited the clinic so people wouldn't recognize me. That was by far the most stressful time of the pregnancy."

Pat carried the triplets until 38 weeks. Then, shortly after 6 a.m. on 1 October 1987, they were delivered by Caesarean. "I remember the doctors taking out the first two babies and announcing that they were boys," said Pat. "They were tiny little scraps of things—it was amazing. Karen was with me and I prayed and prayed the last baby would be a girl. I was so happy when it was. Then I just wanted to be left alone. I was so tired I slept for almost a day. I rested in hospital for another two weeks before going home. There were all sorts of rumours going around about my health. I was very upset on the day I left the clinic to come across a newspaper billboard which said I was dying. I had to phone relatives quickly to reassure them. As for the babies, I felt no longing for them as my own. I never have. In my mind they were always Karen's, and I never had any feelings towards them that were different from my other grandchildren."

For a couple of days after the birth, the boys were kept in incubators, breastfed by Karen, who had undergone treatment which enabled her to produce milk. Paula, the smallest triplet, stayed in the incubator for a month. For Karen, the hard work of triplets was more than compensated by her joy: "My soul-destroying sadness had gone at long last. I'm so proud of my mother. What she did was very characteristic. She is a truly selfless woman."

Nine years on, Pat says: "I see the triplets about every other day. We're all very pleased with the way things turned out. I don't think of what I did as a sacrifice at all. I just saw my daughter in tremendous pain and I wanted to help her."

Britain's first surrogate birth involving a grandmother was on 5 December 1996 in Darlington. Fifty-one-year-old Edith gave birth to her granddaughter Caitlin at 36 weeks. Her daughter, twenty-two-year-old Suzanne, who was born without a womb, was present at the birth and both women wept with joy as a doctor lifted the baby from Edith's body and placed her in Suzanne's arms.

Suzanne said after the birth, "I just can't believe it. My mother is marvellous for doing this for us."

Her husband Chris commented: "Edith has given us the one thing that was missing in our lives. We are so grateful."

Edith, who had two other children and a grandchild, explained that she felt like a normal grandmother. The baby was conceived artificially after Suzanne said that Edith was the only woman she would trust to carry her baby for her.

Suzanne and her mother were given hormone treatment and on 27 March two of Suzanne's embryos were implanted into Edith's womb. Six weeks later a scan confirmed that Edith was carrying Suzanne's child.

Edith said: "Suzanne was worried she would not bond with the baby, but I knew immediately that she had bonded with her straight away. Somehow motherly instinct told me that they were mother and daughter. A nurse at the hospital remarked, 'Edith, I can see love oozing from you. You are just that sort of person.' But it had nothing to do with my own qualities. I carried the baby for my daughter because I love her and don't want her to be hurt."

The pregnancy was an anxious time for Suzanne. She was constantly at her mother's side, helping in every way she could. "I worried about my mother from day one," she said. "Whenever she felt ill, I felt so guilty."

The joint pregnancy had many shared pleasures: the positive pregnancy test, the baby's first kick, the first ultrasound that showed the baby was healthy and the birth itself. Edith had, however, suffered considerably. She told reporters a few days before the baby was born: "It has been harder than I thought. I imagined I would be able to carry this baby as I had my own when I was younger. I did not realize it would take so much out of me."

Barbara Wiedner, who founded Grandmothers For Peace in the spring of 1982 in Sacramento, California, wrote: "We believe that the tremendous power of the love we possess can be an effective force in the struggle to save the world from disaster." Indeed, if older women can harness the qualities of courage, patience and determination acquired in mothering to create a more caring world for their grandchildren, her belief will not have been misplaced.

PART ELEVEN

Alternative Motherhood

Single Mothers by Necessity

I have a real sense of achievement that I did survive
alone, that I did cope. I look at my children, bright and
happy, and I tell myself, 'I did that. Almost everything
they know, I have taught them. I have read to them.' I
am very proud of my children.

Julie, a single parent from Norwich, England

There is undoubtedly still a great deal of pressure, both social and
political, on the single mother. We can all imagine her fears: Will
I be able to cope? What will happen to the children if I fall ill? What if
I'm working full-time and my child falls ill? What about childcare?
Nevertheless, single mothers can and do succeed in rearing well-
balanced and confident children.

Julie, who lives in Norfolk, is not the stereotype of a young
unmarried mother, but a former businesswoman in her thirties who
found her apparently secure world crashing around her ears:

*"I was thirty when I became pregnant. I had been with my partner for
ten years and we were running a successful business, enjoying good
holidays and with no financial worries. It was quite a shock to me at first
having a child as it meant that I could not go where I wanted any more,
that I suddenly had to ask for money. For John, my partner, the idea of
fatherhood was horrifying, although in reality he continued his free
lifestyle without me. John was drinking very heavily. By the time I was
five months pregnant with my son and Jasmine my daughter was
eighteen months old, I warned my partner that unless he stopped
drinking, I would take the children and go. John refused to listen.
We were living in London.*

"At that point, I rang my mother in Norfolk who had been very concerned about the situation and asked her to come and get me. When I moved to Norfolk, I left everything behind. I had no money, no furniture and nowhere to live.

"It was such a struggle. The council would not house me, but I managed to find a rented flat and part of the rent was paid for me. I was really frightened and overnight lost all my confidence. It was a hard struggle until the baby came. I had put off leaving my partner first by a week, then two weeks, then another, because the idea of being on my own seemed so alien, impossible even, I would not be able to cope. One minute it seemed as if I had everything, the next nothing. I was such a strong person before I had children, able to deal with anything, I believed. I used to despise people like myself, single mothers living on benefits, but that was when I had everything. I knew I had made the right decision to leave.

"My personality changed totally too. I was such an outgoing person and used to say when I was young that I would have children but would not need a husband. Alone at thirty-three, I suddenly found I could no longer go down to the shops by myself, or out for an hour in the evenings. In the small village to which I moved, there was a great stigma about my situation. I was a wicked, pregnant woman who had left her husband and deprived the children of a father. At least that's how it seemed to me and certainly that was the message conveyed by everyone.

"I was worried I would not be able to cope with the baby when he came. Jasmine was being very difficult, asking me constantly when her daddy was coming home and where he was. Because she was so young, I told her that he was at work and could not come home for a while. How can you explain to a two-year-old that her father was a drunkard who might harm her? Before baby Ian was born, I went along to a mother and toddler group. Most of the mothers were quite upper-crust and wealthy, but I did make one or two good friends. However, I was always seen as a threat by married women, someone who might be after their husbands. I even found this attitude in the short time I was in the maternity ward after Ian's birth.

"I also found myself the centre of attention for every lecherous male under eighty who assumed I must be easy and desperate for a man.

"I was in total turmoil, not knowing whether I wanted my ex-partner at the birth, because feelings don't just die, whether I wanted my mother there or if I should go through it alone. In the event I went into labour so suddenly that my mother was with me and it was wonderful. She was far more supportive than my partner had been during Jasmine's birth.

"It was painful for me after the birth, seeing the other mothers with their proud husbands walking up and down with the babies. I did not even have a wedding ring, as although my partner and I had been together for ten years we had never married. At thirty-three I was in the same position as an unmarried mother of seventeen. I felt desperately alone, especially when I brought Ian home. I came home the day after the birth and just got on with life.

"I felt very guilty that I was always pushing Jasmine aside, telling her to wait, that I had no time for her. But the baby did not sleep for eight months and even at three years old Jasmine comes into my bed every night. I felt I was becoming a total zombie, that my brain was completely dead. But after the birth of Ian, life was like being on automatic pilot.

"Worst of all my sister's husband turned on me, telling me that I was a scrounger. He knows the problems I have had living on benefits and how I had no choice other than living with an abusive partner. My sister has backed him. I am so angry I will never speak to them again. It was not as if I had ever asked them for anything. The argument has also caused bad feeling with my mother who has been so good to me.

"I have noticed with my son that if there is a roomful of women and one man he will always gravitate to the man, offer him his toys. He is very close to my father. Ian's own father now sees him every two weeks, as John says he has his problem under control. My son sees John as just another male who comes in and out of his life. When I was with John he did not want to know about being a father. The first time he took the children for the afternoon, I was on the phone every five minutes checking they were all right. Because John never cared for them in practical ways, I did not even know if he was capable or if they might be hurt or distressed.

"It is strange. I cannot wait for the children to go, to have some time to *myself, but I cannot wait for them to come back, to see them happy and safe, and I cannot settle while they are away.*

"At one point, when my ex-partner was very unstable, I did not want him to see the children at all as I was worried what he would do or even if he would snatch them away. My solicitor suggested that I took Jasmine and Ian to a Family Centre to meet their father, but I could not bear the children to go to an impersonal place away from the family setting as it would upset them and leave them with bad memories.

"Jasmine talks about her father all the time, draws him pictures at playgroup. He showers her with presents and is able to be the indulgent Father Christmas figure. I do resent the fact John still has everything—the business, the Mercedes and the house—while I am struggling to make ends meet. I am the one who disciplines the children and has to deny them treats.

"My ex-partner has met someone new and the children think his new girlfriend is wonderful. It's Nikki this and Nikki that and I am left on my own with none of their advantages, although I am the innocent party. They would have to shoot me and hang, draw and quarter me before I would let John have custody. John says his problems are in the past, that I have no choice but to trust him. But I know they can recur at any time. He has taken everything away from me and from the children, the comfortable life, the holidays, leaving us on family credit.

"I am just starting to inch my way back into life. I worked for a time years ago in a bar where Singles' Nights were held and we used to giggle about the desperate people eyeing each other up. Now I am on the other side, like a nervous teenager. I am now working a day a week while my mother cares for the children. I have a real sense of achievement that I did survive alone, that I did cope. I look at my children, bright and happy, and I tell myself, 'I did that. Almost everything they know, I have taught them. I have read to them.'

"I am very proud of my children. I know many women who are trapped in unhappy relationships, afraid to leave because they fear they could not cope. They could, although it is no easy choice. Inch by inch I am regaining my confidence and former strength of character. However,

I am becoming strong in a different way because I have overcome the odds and can see a future not only for the children but for myself.

I asked Jane Mattes, coordinator of the American organization Single Mothers by Choice (like Gingerbread in the UK run by and for single mothers, and a tremendous support) about the positive aspects of being a single mother. She replied: "I know loads of guys, my own first partner included, who regard baby as a rival and it seems to bring out quite a primitive destructive response. I do think that living with a loving single parent can be better for a child than living with a couple if the couple includes a hostile or dysfunctional man, but I don't agree that most men are that way."

I wondered if children actually grew up stronger and more independent for seeing a single coping parent.

Jane replied, "Not necessarily. I think if the child's needs are met appropriately in the early years, the child will grow up to be strong and independent. If they aren't the child will hang on to childhood for too long and not be able to be independent. Single parenting can still be a stigma in backwater places in spite of liberalism. But this is less universally true today. Even in backwater places, the reactions are more mixed, not all negative. Single mothering is a valid alternative to traditional two-parent maternity, if the mother is reasonably mature, competent and able to be a good parent. Ditto for a man. I believe that what a child really needs is a good parent who is mature enough to put the child's needs ahead of her/his own and who is also capable of setting limits in a firm and loving way. That's my definition of good parenting, and I don't think the number of parents is as relevant as whether or not the parents have those skills."

Single Mothers by Choice

I experienced a deep feeling of connection to all other mothers, all over the world from the beginning of time. It extended not only to humans but to animals as well. It was not only an emotional and spiritual connection, but also a physical one, as though time and space did not exist. It was almost as though there is only one true mother and we are all part of it.

Helen from Bristol, England, describing her feelings in the early days of single motherhood

There are many situations under which a woman will choose to have and bring up a baby alone. In the case of Julie in the previous chapter the alternative of staying with a drunken husband was not really a choice at all. Other women who become pregnant will detect instantly or during the pregnancy that the birthfather is not the right person to father the child on a daily basis and will choose to become single mothers. In a growing number of cases, a woman who does not have a partner may decide to become a mother and use either artificial insemination or find a male friend with whom she will have sex during her fertile period, but who will have no more contact with the resulting child than any other acquaintance. Then she brings up the child entirely alone.

Kellie, who lives in Kent, was quite young when she became pregnant but realized early on that her boyfriend Matthew would not make a full-time father for her infant. Some people argue that a woman has no right to deprive a baby of his or her natural father. In fact, in many cases where the father is entirely absent the father himself has either expressed reluctance or demonstrated an unwillingness or inability to assume responsibilities. Few totally indifferent, uncaring fathers-to-be are miraculously transformed by the birth process into devoted fathers and it may be advisable for the expectant mother to use her intuition if she is having serious doubts. Kellie explained her decision and the consequences.

"From the moment I found out I was unexpectedly pregnant, I knew I wanted to keep the baby. It was very frightening. Although I knew that I wanted children at some point, I was only nineteen years old and lived at home with my parents. I had a job working as a nanny which hardly paid anything and a steady boyfriend. Life was not perfect but I knew that I could cope with bringing up a child. That sounds naïve, but with the support of my family and friends—and at that point I still included my partner—I knew we would be fine.

"Before the pregnancy Matthew and I had a good relationship and initially he had no objections when I said that I wanted to keep the baby. After the initial shock and despair and the confrontation with our parents we settled into preparing financially and psychologically for our baby.

"These plans for our future lasted only two months because, being in the army, Matthew had to go away. That was when the real problems started. Matthew had received his roster for the next year and it had worked out that he had to be away for eleven out of twelve months. It upset me because he was pleased about travelling and talked about it all the time. He didn't give us a second thought. It was occurring to me that although I might have a partner in name, I would have to bring up my child on my own, even if we stayed together.

"We finally split up when I was four months pregnant. Matthew did not understand why at the time and I had no explanation for him. I was not even sure myself why I was doing it, but it felt right and he made no real attempt to encourage me or to offer support if he stayed.

"Matthew and my mother were close and she kept telling him that it was just my hormones and that I would change my mind in a few weeks, which really annoyed me. Matthew started to get nasty, saying that I had used him to get pregnant. He said that he wanted a blood test when the

baby was born because he did not think that it was his. I was upset about that. All his hostility and spite I found out later were instigated by his mother. I had never met her as she lived on the other side of the country. Matthew later apologized, but the wounds went deep and I was really hurt, and I realized that we did not have a future together.

"When I was five months pregnant Matthew went out to the Falklands for four months. I told him that I was not pushing him away from the baby, and whatever happened between us Matthew would always have the choice to see the baby if he wanted to. Matthew decided that he would come to see the baby whenever he could, but made no real commitments about the future. I settled into pregnancy and started to enjoy it.

"Matthew wrote to me declaring his love, but still no real plans and I just could not cope. I had decided I was going to do it all alone. I wrote back and told Matthew about how the pregnancy was going and what I had bought for the baby, but not about us. In one letter Matthew informed me that he was going to be present for the birth. I was horrified that after all that had happened he still wanted to be there. I was worried about the birth and did not want someone there on whom I could not rely, as it had all been sweet words on his part, but no practical support.

"On 31 January 1995 I gave birth to a beautiful baby boy, Joseph Robert. It was the single most wonderful thing that has ever happened in my life. Everything was perfect. My mum came in with me and was such a comfort to me and gave me all the support I needed. Mum and I were crying. He was her first grandchild. Even the midwife was crying. My sister contacted Matthew but he was at the pub. When he rang back two days later, he was drunk. I had noticed over the previous year he was increasingly becoming drunk. It was then I finally realized that Matthew had a problem with drink as well as with fatherhood.

"Lying in the hospital bed with Joseph asleep next to me the next day, I felt so alone. The other new mothers had their family all around them, dads, uncles, aunts, and I had no one. My father had to work, so did my brother and sister. My mum was not coming in until after lunch because of the visiting times which everyone else conveniently forgot. With tears

streaming down my face I rang my mum, hoping she would be there. It was still only nine o'clock and Mum was not even awake. I sobbed down the phone for her to come and see me. She was there within the hour, by which time I had calmed down. I handed my mother her grandson. The next day we were allowed home. We were met by my family which was really nice. Matthew had still not put in an appearance.

"I remember those first few days at home, mostly because everyone had to go back to work. Joseph was twelve days late. I was so frightened by 'what ifs'. What if he was ill? What if I fell and couldn't get up? What if I couldn't cope? I knew I could, but I think every mother has some sort of irrational fear, especially single mothers.

"Matthew finally came to see Joseph when he was a week old. We both took him to be registered which was nice and I think I still had vestiges of hope, but after two days Matthew told me he had to go home as his father was ill in hospital. It later slipped out that his mother and father were on holiday when Joseph was born and it was just an excuse to leave when the pressure of fatherhood was too much for him.

"After a couple of weeks the visitors slowed down. I wouldn't see or hear from anyone all day. That was when it finally hit me. I had got a baby. I was so happy and so scared at the same time. It was wonderful, even though I hardly got any sleep. What I did not expect was the tremendous feeling of love I had for Joseph. I felt so lucky, happy and proud of what I had. I got used to the sleepless nights, but what I could not get used to was the continual interfering from my parents. In the night my mum would come in and ask me if I was OK, which was fine when Joseph was little, but gradually he got used to his grandma coming in and I could not settle him, only she could. I felt pushed out. I was his mother and he did not want me. I suppose I was a little bit jealous, but who would not be? I felt guilty leaving him to cry because my parents had to get up early for work. They would come in if he cried longer than five minutes so he expected to be picked up as soon as he woke. It made me angry with them and we had lots of arguments over it.

"In the end I took Joseph to a sleep clinic when he was eighteen months old. I had to get it sorted out. I was dead on my feet. I had no energy and I was bad-tempered with my parents all the time. The nurse

suggested that I had a fixed bedtime routine, bath, story, milk, bed, which I had. I had to put Joseph to bed when he was sleepy but still awake, which I did. Then she suggested that I left him to cry for five minutes, go to see to him, then leave him a little longer and so on. I had no problem with this but I knew that my parents would not cope with this. The nurse told me it would take four days to a week and after that I would have no more problems. I went home and told my parents and sister what she had said and they agreed.

"When it came to putting the plan into practice, I had my sister banging on the wall, shouting, 'Shut that kid up.' My parents would fly in banging the door which woke Joseph up even more. It was awful after all their promises that they would support me. I was back to square one after three days.

"Joseph is thirty months old and still waking four times a night. I have not had a full night's sleep since before Joseph was born. All my mother can say is, 'At least it's not six times a night like it used to be.' I may sound ungrateful but I do appreciate what my parents have done for us, in giving us a home.

"In all this time Matthew had not been on the scene and I had made no attempt to contact him as I was determined to bring Joseph up myself. Two weeks after Joseph's first birthday I got a phone call from Matthew. I was half expecting it because a friend of mine had seen Matthew in the local pub. I felt first shock, then anger that he should so casually try to come back into our lives. I asked Matthew if he wanted to see Joseph. When Matthew agreed I said I would meet him in town. I was very nervous and arrived in the coffee shop early so I could see him first. My long hair had been cropped and I put on nice clothes to give me confidence. The first thing Matthew said was, 'Oh, you look great. I though you would look like s***.'

"That confirmed my suspicions. I didn't want him back but I did not want him to see Joseph just to satisfy his curiosity. After an hour he finally mentioned his son. We arranged for Matthew to come to the house at 3 p.m. the next day to see Joseph.

"At four o'clock Matthew finally turned up, making excuses about work. When he saw Joseph he just stood there with his mouth open. It

was strange because Joseph was at the stage where he was shy of strangers, but he looked at Matthew and smiled. Matthew stayed until nine o'clock and really enjoyed playing with Joseph. When he left, he promised he would phone and come round the next day so we could take Joseph to the park. He did not phone for some time and when he finally did we were busy and I told him to ring the next day. He never rang back and that was that. He could treat me badly but I was not having him upset Joseph by his unreliability.

"Joseph and I got back to normal and got on with our lives. We have moved now. I told Matthew we were moving but he did not get in touch and obviously decided against it.

"It is a year now since we saw Matthew and I often wonder what he would think of Joseph. It does not really matter because I am so proud of Joseph and that is what matters. At the moment he is too young to understand that he does not have a father around, but I do not worry about male role models because he has my father and my brother and several uncles. I am back at college now doing business studies in two languages and am a member of Gingerbread. My social life is quite good but once you have a child, even if you have a partner, your life can never return to what it was.

"The one thing that really annoys me is when I tell people that I am a single mother and they automatically say, 'Oh, I'm sorry.' I quickly correct this. There is nothing to be sorry about. I tell them I chose to bring up Joseph on my own and am so far happy and proud of what we have achieved. In the beginning it was hard and still can be. But I am so glad I have Joseph and cannot think of what life was like before him. In my future all I can see is myself and Joseph and as long as we are both happy that is the way it will stay."

"Is the strain of being a lone mother compensated by the joys of creating a child?" I asked Jane Mattes, co-ordinator of Single Mothers by Choice.

She replied, "In my experience the joy is not so much in the creation, although that certainly is a miracle, but in seeing the child grow and thrive."

To my next question—whether choosing to have a child suggests a pretty deep commitment to the child and whether a child finds that a responsibility in later life when Mom might be old and lonely— Jane responded that she thought this was no more true of a lone mother than any other. She commented: "If any mom uses the child to meet her needs that can be a problem. Some parents have a hard time with their daughters becoming single moms at the beginning, but almost all come around when the child is a reality. Most are quite supportive, although they have to grieve over their own dreams for their daughter who isn't going to get married, have the traditional partner, etc. Once in a while, I even hear about some woman's parents urging her to have a child on her own."

Jane started Single Mothers by Choice "to provide a support system for myself and my son. But it took off on its own as people heard about it. Apparently it met a real need for women since it grew consistently and has continued to do so. But the women overall are not radical or even very 'alternative' which is what makes it so shocking in a way. We are predominantly very much mainstream types."

A Single Mother by Artificial Insemination

Jan, a Californian publicity agency executive, told me how her urge to have a child before she was too old had been overwhelming.

"Every guy I met I saw as a potential stud. I got that desperate look in my eyes that would have guys running a mile. I knew I was too upfront, but time was running out. I was forty, divorced, and all the guys I met were either gay or wanted a nice young chick to take home to Momma.

"When I found myself taping the baby ads and replaying them, I knew it was time to act. Money was no object. I could afford a nanny, the best schools, the best healthcare. I figured on taking the first six months after the birth out. I have a house up in the mountains where the air is cool and the smog doesn't reach. I went to the clinic and got myself matched for the right kind of guy, majoring in psychology, young, tall,

blond like my own folks, and first time I got pregnant.

"I was over the moon. My friends had a shower there and then and I went shopping for a dozen babies. The stroller was covered in cute Beatrix Potter animals, the nursery decorated with a sky blue ceiling, with golden cherubs and stars that lit up at night.

"The birth was a dream, two close friends Caroline and Cathy as well as the midwife plus my doula, Rosa, an experienced, trained birther, who talked and hugged me through each bad moment, a kind of mom to the mom. My own parents in Florida were wrapped up in their golf and bridge. Rosa was the mom I had always dreamed of: humorous, supportive and so wise."

Doulas, Greek for servant or slave, are increasingly popular in the US and Canada and, being experienced mothers, provide the wisdom and support traditionally associated with the maternal role. In addition, the doula has expertise and training to support a mother through pregnancy, birth and increasingly the post-partum period.

"The candles glinted on the birthing pool and dolphin music was playing gently over the sound system. The moment of birth was like a huge orgasmic tidal wave and then, after the midwife and Rosa cleaned up, the five of us sat in a circle, Fleur to my breast. I thought I would die with joy.

"The days after were like a dream, Rosa always there, taking over the baby when I was tired, stopping me fretting over every hiccup and sneeze, coaxing the baby to feed. I hoped against hope I could persuade Rosa to stay. The agency weren't happy, saying it was bad if moms got over-attached to their doulas, but Rosa left the agency and moved in. I paid a huge release fee as she had signed up her services for a while and was booked for another mother. Her own kids were teenagers and lived with her ex, though Rosa went to see them quite often, which I hated like anything as I was lost without her.

"Fleur was an angel, sleeping or cooing in her crib, looking up at her magical stars, and after a month I started to miss the excitement of work. When my agency rang up to offer me a week to launch a special account

in LA, I jumped at the chance. I had quit breastfeeding though Rosa scolded me that I ought to stick at it and had exercised back into shape.

"I planned coming back each evening, but with the traffic on the freeways and the late meetings, I only made it once. One week became two, became three. Rosa was so good, sending me little kisses from Fleur and telling me every detail of her day.

"I arrived home for good on the third Friday with a huge furry elephant, twice the size of Fleur. It was late and the lights in the drive were blazing. I found the front door wide open, half-eaten burgers and fries scattered over the TV den and Rosa's kids sprawled on the white floor, fighting and pushing. Fleur was on the floor gurgling, when she should have been in her crib. Rosa bustled in with a tray of cola, saw me, tried to hug me, to explain, but I was so mad I couldn't listen. I was tired and there were strange kids who had taken over my house. They might have trodden on Fleur. Rosa had taken care of her own kids and neglected mine.

"I had so much wanted the homecoming and it was ruined. Rosa tried to explain that her husband was sick and that she had had her kids for the day and was going to drive them home earlier, but I had been late and she had not wanted to take Fleur so far late at night.

"I saw red and it ended with Rosa packing and going, the baby screaming all night. I cried too because I had come to love Rosa as a mom. Worse still I had taken on more work for the next week.

"Rosa refused to accept my calls and returned my flowers. I found an agency nanny but she was young and insisted on working set hours so I was commuting to and fro each day and my boss, a woman in her fifties who had no children, was quick to point out every mistake. My mind was not fully on my work or on the baby. After a succession of nannies I moved to Santa Monica, so I have only an hour's drive each way. I have a good nanny at the moment, but she is making noises about moving on and I have a major shoot planned for an new advert.

"As Fleur gets older and more of a person, I adore her but the strains are unbelievable. I no longer get the top assignments—as a mother I am regarded as less 'workplace-focused' and I can see the younger career women coming up fast behind me. As for the guys they run even faster *when I say I have to get home to my little girl. It is not at all like* Miracle on 34th Street *where the guy falls for the mom and her cute daughter. I suppose I wanted the pregnancy, the fuss, the excitement. My biological clock was ticking away like mad, but I never thought about the real baby rather than the one on the adverts. The cute infants I used to coo over on shoots went home with their moms, leaving me free for drinks or dinner. Now I am the one changing the diapers and watching television night after night alone, while the world passes by at high speed outside the window.*

"It is truly awesome. I am responsible for another human being, not just financially but in every way, and sometimes I feel I can barely take care of myself. I do miss Rosa."

For single mothers especially, a doula can be a lifesaver, especially if there is no partner or relation to help after the birth, to mother the mother at a time when she is vulnerable. Unfortunately, Jan saw Rosa as a permanent fixture and endowed her with expectations that could not be met.

The problem arises when babies are portrayed increasingly as not exactly designer accessories, but the panacea for biological and emotional longings, an answer to loneliness, a formula for instant happiness. Single mothers who choose to have babies alone can be wonderful mothers, so long as they want a child; not just a pregnancy or a baby, but a child that will be around for the rest of their lives.

If a woman is in doubt about whether to go it alone, I would suggest she looks after two or three demanding toddlers or sulky teenagers for at least a weekend in her house or apartment, arranges no special treats or fast-food catering and sees no other adults. After this if she still wants a child as a permanent fixture in her life, then what she feels is real mother love rooted in the everyday world.

Children are noisy, demanding, messy. They are also loving and creative and can take a woman into a world that is both spiritual and magical. Children are not the icing on life's cake, but a lifelong commitment.

Single Mothers and the Psychic Link

> It was as if my hand was pushed back by a powerful force, like someone else's hand pushing against mine, as I moved the plug towards the socket. I put down the plug, moved the baby out of the kitchen and went back to the jug. The side of the jug exploded, peeling open like a sardine can.
>
> *Laurel, a single mother from New Zealand*

Intuitive Birth Bonds

The usual picture of a mother in tune with her baby is of mother and child in spiritual harmony, protected by an adoring father. Yet women who give birth to and rear children alone whether by choice or necessity have intuitions every bit as powerful as mothers in secure relationships. Indeed, the concentration of the mother/child link within the single-parent unit can lead to an intuitive bond that remains throughout life. Children brought up in happy single-parent relationships invariably talk of the special links that made them as children feel treasured and respected as individuals from quite an early age.

Laurel, who lives in Christchurch, New Zealand, described how her son's life was saved by what seems to be maternal intuition, although Laurel is uncertain to whom or to what to attribute the protective force.

"I left my husband during my pregnancy. As my son was a fussy, demanding baby, he was more often in my arms than in a cot. Because I

was on my own with no other responsibilities, my life was entirely devoted to him at this stage. But I did have to make myself a sandwich occasionally and on this particular day I placed him in a bouncinette beside me while I did just that. He was about three months old and we were living in a rented flat.

"I made the sandwich and filled the electric jug. This was a metal jug and two or three weeks old. I placed it on the stove, picked up the plug and began moving it towards the socket on the stove. My hand seemed to resist and the thought flashed through my mind, 'What if the boiling water scalds him?' I bent down to move him out of the kitchen, which was long and narrow. Then I thought, 'No, I'll plug it in and then move him.'

"I picked up the plug again and repeated the motion towards the socket. I felt a stronger resistance this time, almost like the air curtain sometimes used to deter flies from going into a shop. Again I bent to move the baby. Once more reason told me not to be silly and for the third time I picked up the plug. This time it was as if my hand was pushed back by a powerful force, like someone else's hand pushing against mine, as I moved the plug towards the socket. I put down the plug, moved the baby out of the kitchen and went back to the jug.

"This time, although feeling uneasy, I succeeded in putting the plug in the socket. The result was quite spectacular. The side of the jug exploded, peeling open like a sardine can. In the process the protruding rim of a saucepan in front of the jug was melted and projected as a red-hot sizzling pellet on to the floor in the spot where my son had been sitting a minute earlier. The hole it burned into the linoleum was more than enough evidence for me of what it would have done to my baby son's head.

"Although I do not use it, I have kept the saucepan which clearly shows the melted rim from which the potentially lethal bullet came. I have no doubt at all that my son was being looked after by a power which knew what would happen when I put that plug in.

"The warning may have come from my own psychic experience and have had nothing to do with the mother/child link.

"I am still a solo mother in the sense that I never remarried. But my *baby is now a man of twenty-five. I did my degree when my son was at primary school, choosing subjects that fitted with his school hours and writing my assignments after ten at night when he was asleep."*

Helen's links with her daughter Beth were less dramatic than Laurel's but demonstrate an enduring spiritual link that for Helen confirmed the rightness of her decision to keep her baby. Helen told me of her experience and her bonds with Beth.

"I became pregnant at the age of twenty-four during a very brief affair which had no future. I had spent most of the year before my pregnancy travelling and had great plans set up for the next few years of my life, mainly involving travel. At the time I felt that children were something that would happen some time in the distant future if the situation was ever right.

"When I first realized I was pregnant I was devastated, as was the potential father who said straight out that he did not want to be a dad. He felt that I should have an abortion and I also felt that this would be the most sensible option. I tried to consider it very seriously. During the first couple of months of my pregnancy I spent nearly all my time thinking about the options open to me. I desperately wanted to hold on to all my carefully laid plans and was terrified at the prospect of becoming a parent with all the responsibilities it entailed. I think the idea seemed especially frightening to me because I knew I did not have the support of the baby's father.

"I also mistakenly confided in my parents who were shocked and upset and did not feel able to offer me any help. My father thought I should have the baby adopted and would be ruining my life if I kept the infant. I was living with my parents at the time and my father told me via my mother that I could not live with them if I had the baby. My mother, I think, felt that although she would like to offer me emotional support, she would be betraying my father if she did.

"I attended the relevant doctors and hospital appointments necessary to obtain an abortion, but despite everything I still felt as if I was going through the motions. More and more I was envisaging my future as a

434

mother. From the very beginning I had felt like a mother to the baby growing inside me and deep down I think I knew it was already too late for me to go back to being a non-mother. A few days before the abortion was due, I phoned the hospital to say that I was unsure. I had to go in and talk to the doctor again. The operation was delayed for another week to give me more time to consider.

"My most significant pre-birth connection with my baby occurred in that week. I was walking to work early one morning along a stretch of road that I particularly liked, next to the river, and I had a very strong and real vision of myself a few years on with my three- to four-year-old daughter. Her name was Beth and she had dark curly brown hair and her father's very distinctive blue slanting eyes. We were on holiday and were walking along the same stretch of river.

"I knew without a trace of doubt that I should keep my baby and, looking back, I feel as though I was given this vision to help me make the right decision.

"I felt a very strong connection with my baby throughout the remainder of the pregnancy, always thinking of her as my little girl. Beth was born in May 1996 after a short but very intense natural birth and her most distinctive feature was her slanting blue eyes.

"The powerful love that I felt for Beth after the birth was not at all like the instant falling in love that you hear about, but simply a continuation and increasing of the love I already felt. Likewise I did not feel that we bonded after the birth but that we continued the bonding that had started many months before.

"Another memorable experience occurred most intensely in the first euphoric days after the birth and continued for a few months and is very difficult to put into words. It was basically a deep feeling of connection to all other mothers, mothers all over the world from the beginning of time. It extended not only to humans but to animals as well. It was not only an emotional and spiritual connection, but also a physical one, as though time and space did not exist. It was as though I knew all the mothers and all the mothers knew me or I was all mothers and all mothers were me. It was almost as though there is only one true mother and we are all part of it.

"I frequently used to wake in the night before Beth. She has always slept in the same bed as me and is breastfed. She still needs me quite a lot in the night at thirteen months old. Now sometimes she wakes first and sometimes I wake first. A couple of times I have heard her crying while out of normal range of hearing, although each time I have been in the same building. I do not know whether this is a psychic experience or whether my usual hearing range has extended out of necessity. Perhaps it is a case of time and space not really existing in the way that we usually think of them.

"The initially reluctant father has turned out to be a very loving and caring one, seeing Beth regularly and taking part in her care. His family as well as mine have been loving and supportive. I guess everyone needed time to adjust to their new roles."

Marcy Anne, from Christchurch in New Zealand, believes that the love between herself and her daughters was a compensation for financial and external problems the family experienced.

"My daughters and I had become very close because my husband and I had separated and the girls and I were living alone together. Life was very difficult but I tried to ensure our lifestyle stayed roughly the same. I am very close to my younger daughter who I've noticed is particularly sensitive to mood fluctuations. Several years ago Sarah used to sleepwalk, not every night but on nights that I went to bed upset. I always made sure that bedtimes were nice times for the children, with lots of cuddles, stories and poems. I have never left Sarah until she was ready to snuggle down. The routine never varied. She would go to sleep, I would have a bath and go to bed.

"The one moment I would give myself to vent any frustration and anger was when I was alone in my bed. I would get annoyed or upset or cry into my pillow in privacy. Then, like a signal, Sarah would appear in the hallway or in my bedroom sobbing and talking gibberish in a deep sleep but with eyes open. I would coax her back to bed and with some effort would calm her down. Often this would take fifteen or twenty minutes.

"I gradually noticed her night wanderings more often than not coincided with my own emotional outpourings. It did not appear to be my general mood she was responding to but my temporary loss of control or emotional distress which seemed to communicate itself to her in her sleep. In the end I had to stop doing it which was not a bad thing for me either. When I stopped, she stopped. Instead of crying silent tears I tried to meditate and the conscious relaxation seemed to help, as did trying to focus on my inner feelings which eventually bored me to sleep.

"The reverse situation also occurred between my daughter and myself. The girls and I were rarely apart at night and my sister and brother-in-law had asked the children to stay with them in the country. We had been living in a purpose-designed two-family home with my parents who had the first floor of the house while the girls and I occupied the second. The first night the children were away there was a tremendous bother downstairs. As my father is considerably older than my mother and slightly invalid, I assumed he had been unwell during the night. There was a lot of movement, doors opening and closing and water running seemingly for ages as if a lot of cleaning up was going on.

"Normally I would have got up and checked that my mother was coping. However, because I had so many sleepless nights with Sarah and had trouble trying to sleep on that particular night since a neighbour's child was howling next door, I decided to stay where I was unless summoned from below.

"At breakfast the next morning I asked my mother what had been going on during the night. She looked very surprised and asked me what I was talking about. I mentioned the crying, the running water, the doors opening and closing and the long conversations I had heard during the night. My mother insisted that she had not stirred and my father had not stirred. I wondered why she was lying. I did not think the matter was worth pursuing, so changed the subject.

"During the morning my sister rang with a progress report on the children. I waited with bated breath as my sister has no children of her own and this was the first time she had had the girls on her own without me. Everything was fine. Now, that was. The night had been a disaster and I was told that Sarah was not allowed back until she was thirty.

"*At dinner the previous evening Sarah did not want to eat and did not feel well. My sister, due to her inexperience with children, persuaded Sarah to eat. The girls went to bed and eventually fell asleep. Suddenly during the night Sarah woke vomiting. She was only five at the time and was worried that her aunt would be cross with her for being sick in the bed.*

"*Her sister did not wake. Sarah got out of bed and attempted to clear up the mess by herself, with cold water and a flannel. She ran back and forth with the little cloth and the water ran and ran until the constant opening and closing of the doors woke my sister and her husband. They could not believe what they saw and spent the next hour or three cleaning up the mess and changing Sarah's bed.*

"*When I heard the story I realized that it was Sarah, not a neighbour's child, I had heard crying in the night. It was Sarah running through the house, opening and closing doors and endlessly running water. The noises in the night were so near and so coherent that I never thought for a moment there was anything mysterious about them. Psychically I was receiving, but because I did not get up and check the noise I did not realize I was receiving it an hour's drive away.*"

Newspaper articles, television stories and surveys can paint a dark picture of the emotional and psychological well-being of one-parent families. The phenomenon of mother love is much more complicated and it is the devotion, not the circumstances, that is the crucial factor in a child's future welfare.

The Stepmother in Myth and Reality

> When the wicked stepmother appeared, red-hot iron
> shoes were ready for her and she was made to dance in
> them until she fell down dead.
>
> *Snow White*

*S*tepmothers have had a bad press over the years from fairy stories
to folk sayings: in German the idiom to complain of one's
stepmother means to waste one's breath, and to weep at one's
stepmother's grave means to feign sorrow. But this image ignores
the thousands of stepmothers who have done so much for the children
they have taken on: witness Abraham Lincoln's. So why has the
negative image persisted? Let's begin by looking at a Breton legend
that is fairly typical in its view of stepmothers.

*Drýring went to an island and married Barbaik, a pretty young girl. He
lived with her for seven years and became the father of six children. But
death passed through the country and Barbaik, his beautiful flower
without blemish, perished.*

*Drýring went to another island and chose a new wife. Sadly she was
hard and cruel. She saw the bereaved children who looked at her and
cried and roughly pushed them away. She gave them neither drink nor
bread and told them: "You shall have hunger and cold." She took away
their blue cushions and told them: "You shall sleep on the straw." She
took away their bright candles and told them: "You shall stay in the
darkness." That evening the children cried. Lying on her bed, the cold
ground, Barbaik heard them and resolved to return to them. She*

439

approached Our Father and said to him: "Let me go to see my children."
And she continued to beg him until he gave permission for her to return
to the Earth. But he told her that she must return before cockcrow.

Barbaik raised her tired legs and crossed the walls of the cemetery. As
she passed through the village the dogs drew back into their homes and
the air shook with their howls. When she came to her house she found her
eldest girl standing by the door.

"What are you doing there, my dear daughter?" she asked her. "And
where are your brothers and sisters?"

"Why do you call me dear daughter?" replied the child. "You are not
my mother. My mother was beautiful and young, my mother had rosy
cheeks. But you, you are pale as death."

"How could I be beautiful and young? I come from the kingdom of the
dead and so my face is white. How could I have rosy cheeks? I have been
dead so long," said Barbaik and went into her children's room where she
found them crying.

She washed the first, she brushed the hair of the second, she consoled
the third and the fourth, and she took the fifth in her arms as if to suckle
her. Then she said to her eldest girl: "Tell Dryring to come here." When
Dryring came, Barbaik cried in rage: "I left beer and bread here and my
children are hungry. I left blue cushions and my children sleep on the
straw. I left bright candles and my children sleep in the dark. If I have to
return here again there will be trouble for you. Now the red cock crows
and the gates of heaven are opening. Hark, the white cock crows and I
can no longer stay." After that day, whenever Dryring and his wife heard
the dogs bark, they gave the children beer and bread, and every time they
heard the dogs howl they feared they might see the dead mother again.[1]

The story has all the classic ingredients: passive father, cruel
stepmother, and a mother whose love of her children conquers the
grave. This is a motif that recurs again and again in folk tales.

According to some psychologists, making her into the wicked
witch, the alter ego of the Madonna, is an acceptable way of
projecting hostile feelings about one's own mother. Melanie Klein
talks about the concept of the fairy mother and the bad mother who

are one and the same and reflect a child's ambivalence towards his or her mother. "A boy of six made me play the part of the fairy mamma and the bad mamma alternately. As the fairy mamma, I had to heal the fatal wounds he received from a huge wild animal, but the next moment I had to come back as the bad mamma and attack him. He said: 'When the fairy mamma goes out of the room you never know if she will come back as the bad mamma.'"[2]

The wicked stepmother of fairy story provided an acceptable way for a child to come to terms with his ambivalent feelings towards his mother: the good mother would generally have died young and beautiful to be replaced by a hideous stepmother who would meet an unfortunate end. In psychological terms, the child can then resolve his conflicts by projecting them on to the storybook characters and working through them rather than repressing them. Indeed in some very early folk stories and song, the concept of the cruel mother formed the theme.

Wicked Stepmother or Mother at the End of her Tether?

Janet from Surrey told me:

"I have great sympathy with Snow White's stepmother, though I stop short of wanting to devour my stepdaughter's heart. However, I have often contemplated the poisoned apple. I loathe my stepdaughter, though I would never dare admit it to my husband or family.

"Cressida is fifteen. Her mother Annette bleeds my husband Tom dry, although we have two small children. Annette swans around the picture of elegance, while I struggle to keep us fed and clothed. She left Tom for another guy she met at the local amateur dramatic society. That didn't last, so I admit Cressida must be pretty confused.

"When Cressida comes to stay she arrives in a pair of scruffy torn trainers and tells my husband that her mother cannot afford any new ones. I have seen her around the town in her designer stuff. I think she keeps her Cinderella rags for her access visits. But Tom falls for it hook,

line and sinker and I can see my hard-earned salary disappearing down the High Street yet again, as well as the only precious time we get with the children. 'Do they have to come?' Cressida scowls at my daughters and myself as though we had just crawled out of a hole and my husband shrugs apologetically.

"I have to bite my tongue till it bleeds while we go from shop to shop until at last the little princess selects what she will deign to wear and guilt-ridden Daddy pushes our credit cards over the limit yet again.

"Nothing for the girls, of course. Cressida makes such a fuss if we stop for a moment in the toy department. She twines herself round Daddy, whispering in his ear and casting sly glances at me while I trundle behind with the double buggy like the bag lady, the girls whining and bored.

"Every time she comes to stay, Tom and I have a major argument. He accuses me of being jealous and childish, but the minute Cressida arrives the children and I might as well not exist. She throws wet towels all over the bathroom, leaves crisp packets and chocolate biscuit wrappings on her bedroom floor.

"She never asks but just dips into the cupboards and, having snacked all day, pushes the supper around as though it were poisoned. If she was Snow White she would have been too full of junk food to take a bite at the poisoned apple. I am just the servant who cooks and clears while she sits like royalty and doesn't even clear her plate away. Mummy, needless to say, is a brilliant cook. Tom and Cressida sit and reminisce over the wonderful meals the three of them shared.

"Cressida is the image of her mother, and when I see her head close to Tom it is like a knife going through my heart. Annette will phone always in the middle of a meal and does not even address me. 'Is our daughter there?'

"I can hear Cressida complaining and laughing in her high-pitched spiteful way, then Tom goes to the phone and positively oozes charm. I wonder, if they are so attached, why his wife left him. Cressida also makes trouble for our girls, screaming if they touch any of her things and complaining to her father that I always take their part. I know she pinches them and says nasty things when I am not around. I have seen the marks, but if I ask her why they are crying she just smirks.

"It is as if we have changed places and I am the harassed middle-aged wife and his ex is the glamorous femme fatale *I used to be. I have tried to talk to Cressida but she just ignores me unless her father is present. Then she is all sweetness and light.*

"Now Cressida wants to go to France on a school trip, so she wants new clothes and spending money. This means yet again that our girls will be lucky to get a week in a caravan. I have tried to explain to Tom how I feel, but we always end up quarrelling and he always takes Cressida's part, saying she is only a child and that it is up to me to make an effort. She is driving a wedge between us. I used to think I loved all children until I met Cressida. There is a Poisoned Apple Society in the States. Maybe I'll found one here."

A Happy Ending

The other side of the coin is the story of Meena, a Hindu stepmother, who lives in north London. She told me of her rewarding relationship with her new family.

"I have two stepsons. I married their father a year ago. They are nine and six years old and at last we are getting there as a family. At first it was overwhelming moving in with the children, although I had known them for a year before we married. I spent a great deal of time with the boys in their home before our wedding, gradually assuming responsibility for their care. Their mother divorced my husband and the children lived full-time with their father. When my husband first took me to the house, the boys were not sure of me and asked questions like, 'Isn't she going home yet?'

"The older boy was seven at the time. At first I treated the children as friends, now I treat them as my own. There is no problem. At first I felt very guilty about shouting at the boys. but it had to be done. My husband finds it hard to discipline the children and is very soft with them. At first he was very protective towards them which was frustrating, because he did not realize how badly the boys were behaving. I talked to him about

443

the problem and how difficult it was when he tried to interfere. Now he is quite relaxed about my role, the boys are happier and more settled and we all have a good relationship which is very positive.

"All women can be mothers even if they do not give birth to children. Women are naturally intuitive and can sense unhappiness in children and know instinctively how to make them feel better. It takes determination to think of yourself as a mother if you come to the role as I did, but it becomes easier with practice. At first I used to get paranoid about other mothers, watching them with their children and thinking, 'Is she a better mother than I am?' Then a close friend assured me I was doing incredibly well and should relax.

"The children have never once said 'You are not our real mother' and have always called me Mum from the day I married their father. Indeed, everybody regards them as my children because their real mother only sees them once a week. She walked out of the marriage and so does not have the glory of being their mother. In traditional Indian society a woman who divorces is downgraded, the new wife becomes number one and the first wife is erased for ever. The new wife is regarded as the mother if she takes over the children. I was not frightened of becoming an instant mother. A lot of new stepmothers feel very anxious and that in itself can cause pressures. I have achieved so much in the year we have all been together, I sometimes forget I was ever the stepmother.

"My own parents have accepted the children happily, although they were against the marriage initially. They would have preferred an arranged marriage. But I loved my husband and was determined to go ahead. They were worried that I was taking on too much, marrying a man with children, as I was only twenty-three. My parents, aunts and uncles spread lots of doom and gloom and said I did not know what I was doing, but now they have seen how well it has worked. My husband's family are very liberated and there have been no pressures. They accepted me as the children's mother from the first."

Meena's own determination has been a major factor in making her step-relationship so successful, and she took a year to get to know the children before moving in. It has also perhaps helped that she has a clearly defined role in the children's lives, supported by her husband.

Merryl from Quebec was a stepchild herself and so was well aware of the pitfalls.

"I remember as a child of divorced parents when I was at my dad and stepmom's home, I missed the other people in my life and felt vaguely guilty in case they were missing me. Then no sooner had I got to my mom and stepdad's house than I was wondering how the others were handling my absence.

"How we as step-parents handle the absent biological parent is the most central issue. Worst of all can be if we fail to acknowledge the other person or to ask about their well-being. We ask 'How's your puppy or school work?' but never 'How's your mom?'

More than a third of all American children are expected to live in a stepfamily before the age of eighteen. James Bray, PhD, a researcher and clinician at the Department of Family Medicine at Baylor College of Medicine, has worked for nine years on a study of the impact of step-families upon the emotional and behavioural welfare of children. He discovered that one area of potential conflict for both adults and children occurred on the remarriage of one of the parents, when unresolved anger and pain from the previous marriage could easily surface. Dr Bray said that on discovering that a parent was getting remarried, a child was forced to give up hope that the parents would reconcile. A mother might make a stormy relationship with her ex-husband worse after learning of his plans to remarry, because she felt hurt or angry.

Dr Bray said that it was necessary to have a final emotional divorce. Furthermore, there should be non-confrontational discussions as to the role the step-parent would play in raising their new spouse's children. He also pointed out that young children could feel abandoned as a parent devoted time and energy to the new spouse that had previously been concentrated on the child. Adolescents were often, because of their own awakening sexuality, disturbed by "an active romance in their family".

Dr Bray found from his research that forming a step-family with young children was easier than forming one with adolescent children, because the need for independence experienced by all adolescents was "at odds with the developmental push of the new step-family for closeness and bonding".

He suggested that step-parents should first establish a relationship with the children that is more akin to a friend or camp counsellor than a disciplinarian. Couples can also arrange for each spouse to develop a list of basic household rules to be agreed with the children. The new step-parent is thereby following house rules, rather than inadvertently undermining the authority of the other parent. Dr Bray warns that parents should not speak against their ex-spouses in front of the child because it "undermines the child's self-esteem and may even put the child in a position of defending a parent".

"Under the best conditions, it may take two to four years for a new stepfamily to adjust to living together," Dr Bray concluded. While he saw psychological intervention as helpful, many step-parents find that their own personal efforts, given patience and goodwill, do win through and that if any outside help is required, then a good self-help group with other step-parents to talk and laugh with can defuse most difficult situations.

Maternal love is neither purely biological nor exclusive. Just as a child can love a mother and grandmother, so he or she can come to relate closely and positively with two mothers.

The Stepmother and the Psychic Bond

Just as intuitive links can exist where there is no genetic link in the adoptive situation, so a warm and intuitive relationship can spring up in the step-relationship. Gibert Attard, a French parapsychologist, sent me the following account from a close friend of his.

"I had excellent relations with my stepmother whom the family called Mammy Blue because she had such beautiful eyes. She was taken to

446

hospital with cardiovascular trouble and I was told that it was not worth visiting her as she was unconscious. I telephoned every day for news. Some days before her illness she had telephoned me, very depressed, and I told her, 'Listen, Mammy, come and spend a few days with me.' But it was February and she did not want to travel alone. She lived 700 kilometres (438 miles) from me. But she said she was sending me a parcel—she often sent me little things for the children.

"After Mammy had been in hospital for some time, I was told that she had regained consciousness. I sent her a big bouquet. When I telephoned the hospital I was told that Mammy was lucid enough to understand that I had sent them. The next day was Sunday, Mother's Day. My stepmother usually phoned me every Sunday at around 11 a.m. That Sunday I knew that I could not get her directly on the phone as only messages were being relayed. I was very busy and was going to ring that afternoon, but something made me call her at the usual hour.

"The duty nurse told me Mammy was very happy, that she had regained consciousness and was lucid and had her big bouquet next to her.

"Ten minutes later the nurse phoned to say that Mammy was dead. It seems that she had waited for my call so that she could die in peace. I still ask myself if I would have felt guilty if I had phoned in the afternoon and not the morning?

"While she was in her coma I had received her parcel which contained books, curtains and a radio alarm clock which I put in the wardrobe. The day after her death I set my alarm clock for seven. When it went off, I was surprised to find the house quiet and dark. For some reason it had gone off in advance. I reset the alarm but by the evening it had gained an hour. I could not trust this alarm clock so I got out Mammy's radio alarm. I did not choose any particular radio station but just set the alarm for seven o'clock and said, 'Well, Mammy, it's you who will wake me up.'

"The next day to my great surprise the radio woke me at seven o'clock with the song 'Mammy Blue'. I was staggered because I had not heard this song for years. Two or three days later I left for work a little late. Usually I have cassettes in my car rather than listen to the radio but that morning, as I was late, I didn't have time to find a cassette. I put on the radio at random and again I heard the song 'Mammy Blue'. Some days later I went into a shop and again I heard 'Mammy Blue'.

"Mammy had not had a proper burial because she had left her body to science. Sad to say her family had not had a mass said for her. I had mass said and after that I did not hear from her again.

"Some months later, my stepsister telephoned me. 'Do you still hear "Mammy Blue"?' she asked me. 'Now I keep hearing the song.'

"My stepsister had a mass said and from then on she did not hear the song again. Mammy Blue had no funeral because the medical faculty did not say what it had done with her remains. But as she did not have a tomb, she had perhaps her own fashion of ensuring that her soul could rest in peace."

PART TWELVE

The Cruel Mother

There was a lady lived in York,
All alone and a loney.

A farmer's son he courted her
Down by the greenwood sidey.

He courted her for seven long years.
At last she proved in child by him.

She pitched her knee against a tree
And there she found great misery.

She pitched her back against a thorn,
And there it was the babe was born.

She drew the fillet off her head.
She bound the baby's hands and legs.

She drew a knife both long and sharp.
She pierced the baby's innocent heart.

She wiped the knife upon the grass.
The more she wiped the blood run fast.

She washed her hands all in the spring,
Thinking to turn a maid again.

As she was going to her father's hall,
She saw three babes a-playing at ball.

One dressed in silk, the other in satin,
The other star-naked as ever was born.

O dear baby, if you was mine,
I'd dress you in silk and satin so fine.

O, dear mother, I once was thine.
You never would dress me coarse or fine.

The coldest earth it was my bed.
The green grass was my coverlet.

Women Who Cannot Mother

The ambulance men were laughing and cracking jokes about this loony woman. I told them to stop it, that it was my mother they were laughing at, but they just laughed all the more. I was sobbing because she was so ill. We were met at the door by a nurse with a bunch of keys at her waist. It was like another world. I booked my mother in and she was taken away.

Antonia on her mother's admission to a mental hospital

*A*ntonia's mother was not cruel, but through no fault of her own was unable to mother her daughter. As recently as thirty or forty years ago, some women were still "locked away" and perhaps given electroconvulsive therapy (ECT) for what was initially post-natal depression and ended up years later as incurable psychotic illness. Antonia told me:

"I should not have been born. I was an only child. My mother was three-quarters of the way though her pregnancy when she discovered she was expecting me. She had a good career and was going places. Children did not figure in her plans. In spite of this she was delighted to be pregnant. I was born by Caesarean section which thirty-six years ago was a major operation. My mother was sedated for a couple of days. Nevertheless she adored me then.

"When I was two years old, my father became very ill with pneumonia and my mother became very worried about him. With me to cope with as well, Mum rapidly became very depressed. Worse still, she thought she was pregnant again. The doctor examined my mother and told her she was having a very early menopause. Although relieved,

451

she was also deeply distressed and became even more depressed. It would seem Mum was suffering from post-natal depression, but in those days such conditions were not recognized and she was admitted to a mental hospital, a huge Gothic monstrosity like a prison.

"My father was not very assertive and left to cope with a two-year-old, so he just accepted what was happening without question. Mum thought it was a normal ward until suddenly she found she was locked away. She was very conscious of her appearance, but her makeup and mirror were taken away from her, in case she hurt herself with them, it was said, although she had not tried to harm herself or anyone else.

"Mum had only ever been in hospital to have me and she was terrified. She was in there for quite a while and given ECT. It was a total nightmare for her. When she came out she seemed recovered, but my father fell seriously ill with pneumonia, was admitted to hospital and died of heart failure. Although my mother had a good family, they could not cope with mental illness. Mum had a struggle to manage financially and once I was at school she was lonely. Mum had a serious breakdown, as her condition was then called, every three or four years, usually brought on by some sentimental occasion such as Christmas or an anniversary. She always found such occasions hard to bear.

"At Christmas we would not have any decorations and she would forget to take the chicken for dinner out of the refrigerator. One year she burned my Christmas presents. The Christmas when I was seven, she dropped a dish and that set her off. She sat in her chair talking to my dead Nan. I said, 'Come on, Mum, let's get the dinner,' and we carried on with Christmas.

"However, Mum was soon whisked off to hospital again. I would go up the eighteen wooden stairs to my aunt's flat where it was like entering a different world, everything jolly and normal. I would not be taken to see my mother in those days. That stay I remember Mum had a toothache. My mother had lovely pearly teeth. The dentist took several of them out and gave her false ones. She was maddened beyond belief at this attack on her person.

"I used to have terrible problems at school with the other children. They used to tease me that my mum was not right in the mind. It used to

452

hurt inside when my friends laughed at my mother. I used to say, 'That's not my mother. That's my nan. My mother is beautiful, but she's at home. My nan is dotty.'

"It did not seem to matter so much to have a dotty gran. I remember once a friend saying she saw my mum out in the High Street wearing only one shoe. I felt like dying. I was so ashamed of her. I never had friends round. We might pop into the house for a quick drink of water but that was all. I never knew what I would find, what she would say.

"Once I was fifteen, I assumed responsibility for my mother's illness. I went in the ambulance with her to hospital. We had a long wait as an ambulance had to come from a special depot. I paced the floor waiting for it to arrive with Mum shouting, 'Who the hell are you?'

" 'Come on, Mum. You know who I am.'

" 'I want my daughter. Where is my Antonia? I want my daughter.'

"Now I think I can understand. She wanted not this Antonia who was having her committed, who had ruined her life, but the lovely baby Antonia, before all the trouble, before my father's death, before her being put away. Many tears were shed as we waited.

"My mother always insisted on taking carrier bags of goodies for the staff. She rushed about the kitchen, packing pints of milk, tea bags, butter. On this occasion she was trying to make tea and was flooding the kitchen, spilling food and drink everywhere and got her clothes covered. At last the ambulance came.

"I will never forget that journey. Mum tried to smoke in the ambulance. I was telling her she shouldn't and she started to swear, which she only did when she was ill. The ambulance men were laughing and cracking jokes about this loony woman. I told them to stop it, that it was my mother they were laughing at, but they just laughed all the more. I was sobbing because she was so ill. We were met at the door by a nurse with a bunch of keys at her waist. It was like another world. I booked my mother in and she was taken away.

"When I visited my mother a week later, she insisted she was coming home. There were old people rocking to and fro in their chairs. People would come up and say, 'Have you got anything for me?' Even now I have a horror of visiting hospitals of any kind.

"I had taken Mum to hospital with half a dozen dresses, money, cigarettes and her watch, but when I saw her, all her possessions were gone. I saw an old lady walking down the ward wearing one of my mother's dresses, but the staff refused to listen. I rummaged through her locker, looking for her belongings. At fifteen I did not really know what else to do. Sometimes Mum would escape from the hospital and catch a bus somewhere and be missing for days. We would get a phone call from the hospital to say that she had run away. Although I was spared this knowledge when I was younger, as I grew older I used to worry what had happened to her.

"I tried to talk to the doctors about her condition, but not one of them ever asked how I was, how I was coping or who was caring for me. When I was sixteen I left school and Mum seemed to improve for about two years. But it was still very difficult. If there was a knock on the door and it was a friend for me, I had to rush to get there first or Mum would say I was out. Once she told the neighbours when I was fifteen that I had had an abortion, although I did not even have a boyfriend and was a virgin. My mother was obsessed with pregnancy and unwanted babies. She never had another relationship after my father and saw her pregnancy as the cause of all the subsequent sorrows and suffering. I regret the things I said to her as a teenager but I was so provoked. I had not asked to be born.

"The periods in hospital continued, together with the disappearances. I became pregnant ten years after I was married. I was worried about telling my mother. When I told her she just said 'That's not good', and refused to acknowledge my pregnancy further.

"Mum went into hospital again towards the end of my pregnancy and refused to see me when I visited, saying I was not her Antonia as her Antonia was slim. Mum would not even speak to me on the telephone, though I rang every day. She went missing when I was two days overdue. I really believed she was dead this time, as it was a cold autumn. She had escaped three times in five weeks. I was distraught and only heard just before I went into labour that she was safe.

"When my aunt went to inform Mum that baby Maria had been born, my mother hid under the blankets and asked, 'Is Antonia dead?'

"I had sent my mother a letter about the baby's weight and that she was well. Suddenly, Mum asked where the baby was and from that moment took on a new lease of life, showered and changed her clothes for the first time in five weeks. I went to see my mother when Maria was ten days old. My husband stayed with the baby in the car. I was quite slim again and my mother told the nurses, 'There's my daughter.'

"Mum asked if I had brought her anything. Then she said, 'I'm a gran. Where's the baby?'

"I took Mum outside to the car but was worried about her holding the baby. She had never hurt anyone but I had no idea how Mum would react to my infant, if it would stir painful memories.

"My husband handed her the baby. Mum's eyes filled with tears. It was the first time I had ever seen her cry. Everyone else cried for Mum and because of her. She had not even cried when my father died. Mum asked me about the baby's feeds and then said, 'You'd better take her home for her lunch.' She came out of hospital a month later.

"When I came home with the baby I shed tears. It hit me, the overwhelming responsibility of motherhood and my love for baby Maria. The baby cried a lot because she was so active and I became very tired, but I was afraid of letting go with my own emotions because of my mother. My husband assures me I am not like my mother, but the fear is always there, ticking away, if I become even slightly upset.

"We go and see my mother once a week. She did not cuddle the baby, because when she tried the baby cried and Mum went completely rigid. After that the baby would cry and she would get uptight. Once Maria was eighteen months old and could say a few words, Mum found it easier to relate to her.

"I have explained to Maria as she gets older that Nanny isn't very well. I notice the vacant expression in Mum's eyes when she is with Maria, but so far my daughter has not commented. My mum is a million miles away from the grandmothers who sit on the floor and play with their grandchildren, who babysit and take them out for treats. Maria will give my mother drawings she has done, and if I prompt Mum she will respond and Maria is happy.

"Mum has been diagnosed as a manic schizophrenic and is the most

complex case the consultant says he has ever seen. Mum has been out of hospital for four years since Maria's birth, although she is on permanent medication and there is a psychiatric nurse whom I can call on in crises. We see the consultant every two months, but my mother just says yes and no and never explains how she really is or what she is feeling and he never asks. I wonder how much of her illness was aggravated by her early mistreatment when she suffered from post-natal depression. I feel so much is waiting to be said between us, but there are topics I have to steer away from. I question whether in all those years someone could have acknowledged her pain and talked to her.

"I also want someone to say to me, 'How are you feeling?' I keep it all light-hearted to the outside world, tell them the funny bits, but it hurts so much inside. I had no mother, no father, and saw my relations only when my mother was away, because of their attitude towards her illness. I have made a good life for myself and I have become very strong and capable, but nothing can compensate for the lost years.

"One legacy is that I am always punctual. My mother needed to know exactly when and where I would be and does even now. It is something she can control in her chaotic world and so can I. I panic if I am not on time. Even now I always go at the same time and the same day to Mum's house and she is invariably watching television or making tea when I arrive. My aunt says I should go at another time as I might see a very different picture and Mum's coping may all be show for me. I refuse to spy on my mother. Mum has had enough surveillance already. Perhaps it suits me too, that I can believe she is coping. I have to.

"My mother was seventy-three in March. I think 'What a waste of her life'. My mother is my daughter as well as Maria. I am her parent. I do her chores, ask how she is, and will go on taking care of her until she dies. Sometimes I wish Mum would die for her own sake and for mine but then I feel ashamed. If she died she would make herself happy and me happy, because while she is there the volcano is still waiting to erupt."

Antonia's mother was not a bad mother in the sense that she deliberately hurt or neglected her daughter. She was unable to alter her behaviour and so Antonia suffered and still suffers from the burden of a mother who cannot respond to the needs of her daughter and granddaughter.

However, Tony's mother was deliberately cruel and neglectful. Tony, now in his fifties, drives convoys to Bosnia and Russia and runs the British Humanitarian Aid Society. He is a former soldier and commercial lorry driver. His early recollections are still painful:

"I have only two memories of my mother before I was four years old. One was when she broke a yard broom over my shoulders. The other is of her hitting me on the head with a metal bucket. I still bear the scar where my head was cut open. I have no recollection of her first cruelty but I have been told that when I was two I stole some bread and my mother held my hands in an old-fashioned mangle. Because I was so young my bones were soft and my hands recovered.

"When I was five I recall my mother driving away with a man in a black car and waving. Because my brothers and I all had different fathers we were sent to different orphanages. I was sent to a spinster I called Aunty. She was into sex games and would sit on the bed and make me watch her masturbate. When I was twelve she made me do it as well.

"If anyone came from the authorities I would say I was happy. No one would have believed me. Besides I was fed and clothed and it was better than being in an orphanage. I did not know any different way of life, but when the other children at school talked about sex I would think, 'You do not know anything.'

"When I was fifteen my mother came back into my life, sobbing that she had been a bad mother and was sorry and wanted to make it all up to me. For a week she was very loving and then turned to me and said, 'Get out to work, you lazy ****, and earn some money for me.'

"That day I joined the Army as a boy soldier and never saw her again. I have no idea if she is still alive and do not care. I never saw Aunty again or tried to contact her. As for my brothers, the five of us eventually met up years later but it is too late. We exchange Christmas and birthday cards but we are strangers except for the fact that we all shared the same mother.

"Mothers do not have a right to love from their children. They have to earn it."

Tony now spends time with children in war zone orphanages who have lost their mothers and has made many warm relationships with them. He has lost touch with his own children after a failed marriage.

Much maternal sickness and neglect can be explained in terms of depressive illness, but mothering can be difficult and lonely for anyone, especially where there are financial problems and a lack of support and relief from unremitting childcare. There can be few women who have not screamed at their children or shaken a child in a fit of despair. Alas, becoming a mother does not automatically turn a woman into a saint!

Mothers Who Disappear

Some people never know their mothers, not because they have died but because they have deliberately chosen not to know their offspring. Alison, who lives in Cornwall, told me:

"It did not occur to me for many years that I had no mother, at least no mother I thought about at all. I was well looked after by my granny in Glasgow, although from time to time I was shunted about to various aunts and uncles who were themselves childless.

"Then my father who saw me from time to time sent for me to go and live with him and his intended new wife in Kent and all this at the height of the Blitz. I learned that he had divorced my mother who had apparently been suffering from melancholia following my birth in July 1933 and had spent many years in a mental institution in Maidstone. This today would be classed as post-natal depression and be curable.

"The marriage was a disaster for my journalist father and this new wife who was in her forties, but especially so for me who had been uprooted from a good lifestyle in Scotland. I had been chauffeur-driven to a select private school and now was plunged into a different world.

"Before they wed, I called my father's new wife Smithy which was a shortened from of her surname. As soon as she could, she insisted that I called her Mummy. As I had never called anyone Mummy before, the word stuck in my throat. A son was born to them, although since there is about eleven years' difference between us I feel no kinship, which is sad.

"I spent the year between fourteen and fifteen years of age with my uncle and aunt in Denmark where I enjoyed a good lifestyle. I could have stayed longer but my stepmother had been ill and wanted me to come home and look after her, which was really unnecessary. Returning home was disastrous after such a wonderful year in Scandinavia.

"Life was very unhappy and I packed my bags and left even though I was only sixteen years old and earning thirty shillings a week as a trainee journalist. I was at this time engaged to my first husband, a national serviceman at the time and also a trainee journalist.

"One day my father told me that my mother had recovered sufficiently to go and live with her sister in Kent but that I must not discuss this with my stepmother. Goodness knows why, but I never questioned my father about my mother, even though when I got angry I remember saying to him that I wished I had never been born, then my mother would have been all right.

"What I shall never understand is why I was cut off entirely from my mother's family. I feel cheated that I know nothing about her family. There must have been some family quarrel that resulted in my father placing me with his own mother who was quite elderly.

"Now I will never know as my mother would have been over a hundred years old. I feel like a jigsaw with a large chunk missing. If only I had questioned my father, I would have known more about her and whether I took after her or not. Surely she must have wanted to know all about me and my five children? It is like a blankness, and when women say to me they do not get on with their mothers I think to myself how lucky they are to have a mum. I want to know which of her characteristics I have inherited, brains or beauty. I know that she played the piano and I once had one of the school prizes awarded to her for an English examination.

"When I go to hospital and I am asked if there has been any cancer on

459

my mother's side or whether there has been any heart disease, what can I say? When my twin son and daughter were born I was on the brink of death from eclampsia and have no memory of their birth at all. But the first thing I asked the midwife was 'Did I lose my memory?' as I grew up believing that this was what had happened to my mother. It was a stupid question because if I had lost my memory I would not have been able to ask the question. But it was a real worry that I might end up the same. Many years later my twin daughter herself gave birth to twins and suffered from post-natal depression and I have wondered if this was an inherited gene.

"So what has all this revealed? Sadness that I was not told anything much about my mother and now it is too late to find out. My children and I are bonded very closely and together with my second husband and my four grandsons they are the most important beings in the world to me.

"I have a guilty admission that I never made any attempt to find my mother. I was frightened of what I might find—a mentally ill woman who was getting on in years and who might possibly become my responsibility—and so I did nothing. With five children to bring up life was particularly hectic, and by the time they had all left I did not think about her very often.

"Sometimes days and even weeks go by without my wondering, wondering and wondering about her and thinking how sad her life must have been. Perhaps she thought I had died or did not even remember me. A final irony—my aunt told me that my mother was rather a depressive type of person and it was thought that having a baby might cure her."

Mothers Who Kill

Damon did not die immediately. He opened his eyes and saw
who was murdering him. He saw her. He saw his mother.
Prosecutor in the case of a mother who
killed her five-year-old child

*D*arlie Routier seemed to live the American dream. She was
twenty-seven, mother to three children, good-looking, and her
husband had his own business. They had a house with a big garden
with a fountain, a Jaguar in the drive and a motor cruiser. The dream
was shattered when two of her children were murdered in June 1996.

Darlie claimed that an intruder had broken into the family's home
in Rowlett, Texas, and stabbed Damon aged five and Devon, six. He
had also slashed her neck, arms and abdomen. Police began
searching for the murderer and Darlie held a tearful birthday party
by her sons' grave.

But doubts began to grow in the minds of the police. None of the
ornaments in the house had been damaged in the attack and the only
bloody footprints found were Darlie's own. In the kitchen drawer
detectives found the knife allegedly used by the intruder to cut open
a window screen in the garage. The knife used in the killings bore
only Darlie's fingerprints. When the alleged intruder attacked Darlie
he was careful not to slash her breasts which had had a $5,000
implant operation to restore her figure after the birth of her third son
eight months earlier.

Twelve days after the murder Darlie was arrested and brought to
trial. There it was revealed that while Darlie and her husband Darin
appeared to have all they needed materially, they had no savings or

pension plan and were having problems with extensive credit card and tax debts. The day before the murders, they had been refused a loan of $5,000. The jurors heard that after Darlie's third son Dover was born she became obsessed with the idea that she was losing her looks. She had a breast implant and took slimming pills.

The prosecutor said: "Damon did not die immediately. That's the most horrible part of this case. He opened his eyes and saw who was murdering him. He saw her. He saw his mother."

On 2 February 1997 Darlie was found guilty of Damon's murder and was sentenced to death by lethal injection. Did her obsession about losing her looks spring only from inside herself or was it some casual remark from someone close to her that drove her to destroy the children she blamed for taking away the approval won by her former beauty? Her youngest child was only eight months old. Was she suffering from severe post-natal depression but felt unable to seek help?

The trial shook America, which was still struggling to come to terms with the case of Susan Smith. She was another mother who had appeared to love her two young sons and had pleaded for their return after they were allegedly snatched by a carjacker. Smith had appeared on television daily and videos had been shown of her at the children's party. The pictures pulled at the heartstrings of American parents. Then she confessed that she had herself driven to a lake and let the car roll in with the children asleep on the back seat.

Smith, a divorcee, had suffered a break-up with her boyfriend shortly before she committed the crime. But her reasons for what she did, like Routier's, remain obscure.

In Greek mythology Medea, who helped the hero Jason in his search for the Golden Fleece, had two children by him and then was abandoned. The faithless Jason sought to marry Glauke, daughter of the Corinthian King Kreon, so that he might found a dynasty for his sons. After killing the bride with a magic ointment, Medea murdered her own sons so that they would not fulfil Jason's dynastic ambitions or be slaughtered by those who wished to avenge the death of Glauke. She escaped in the Chariot of the Sun, carrying the bodies of her dead sons. In Euripides' tragedy, Medea looks at her sleeping infants and says, "I will slay them—I, the mother that bore them. O heart of mine, steel thyself! Why do I hesitate to do the awful deed that must be done? Come, take the sword, thou wretched hand of mine! Take it, and advance to the post whence starts thy life of sorrow! Away with cowardice! Give not one thought to thy babes, how dear they are or how thou art their mother. This one brief day forget thy children dear, and after that lament; for though thou wilt slay them yet they were thy darlings still, and I am a lady of sorrows."

Can killing a child ever be justified to spare it a worse fate? Erla Hulda Halldorsdottir, an Icelandic librarian and researcher, posed this question to me. "I am sure that some people do not see the following story from our past as mother love, but cruelty. In the eighteenth century there were outlaws in Iceland, people who lived in the mountains, in caves and small earth houses, and stole sheep and cattle from the farmers. If the farmers suspected where the outlaws were they tried to capture them. Two of the most famous bandits were Eyvindur and Halla, a man and woman who had been outlaws for decades. They had been captured but always managed to escape again. When Halla was pregnant she was easily captured. When their daughter was between one and two years old, farmers came suddenly to Halla and Eyvindur's refuge. They ran away but realized that they could not escape with the child. Instead of leaving the child behind where she would have been captured by the farmers, Halla threw her daughter either down a cliff or into a waterfall (there are different versions of the story). Asgrimur Jonsson painted a beautiful picture of Halla with her baby girl in her arms on her way to drown her. This incident is not always seen as mother's love, but if one thinks about Icelandic society in the eighteenth century, killing the child was the best thing for her. She would have been raised as a criminal's daughter, an orphan with no money of her own. That meant that the farmer who said he could have the child in his home for the smallest amount of money paid by the authorities would have got to keep her. Most of these children had to work very hard, got few clothes, were given less to eat than the others, were beaten and were often treated like animals. They seldom got any education that was necessary for their confirmation. In fact education was very poor among the majority of the nation at that time, but for those penniless orphans it was usually worse."

Cases of mothers slaying their children in the developed world, where their infants are not threatened by external dangers, are mercifully rare and there is usually intense stress immediately beforehand from circumstances which may or may not be linked to the child. In one case in the north of England, a woman drove the family car into a dock, killing herself and the children after her husband had left her for another woman. The fact the woman feels unsupported and desperate for whatever reason seems to override her natural protective instincts towards her young.

Yet Emma appeared to have everything. She was the daughter of a millionaire with her own apartment in London. Nevertheless, she gave birth alone and appears to have lost touch with reality in the confused hours surrounding the event. Emma had the baby in her Kensington basement flat. The actual circumstances are uncertain but after the birth Emma covered the baby's face with a flannel, put a pair of her boyfriend's pyjama bottoms around the infant's neck, covered his face with a pillow, was very sick and then went to work as usual. When Emma returned from work she removed the pillow. She did not think the baby was alive. She rang her brother and told him she was in trouble, but not what the problem was. Her brother took her back to the family home in Kent, not knowing she was carrying her dead baby.

When Emma returned to her flat, she hid the baby's body in the freezer where it was discovered four weeks later by her brother. Emma was totally confused about whether and at what point the baby had been alive. "I feel numb, confused. I did not want people to know. They didn't know I was pregnant," Emma told the police when she admitted what she had done and said she had felt she had no option. In court she said: "It's in my head. There is no connection between what is in my head and what is in my mouth." She was given three years' probation on condition she received psychiatric treatment.

Clare Delpech, secretary of the Association for Post-Natal Illness, commented that cases like Emma's were extremely rare. "Most cases do not involve a mother actively killing her baby. Unless you wrap up a baby and keep it warm and fed it won't live, and this is what often happens. There may have been a dissociative connection in this case. Emma may have been rich but it looks as if she was incredibly isolated. Tragically, she has got to live with this for the rest of her life, and for that I have endless sympathy with her."

Dissociative illness is a rare condition that can occur just after childbirth, or even in the late stages of pregnancy, which produces a shock-like state where the mother dissociates herself from reality. In this state a mother cannot comprehend the existence of her infant or realize that the infant has been born. In such cases the child, if born to the mother when she is alone and unsupported, will usually die of neglect rather than be killed.

In Emma's case her troubled past may have compounded or even triggered the disorder. The infant who died was not her first child. After an apparently idyllic childhood, Emma suffered from depression as a teenager. At Edinburgh, where she was an undergraduate, she began a relationship with another student, who fathered her two babies. In 1994 when she was nineteen she took an overdose and dropped out of university. She became pregnant for the first time in the same year.

Too frightened to tell her family or boyfriend, Emma admitted herself to hospital in February 1995 where she gave birth to her first son. When Emma told her boyfriend about the baby, both families put her under pressure to have the baby adopted. This was a prolonged process which caused Emma great distress. She became pregnant again shortly afterwards, but it was not until February 1996 that she telephoned her boyfriend, now working abroad, to tell him about their pregnancy. They both agreed an abortion would be best, and he believed Emma had gone ahead with it.

Munchausen's Syndrome by Proxy, the disorder in which carers cause harm to others to gain attention for themselves, has been implicated in the death of several children in recent years. One victim of this syndrome was four-year-old Christopher from England's West Midlands, who was killed by his mother, Caroline. She put salt into his blackcurrant drinks, 125 mg in all over the ten-day period of his half-term holiday from nursery school. Christopher died in hospital in his mother's arms, shortly before midnight on 29 February 1996, from a brain swelling caused by the abnormally high level of salt in his body.

Caroline later confessed to administering the salt solution, although she insisted she had not meant to kill her son but merely to quieten him, because she was worn out caring for her two children. Her second son Adrian, born in 1994, was unharmed. Caroline herself had been abandoned by her mother when she was seven months old and passed around the remainder of the family during her childhood, ending up with two sets of foster parents and eventually in a children's home for a while. Of Christopher's death, Caroline tried to explain: "I never wanted him to die. I just wanted him to feel poorly. The salt made him go to sleep and then I could get some rest."

After Christopher's death his stepfather found carefully wrapped birthday presents, including one for Christopher whose birthday was seven months later. Brochures arrived from a number of schools into which Caroline was considering enrolling Christopher, suggesting that his death was not premeditated.

Neighbours and family members said Caroline was a good mother, giving lovely birthday parties, even offering to care for a friend's children. Is a good mother one who gives lovely parties? And is the mother screaming at her children in a supermarket or apparently allowing them to run unattended in a public place a bad mother or just an exhausted one? All the professional advice, assessment and counselling in the world cannot compare with the offer of a helping hand.

PART THIRTEEN

Animal Mothers

Maternal Instinct in Animals

> I can say with firm conviction that of all creatures the one
> nearest to man in the fineness of its perceptions and in its
> capacity to render true friendship, is a bitch. Strange that
> in English her name has become a term of abuse.
> *Konrad Lorenz,* King Solomon's Ring

Maternal Love

In September 1996, in the New York City borough of Brooklyn, a
stray cat raced into a burning building to rescue her five four-week-
old kittens, one by one. With her eyes blistered shut and her paws
burned, she made a head count of her young ones, touching each
one with her nose to make sure they were all safe.

"What she did was she ran in and out of that building five times,
got them all out, and then started moving them one by one across
the street," said firefighter David Giannelli, who took the animals to
North Shore Animal League Shelter in Brooklyn.

"She's a wonderful, gentle animal who did a courageous thing,"
said Marge Stein, the shelter's manager of adoption services. "It
shows with all creatures, animals or people, there's no way of
measuring a mother's love."

Mother animals will fight to the death for their young. In some
remote parts of Britain the method of stopping a young sheepdog
from attacking lambs is to put him in a pen with a ewe and her
newborn lamb. It is said that a ewe will defend her young against a
creature twice her size.

Liz Nerval, an expert dog breeder who lives on the Isle of Wight, told me: "A mother wolf will apparently let a predator into her lair, but will be waiting at the side and drag the attacker out into the open, so that he is caught off guard. I saw this same defensive tactic used by one of my bitches who apparently left her puppies when a stranger she did not trust came into the room. She was hiding between the chair and radiator. I warned the man not to touch the puppies, but he insisted the mother had left them and so could not mind. As he picked one of the puppies up, the bitch came round the side and bit him in the calf. She had not remained in front of the puppies barking, as this would have frightened them, but followed the primitive protective pattern. A good animal mother—and not all are—will go to any lengths to protect her young."

The Psychic Link

A naturalist specializing in the observation of foxes undertook a long-term study of a particular fox family located near a creek in a ravine. One beautiful sunny afternoon he noticed the vixen doing something he had never seen a fox do. The mother suddenly left her burrow and kin, went up the hillside some 30 yards and began busily digging another burrow. She then carried each of the cubs up the hill to the new den. Several hours later the reason for this atypical act became clear. Although the weather remained beautiful, a flash flood caused by a cloudburst many miles upstream suddenly filled the ravine. Had the family remained where they were they would certainly have drowned.[1]

Alison, who lives in the west of England, told me how Maddy, her Pembroke corgi bitch, anticipated danger and so averted a potential disaster.

"Maddy had a lovely litter of seven puppies at barely two years old, a little younger than I normally whelp. She was an excellent mother but by four weeks and weaning was happy to pop in for a milk top-up feed and check all was well. She rarely wanted to stay for more than five or ten

minutes. The puppies were by now in the outside kennel by day with a large run with access to the garden and grounds by a connecting gate kept shut so that they would not get out.

"One morning I woke with a bad sick migraine. Friends kindly got the dogs up, fed the puppies and took them to the outside kennel. The kitchen door was also left open to allow the older dogs access to the garden.

"At some time later during the morning, I surfaced to realize that Maddy was not with me as the other dogs were and a nasty niggling thought occurred. Had I shut the kennel run gate last night when bringing in the five-week-old puppies for the night? There had been some puppy thefts in the area and I realized in the three hours or so that the puppies had been outside they could be anywhere. In some anxiety I looked out of the window and the run gate was indeed wide open and no sign of Maddy or the puppies.

"I rushed outside frantically looking for some sign of a puppy. I got to the kennel run and then Maddy poked her head out of the kennel and, on seeing me, came out, followed by all the puppies. She had been lying in front of the kennel access, not allowing a puppy out, for more than three hours.

"How had that bitch realized I was out of action, that the kennel run gate was open and that she had to keep them indoors until I came to take charge? After the incident she was again happy just to pop in on them at intervals."

As with human mothers faced with a potential crisis, Maddy, who was not an anxious mother, changed her pattern of behaviour from healthy neglect to vigilance, knowing that her puppies needed her to keep them safe.

Grandmother Love

An animal grandmother can form strong bonds with her grand-children. Derek, a dog breeder on the south coast of England, told me about the cross-generation link.

"I have an eight-year-old cavalier bitch called Carrie. She did not like other dogs, but eventually she became pregnant and had a litter which she fed and cleaned. She was not a particularly good mother. She later had a second litter and proved a better mother.

"We kept one of the bitches called Bonnie, and although Bonnie was three and a half Carrie insisted on cleaning her and caring for her. Bonnie had a litter of six puppies and we put them in the outer part of the house as it was summer. They were born about eight o'clock at night. The next morning Carrie was crying and scratching at the door furiously, but refused to go for her customary walk. Instead she jumped in with the pups, came into milk and watched and cleaned and fed the babies, turn and turn about, with Carrie throughout the day and night. They each took turns of two hours. When it was her turn to look after the pups, Carrie would gently nudge Bonnie out.

"I had two other slightly older litters and when they were old enough I put the three litters together. Bonnie and Carrie went with them and if any of the older puppies came too close to her litter Carrie would gently nudge them away. If she felt 'her puppies' should not run about, she would bring them back until she decided it was time to exercise them. Indeed, she carried on mothering the pups long after Bonnie had given up, refusing to go on walks or sleep in her customary place in my bedroom, as long as they remained."

Fostering

One of the most common reasons for one animal to foster another's offspring is when the young creature is abandoned by its natural mother. There is an assumption that all females, animal and human, are genetically programmed to be good mothers. The reality is more complex and involves, even in animals, emotions as well as reflexes.

Valerie, who lives in Essex, described Bertha, her canine earth mother.

"Until a few years ago, I bred whippets, labradors and Pekinese. One

472

Pekinese bitch was an especially bad mother. She would not allow her puppies to go near her food bowl and when they did killed two of them. She then refused to go back with the three surviving puppies and attacked them.

"Bertha, a whippet, was in a false pregnancy at the time and had often helped out other mothers with their puppies. Bertha will take over any puppies whatever the breed. She had helped Tigger, another whippet, with eight puppies, to rear them. I knew the Pekinese babies would die unless Bertha would help. I picked up the surviving puppies and asked Bertha if she would look after them, explaining that they would die without her help.

"Without hesitation, she at once took the puppies, fed, cleaned and slept with them and they suckled from her as if they were her own. Hers were the only litter of Pekinese I had ever reared. The tiny Pekes followed Bertha everywhere. Cheeky, their birthmother, would chase them if she saw them and actually attacked the female puppy and damaged her eye. Bertha died a year ago having had three litters of her own.

"A friend called Poppy, who lived in South Wales and has now died, bred a lot of animals. Her whippet bitch died when she was giving birth to a puppy who was subsequently reared by her rabbit. The rabbit suckled the young whippet until it was too big to fit in the hutch. The whippet always regarded the rabbit as its mother, which is amazing since whippets usually kill rabbits.

"Why do animals rear creatures of other breeds and species? They are like humans who see orphans abroad in orphanages and long to adopt them. If a baby needs help the mothering instinct is aroused in most animal and human mothers."

Cross-Species Fostering and Adoption

Valerie's story of the whippet reared by a rabbit illustrates the fascinating phenomenon of cross-species fostering between animals more usually perceived as predator and prey. Newspaper photographs of cats mothering chicks are guaranteed to appeal to the sentiments of readers. Yet the phenomenon is quite common. Kath, who lives on the Isle of Wight, has experienced several examples of maternal love and concern overriding inbuilt destructive instincts with her own animals.

"The mother of four papillon puppies died when they were three weeks old. My friend had a tortoiseshell cat with one kitten. She brought the cat and kitten to my house, as I was desperate not to lose the puppies as well. The cat took to them quite happily and fed the four puppies and her own kitten for six weeks. She had never encountered a dog in her life. This was in August 1962. I still treasure the photographs.

"Some years later another papillon bitch of mine Kate lost her only puppy. My friend brought the distraught bitch two kittens and the papillon happily fed these until they were seven or eight weeks old. Even after the kittens were weaned, the three remained bonded and Kate would clean and protect the cats and they would go into her kennel to find her.

"Penny, another papillon bitch, had her puppy die when it was only two days old. She stole a kitten from the cat's litter and reared it instead. Again dog and cat remained friends. I have several bitches who have washed and cared for baby rabbits most lovingly."

Jane from Dorset provided another example of mother love overcoming what might be considered innate cross-species hostility.

"I had a bull terrier bitch who hated cats. But she fostered two kittens aged about ten days old which were found abandoned in a cardboard box in a ditch, their eyes still shut. She had not had a litter for three years but she came into milk and continued to feed them and wash them for about eighteen months. To her dying day she chased and would have murdered all cats—except her children."

But the most amazing example of cross-species adoption I have come across occurred in Maine in February 1997. Butch went rabbit hunting with his three-year-old beagle, Dodger. But Dodger ran off and even though the dog was wearing a radio, Butch was unable to find him.

After two days searching, Butch found Dodger's tracks and followed them to a snow-covered brush pile. When he called the dog, Dodger appeared from a hole. But when he was halfway out a huge black bear reached up, grabbed the dog's legs in her mouth and pulled him back into the den. Butch fled, fearing the dog would certainly be killed.

The following day Butch returned with a state game warden and was relieved to find Dodger still alive although they could not get him out. On 10 February, Butch returned with more game wardens. After a gentle tugging contest with the mother bear, one of them was able to seize Dodger's collar and drag him out. The mother bear followed, but when she saw the people she went off into the woods. Two tiny bear cubs, left in the den, were wrapped in blankets by the wildlife team. The following morning, the bear was seen back with her young.

Wardens have speculated that the dog entered the den to escape the bitter cold, and when the drowsy mother awoke she assumed he was one of her cubs and tried to prevent him from wandering. Without the bear's warmth, it is unlikely the dog would have survived. The smell of sour milk on Dodger's breath meant that he had probably been fed along with the bear cubs.

The Animal/Human Link

Mila screamed, "Don't take my babies," and her husband
appeared with a machete and dared the ranger to take the
orang-utans. She saw them as family members and she
and her husband reacted as any parents would if someone
tried to take their children.

Incident in Borneo

Mothering Animals

Rescue workers in remote areas of Borneo have discovered that
childless couples take baby orang-utans from the jungle or buy
orphans at high prices, shave and dress them and rear them as human
infants.

"These lovely animals are so human-like in appearance and
mannerisms that for some people it's almost a natural step for
them to take one in and raise it as their baby," said Annelisa
Kilbourn, a British vet who works at the Sepilok Orang-utan
Rehabilitation Centre in north-east Borneo. The problem for
rangers working with the centre is to rescue the ape babies before
they outgrow their loveable phase and are thrown out of the house or
killed for displaying behaviour that would be normal in the wild but
is unmanageable in a domestic setting. Rangers have been threatened
with death when they have staged a raid to take away a loved orang-
utan, man's closest relative and the beloved child of a childless
couple.

Childless and apparently infertile, Petrus and his wife Mila
from East Timor, Indonesia, were living in a wooden shack on a

476

palm oil plantation in north-east Borneo when they adopted two baby orang-utans whom they named Douglas and Fernando. Mila shaved off the apes' red body hair and rubbed talculm powder into their skin to make them look fairer. She fed them warm milk through a bottle, holding them close to her breast.

After the orang-utans were seized, Mila explained why she took them in: "I was dying inside. The wives of all the other workers on the plantation had their children and, when their husbands were away, they had their babies to keep them happy and I had no one. When I had Douglas and Fernando they were the children I could never have. They responded to my affection and gave it back to me. There was nothing wrong. They did not have a mother and I gave them a mother's love." Mila was heartbroken when a ranger came to take her "babies" who were lying underneath a coverlet on the bed having an afternoon rest. "You can't take them, they are my children," she wept. "Don't take my babies." Petrus threatened the ranger with a machete.

Dr Bosi, the manager of the rehabilitation centre, said: "The woman regarded the orang-utans as family members and she and her husband reacted as any parents would if someone tried to take their children."

Are the mothers in Borneo different from the eccentric childless Englishwoman and amateur scientist Gertrude Lintz who, while living in Brooklyn, New York, for several decades reared primates as her children?

Gertrude was born in 1889 but was taken to live in New York a few years later. One of her few memories of England was of London Zoo and her distress at the caged animals, especially the lions. She married in 1914 and moved to an estate overlooking the Hudson River where she bred giant St Bernard dogs. In the 1920s an animal dealer arrived with the first chimp, captured in West Africa. Gertrude called her Maggie.

Maggie and the subsequent chimps lived in a nursery with their own toys and smart clothes, and would sometimes ride in the back of Gertrude's car. They would be taken to stores on Fifth Avenue to buy white kid boots, and brought down for afternoon tea wearing velvet suits. In 1931 Gertrude adopted a tiny and very sick gorilla called Massa who made a remarkable recovery thanks to her diligent nursing. By now she owned the largest private collection of primates in the world. In the same year another gorilla Buddy arrived; also close to death because he had been sprayed with acid. Buddy grew up to trust only Gertrude. She took her apes to the 1933 Chicago World Fair and toured Canada where the "family" was mobbed.

Problems arose as the gorillas grew. In 1935 Gertrude was badly mauled by Massa, who had been moved to a specially constructed compound in the grounds. She needed seventy stitches. He was sent to the Philadelphia Zoo and Buddy, who also became unmanageable, went to a circus. Although Gertrude made sure that Buddy was given a large luxurious cage, she could not forgive herself for betraying her children. She died almost penniless in a Florida nursing home in the early 1960s.

It is too glib to write off women who take care of animals as "frustrated mothers". Sadie Grant-James who runs an animal sanctuary for orphaned and injured creatures at her home in Sleaford in Lincolnshire is quite the opposite. She has been a very successful mother to her daughters and to foster children.

"I began caring for animals and birds as a child, because my uncle ran a pet shop and I would nurse all the weak, unwanted animals. When I moved to Wales as a young adult, people seemed to know instinctively that I loved animals and would bring any that had problems to my door.

"At first I used to read books on animal care, but gradually learned to follow my own instincts and trust them, just as a mother does. I have pulled many animals back from almost certain death by trusting my own intuitive wisdom. I can look at any animal and tell if it wants to carry on. If it does, then I will go to death and back with it to save its life.

"I naturally tune with children in the same way. I raised my two girls on my own, but I used to take them dancing and swimming and often other people's children as well. I also ended up with four foster children who just stayed because they felt cherished and wanted, which they were.

"With my two girls there is an incredible bond of love, like a magnet between us. Once when I had gone to Wales for a few days, I had a sudden dreadful feeling that Becky was hurt, although I had only been gone half a day. I rang home and my other daughter answered. I asked where Becky was. She laughed because I had only just left and Becky was twenty-two, not a baby. I said, 'She's hurt her head.'

"My daughter laughed and told me, 'Becky's off playing golf.' At that moment she looked out of the window, 'No, she's coming up the path.' And so she was—with a lump the size of a golf ball on her head where she had been hit by a flying ball. 'Mother—you're a mother,' was my daughter's comment.

"My animals also are remarkably caring. I had a mother hedgehog who had four of her own babies. They died and I replaced them with orphan hedgehogs whom she fed and cleaned beautifully. All in all she mothered twenty-two orphan babies. Even as they got bigger and started feeding independently she still looked after them. She was a wonderful mother, quite exceptional, and I could always rely on her to adopt any orphans and rear them so that they could go off into the wild. With the last four she became so attached that when they went off into the wild she followed them. She looked back, as hedgehogs do when they depart, and I told her to remember me and call if she was passing."

Animals Who Mother Humans

Myths abound of the intriguing adoption of human infants by animal mothers. The most famous cases in fiction are Rudyard Kipling's Mowgli and Edgar Rice Burrough's Tarzan of the apes. But the stories go back to the legendary founders of Rome, Romulus and Remus. According to myth they were the sons of the God of War, Mars, and Rhea Silvia. Because the latter had broken her vestal vows she was condemned to death and her sons were left in the wilderness to die. But the infants were suckled by a she-wolf and brought up to be shepherds. Eventually the brothers joined with others to found a city on the hill.

There have been real cases of such adoptions.[1] The girl now known as the Little Nun of Songi was found in 1731 in the Champagne district of France when she was about ten, eating green shoots. She was well adapted to forest living and had developed extra-strong thumbs with which to swing from tree to tree. She became a nun and was taught to say, "Why should God have searched for me and saved me from the power of wild animals and made me a Christian? Would he have done this in order to leave me and make me die from hunger? This is not possible. He is my father and the Virgin Mary is my mother and they will take care of me."

During one of his evangelical trips to Midnapore, India, in 1920 the Reverend A. Singh heard of two malevolent *manush-baghas*, small ghostly creatures with blazing eyes that haunted villagers from the forests near Denganalia and were always accompanied by a female wolf. Their lair was located in an abandoned ant heap. The Reverend Singh decided after two fleeting glimpses that the ghosts were human children running on all fours. He arranged for local tribesmen to dig the lair out and on 17 October the ant heap was surrounded by beaters and diggers. Two wolves ran out as soon as the digging started and broke through the cordon. A third wolf, a female, appeared and, according to Singh's journal, instead of running away made for the diggers, scattering them to all sides before diving back into the hole. She came out again and raced round, growling furiously and pawing the ground. Lowering her head with bared teeth and ears flattened against her neck, her tail whipping from side to side, she refused to leave the spot, and was killed by bowmen.

The ant heap was opened and the two children found huddled in a ball with two wolf cubs. After a fierce struggle they were separated. The wolf cubs were sold and the children were taken to Midnapore

Orphanage. The younger, aged about three at the time of her discovery, died within a year. The older girl, Kamala, who was about five, lived for nine years, eventually learning to stand upright, to eat by hand and speak about thirty words of English. Her dying words to Singh's wife were, "Mama, the little one hurts."

Afterword

Mother love is loving your mother and your mother
loving you whatever happens for ever, because she is your
mother and you are her child.

Jack Eason, aged thirteen

*M*other love begins with wanting a child so badly that it
hurts. Not because all your friends are having one, not
because babies are cute, or even because the biological clock is ticking
like a time bomb, but because you already love the embryonic toddler,
teenager and adult who are waiting to unfold from the as yet unfused
cells of creation. Mother love is keeping faith with that child when he or
she is sick, grumpy, ungrateful and frankly awful; being incredibly
proud that you have reared a human being who is kind and gentle,
brave and wise, and then letting the child go, maybe across the world,
knowing that your love, if not conventional communication, will keep
you close. It is accepting and forgiving your own fallibility and that of
your mother, for images of perfection, whether that of Madonna or
Media Mom, can intrude on real feelings and true-life relationships.

I began this book with the desire to celebrate motherhood in all its
aspects. I have been overwhelmed not only by the response I
received to my appeals, but also by the fact that almost everyone
I met in my daily world had a mothering experience that they
wanted to share.

Most of these were endowed with great emotion: joy or sorrow,
often a mixture of both. Whether we love our mothers, hate them or
are ambivalent, they gave us life and most of them provided love and
security to launch us on our path. If the mothering experience has
been totally negative, we are not condemned to a repetition of our

mothers' mistakes, but can reshape the destiny they imperfectly moulded.

It is only now, as I approach fifty and am a mother myself, that I am beginning to appreciate the sacrifices my own mother made for me and the enduring values she passed on. They transcend any mistakes, any unkindness or possessiveness that stemmed from the disappointments of her own life spent in a tiny terrace house in the back streets of Birmingham, trapped in a desperately unhappy marriage. More than anything, she wanted to be a writer. Every week she would send a short story to the *Birmingham Evening Mail* and every week would receive a polite rejection. I do not think the newspaper actually published short stories, but the hope kept her going.

Sometimes when I look in the mirror I see her face in mine, her smile, a frown or a fleeting gesture. My lips formulate words she once spoke. In a sense I have re-created her into the ideal. Her sayings and eccentric ways have entered the family mythology. She insisted on cleaning the house from top to bottom on the day it was bulldozed for slum clearance, so that we wouldn't "show ourselves up", her favourite expression.

When my mother bought her first tiny car when I was seventeen, we all crammed in; myself, my dad, my brother, my aunt and the basset-hound, until the springs groaned. On outings Mom would make us bounce up and down, even the dog, when we came to hills so that the car would go faster. I have the book my mother wrote when she was ten years old on her first day trip from inner Birmingham to the countryside. It is pressed with flowers and leaves and recounts every moment of the seven-mile train journey as though she were travelling across the globe.

I remember her appalling rock cakes that my dad said would have won the war if they had been used as missiles. She would often recall how, when she was made a tram conductress during the war, on her first day she entangled the pole in the wires and brought down the entire system in the local tram depot.

I can laugh now, but was mortified the day she informed my

incredibly snooty friends from the school to which I won a scholarship that they had to go to the toilet in the hut in the garden, because an enemy sniper had blown our bathroom off the side of the house. When my mother, almost six foot tall and fifteen stone, worked as an insurance agent in the notorious red light district of Birmingham in which we lived, she flattened a small gentleman who accosted her and suggested that she might like to come inside his custom-built van with curtains and a mattress for a "nice time".

In my children I can see her too, especially in my daughters, and Miranda, my youngest girl, has frequently been visited by Granny Beryl who died twenty years before she was born. I see in the girls, too, my mother's exact stance, her way of pursing her lips when she was annoyed. She is ever-present.

The freezer is merrily defrosting, having been left open by one of my offspring on an ice cream raid. There is a mountain of washing and the line is creaking to overflowing in the pouring rain. The cat, having been parted from her kittens, is mewing piteously and pulling at my heart strings. On my desk is a missive from my bank manager, informing me we must subsist on bread and water for the next ten years to reduce the overdraft, and I have not yet bought the school uniforms for the coming term.

My mother's face comes into my mind.

"What's for tea?" I ask her, as I did when I was a child.

"Bread and pullet."

"What's bread and pullet?" I demand for the thousandth time.

"Pull it open and you'll see what's inside—nothing."

My children ask me why I am sitting at my computer alone, laughing. I tell them my mom's joke and they wander off, shaking their heads. It isn't any funnier forty years on, but I keep smiling and decide we'll go out for tea to celebrate. Mother love is the most natural state in the world, the most mystical and mundane. Like bread and pullet, if you take mother love apart to analyze its contents, there's nothing to measure. Yet it lies at the heart of human existence and is the purest and most enduring form of love.

Notes

INTRODUCTION

1. Ehrenreich, Barbara and English, Deirdre, *Witches, Midwives and Nurses, A History of Women Healers* (The Feminist Press, 1973)

PART ONE

The Lifesaving Link

1. Jaffe, Aniela, *From the Life and Work of C.J. Jung* (Hodder & Stoughton, 1967)
2. Jones, Carl, *From Parent to Child: The Psychic Link* (Warner Books, 1989)

The Continuing Connection

1. Frazer, James George, *The Golden Bough* (Papermac, 1987)
2. Sheldrake, Rupert, *Seven Experiments That Could Change The World* (Fourth Estate, 1996)

The Link of Love

1. Morris, J.D., Roll, W.G. and Morris, R.L. (eds), *The Effect of Chronological Age on GESP Ability in Research in Parapsychology* (Scarecrow Press, 1977)

PART THREE

The Virgin Mary, Perfection of Motherhood

1. Voragine, Jacobus, trs. William Granger Ryan, *The Golden Legend* (Princeton University Press, 1993)

PART FOUR

Mothers in Myth and Literature

1. Spink, Kathryn, *Mother Teresa, An Authorised Biography* (HarperCollins, 1997)
2. Brown, Christy, *My Left Foot* (Secker & Warburg, 1972)

3. Paskin, Barbara, *Dudley Moore* (Sidgwick & Jackson, 1997)

4. King, F. Truby, *Feeding and Care of the Baby* (Oxford University Press, 19???)

5. Watson, John B., *Psychological Care of the Infant and Young Child* (W. Norton & Co., 1928)

6. Scott, Marion M., *Beethoven* (J.M. Dent & Son, 1974)

PART FIVE

Mothers and Reincarnation

1. Watson, John B., *op. cit.*

2. Stevenson, Ian, *Twenty Cases Suggestive of Reincarnation* (1966; revised edition University of Virginia Press, 1974)

The Mother as Seer

1. Snow, Chet B., *Dreams of the Future* (Thorsons 1991)

PART SIX

Birth and Beyond

1. Sidenbladh, Eric, *Water-Babies* (A. & C. Black, 1983)

The Magic of Birth in the Modern World

1. Stanway, Andrew and Penny, *Choices in Childbirth* (Pan, 1984)

2. In the *New Scientist*, 5 August 1989

Shared Experiences

1. Brazelton, T. Berry, *Implications of Infant Development among Mayan Indians of Mexico* (Academic Press, 1977)

2. Raphael, Dona and Davis, Flora, *Only Mothers Know* (Greenwood Press, 1985)

PART EIGHT

The Pain of Parting

1. Stiffler, LaVonne Harper, *Synchronicity and Reunion* (FEA Publishing, 1992)

PART ELEVEN

The Stepmother in Myth and Reality

1. Translated from Souvestre, Emile, *Le Foyer Breton*

2. Klein, Melanie, *The Psychoanalysis of Children* (Virago Press, 1989)

PART THIRTEEN

Maternal Instinct in Animals

1. Pearce, J.C., *The Magical Child* (E.P. Dutton, 1977)
2. Malson, Lucien, trs. E. Fawcett and others, *Les Enfants Sauvages* (NLB 1972)

Suggested Additional Reading

Adoption Wisdom, Marlou Russell (Broken Branch Productions, 1996)

Alone of All her Sex, The Myth and Cult of the Virgin Mary, Marina Warner (Pan, 1985)

Birth Without Violence, Frederick Leboyer (Alfred A. Knopf, 1976)

Child Care and the Growth of Love, John Bowlby (Penguin, 1968)

Children's Minds, Margaret Donaldson (Flamingo, 1985)

The Cult of the Virgin Mary, Michael Carroll (Princeton University Press, 1986)

Discover Your Past Lives, Cassandra Eason (Quantum, 1996)

Dream Babies, Christina Hardyment (Jonathan Cape, 1983)

Elizabeth, Sarah Bradford (Heinemann, 1996)

The Family in the Western World, Beatrice Gottlieb (Oxford University Press, 1993)

The Feminist Companion to Mythology, edited by Carolyne Larrington (Pandora, 1992)

For her Own Good, Barbara Ehrenreich and Deirdre English (Pluto Press, 1979)

Freud and the Post Freudians, J.A.C. Brown (Penguin, 1997)

Ghost Encounters, Cassandra Eason (Blandford, 1997)

The Goddess, Caitlin Matthews (Element Books, 1989)

Larousse Encyclopaedia of Mythology (Prometheus Press, 1960)

Lost Children of the Empire, Philip Bean and Joy Melville (Unwin Hyman 1989)

The Mammoth Book of Ancient Wisdom, Cassandra Eason (Robinson, 1997) (published in the US as *The Handbook of Ancient Wisdom* by Sterling Books, 1997)

The Mammoth Book of Symbols (Robinson, 1996)

Maternal Deprivation Reassessed, Michael Rutter (Penguin, 1975)

Mediaeval Women, Henrietta Leyser (Phoenix Books, 1996)

Miracles, Cassandra Eason (Piatkus, 1997)

Modern Man in Search of a Soul, C.G. Jung (Routledge & Kegan Paul, 1978)

The Myth of the Goddess, Anne Baring and Jules Cashford (Penguin, 1993)

The Myth of Irrationality, John McCrone (Macmillan, 1993)

The Myths of Motherhood, Shari L. Thurer (Penguin, 1994)

Native American Art and Folklore, edited by David Campbell (Crescent Books, 1993)

Night-time Parenting, William Sears (La Leche International, 1985)

The Oxford Dictionary of Saints, David Hugh Farmer (Clarendon Press, 1978)

Pagan Celtic Britain, Anne Ross (Cardinal, 1974)

Parent-Child Telepathy, Berthold Eric Schwarz (Garrett Publications, 1971)

Patterns of Infant Care in an Urban Community, John and Elizabeth Newson (Allen & Unwin, 1963)

Psychic Power of Children, Cassandra Eason (Foulsham, 1994)

Reincarnation, The Phoenix Fire Mystery, Joseph Head and S.L. Cranston (Crown Publishers, 1978)

The Secret Life of the Unborn Child, Thomas R.Verny (Dell, 1981)

The Science of Animal Behaviour, Peter L. Broadhurst (Penguin, 1973)

Sophia, Goddess of Wisdom, Caitlin Matthews (Grafton Books, 1991)

Soviet Women, Francine du Plessix Gray (Doubleday, 1990)

Victoria R, Elizabeth Longford (Weidenfeld & Nicolson, 1967)

The Virgin, Geoffrey Ashe (Routledge & Kegan Paul, 1976)

The White Goddess, Robert Graves (Faber & Faber, 1988)

Why Zebras Don't Get Ulcers, Robert M. Sapolsky (W.H. Freeman, 1994)

Women in England 1500–1760, Anne Laurence (Phoenix Books, 1996)

Women in Prehistory, Margaret Ehrenberg (British Museum Press, 1995)

The World Religions, Ninian Smart (Cambridge University Press, 1992)

Yesterday's Children, The Extraordinary Search for my Past Life Family, Jenny Cockell (Piatkus, 1996)

Index